D0127149

9-11

emergency
relief

9-11
emergency
relief

9-11: Emergency Relief

✳

FIRST PRINTING, 2002

ISBN 1-891867-12-1

Published by Alternative Comics
503 NW 37th Avenue
Gainesville, FL 32609-2204
3 5 2 . 3 7 3 . 6 3 3 6
jmason@indyworld.com
www.indyworld.com

The publisher's profit from this book will
be donated to the American Red Cross.

design: Chris Pitzer
            editor: Jeff Mason

You can always find a comic book
store in your area by calling toll free
1-888-COMIC-BOOK.

✳

Printed in Canada by Quebecor Printing.

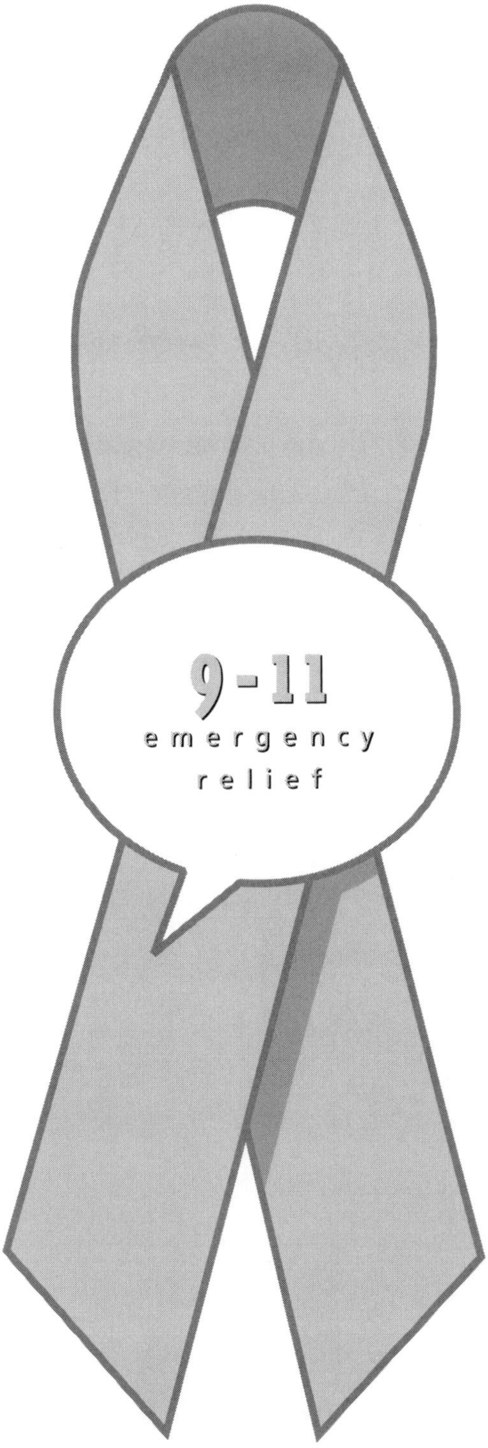
9-11
emergency
relief

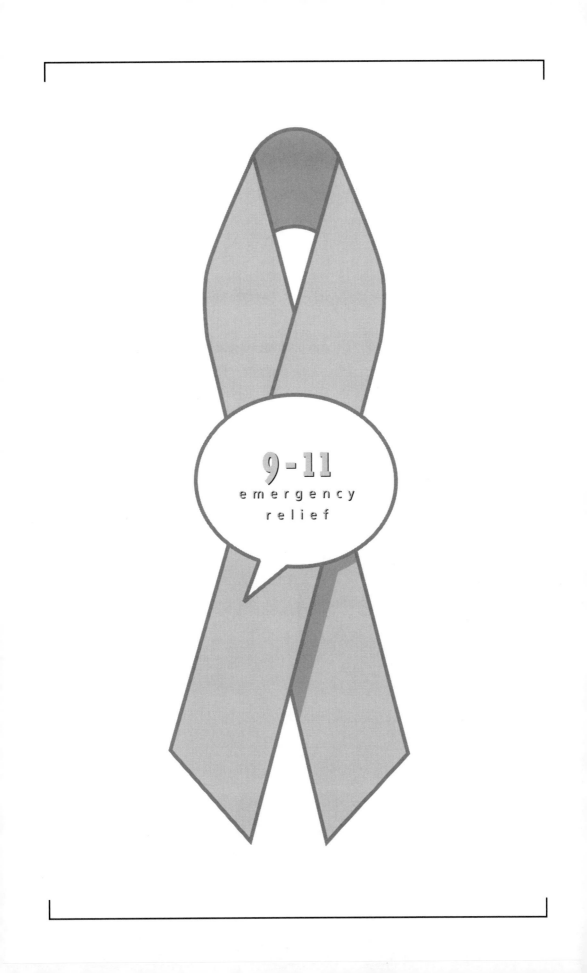

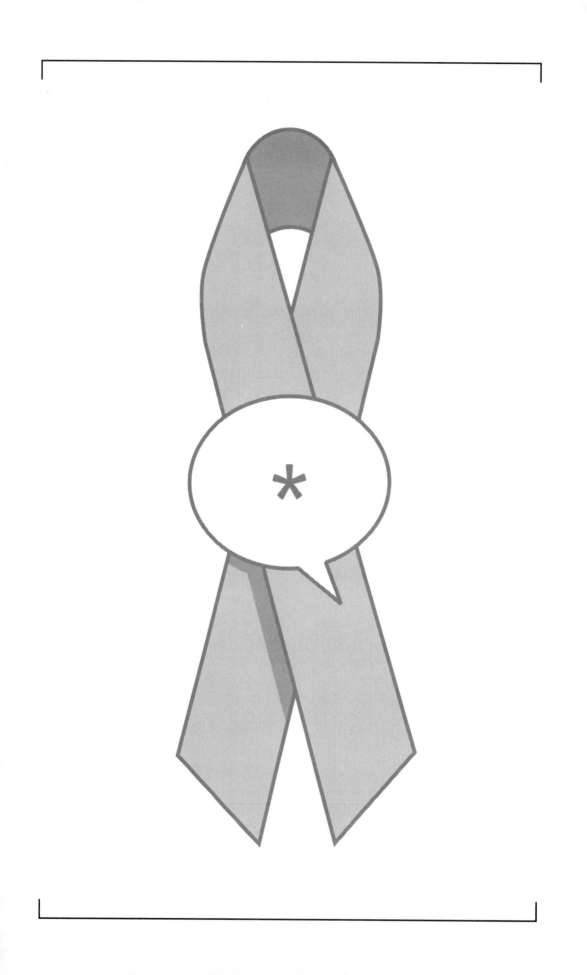

It is singular how soon we lose the impression

of what ceases to be constantly before us.

A year impairs, a luster obliterates.

There is little distinct left without an effort of memory,

then indeed the lights are rekindled for a moment —

but who can be sure that the

Imagination is not the torch-bearer?

* Lord Byron (1788-1824)

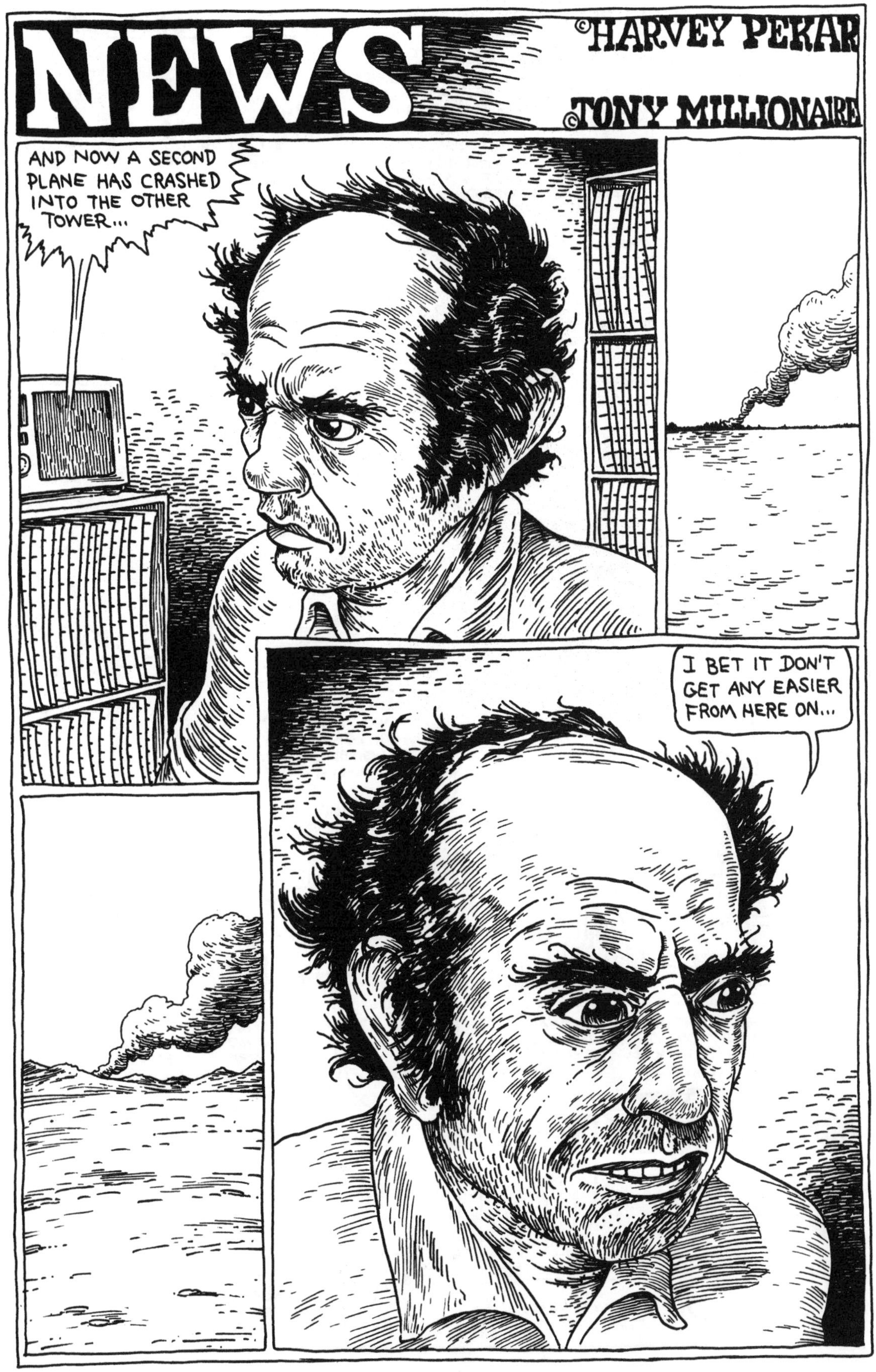
NEWS
©HARVEY PEKAR
©TONY MILLIONAIRE
AND NOW A SECOND PLANE HAS CRASHED INTO THE OTHER TOWER...
I BET IT DON'T GET ANY EASIER FROM HERE ON...

My Very First Flag

By Jeff Smith

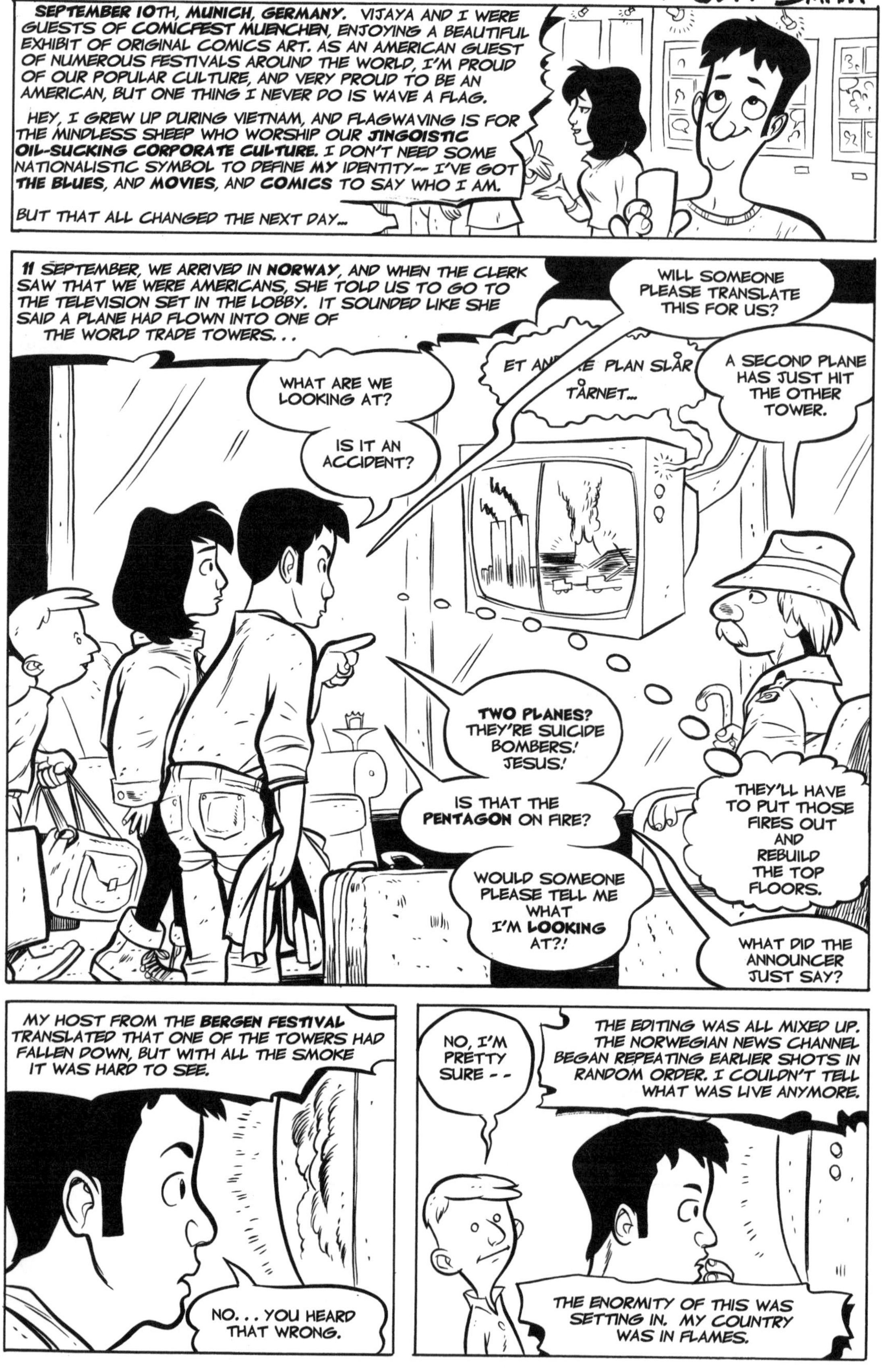
SEPTEMBER 10TH, MUNICH, GERMANY. VIJAYA AND I WERE GUESTS OF COMICFEST MUENCHEN, ENJOYING A BEAUTIFUL EXHIBIT OF ORIGINAL COMICS ART. AS AN AMERICAN GUEST OF NUMEROUS FESTIVALS AROUND THE WORLD, I'M PROUD OF OUR POPULAR CULTURE, AND VERY PROUD TO BE AN AMERICAN, BUT ONE THING I NEVER DO IS WAVE A FLAG.
HEY, I GREW UP DURING VIETNAM, AND FLAGWAVING IS FOR THE MINDLESS SHEEP WHO WORSHIP OUR JINGOISTIC OIL-SUCKING CORPORATE CULTURE. I DON'T NEED SOME NATIONALISTIC SYMBOL TO DEFINE MY IDENTITY-- I'VE GOT THE BLUES, AND MOVIES, AND COMICS TO SAY WHO I AM.
BUT THAT ALL CHANGED THE NEXT DAY...
11 SEPTEMBER, WE ARRIVED IN NORWAY, AND WHEN THE CLERK SAW THAT WE WERE AMERICANS, SHE TOLD US TO GO TO THE TELEVISION SET IN THE LOBBY. IT SOUNDED LIKE SHE SAID A PLANE HAD FLOWN INTO ONE OF THE WORLD TRADE TOWERS...
WILL SOMEONE PLEASE TRANSLATE THIS FOR US?
WHAT ARE WE LOOKING AT?
IS IT AN ACCIDENT?
ET AN E PLAN SLÅR TÅRNET...
A SECOND PLANE HAS JUST HIT THE OTHER TOWER.
TWO PLANES? THEY'RE SUICIDE BOMBERS! JESUS!
IS THAT THE PENTAGON ON FIRE?
WOULD SOMEONE PLEASE TELL ME WHAT I'M LOOKING AT?!
THEY'LL HAVE TO PUT THOSE FIRES OUT AND REBUILD THE TOP FLOORS.
WHAT DID THE ANNOUNCER JUST SAY?
MY HOST FROM THE BERGEN FESTIVAL TRANSLATED THAT ONE OF THE TOWERS HAD FALLEN DOWN, BUT WITH ALL THE SMOKE IT WAS HARD TO SEE.
NO... YOU HEARD THAT WRONG.
NO, I'M PRETTY SURE - -
THE EDITING WAS ALL MIXED UP. THE NORWEGIAN NEWS CHANNEL BEGAN REPEATING EARLIER SHOTS IN RANDOM ORDER. I COULDN'T TELL WHAT WAS LIVE ANYMORE.
THE ENORMITY OF THIS WAS SETTING IN. MY COUNTRY WAS IN FLAMES.

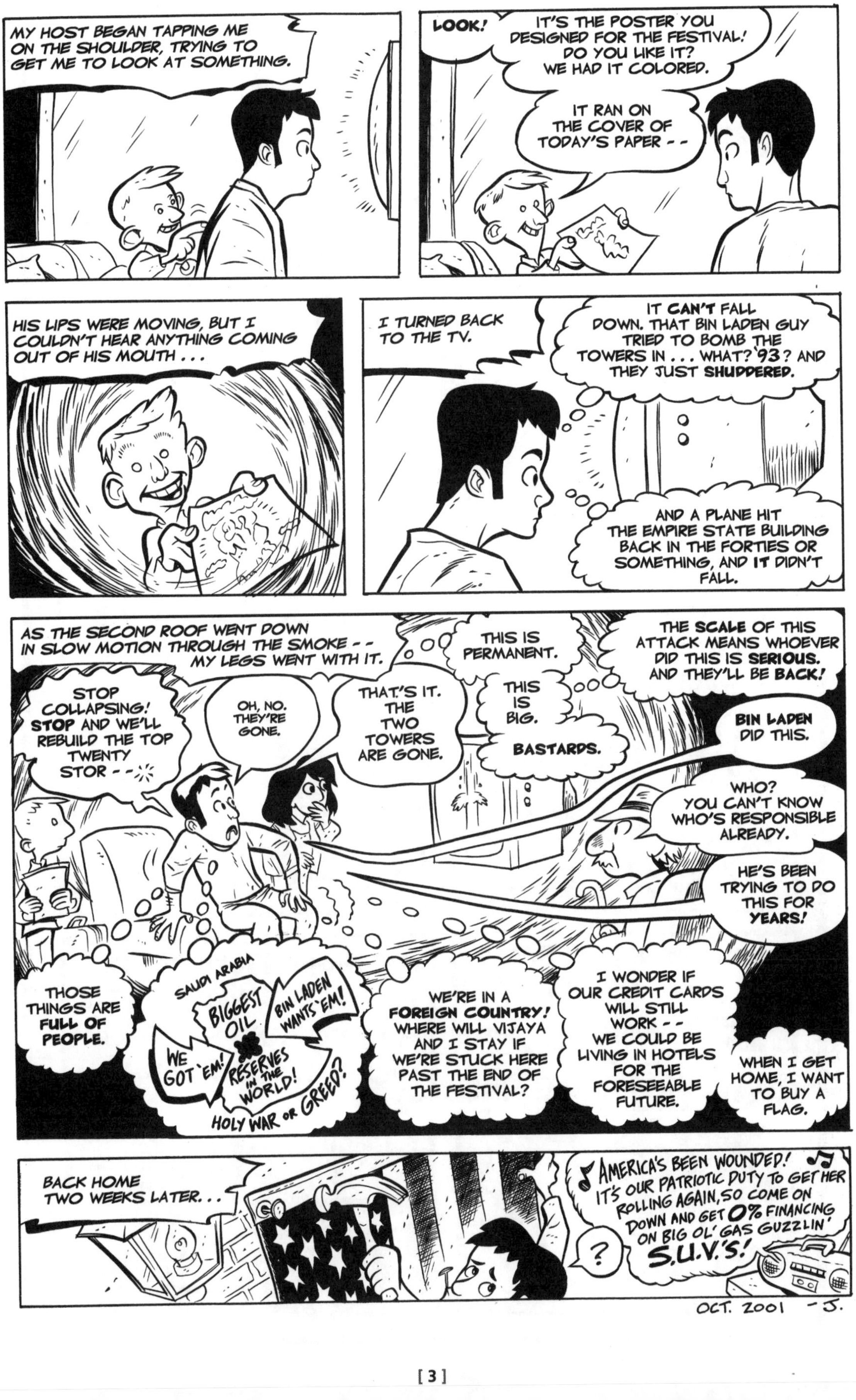
MY HOST BEGAN TAPPING ME ON THE SHOULDER, TRYING TO GET ME TO LOOK AT SOMETHING.
LOOK!
IT'S THE POSTER YOU DESIGNED FOR THE FESTIVAL! DO YOU LIKE IT? WE HAD IT COLORED.
IT RAN ON THE COVER OF TODAY'S PAPER - -
HIS LIPS WERE MOVING, BUT I COULDN'T HEAR ANYTHING COMING OUT OF HIS MOUTH . . .
I TURNED BACK TO THE TV.
IT CAN'T FALL DOWN. THAT BIN LADEN GUY TRIED TO BOMB THE TOWERS IN . . . WHAT? '93? AND THEY JUST SHUDDERED.
AND A PLANE HIT THE EMPIRE STATE BUILDING BACK IN THE FORTIES OR SOMETHING, AND IT DIDN'T FALL.
AS THE SECOND ROOF WENT DOWN IN SLOW MOTION THROUGH THE SMOKE - - MY LEGS WENT WITH IT.
THIS IS PERMANENT.
THE SCALE OF THIS ATTACK MEANS WHOEVER DID THIS IS SERIOUS. AND THEY'LL BE BACK!
STOP COLLAPSING! STOP AND WE'LL REBUILD THE TOP TWENTY STOR - -
OH, NO. THEY'RE GONE.
THAT'S IT. THE TWO TOWERS ARE GONE.
THIS IS BIG.
BASTARDS.
BIN LADEN DID THIS.
WHO? YOU CAN'T KNOW WHO'S RESPONSIBLE ALREADY.
HE'S BEEN TRYING TO DO THIS FOR YEARS!
THOSE THINGS ARE FULL OF PEOPLE.
SAUDI ARABIA
BIGGEST OIL RESERVES IN THE WORLD!
WE GOT 'EM!
BIN LADEN WANTS 'EM!
HOLY WAR OR GREED?
WE'RE IN A FOREIGN COUNTRY! WHERE WILL VIJAYA AND I STAY IF WE'RE STUCK HERE PAST THE END OF THE FESTIVAL?
I WONDER IF OUR CREDIT CARDS WILL STILL WORK - - WE COULD BE LIVING IN HOTELS FOR THE FORESEEABLE FUTURE.
WHEN I GET HOME, I WANT TO BUY A FLAG.
BACK HOME TWO WEEKS LATER . . .
AMERICA'S BEEN WOUNDED! IT'S OUR PATRIOTIC DUTY TO GET HER ROLLING AGAIN, SO COME ON DOWN AND GET 0% FINANCING ON BIG OL' GAS GUZZLIN' S.U.V.'S!
?

OCT. 2001 -J.

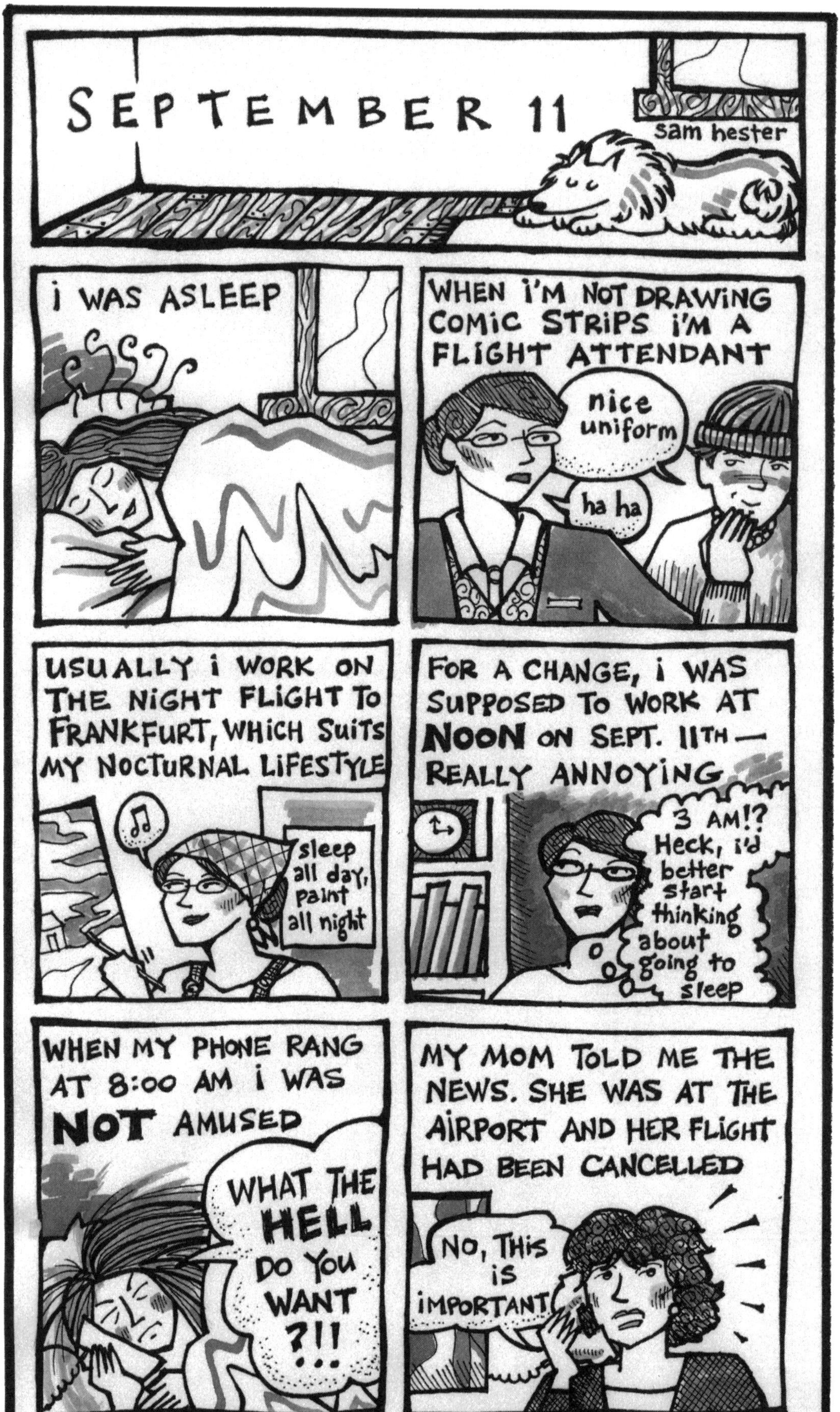
SEPTEMBER 11
sam hester
i WAS ASLEEP
WHEN i'M NOT DRAWING COMIC STRIPS i'M A FLIGHT ATTENDANT
nice uniform
ha ha
USUALLY i WORK ON THE NIGHT FLIGHT TO FRANKFURT, WHICH SUITS MY NOCTURNAL LIFESTYLE
sleep all day, paint all night
FOR A CHANGE, i WAS SUPPOSED TO WORK AT NOON ON SEPT. 11TH — REALLY ANNOYING
3 AM!? Heck, i'd better start thinking about going to sleep
WHEN MY PHONE RANG AT 8:00 AM i WAS NOT AMUSED
WHAT THE HELL DO YOU WANT ?!!
MY MOM TOLD ME THE NEWS. SHE WAS AT THE AiRPORT AND HER FLIGHT HAD BEEN CANCELLED
NO, THIS iS iMPORTANT

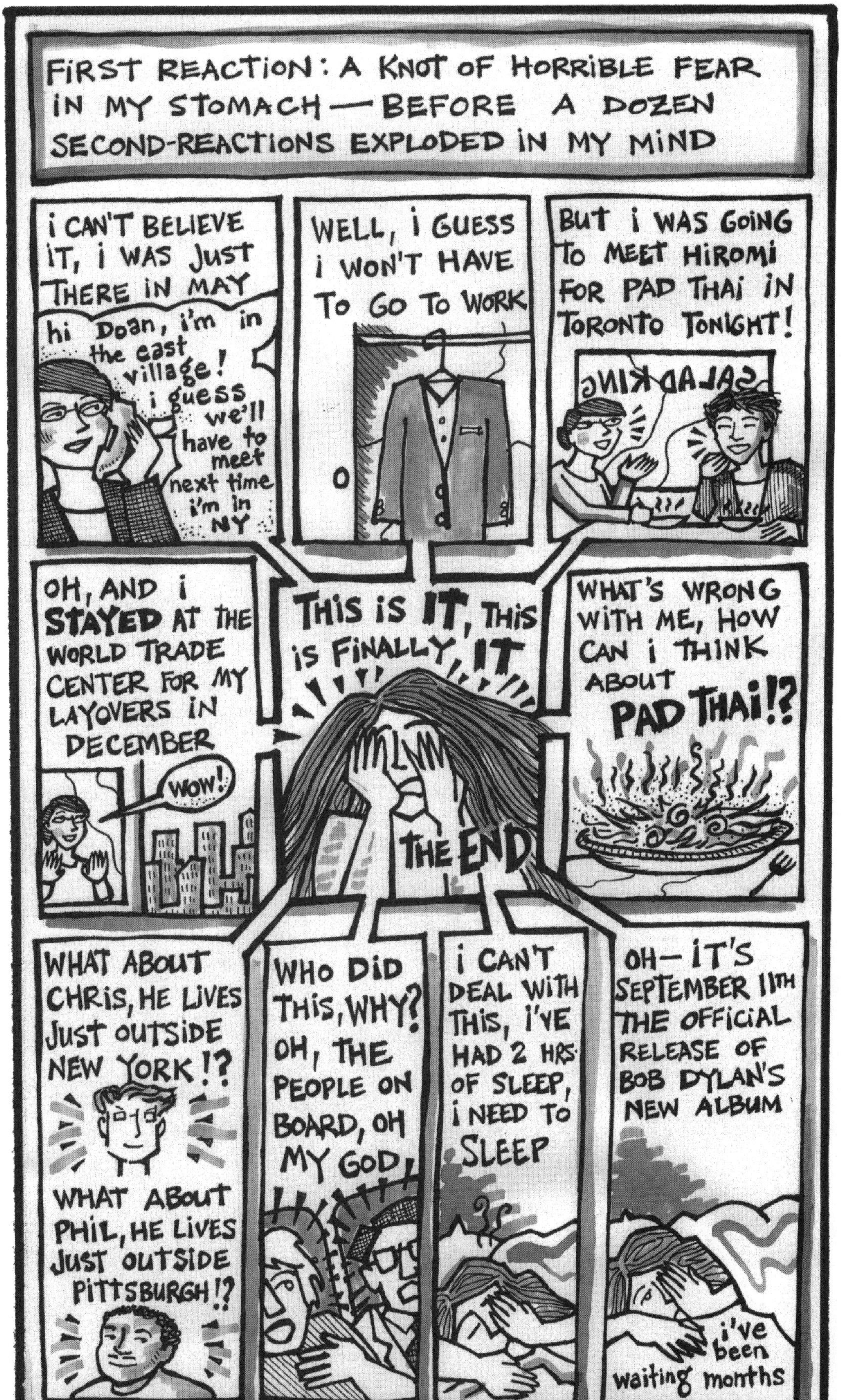
FIRST REACTION: A KNOT OF HORRIBLE FEAR IN MY STOMACH — BEFORE A DOZEN SECOND-REACTIONS EXPLODED IN MY MIND
I CAN'T BELIEVE IT, I WAS JUST THERE IN MAY
hi Doan, i'm in the east village! i guess we'll have to meet next time i'm in NY
WELL, I GUESS I WON'T HAVE TO GO TO WORK
BUT I WAS GOING TO MEET HIROMI FOR PAD THAI IN TORONTO TONIGHT!
SALAD KING
OH, AND I STAYED AT THE WORLD TRADE CENTER FOR MY LAYOVERS IN DECEMBER
WOW!
THIS IS IT, THIS IS FINALLY IT
THE END
WHAT'S WRONG WITH ME, HOW CAN I THINK ABOUT PAD THAI!?
WHAT ABOUT CHRIS, HE LIVES JUST OUTSIDE NEW YORK!?
WHAT ABOUT PHIL, HE LIVES JUST OUTSIDE PITTSBURGH!?
WHO DID THIS, WHY? OH, THE PEOPLE ON BOARD, OH MY GOD,
I CAN'T DEAL WITH THIS, I'VE HAD 2 HRS. OF SLEEP, I NEED TO SLEEP
OH— IT'S SEPTEMBER 11TH THE OFFICIAL RELEASE OF BOB DYLAN'S NEW ALBUM
i've been waiting months

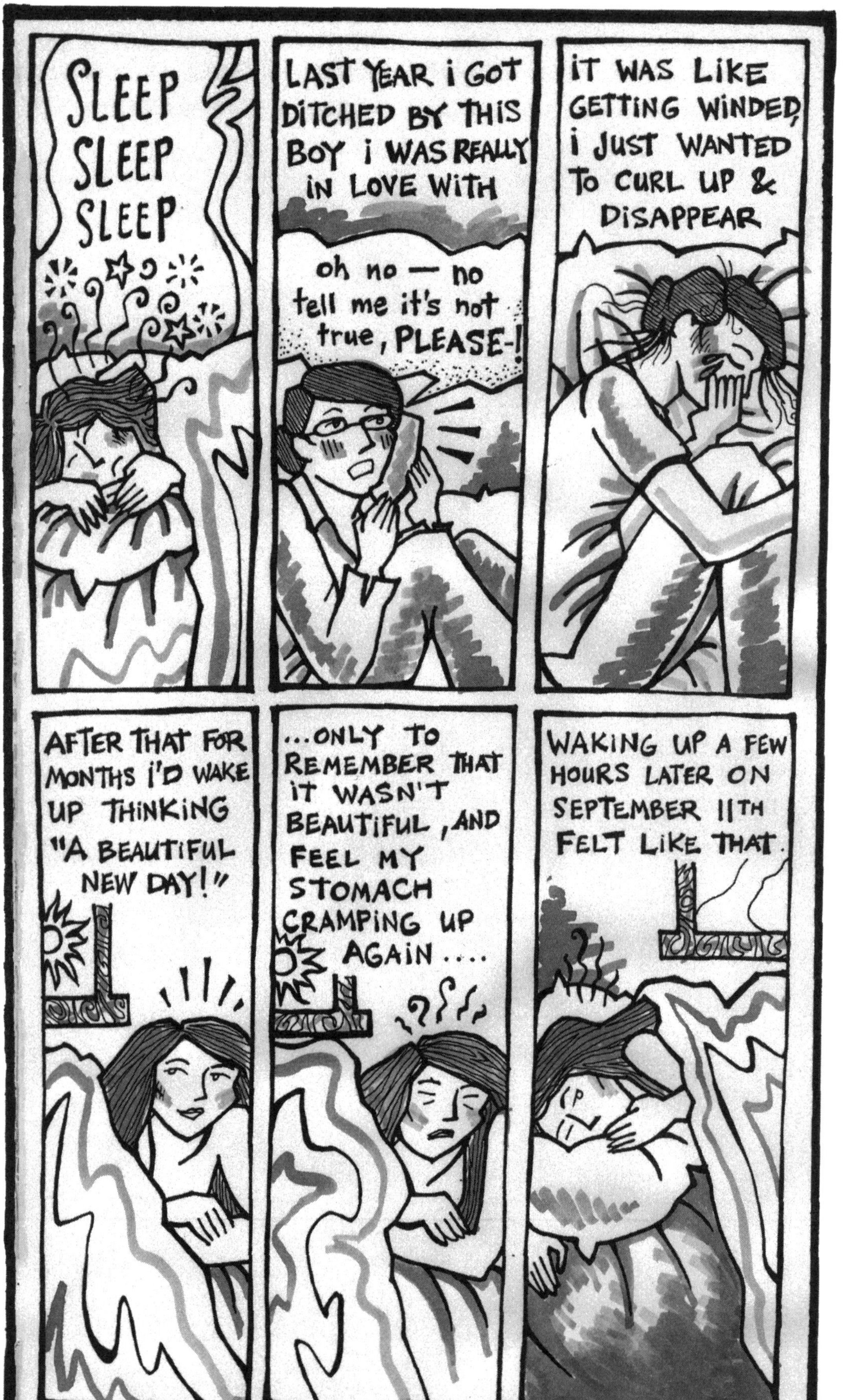
SLEEP SLEEP SLEEP
LAST YEAR i GOT DITCHED BY THIS BOY i WAS REALLY IN LOVE WITH
oh no — no tell me it's not true, PLEASE-!
iT WAS LIKE GETTING WINDED, i JUST WANTED TO CURL UP & DiSAPPEAR
AFTER THAT FOR MONTHS i'D WAKE UP THiNKiNG "A BEAUTiFUL NEW DAY!"
...ONLY TO REMEMBER THAT iT WASN'T BEAUTiFUL, AND FEEL MY STOMACH CRAMPING UP AGAIN....
WAKiNG UP A FEW HOURS LATER ON SEPTEMBER 11TH FELT LiKE THAT.

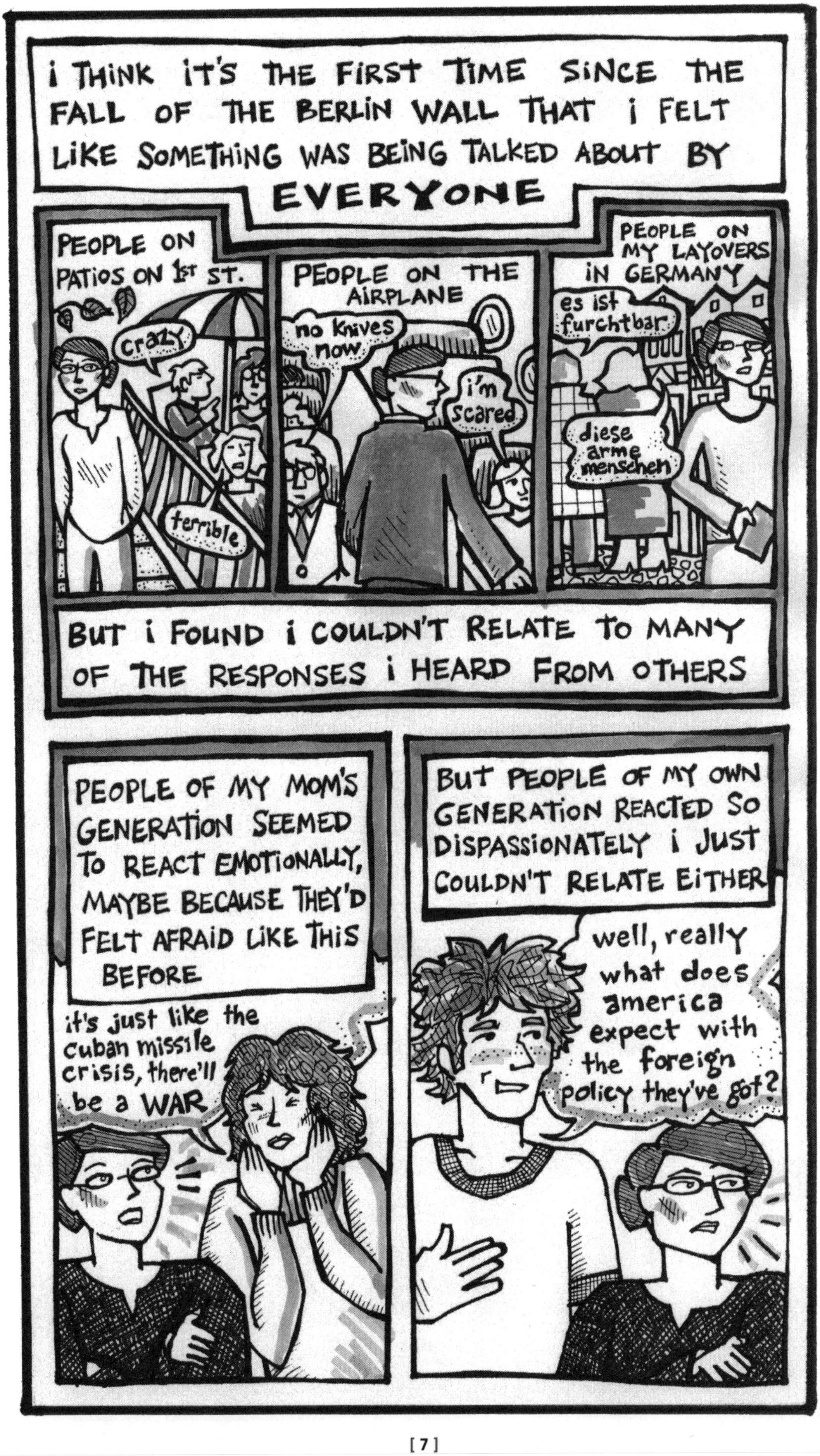
i THINK iT'S THE FIRST TIME SINCE THE FALL OF THE BERLIN WALL THAT i FELT LIKE SOMETHING WAS BEING TALKED ABOUT BY
EVERYONE
PEOPLE ON PATIOS ON 1st ST.
crazy
terrible
PEOPLE ON THE AIRPLANE
no knives now
i'm scared
PEOPLE ON MY LAYOVERS IN GERMANY
es ist furchtbar
diese arme menschen
BUT i FOUND i COULDN'T RELATE TO MANY OF THE RESPONSES i HEARD FROM OTHERS
PEOPLE OF MY MOM'S GENERATION SEEMED TO REACT EMOTIONALLY, MAYBE BECAUSE THEY'D FELT AFRAID LIKE THIS BEFORE
it's just like the cuban missile crisis, there'll be a WAR
BUT PEOPLE OF MY OWN GENERATION REACTED SO DISPASSIONATELY i JUST COULDN'T RELATE EITHER
well, really what does america expect with the foreign policy they've got?

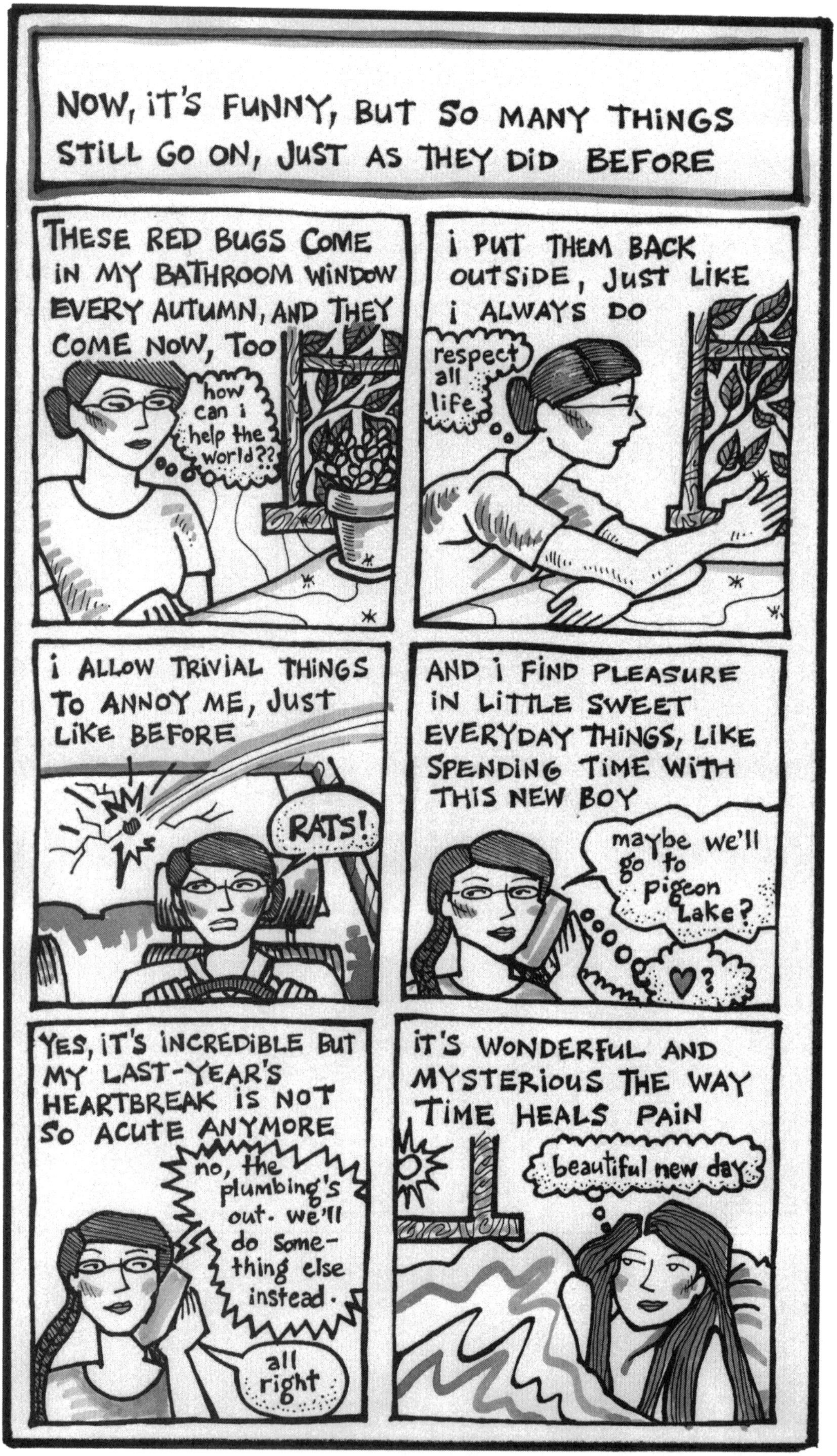

NOW, iT'S FUNNY, BUT SO MANY THiNGS STILL GO ON, JUST AS THEY DiD BEFORE
THESE RED BUGS COME iN MY BATHROOM WiNDOW EVERY AUTUMN, AND THEY COME NOW, TOO
how can i help the world??
i PUT THEM BACK OUTSiDE, JUST LiKE i ALWAYS DO
respect all life
i ALLOW TRiViAL THiNGS TO ANNOY ME, JUST LiKE BEFORE
RATS!
AND i FiND PLEASURE iN LiTTLE SWEET EVERYDAY THiNGS, LiKE SPENDiNG TiME WiTH THiS NEW BOY
maybe we'll go to pigeon Lake?
?
YES, iT'S iNCREDiBLE BUT MY LAST-YEAR'S HEARTBREAK iS NOT SO ACUTE ANYMORE
no, the plumbing's out. we'll do something else instead.
all right
iT'S WONDERFUL AND MYSTERiOUS THE WAY TiME HEALS PAiN
beautiful new day

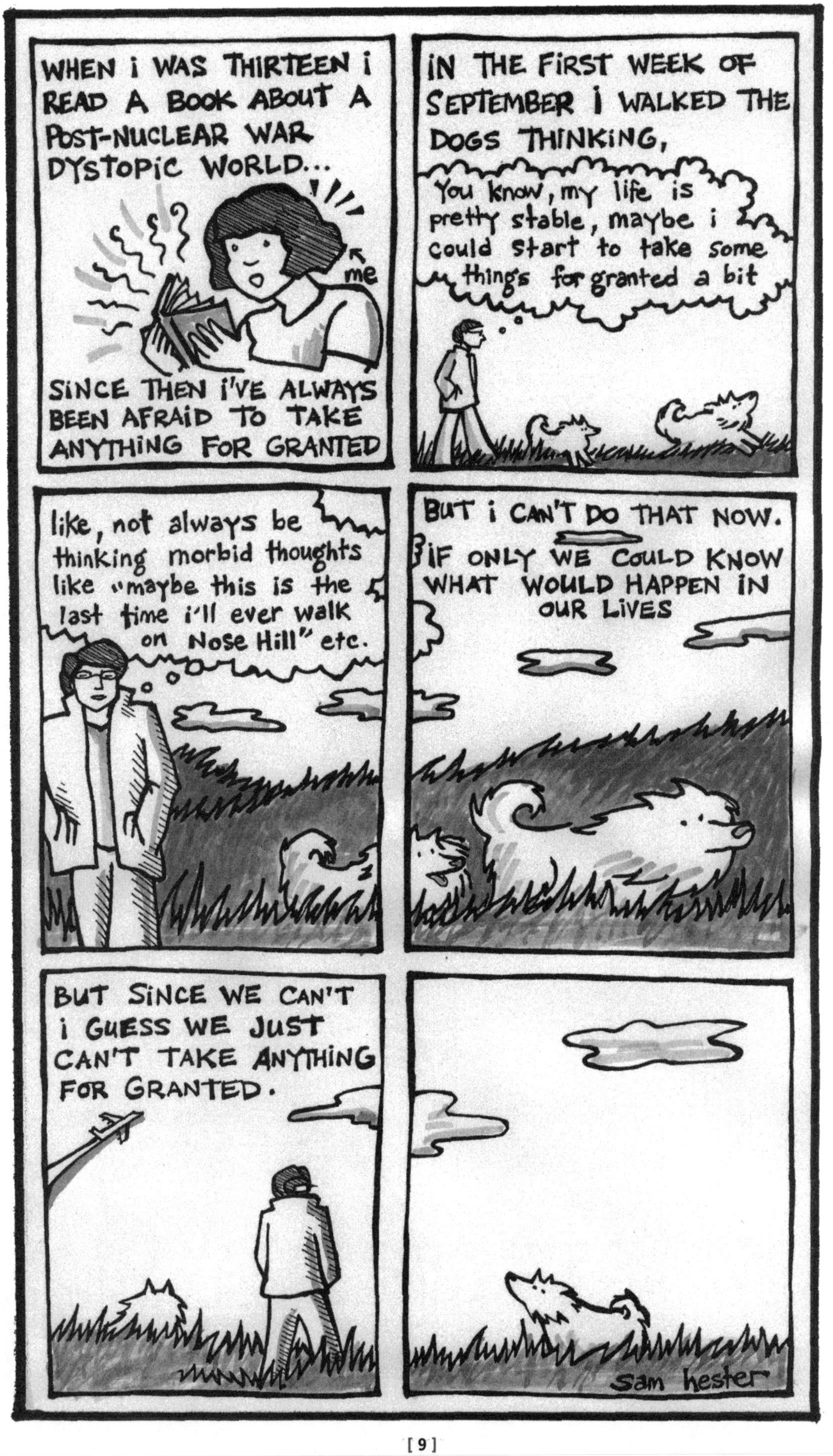
WHEN i WAS THIRTEEN i READ A BOOK ABOUT A POST-NUCLEAR WAR DYSTOPIC WORLD...
me
SINCE THEN i'VE ALWAYS BEEN AFRAID TO TAKE ANYTHING FOR GRANTED
iN THE FiRST WEEK OF SEPTEMBER i WALKED THE DOGS THINKiNG,
You know, my life is pretty stable, maybe i could start to take some things for granted a bit
like, not always be thinking morbid thoughts like "maybe this is the last time i'll ever walk on Nose Hill" etc.
BUT i CAN'T DO THAT NOW.
iF ONLY WE COULD KNOW WHAT WOULD HAPPEN iN OUR LiVES
BUT SiNCE WE CAN'T i GUESS WE JUST CAN'T TAKE ANYTHING FOR GRANTED.
sam hester

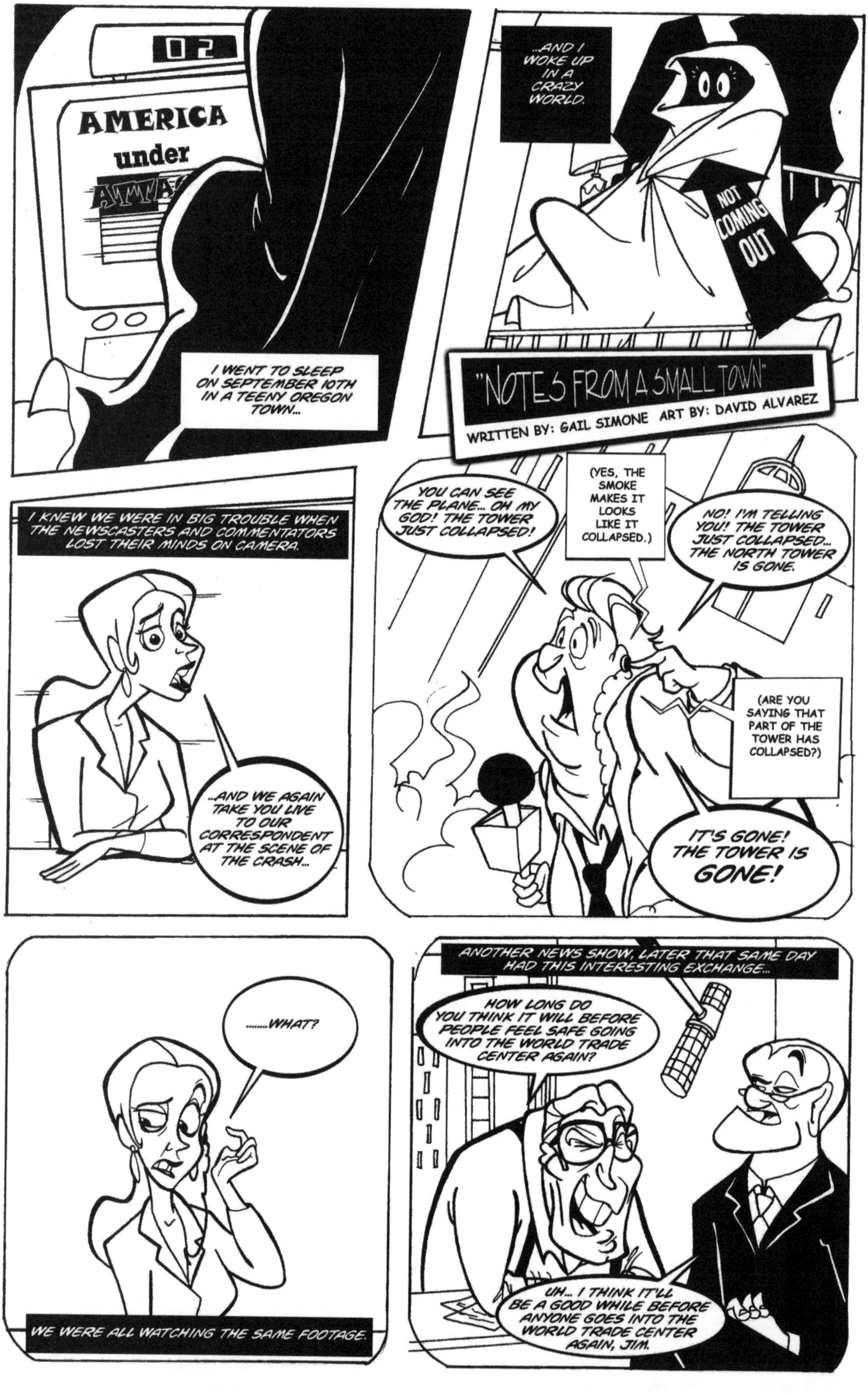
0 2
AMERICA under ATTA
I WENT TO SLEEP ON SEPTEMBER 10TH IN A TEENY OREGON TOWN...
...AND I WOKE UP IN A CRAZY WORLD.
NOT COMING OUT
"NOTES FROM A SMALL TOWN"
WRITTEN BY: GAIL SIMONE ART BY: DAVID ALVAREZ
I KNEW WE WERE IN BIG TROUBLE WHEN THE NEWSCASTERS AND COMMENTATORS LOST THEIR MINDS ON CAMERA.
...AND WE AGAIN TAKE YOU LIVE TO OUR CORRESPONDENT AT THE SCENE OF THE CRASH...
YOU CAN SEE THE PLANE... OH MY GOD! THE TOWER JUST COLLAPSED!
(YES, THE SMOKE MAKES IT LOOKS LIKE IT COLLAPSED.)
NO! I'M TELLING YOU! THE TOWER JUST COLLAPSED... THE NORTH TOWER IS GONE.
(ARE YOU SAYING THAT PART OF THE TOWER HAS COLLAPSED?)
IT'S GONE! THE TOWER IS GONE!
........WHAT?
WE WERE ALL WATCHING THE SAME FOOTAGE.
ANOTHER NEWS SHOW, LATER THAT SAME DAY HAD THIS INTERESTING EXCHANGE...
HOW LONG DO YOU THINK IT WILL BEFORE PEOPLE FEEL SAFE GOING INTO THE WORLD TRADE CENTER AGAIN?
UH... I THINK IT'LL BE A GOOD WHILE BEFORE ANYONE GOES INTO THE WORLD TRADE CENTER AGAIN, JIM.

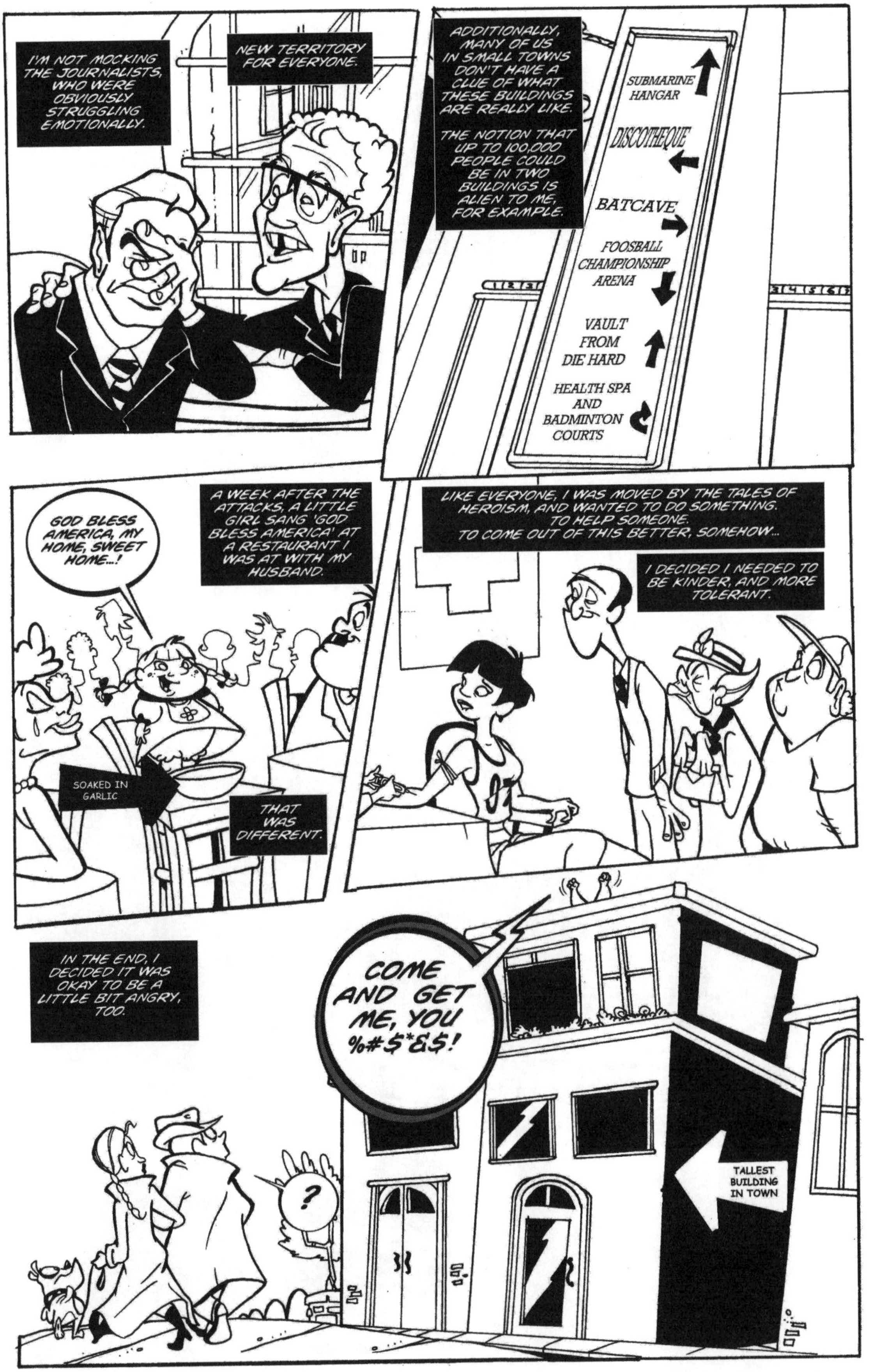
I'M NOT MOCKING THE JOURNALISTS, WHO WERE OBVIOUSLY STRUGGLING EMOTIONALLY.
NEW TERRITORY FOR EVERYONE.
ADDITIONALLY, MANY OF US IN SMALL TOWNS DON'T HAVE A CLUE OF WHAT THESE BUILDINGS ARE REALLY LIKE.
THE NOTION THAT UP TO 100,000 PEOPLE COULD BE IN TWO BUILDINGS IS ALIEN TO ME, FOR EXAMPLE.
SUBMARINE HANGAR
DISCOTHEQUE
BATCAVE
FOOSBALL CHAMPIONSHIP ARENA
VAULT FROM DIE HARD
HEALTH SPA AND BADMINTON COURTS
A WEEK AFTER THE ATTACKS, A LITTLE GIRL SANG 'GOD BLESS AMERICA' AT A RESTAURANT I WAS AT WITH MY HUSBAND.
GOD BLESS AMERICA, MY HOME, SWEET HOME...!
SOAKED IN GARLIC
THAT WAS DIFFERENT.
LIKE EVERYONE, I WAS MOVED BY THE TALES OF HEROISM, AND WANTED TO DO SOMETHING. TO HELP SOMEONE. TO COME OUT OF THIS BETTER, SOMEHOW...
I DECIDED I NEEDED TO BE KINDER, AND MORE TOLERANT.
IN THE END, I DECIDED IT WAS OKAY TO BE A LITTLE BIT ANGRY, TOO.
COME AND GET ME, YOU %#$*&$!
?
TALLEST BUILDING IN TOWN

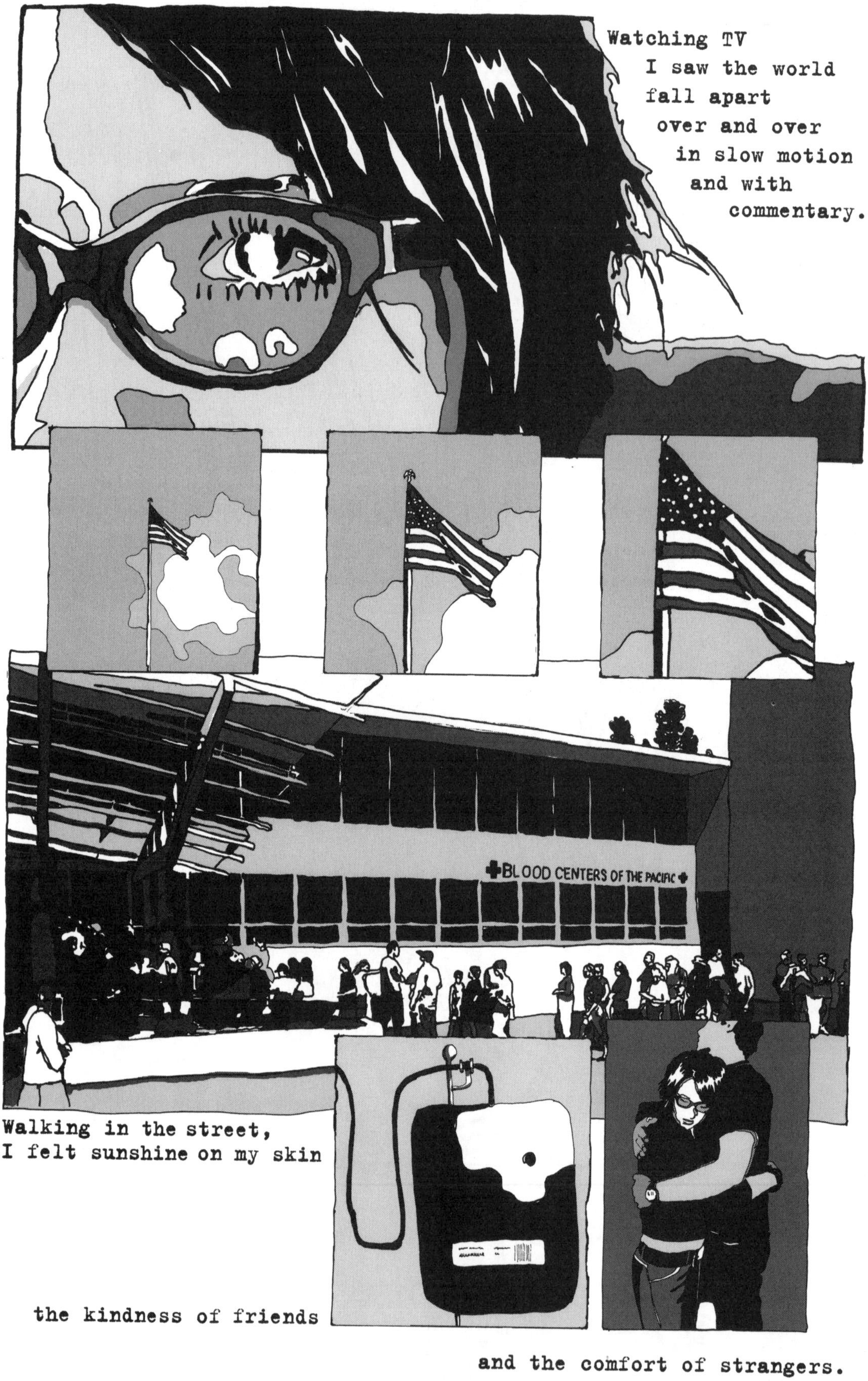
Watching TV
I saw the world
fall apart
over and over
in slow motion
and with
commentary.
BLOOD CENTERS OF THE PACIFIC
Walking in the street,
I felt sunshine on my skin
the kindness of friends
and the comfort of strangers.

By Jessica Abel ©2001
So, did you work it out for SPX with Tom & Leela?
Yeah, they've got room. What are you guys doing?
Ohmigod! Cute attack!
I know!
We're sharing with Jason and Myla.
We're renting a car, too.
Oh, that's a good idea.
Yeah, I've got a lot of originals and stuff to bring.
Will your new book be out?
Supposedly. Cross your fingers.
Ha ha! Yeah...

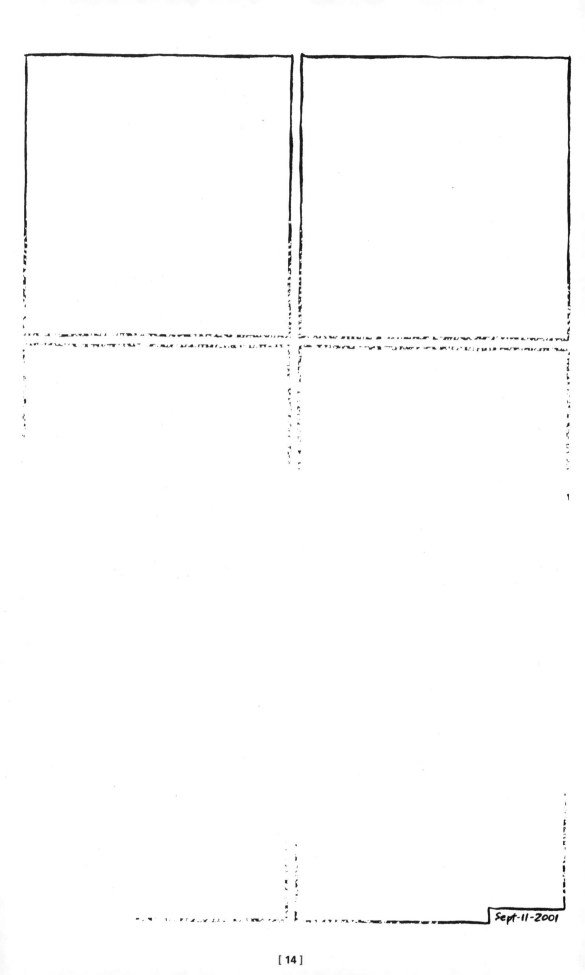

Sept-11-2001

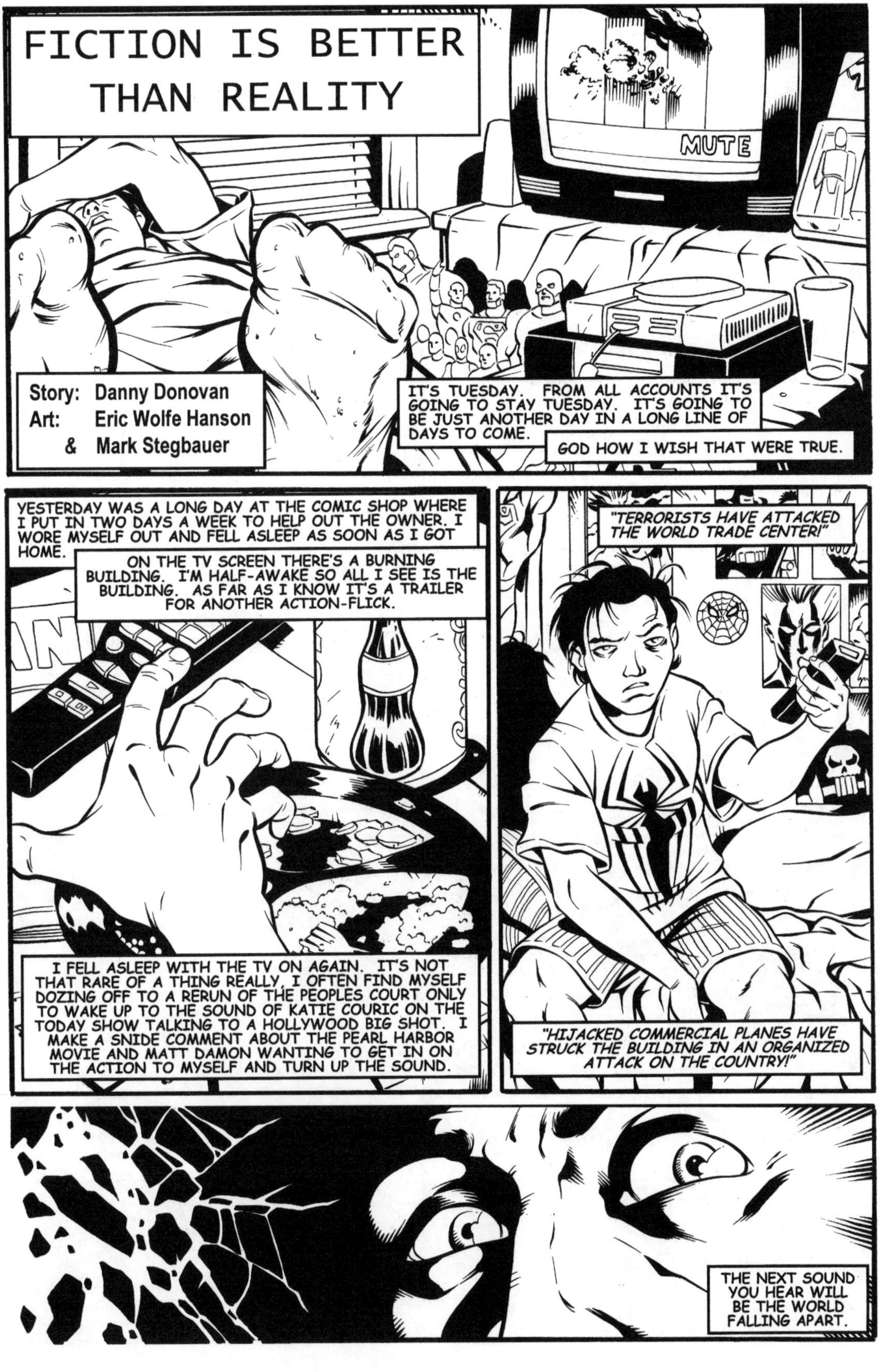
FICTION IS BETTER THAN REALITY
MUTE
Story: Danny Donovan
Art: Eric Wolfe Hanson
& Mark Stegbauer
IT'S TUESDAY. FROM ALL ACCOUNTS IT'S GOING TO STAY TUESDAY. IT'S GOING TO BE JUST ANOTHER DAY IN A LONG LINE OF DAYS TO COME.
GOD HOW I WISH THAT WERE TRUE.
YESTERDAY WAS A LONG DAY AT THE COMIC SHOP WHERE I PUT IN TWO DAYS A WEEK TO HELP OUT THE OWNER. I WORE MYSELF OUT AND FELL ASLEEP AS SOON AS I GOT HOME.
ON THE TV SCREEN THERE'S A BURNING BUILDING. I'M HALF-AWAKE SO ALL I SEE IS THE BUILDING. AS FAR AS I KNOW IT'S A TRAILER FOR ANOTHER ACTION-FLICK.
I FELL ASLEEP WITH THE TV ON AGAIN. IT'S NOT THAT RARE OF A THING REALLY, I OFTEN FIND MYSELF DOZING OFF TO A RERUN OF THE PEOPLES COURT ONLY TO WAKE UP TO THE SOUND OF KATIE COURIC ON THE TODAY SHOW TALKING TO A HOLLYWOOD BIG SHOT. I MAKE A SNIDE COMMENT ABOUT THE PEARL HARBOR MOVIE AND MATT DAMON WANTING TO GET IN ON THE ACTION TO MYSELF AND TURN UP THE SOUND.
"TERRORISTS HAVE ATTACKED THE WORLD TRADE CENTER!"
"HIJACKED COMMERCIAL PLANES HAVE STRUCK THE BUILDING IN AN ORGANIZED ATTACK ON THE COUNTRY!"
THE NEXT SOUND YOU HEAR WILL BE THE WORLD FALLING APART.

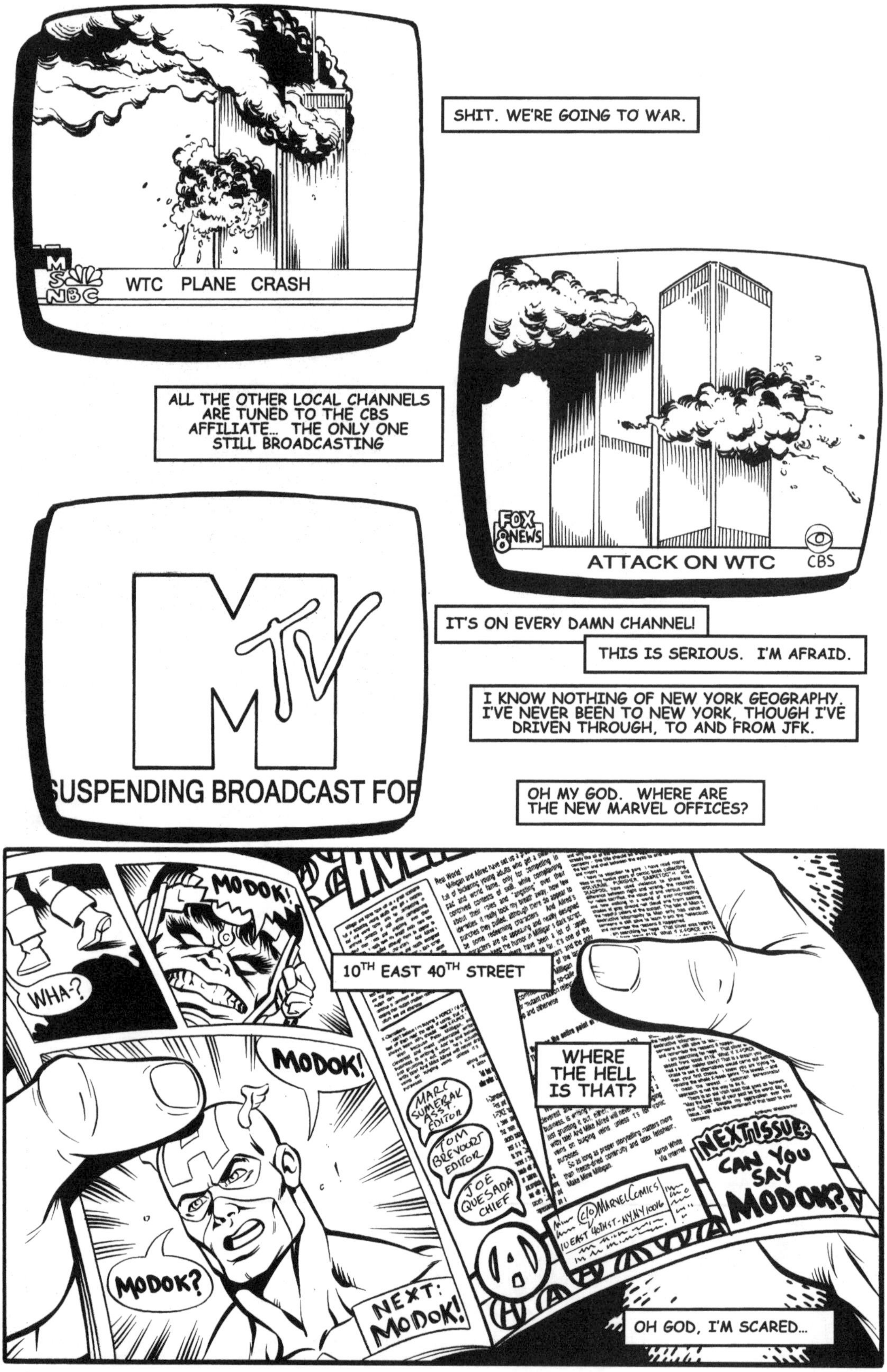
WTC PLANE CRASH
MSNBC
SHIT. WE'RE GOING TO WAR.
FOX 8 NEWS
ATTACK ON WTC
CBS
ALL THE OTHER LOCAL CHANNELS ARE TUNED TO THE CBS AFFILIATE... THE ONLY ONE STILL BROADCASTING
MTV
SUSPENDING BROADCAST FOR
IT'S ON EVERY DAMN CHANNEL!
THIS IS SERIOUS. I'M AFRAID.
I KNOW NOTHING OF NEW YORK GEOGRAPHY. I'VE NEVER BEEN TO NEW YORK, THOUGH I'VE DRIVEN THROUGH, TO AND FROM JFK.
OH MY GOD. WHERE ARE THE NEW MARVEL OFFICES?
WHA-?
MODOK!
10TH EAST 40TH STREET
MODOK!
WHERE THE HELL IS THAT?
MARC SUMERAK ASST. EDITOR
TOM BREVOORT EDITOR
JOE QUESADA CHIEF
MODOK?
NEXT: MODOK!
C/O MARVEL COMICS 10 EAST 40TH ST - NY, NY 10016
NEXT ISSUE: CAN YOU SAY MODOK?
OH GOD, I'M SCARED...

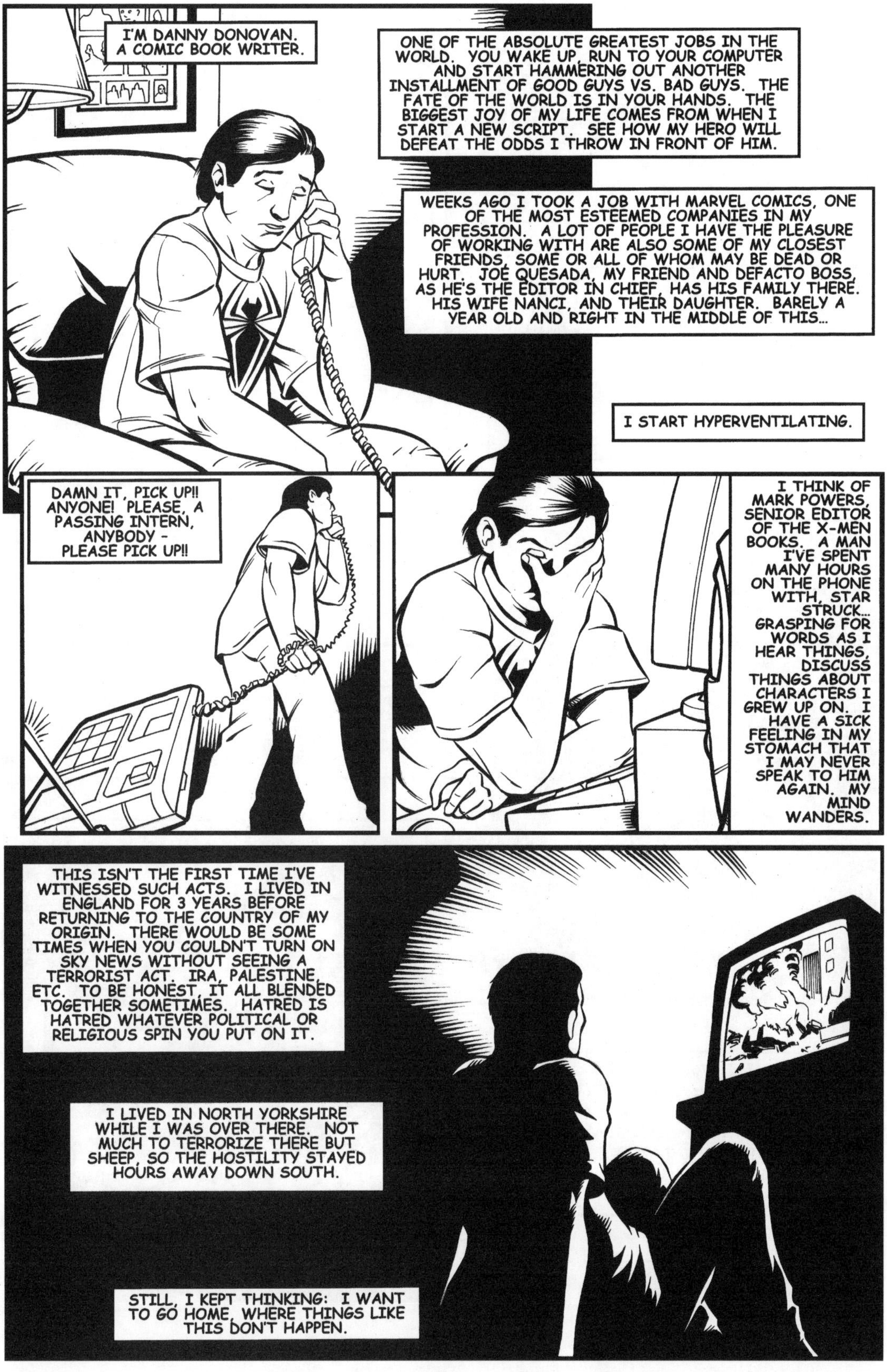
I'M DANNY DONOVAN. A COMIC BOOK WRITER.
ONE OF THE ABSOLUTE GREATEST JOBS IN THE WORLD. YOU WAKE UP, RUN TO YOUR COMPUTER AND START HAMMERING OUT ANOTHER INSTALLMENT OF GOOD GUYS VS. BAD GUYS. THE FATE OF THE WORLD IS IN YOUR HANDS. THE BIGGEST JOY OF MY LIFE COMES FROM WHEN I START A NEW SCRIPT. SEE HOW MY HERO WILL DEFEAT THE ODDS I THROW IN FRONT OF HIM.
WEEKS AGO I TOOK A JOB WITH MARVEL COMICS, ONE OF THE MOST ESTEEMED COMPANIES IN MY PROFESSION. A LOT OF PEOPLE I HAVE THE PLEASURE OF WORKING WITH ARE ALSO SOME OF MY CLOSEST FRIENDS, SOME OR ALL OF WHOM MAY BE DEAD OR HURT. JOE QUESADA, MY FRIEND AND DEFACTO BOSS, AS HE'S THE EDITOR IN CHIEF, HAS HIS FAMILY THERE. HIS WIFE NANCI, AND THEIR DAUGHTER. BARELY A YEAR OLD AND RIGHT IN THE MIDDLE OF THIS...
I START HYPERVENTILATING.
DAMN IT, PICK UP!! ANYONE! PLEASE, A PASSING INTERN, ANYBODY - PLEASE PICK UP!!
I THINK OF MARK POWERS, SENIOR EDITOR OF THE X-MEN BOOKS. A MAN I'VE SPENT MANY HOURS ON THE PHONE WITH, STAR STRUCK... GRASPING FOR WORDS AS I HEAR THINGS, DISCUSS THINGS ABOUT CHARACTERS I GREW UP ON. I HAVE A SICK FEELING IN MY STOMACH THAT I MAY NEVER SPEAK TO HIM AGAIN. MY MIND WANDERS.
THIS ISN'T THE FIRST TIME I'VE WITNESSED SUCH ACTS. I LIVED IN ENGLAND FOR 3 YEARS BEFORE RETURNING TO THE COUNTRY OF MY ORIGIN. THERE WOULD BE SOME TIMES WHEN YOU COULDN'T TURN ON SKY NEWS WITHOUT SEEING A TERRORIST ACT. IRA, PALESTINE, ETC. TO BE HONEST, IT ALL BLENDED TOGETHER SOMETIMES. HATRED IS HATRED WHATEVER POLITICAL OR RELIGIOUS SPIN YOU PUT ON IT.
I LIVED IN NORTH YORKSHIRE WHILE I WAS OVER THERE. NOT MUCH TO TERRORIZE THERE BUT SHEEP, SO THE HOSTILITY STAYED HOURS AWAY DOWN SOUTH.
STILL, I KEPT THINKING: I WANT TO GO HOME, WHERE THINGS LIKE THIS DON'T HAPPEN.

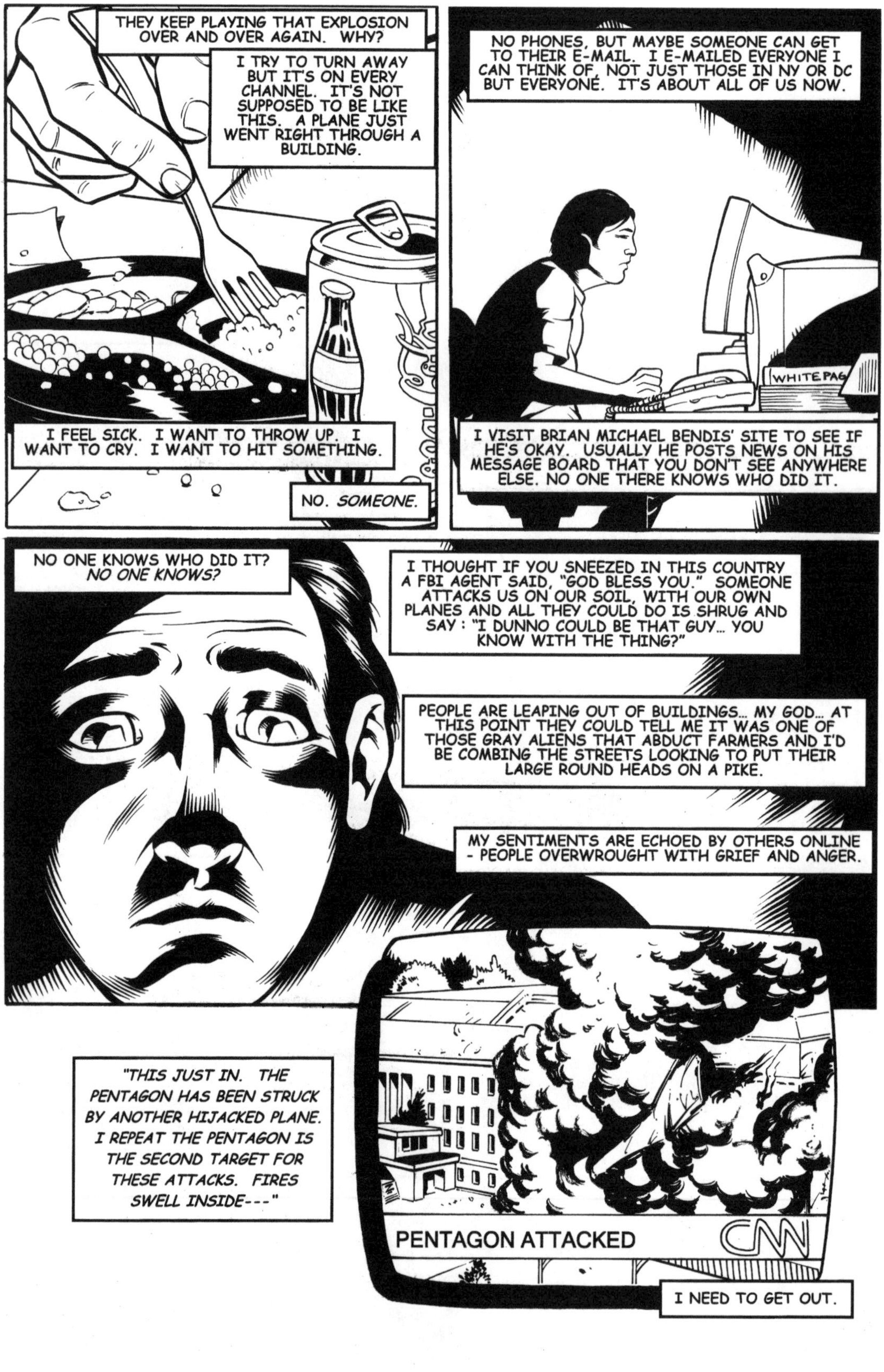
THEY KEEP PLAYING THAT EXPLOSION OVER AND OVER AGAIN. WHY?
I TRY TO TURN AWAY BUT IT'S ON EVERY CHANNEL. IT'S NOT SUPPOSED TO BE LIKE THIS. A PLANE JUST WENT RIGHT THROUGH A BUILDING.
I FEEL SICK. I WANT TO THROW UP. I WANT TO CRY. I WANT TO HIT SOMETHING.
NO. *SOMEONE.*
NO PHONES, BUT MAYBE SOMEONE CAN GET TO THEIR E-MAIL. I E-MAILED EVERYONE I CAN THINK OF, NOT JUST THOSE IN NY OR DC BUT EVERYONE. IT'S ABOUT ALL OF US NOW.
WHITE PAG
I VISIT BRIAN MICHAEL BENDIS' SITE TO SEE IF HE'S OKAY. USUALLY HE POSTS NEWS ON HIS MESSAGE BOARD THAT YOU DON'T SEE ANYWHERE ELSE. NO ONE THERE KNOWS WHO DID IT.
NO ONE KNOWS WHO DID IT? *NO ONE KNOWS?*
I THOUGHT IF YOU SNEEZED IN THIS COUNTRY A FBI AGENT SAID, "GOD BLESS YOU." SOMEONE ATTACKS US ON OUR SOIL, WITH OUR OWN PLANES AND ALL THEY COULD DO IS SHRUG AND SAY : "I DUNNO COULD BE THAT GUY... YOU KNOW WITH THE THING?"
PEOPLE ARE LEAPING OUT OF BUILDINGS... MY GOD... AT THIS POINT THEY COULD TELL ME IT WAS ONE OF THOSE GRAY ALIENS THAT ABDUCT FARMERS AND I'D BE COMBING THE STREETS LOOKING TO PUT THEIR LARGE ROUND HEADS ON A PIKE.
MY SENTIMENTS ARE ECHOED BY OTHERS ONLINE - PEOPLE OVERWROUGHT WITH GRIEF AND ANGER.
"THIS JUST IN. THE PENTAGON HAS BEEN STRUCK BY ANOTHER HIJACKED PLANE. I REPEAT THE PENTAGON IS THE SECOND TARGET FOR THESE ATTACKS. FIRES SWELL INSIDE---"
PENTAGON ATTACKED
CNN
I NEED TO GET OUT.

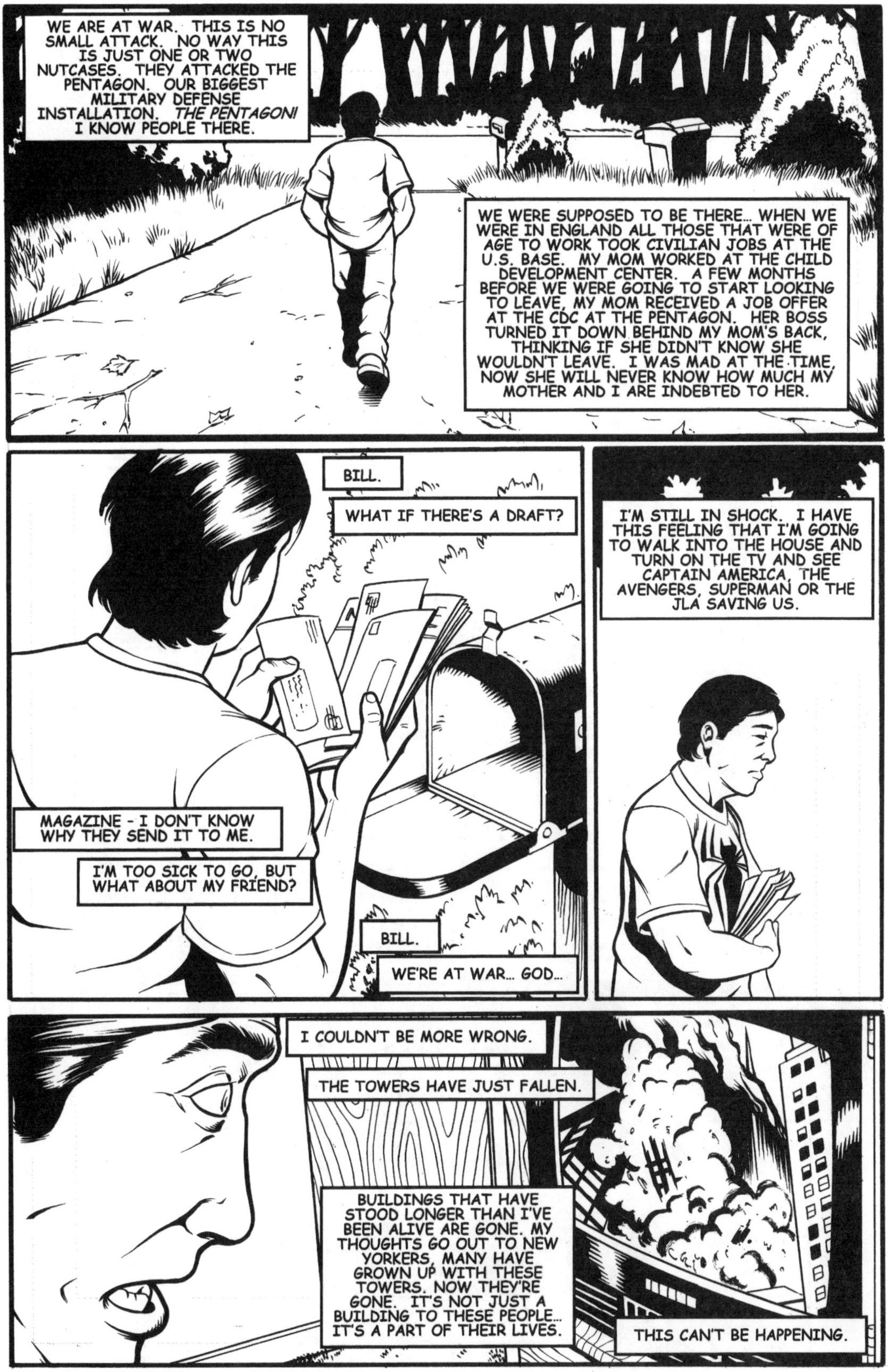
WE ARE AT WAR. THIS IS NO SMALL ATTACK. NO WAY THIS IS JUST ONE OR TWO NUTCASES. THEY ATTACKED THE PENTAGON. OUR BIGGEST MILITARY DEFENSE INSTALLATION. *THE PENTAGON!* I KNOW PEOPLE THERE.
WE WERE SUPPOSED TO BE THERE... WHEN WE WERE IN ENGLAND ALL THOSE THAT WERE OF AGE TO WORK TOOK CIVILIAN JOBS AT THE U.S. BASE. MY MOM WORKED AT THE CHILD DEVELOPMENT CENTER. A FEW MONTHS BEFORE WE WERE GOING TO START LOOKING TO LEAVE, MY MOM RECEIVED A JOB OFFER AT THE CDC AT THE PENTAGON. HER BOSS TURNED IT DOWN BEHIND MY MOM'S BACK, THINKING IF SHE DIDN'T KNOW SHE WOULDN'T LEAVE. I WAS MAD AT THE TIME, NOW SHE WILL NEVER KNOW HOW MUCH MY MOTHER AND I ARE INDEBTED TO HER.
BILL.
WHAT IF THERE'S A DRAFT?
MAGAZINE - I DON'T KNOW WHY THEY SEND IT TO ME.
I'M TOO SICK TO GO, BUT WHAT ABOUT MY FRIEND?
BILL.
WE'RE AT WAR... GOD...
I'M STILL IN SHOCK. I HAVE THIS FEELING THAT I'M GOING TO WALK INTO THE HOUSE AND TURN ON THE TV AND SEE CAPTAIN AMERICA, THE AVENGERS, SUPERMAN OR THE JLA SAVING US.
I COULDN'T BE MORE WRONG.
THE TOWERS HAVE JUST FALLEN.
BUILDINGS THAT HAVE STOOD LONGER THAN I'VE BEEN ALIVE ARE GONE. MY THOUGHTS GO OUT TO NEW YORKERS, MANY HAVE GROWN UP WITH THESE TOWERS. NOW THEY'RE GONE. IT'S NOT JUST A BUILDING TO THESE PEOPLE... IT'S A PART OF THEIR LIVES.
THIS CAN'T BE HAPPENING.

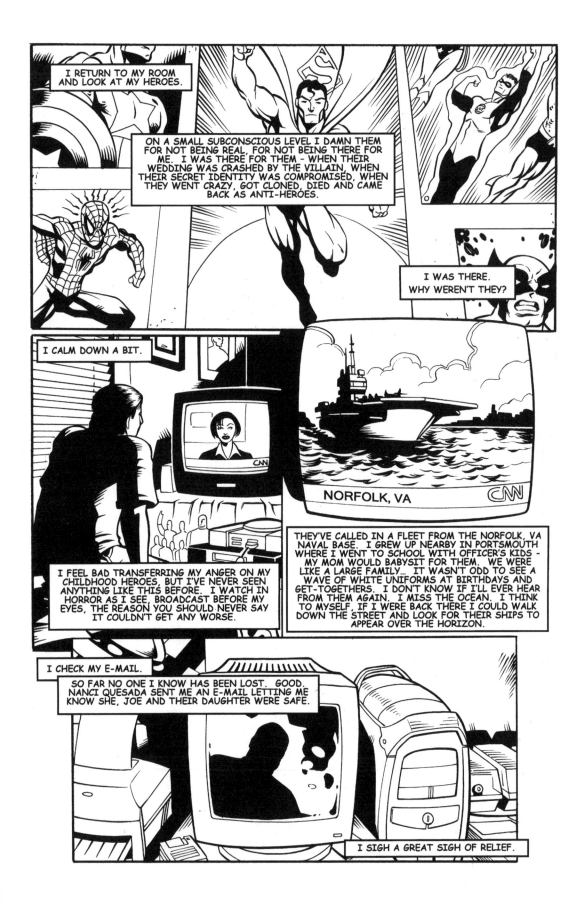

I RETURN TO MY ROOM AND LOOK AT MY HEROES.

ON A SMALL SUBCONSCIOUS LEVEL I DAMN THEM FOR NOT BEING REAL, FOR NOT BEING THERE FOR ME. I WAS THERE FOR THEM - WHEN THEIR WEDDING WAS CRASHED BY THE VILLAIN, WHEN THEIR SECRET IDENTITY WAS COMPROMISED, WHEN THEY WENT CRAZY, GOT CLONED, DIED AND CAME BACK AS ANTI-HEROES.

I WAS THERE. WHY WEREN'T THEY?

I CALM DOWN A BIT.

NORFOLK, VA

I FEEL BAD TRANSFERRING MY ANGER ON MY CHILDHOOD HEROES, BUT I'VE NEVER SEEN ANYTHING LIKE THIS BEFORE. I WATCH IN HORROR AS I SEE, BROADCAST BEFORE MY EYES, THE REASON YOU SHOULD NEVER SAY IT COULDN'T GET ANY WORSE.

THEY'VE CALLED IN A FLEET FROM THE NORFOLK, VA NAVAL BASE. I GREW UP NEARBY IN PORTSMOUTH WHERE I WENT TO SCHOOL WITH OFFICER'S KIDS - MY MOM WOULD BABYSIT FOR THEM. WE WERE LIKE A LARGE FAMILY... IT WASN'T ODD TO SEE A WAVE OF WHITE UNIFORMS AT BIRTHDAYS AND GET-TOGETHERS. I DON'T KNOW IF I'LL EVER HEAR FROM THEM AGAIN. I MISS THE OCEAN. I THINK TO MYSELF, IF I WERE BACK THERE I COULD WALK DOWN THE STREET AND LOOK FOR THEIR SHIPS TO APPEAR OVER THE HORIZON.

I CHECK MY E-MAIL.

SO FAR NO ONE I KNOW HAS BEEN LOST. GOOD. NANCI QUESADA SENT ME AN E-MAIL LETTING ME KNOW SHE, JOE AND THEIR DAUGHTER WERE SAFE.

I SIGH A GREAT SIGH OF RELIEF.

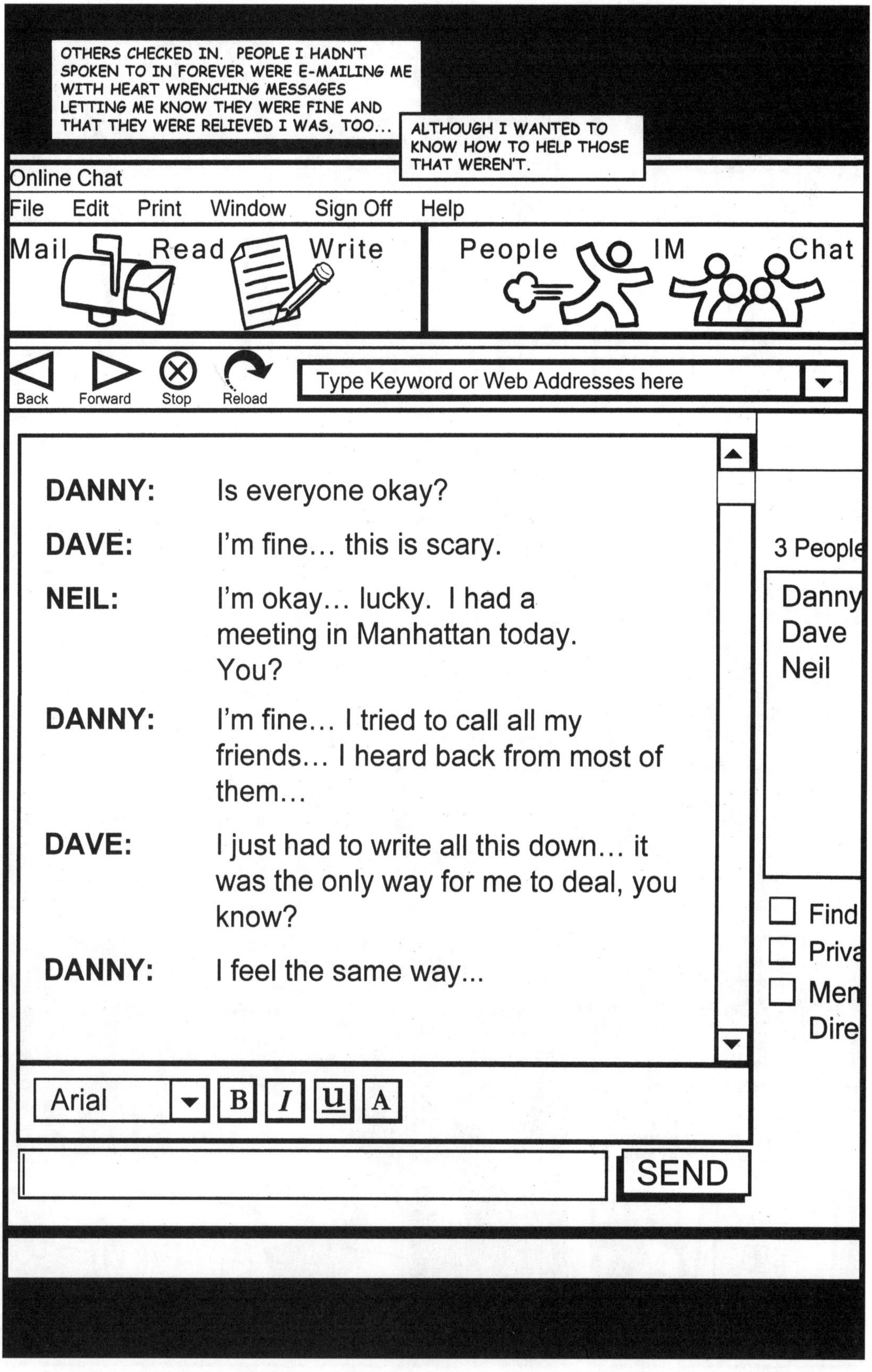
OTHERS CHECKED IN. PEOPLE I HADN'T SPOKEN TO IN FOREVER WERE E-MAILING ME WITH HEART WRENCHING MESSAGES LETTING ME KNOW THEY WERE FINE AND THAT THEY WERE RELIEVED I WAS, TOO...
ALTHOUGH I WANTED TO KNOW HOW TO HELP THOSE THAT WEREN'T.
Online Chat
File Edit Print Window Sign Off Help
Mail Read Write
People IM Chat
Back Forward Stop Reload
Type Keyword or Web Addresses here
DANNY: Is everyone okay?
DAVE: I'm fine… this is scary.
NEIL: I'm okay… lucky. I had a meeting in Manhattan today. You?
DANNY: I'm fine… I tried to call all my friends… I heard back from most of them…
DAVE: I just had to write all this down… it was the only way for me to deal, you know?
DANNY: I feel the same way...
3 Peopl
Dann
Dave
Neil
Find
Priv
Men
Dire
Arial
B I U A
SEND

"SLEEPING THROUGH A NIGHTMARE" ©2001 JEN SORENSEN

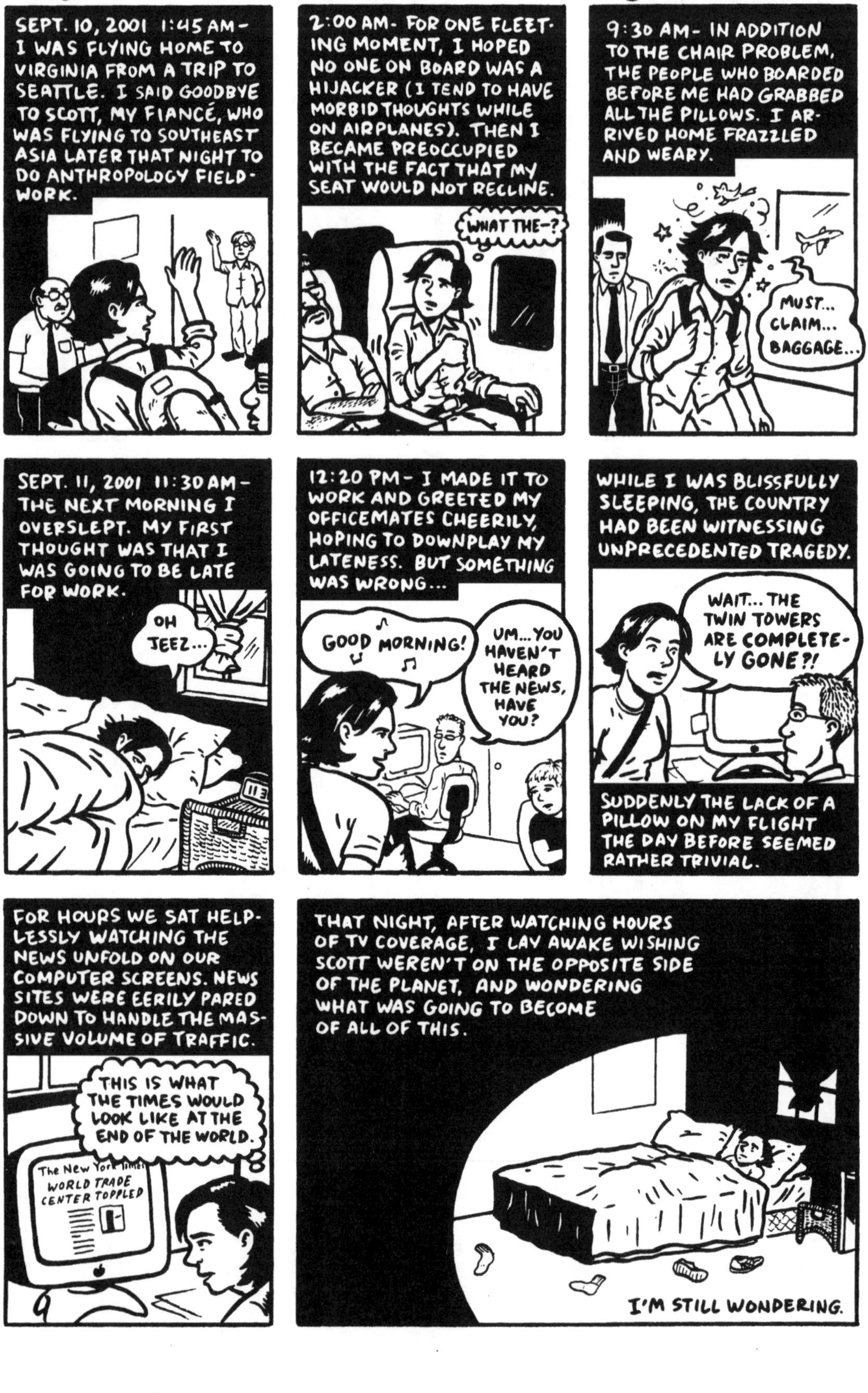
SEPT. 10, 2001 1:45 AM - I WAS FLYING HOME TO VIRGINIA FROM A TRIP TO SEATTLE. I SAID GOODBYE TO SCOTT, MY FIANCÉ, WHO WAS FLYING TO SOUTHEAST ASIA LATER THAT NIGHT TO DO ANTHROPOLOGY FIELD-WORK.
2:00 AM - FOR ONE FLEETING MOMENT, I HOPED NO ONE ON BOARD WAS A HIJACKER (I TEND TO HAVE MORBID THOUGHTS WHILE ON AIRPLANES). THEN I BECAME PREOCCUPIED WITH THE FACT THAT MY SEAT WOULD NOT RECLINE.
WHAT THE-?
9:30 AM - IN ADDITION TO THE CHAIR PROBLEM, THE PEOPLE WHO BOARDED BEFORE ME HAD GRABBED ALL THE PILLOWS. I ARRIVED HOME FRAZZLED AND WEARY.
MUST... CLAIM... BAGGAGE...
SEPT. 11, 2001 11:30 AM - THE NEXT MORNING I OVERSLEPT. MY FIRST THOUGHT WAS THAT I WAS GOING TO BE LATE FOR WORK.
OH JEEZ...
12:20 PM - I MADE IT TO WORK AND GREETED MY OFFICEMATES CHEERILY, HOPING TO DOWNPLAY MY LATENESS. BUT SOMETHING WAS WRONG...
GOOD MORNING!
UM... YOU HAVEN'T HEARD THE NEWS, HAVE YOU?
WHILE I WAS BLISSFULLY SLEEPING, THE COUNTRY HAD BEEN WITNESSING UNPRECEDENTED TRAGEDY.
WAIT... THE TWIN TOWERS ARE COMPLETELY GONE?!
SUDDENLY THE LACK OF A PILLOW ON MY FLIGHT THE DAY BEFORE SEEMED RATHER TRIVIAL.
FOR HOURS WE SAT HELPLESSLY WATCHING THE NEWS UNFOLD ON OUR COMPUTER SCREENS. NEWS SITES WERE EERILY PARED DOWN TO HANDLE THE MASSIVE VOLUME OF TRAFFIC.
THIS IS WHAT THE TIMES WOULD LOOK LIKE AT THE END OF THE WORLD.
The New York Times
WORLD TRADE CENTER TOPPLED
THAT NIGHT, AFTER WATCHING HOURS OF TV COVERAGE, I LAY AWAKE WISHING SCOTT WEREN'T ON THE OPPOSITE SIDE OF THE PLANET, AND WONDERING WHAT WAS GOING TO BECOME OF ALL OF THIS.
I'M STILL WONDERING.

School Daze

by Brian Clopper

SEPTEMBER 11TH WAS A DAY THAT THE MEASURE OF MANKIND WAS TAKEN.

THE FOLLOWING COMIC DESCRIBES MY LIMITED EXPERIENCES FROM THAT TRAGIC DAY.

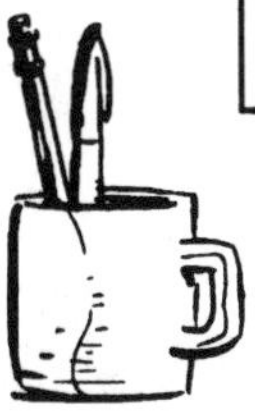

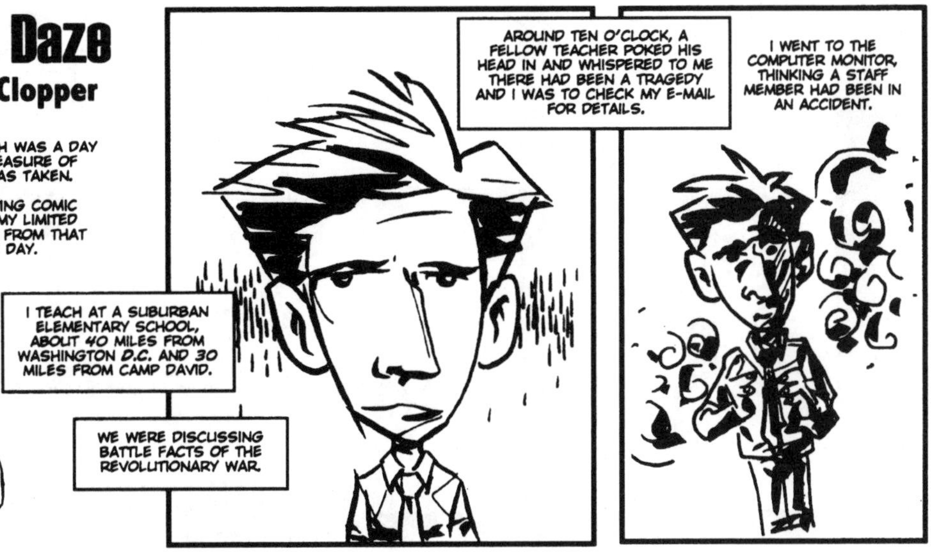
I TEACH AT A SUBURBAN ELEMENTARY SCHOOL, ABOUT 40 MILES FROM WASHINGTON D.C. AND 30 MILES FROM CAMP DAVID.
WE WERE DISCUSSING BATTLE FACTS OF THE REVOLUTIONARY WAR.
AROUND TEN O'CLOCK, A FELLOW TEACHER POKED HIS HEAD IN AND WHISPERED TO ME THERE HAD BEEN A TRAGEDY AND I WAS TO CHECK MY E-MAIL FOR DETAILS.
I WENT TO THE COMPUTER MONITOR, THINKING A STAFF MEMBER HAD BEEN IN AN ACCIDENT.

MY STUDENTS CONTINUED TO WORK ON THEIR ASSIGNMENT.

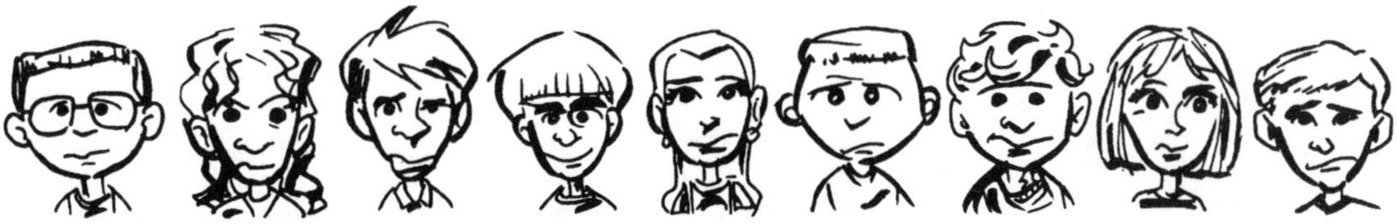

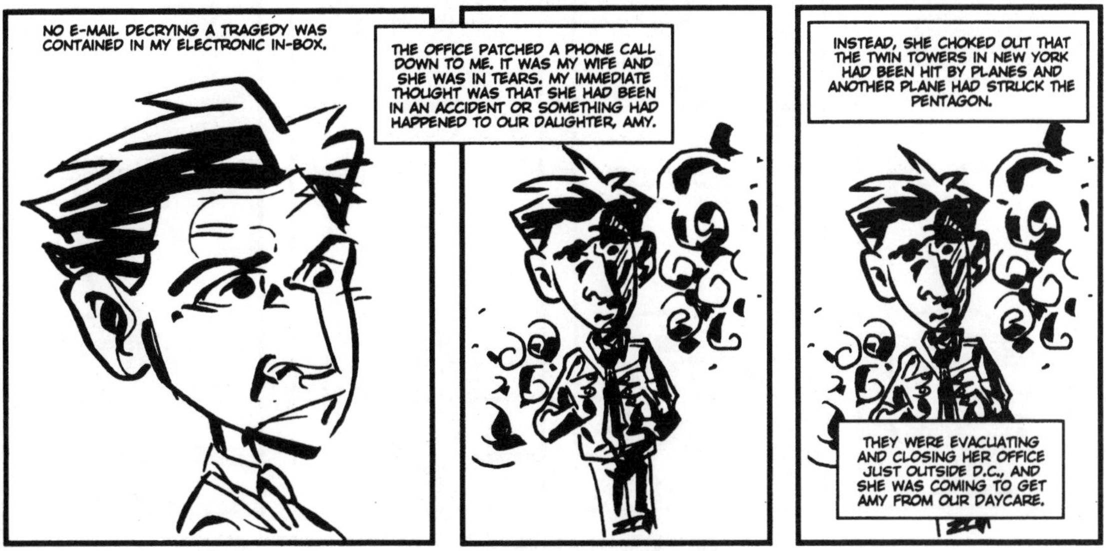
NO E-MAIL DECRYING A TRAGEDY WAS CONTAINED IN MY ELECTRONIC IN-BOX.
THE OFFICE PATCHED A PHONE CALL DOWN TO ME. IT WAS MY WIFE AND SHE WAS IN TEARS. MY IMMEDIATE THOUGHT WAS THAT SHE HAD BEEN IN AN ACCIDENT OR SOMETHING HAD HAPPENED TO OUR DAUGHTER, AMY.
INSTEAD, SHE CHOKED OUT THAT THE TWIN TOWERS IN NEW YORK HAD BEEN HIT BY PLANES AND ANOTHER PLANE HAD STRUCK THE PENTAGON.
THEY WERE EVACUATING AND CLOSING HER OFFICE JUST OUTSIDE D.C., AND SHE WAS COMING TO GET AMY FROM OUR DAYCARE.

I COULD TELL SHE NEEDED ME.

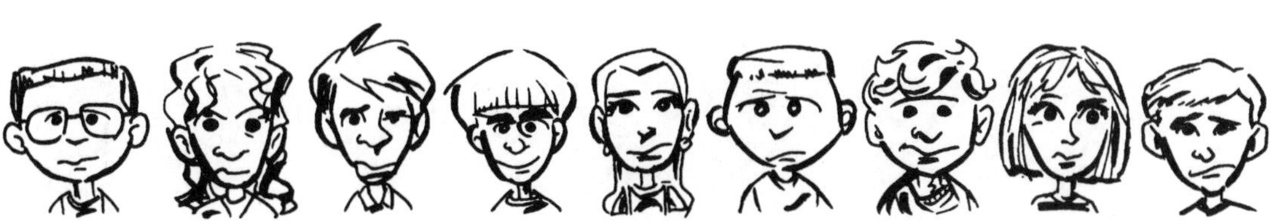

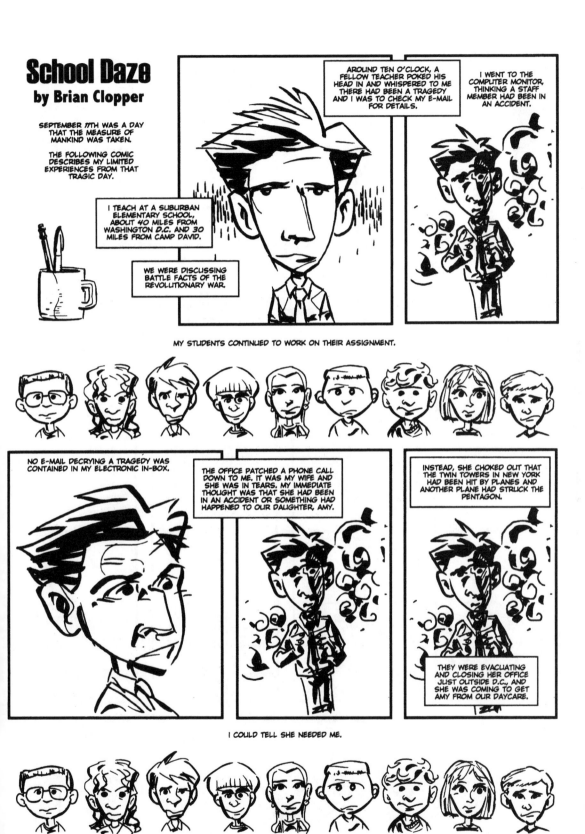

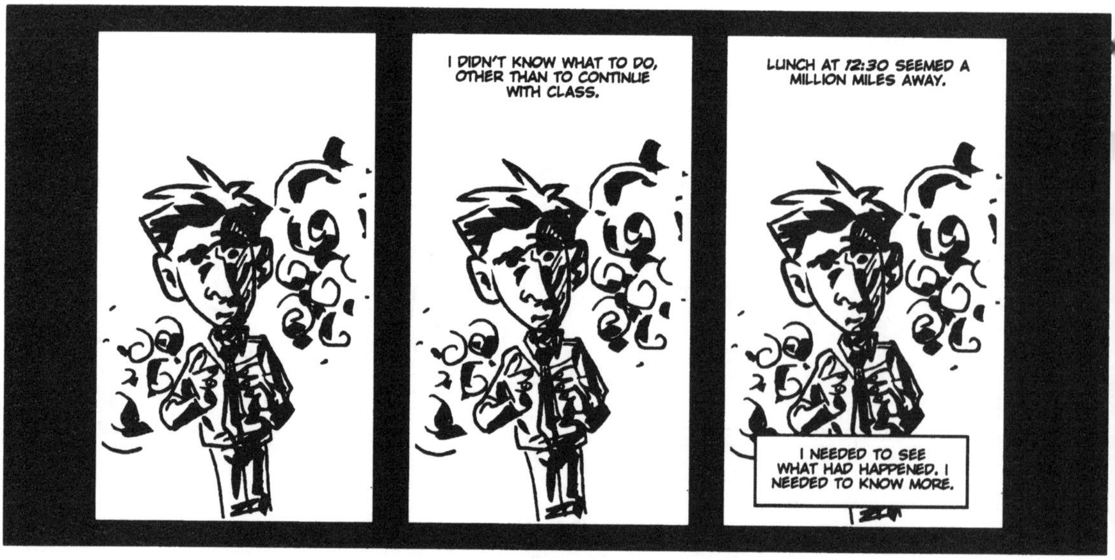
I DIDN'T KNOW WHAT TO DO, OTHER THAN TO CONTINUE WITH CLASS.
LUNCH AT 12:30 SEEMED A MILLION MILES AWAY.
I NEEDED TO SEE WHAT HAD HAPPENED. I NEEDED TO KNOW MORE.

I CHECKED MY E-MAIL, AND OUR ADMINISTRATION HAD SENT OUT A VERY BRIEF ALERT OF THE EVENTS WITH A DECLARATION THAT WE WERE NOT TO INFORM THE STUDENTS.

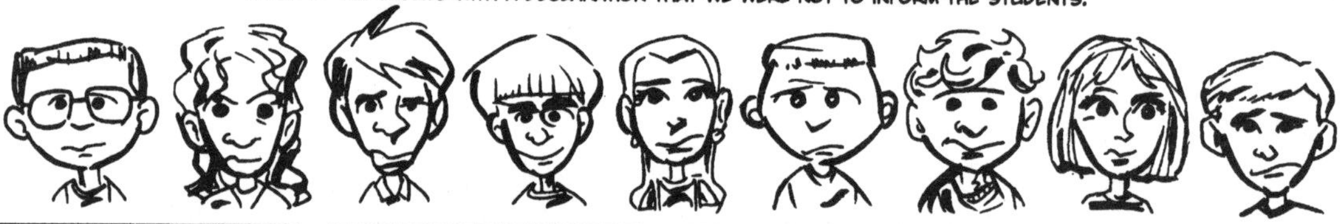

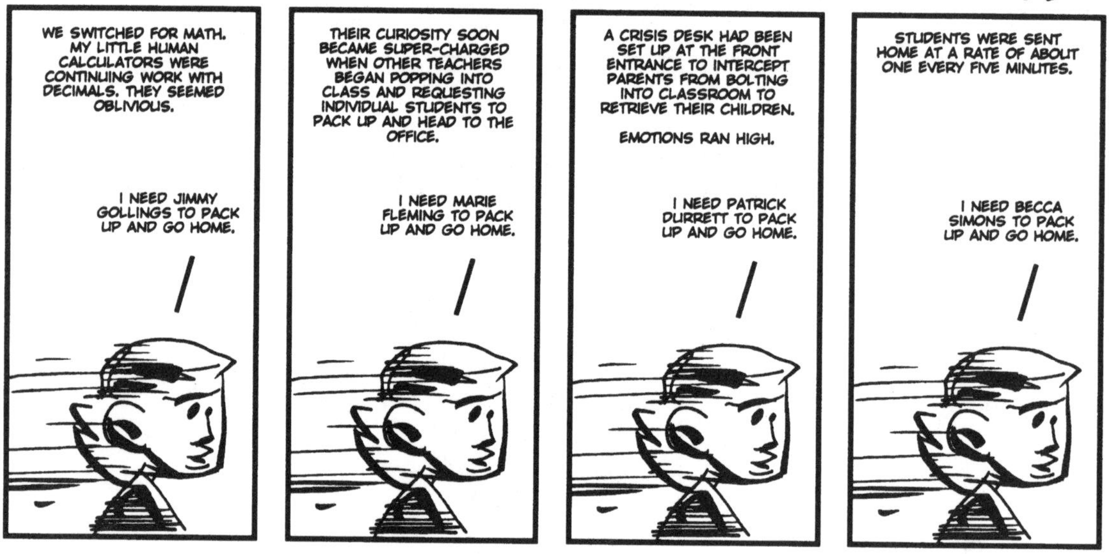
WE SWITCHED FOR MATH. MY LITTLE HUMAN CALCULATORS WERE CONTINUING WORK WITH DECIMALS. THEY SEEMED OBLIVIOUS.
I NEED JIMMY GOLLINGS TO PACK UP AND GO HOME.
THEIR CURIOSITY SOON BECAME SUPER-CHARGED WHEN OTHER TEACHERS BEGAN POPPING INTO CLASS AND REQUESTING INDIVIDUAL STUDENTS TO PACK UP AND HEAD TO THE OFFICE.
I NEED MARIE FLEMING TO PACK UP AND GO HOME.
A CRISIS DESK HAD BEEN SET UP AT THE FRONT ENTRANCE TO INTERCEPT PARENTS FROM BOLTING INTO CLASSROOM TO RETRIEVE THEIR CHILDREN.
EMOTIONS RAN HIGH.
I NEED PATRICK DURRETT TO PACK UP AND GO HOME.
STUDENTS WERE SENT HOME AT A RATE OF ABOUT ONE EVERY FIVE MINUTES.
I NEED BECCA SIMONS TO PACK UP AND GO HOME.

THE REMAINING STUDENTS WERE GETTING ANXIOUS.

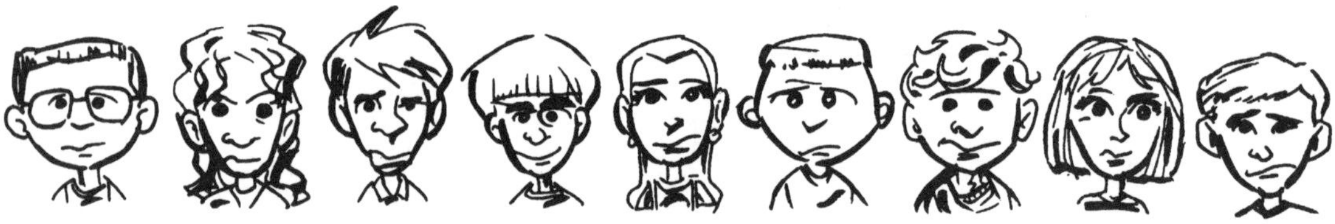

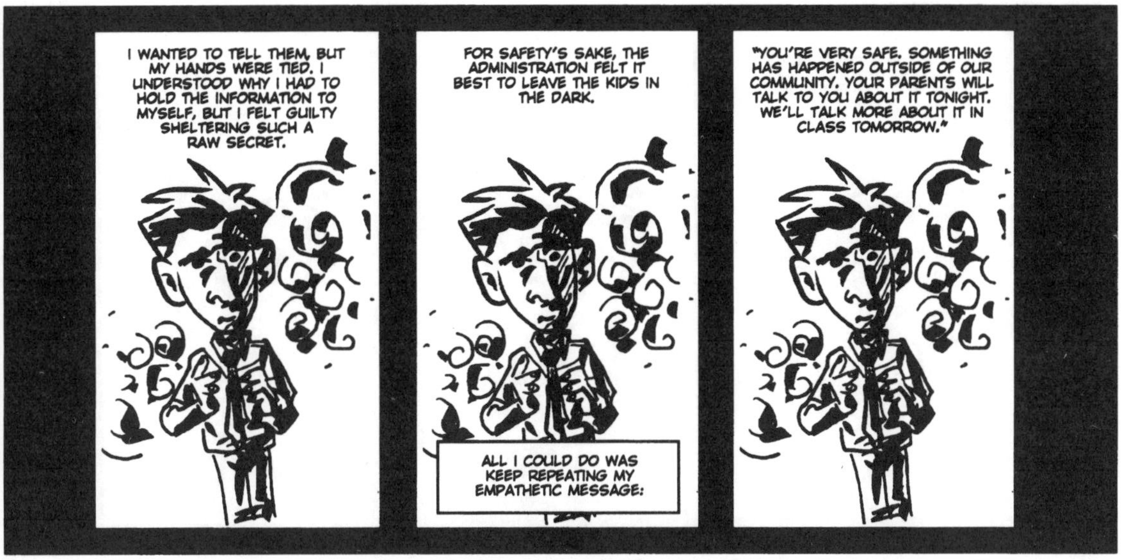
I WANTED TO TELL THEM, BUT MY HANDS WERE TIED. I UNDERSTOOD WHY I HAD TO HOLD THE INFORMATION TO MYSELF, BUT I FELT GUILTY SHELTERING SUCH A RAW SECRET.
FOR SAFETY'S SAKE, THE ADMINISTRATION FELT IT BEST TO LEAVE THE KIDS IN THE DARK.
ALL I COULD DO WAS KEEP REPEATING MY EMPATHETIC MESSAGE:
"YOU'RE VERY SAFE. SOMETHING HAS HAPPENED OUTSIDE OF OUR COMMUNITY. YOUR PARENTS WILL TALK TO YOU ABOUT IT TONIGHT. WE'LL TALK MORE ABOUT IT IN CLASS TOMORROW."

BUT MY MESSAGE NAGGED AT ME. IT ***WAS OUR*** COMMUNITY.

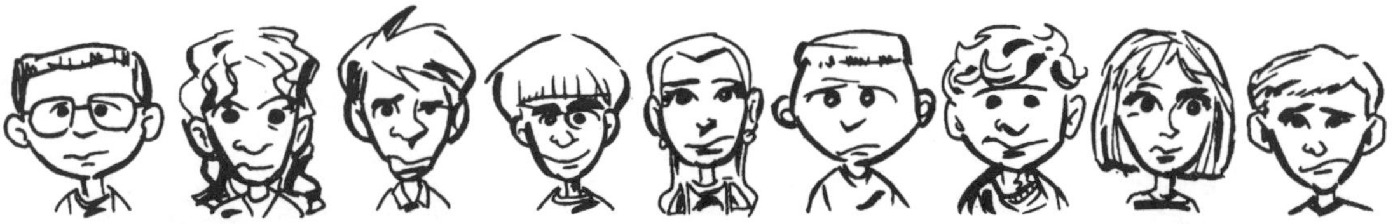

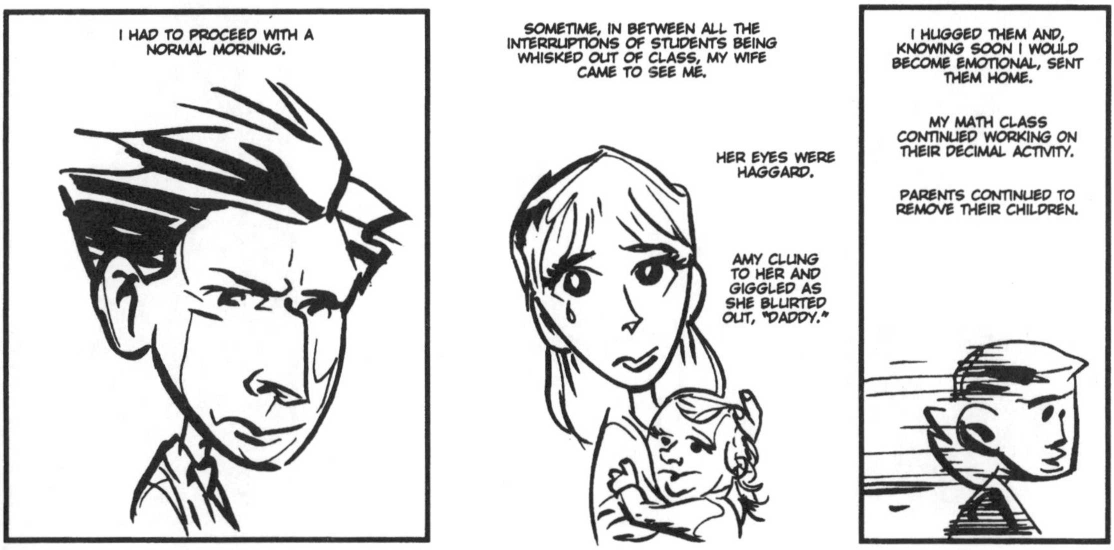
I HAD TO PROCEED WITH A NORMAL MORNING.
SOMETIME, IN BETWEEN ALL THE INTERRUPTIONS OF STUDENTS BEING WHISKED OUT OF CLASS, MY WIFE CAME TO SEE ME.
HER EYES WERE HAGGARD.
AMY CLUNG TO HER AND GIGGLED AS SHE BLURTED OUT, "DADDY."
I HUGGED THEM AND, KNOWING SOON I WOULD BECOME EMOTIONAL, SENT THEM HOME.
MY MATH CLASS CONTINUED WORKING ON THEIR DECIMAL ACTIVITY.
PARENTS CONTINUED TO REMOVE THEIR CHILDREN.

SCHOOL, OUR RANKS DIMINISHED, MARCHED ON.

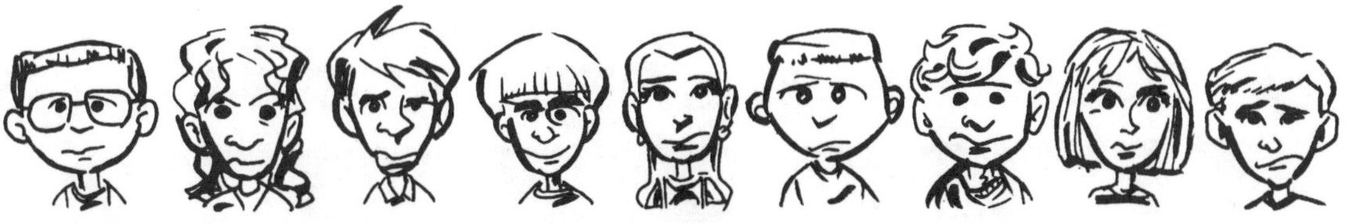

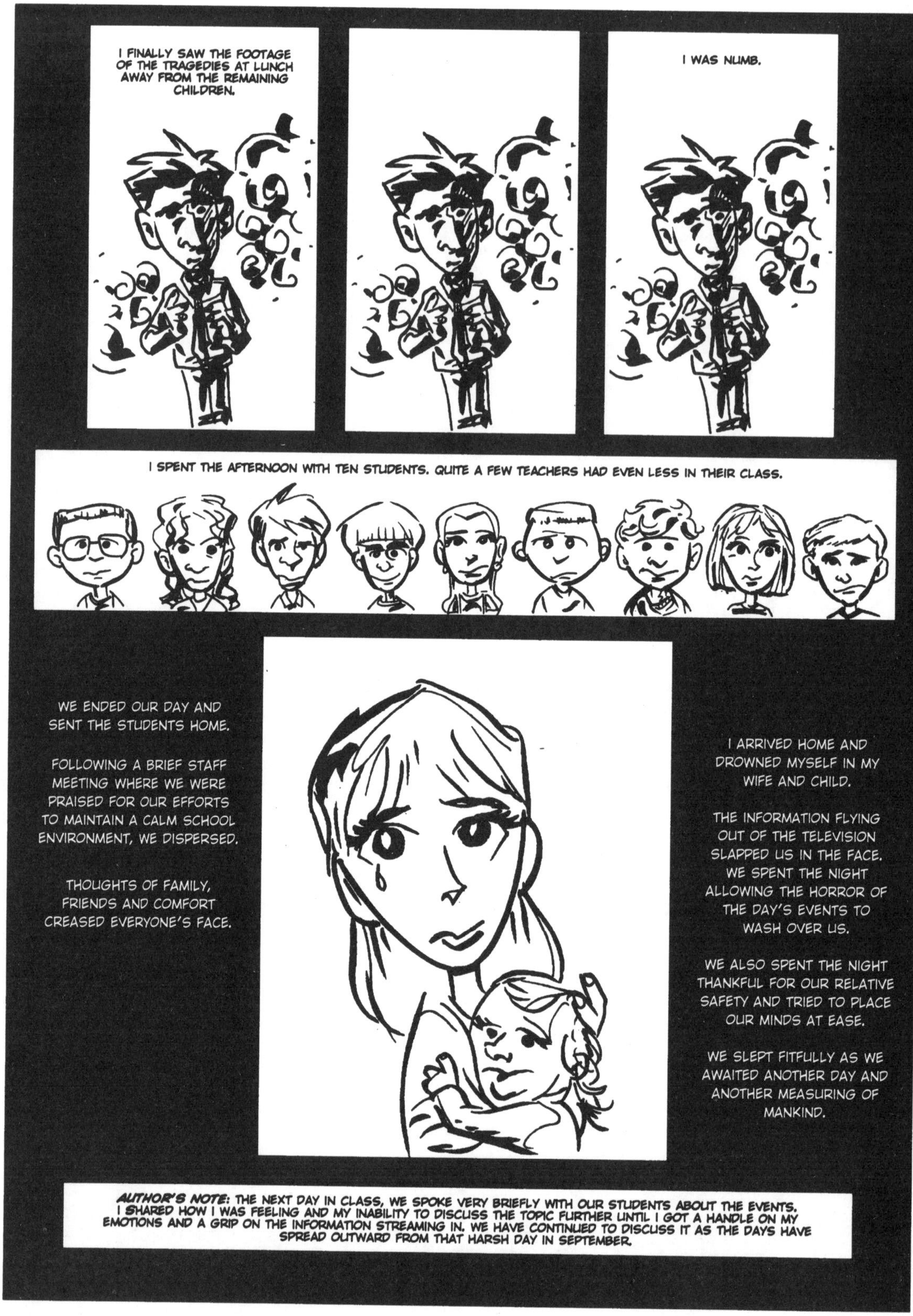
I FINALLY SAW THE FOOTAGE OF THE TRAGEDIES AT LUNCH AWAY FROM THE REMAINING CHILDREN.
I WAS NUMB.
I SPENT THE AFTERNOON WITH TEN STUDENTS. QUITE A FEW TEACHERS HAD EVEN LESS IN THEIR CLASS.
WE ENDED OUR DAY AND SENT THE STUDENTS HOME.
FOLLOWING A BRIEF STAFF MEETING WHERE WE WERE PRAISED FOR OUR EFFORTS TO MAINTAIN A CALM SCHOOL ENVIRONMENT, WE DISPERSED.
THOUGHTS OF FAMILY, FRIENDS AND COMFORT CREASED EVERYONE'S FACE.
I ARRIVED HOME AND DROWNED MYSELF IN MY WIFE AND CHILD.
THE INFORMATION FLYING OUT OF THE TELEVISION SLAPPED US IN THE FACE. WE SPENT THE NIGHT ALLOWING THE HORROR OF THE DAY'S EVENTS TO WASH OVER US.
WE ALSO SPENT THE NIGHT THANKFUL FOR OUR RELATIVE SAFETY AND TRIED TO PLACE OUR MINDS AT EASE.
WE SLEPT FITFULLY AS WE AWAITED ANOTHER DAY AND ANOTHER MEASURING OF MANKIND.
AUTHOR'S NOTE: THE NEXT DAY IN CLASS, WE SPOKE VERY BRIEFLY WITH OUR STUDENTS ABOUT THE EVENTS. I SHARED HOW I WAS FEELING AND MY INABILITY TO DISCUSS THE TOPIC FURTHER UNTIL I GOT A HANDLE ON MY EMOTIONS AND A GRIP ON THE INFORMATION STREAMING IN. WE HAVE CONTINUED TO DISCUSS IT AS THE DAYS HAVE SPREAD OUTWARD FROM THAT HARSH DAY IN SEPTEMBER.

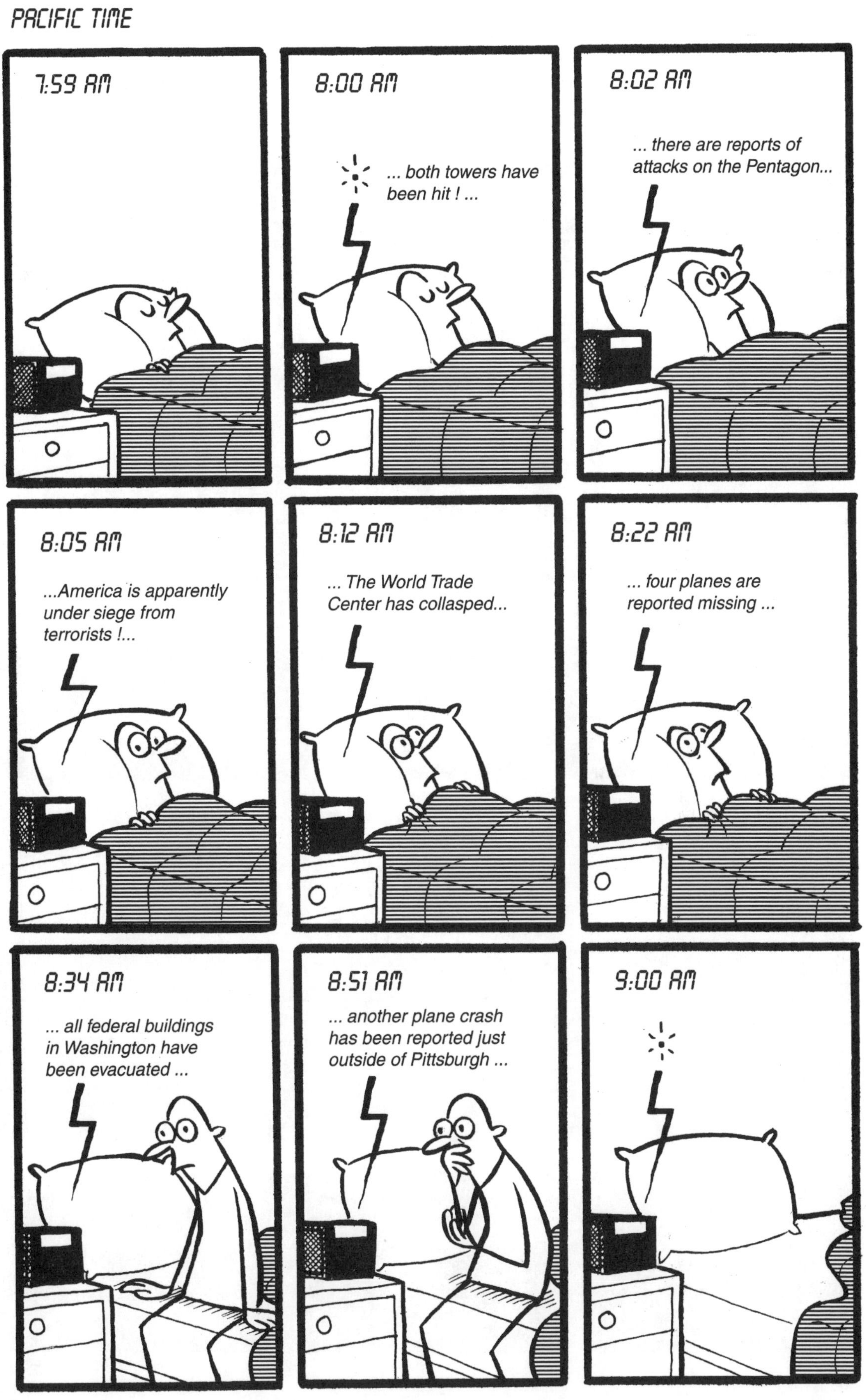
PACIFIC TIME
7:59 AM
8:00 AM
... both towers have been hit ! ...
8:02 AM
... there are reports of attacks on the Pentagon...
8:05 AM
...America is apparently under siege from terrorists !...
8:12 AM
... The World Trade Center has collasped...
8:22 AM
... four planes are reported missing ...
8:34 AM
... all federal buildings in Washington have been evacuated ...
8:51 AM
... another plane crash has been reported just outside of Pittsburgh ...
9:00 AM

I'VE ALWAYS THOUGHT SEPTEMBER WAS A BAD MONTH. AS A CHILD, SEPTEMBER IS THE MONTH WHERE THAT LIMITLESS, INCREDIBLE FREEDOM OF THE SUMMER FALLS TO THE IMPLACABLE ROUTINE OF SCHOOLWORK AND MINDLESS TEDIUM. BUT IT GOES DEEPER THAN THAT, FAR DEEPER, INTO THOSE PLACES IN US WE RARELY TALK ABOUT...

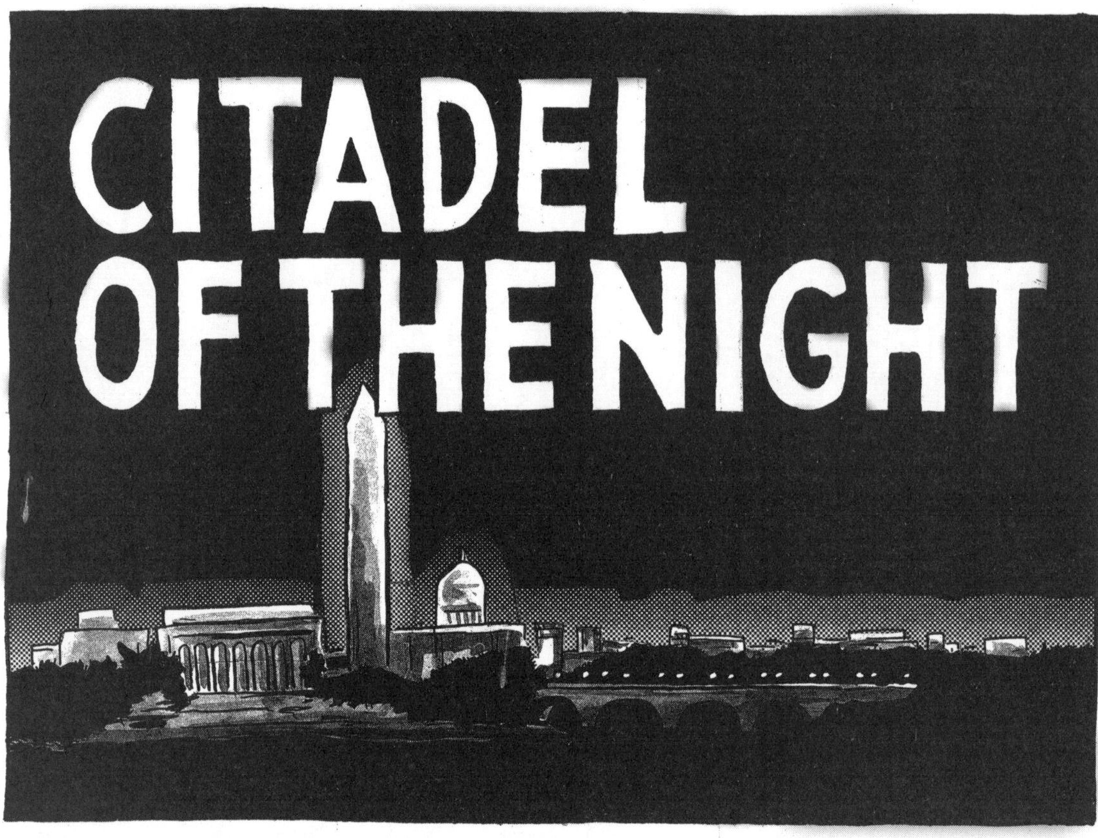
CITADEL
OF THE NIGHT

I LIVE JUST OUTSIDE OF D.C., JUST ON THE OTHER SIDE OF THE BELTWAY, REALLY, IN THE MARYLAND SUBURBS, IN A NICE APARTMENT COMPLEX.

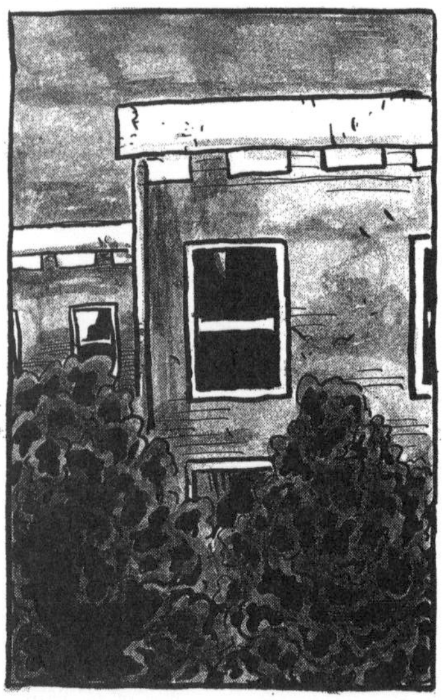

PART OF MY DRIVE TO WORK IS THROUGH THE BELTSVILLE AGRICULTURAL CENTER, SEVERAL THOUSAND ACRES OF BEAUTIFUL, PURE FARMLAND BUTTING UP AGAINST THE DC BELTWAY.

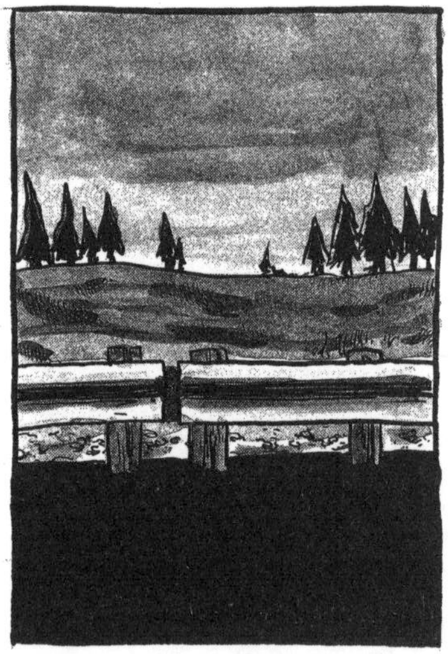

IT'S AMAZING TO SEE SUCH LUSH, SUCH PERFECT LAND EXIST AGAINST THE BACKDROP OF WASHINGTON. THERE ARE NO REAL WORDS TO DESCRIBE IT.

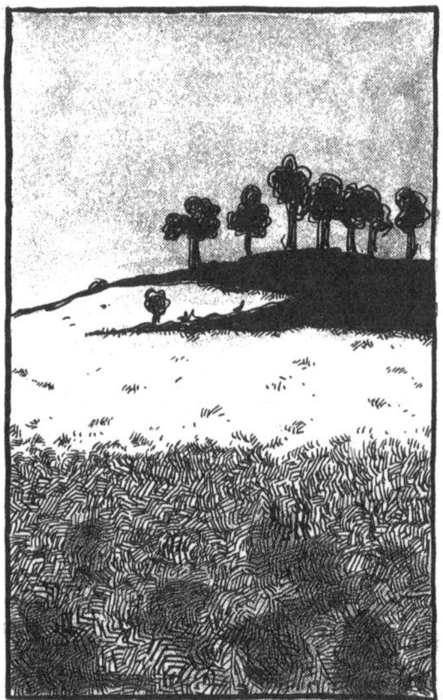

KNOWLE / JENSEN 2001

I THINK, ON OCCASION, THAT THE AGRICULTURAL CENTER IS THE ONLY REASON I MAKE IT INTO WORK MOST DAYS - THAT THE TRANQUIL, SERENE HEART OF THAT PLACE IS THE ONLY REASON I CAN FIND THE COURAGE TO DRIVE THOSE LONG MILES TO THE DC METRO STATION, TO BOARD THAT DANK, GREY TRAIN.

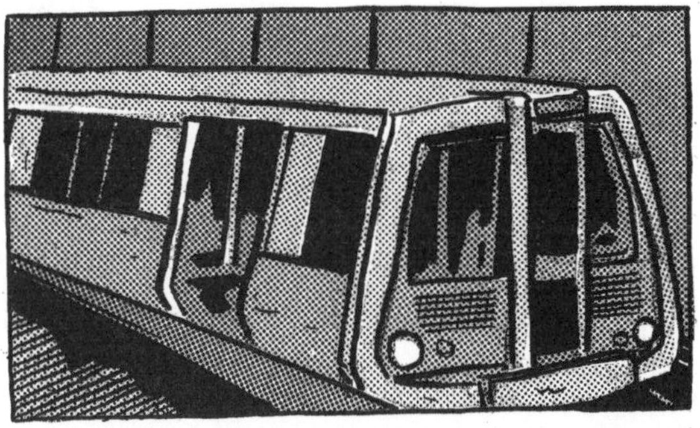

THIS WEEK, THE QUIET BACKROADS OF THE CENTER WERE CLOSED, BARRICADED TO HOLD AGAINST THE HORRORS OF THE WORLD.

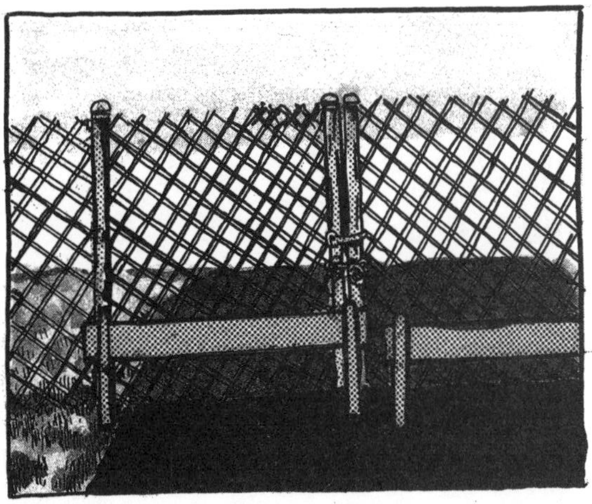

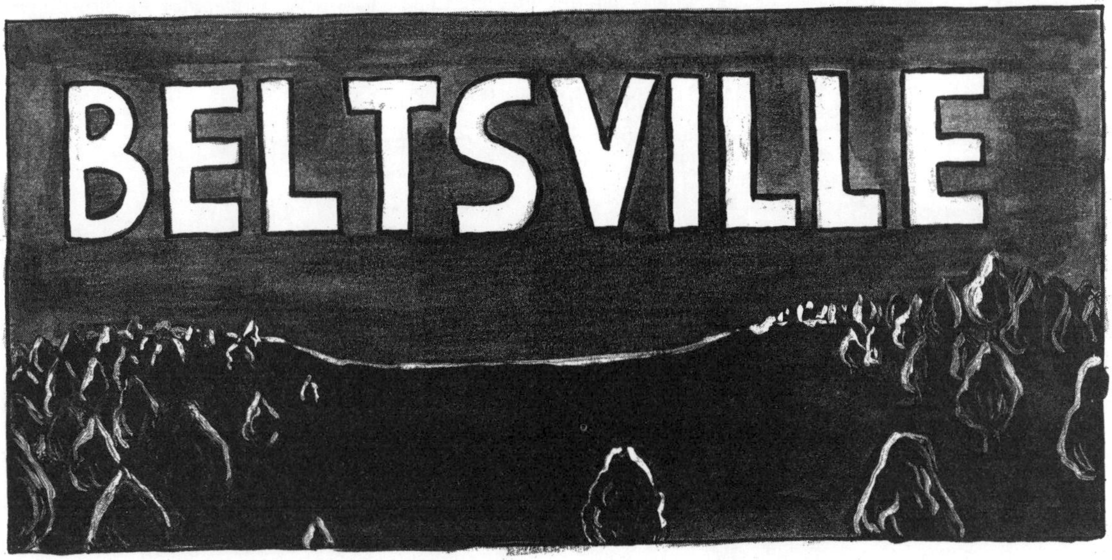
BELTSVILLE

THERE IS ONLY ONE OTHER PLACE I HAVE SEEN, IN THIS BRIEF LIFE, THAT COMPARES TO THE TRANQUILITY OF BELTSVILLE.

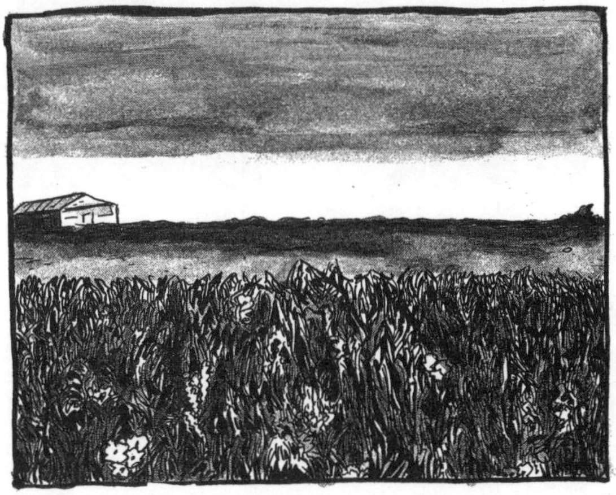

THAT PLACE, SEVERAL HUNDRED MILES FROM THE PRESENT-DAY HORROR OF DOWNTOWN MANHATTAN, IS ATTICA.

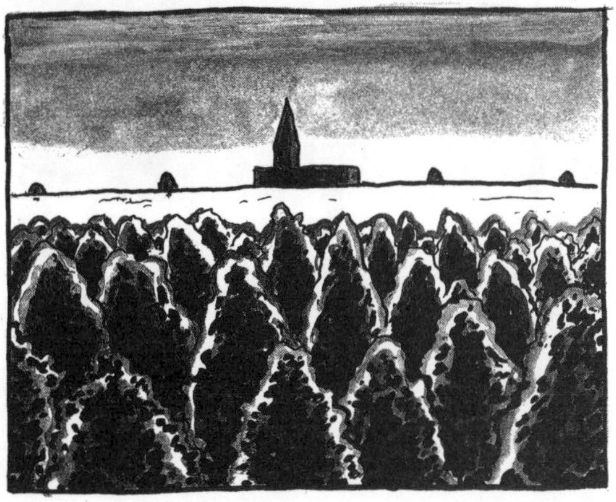

AMIDST THE ROLLING FARMLANDS OF UPSTATE NEW YORK, YOU CAN STILL SEE HER - CALLED BY SOME THE HARDEST PRISON IN AMERICA. FOR ME, IT WAS A PLACE OF CHILDHOOD FANTASY, THE AMERICAN DREAM INSCRIBED IN SMALL TOWN STREETS. AND YET, THIRTY YEARS AGO, THIS PAST WEEK, SHE WAS HOST TO THE WORST PRISON RIOTS IN AMERICAN HISTORY.

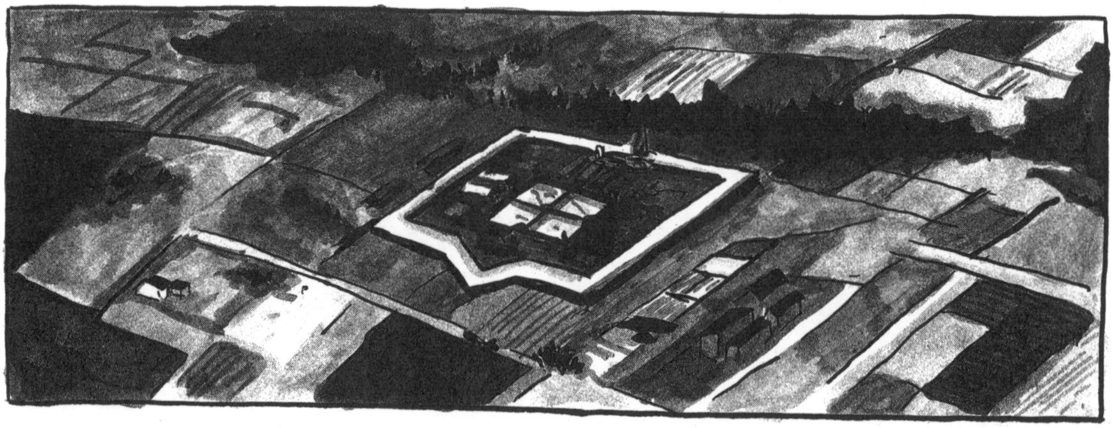

THE STREETS OF ATTICA ARE DRAWN FROM SOME NORMAN ROCKWELL VERSION OF AMERICA, A PLACE WHERE YOUR NEIGHBORS ARE YOUR CLOSEST FRIENDS AND NO ONE LOCKS THEIR DOORS AT NIGHT. I WOULD VISIT THERE, TWICE A YEAR, TO SEE MY GRANDPARENTS. IT WAS NOT UNTIL A FEW YEARS AGO THAT I WOULD DISCOVER WHAT HAD TRANSPIRED BEHIND THAT FACADE.

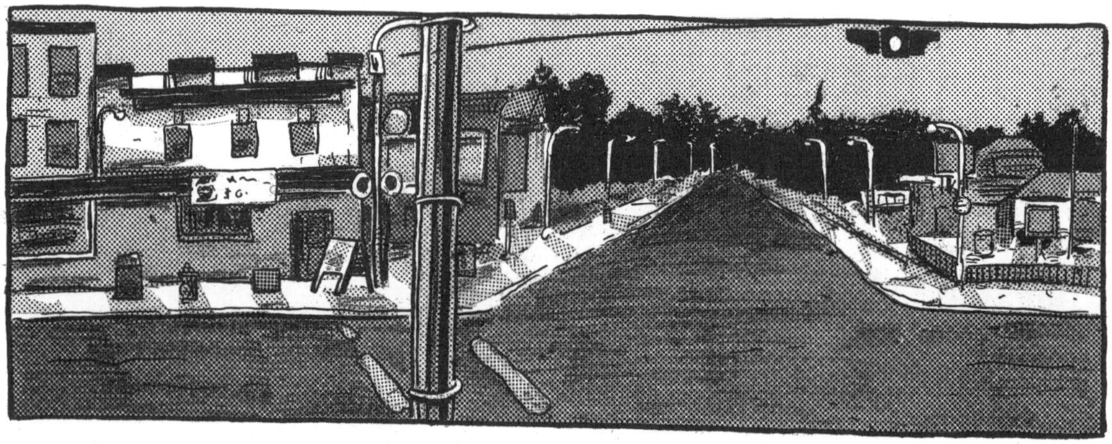

MY MOTHER'S FATHER, ARTHUR SMITH, WAS A GUARD TAKEN PRISONER DURING THE RIOTS.

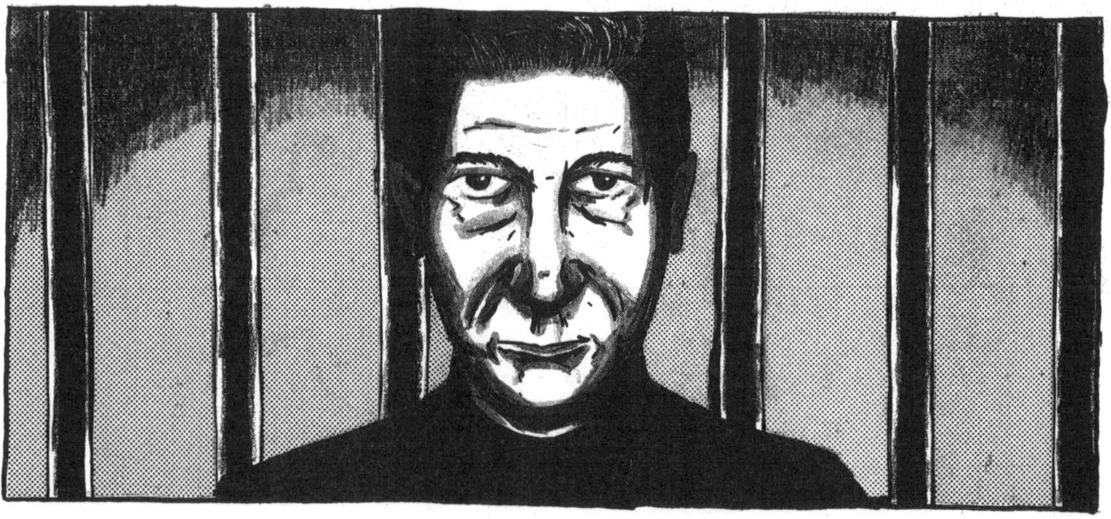

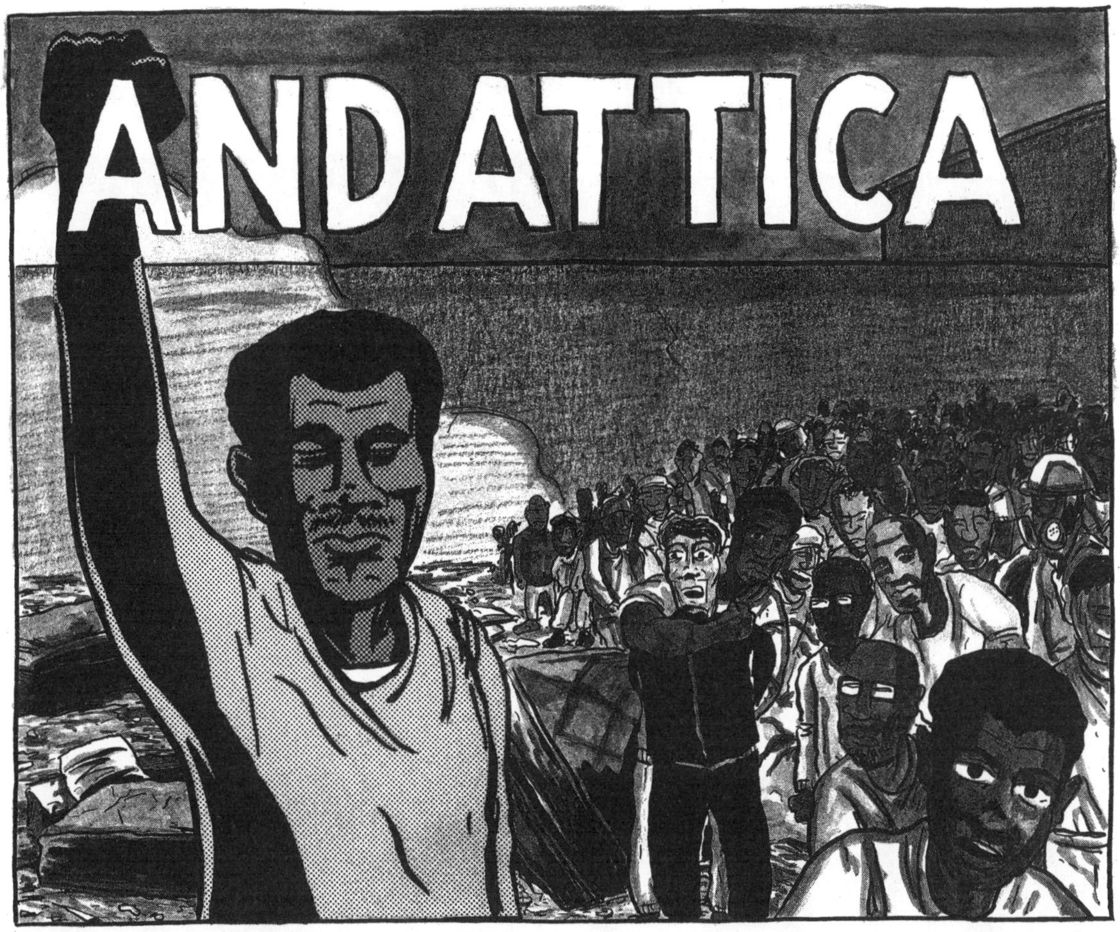
AND ATTICA

AMERICA'S PRISON SYSTEM SEEMS TO MIRROR OUR FOREIGN POLICY- DO WHAT YOU CAN TO HELP, BUT BE PREPARED TO WRITE SOME OFF. I AM PROUD TO SAY THAT MY GRANDFATHER NEVER SUBSCRIBED TO THIS VIEW OF HUMANITY, AND I CAN ONLY PRAY THAT I CAN SAY THE SAME.

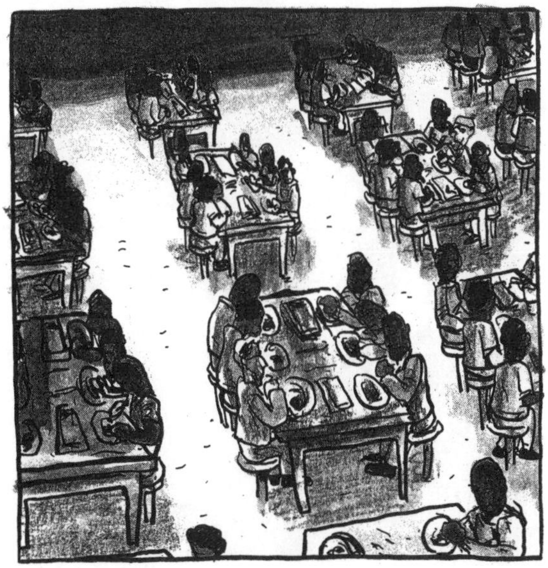

MY GRANDFATHER WAS IN CHARGE OF THE CHRISTMAS USO SHOW. THEY WOULD BRING IN BEAUTIFUL YOUNG WOMEN AND FUNNY COMEDIANS TO HELP THE CONVICTS WHILE AWAY THEIR TIME, IF EVEN FOR A SINGLE NIGHT, WHILE TRAPPED BEHIND THOSE INESCAPABLE WALLS. HE SAW IT AS A MATTER OF PRIDE, A HUMANITARIAN EFFORT FOR THOSE MEN WHO HAD THEIR HUMANITY STRIPPED FROM THEM.

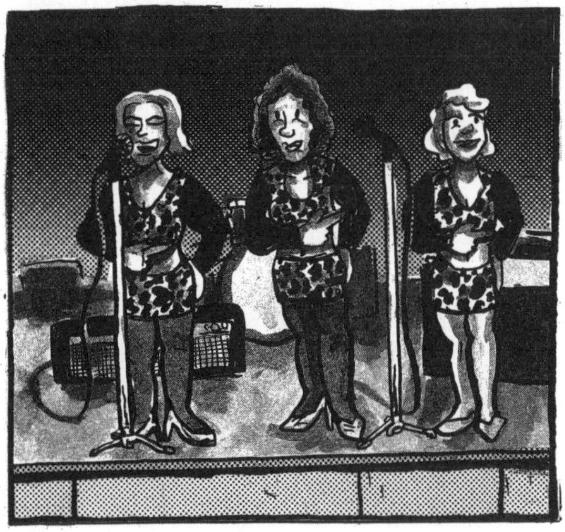

AND THEN CAME THE RIOT. MY GRANDFATHER WAS ON BLOCK A AT THE TIME; THE MEN WHO REVOLTED WERE INMATES OF D BLOCK. HE WAS CAPTURED, HORRIBLY TORTURED, AND GIVEN OVER TO A BLOCK FOR EXECUTION.

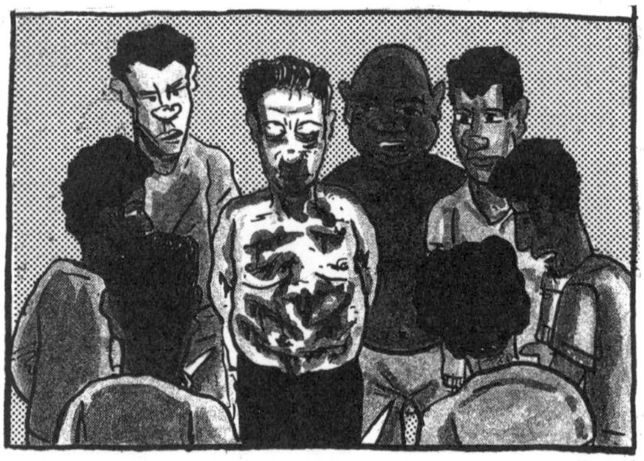

BUT SOMETHING HAPPENED; THE INMATE WHO TOOK MY GRANDFATHER FROM THE CUSTODY OF BLOCK D DISGUISED HIM AS A FELLOW INMATE AND HID HIM IN BLOCK A.

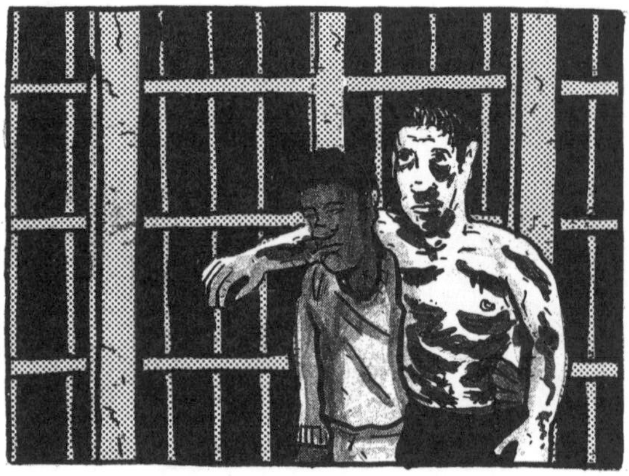

THE INMATE ALSO SAVED THE LIFE OF ANOTHER GUARD AT MY GRANDFATHER'S INSISTENCE. THE WORD LEAKED, AS IT DOES IN SUCH PLACES, BUT THE MAN WHO HID MY GRANDFATHER WOULD NOT RELENT.

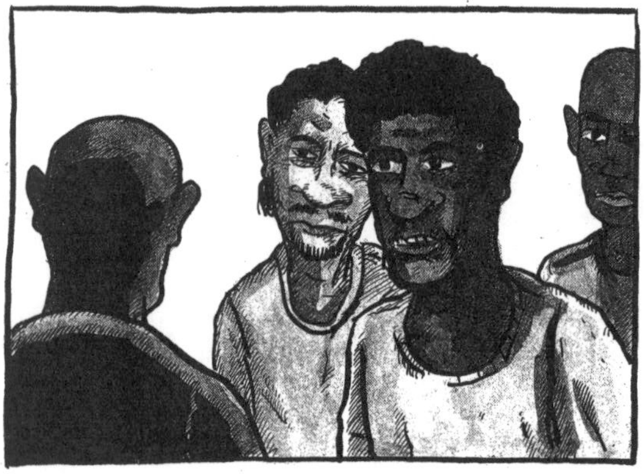

HE WAS KILLED BY HIS FELLOW INMATES, TAKING THE LOCATION OF THE HIDDEN AND PROTECTED GUARDS TO HIS GRAVE. THIS SACRIFICE, IN THE FACE OF UNSPEAKABLE HORROR, SAVED MY GRANDFATHER'S LIFE.

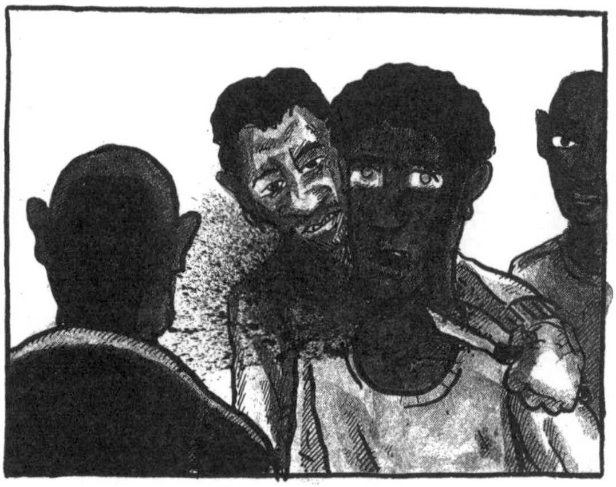

THE NEXT DAY, STATE TROOPERS, UNDER THE ORDER OF THE GOVERNOR OF NEW YORK, RETOOK ATTICA. INMATES AND GUARDS ALIKE FELL BEFORE THE BULLETS FLUNG FROM ATOP THE WALLS OF THE COMPOUND. THE PRISON WAS RE-TAKEN, AT A COST NO ONE SHOULD EVER HAVE TO BEAR.

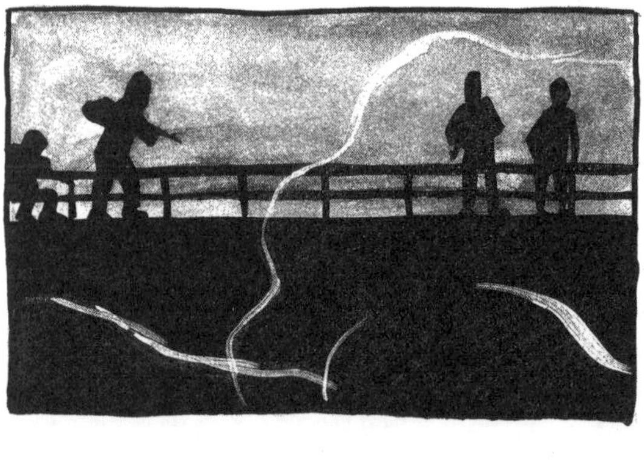

THEY WOULD NEVER HAVE THE USO SHOW FOR THE PRISONERS AGAIN.

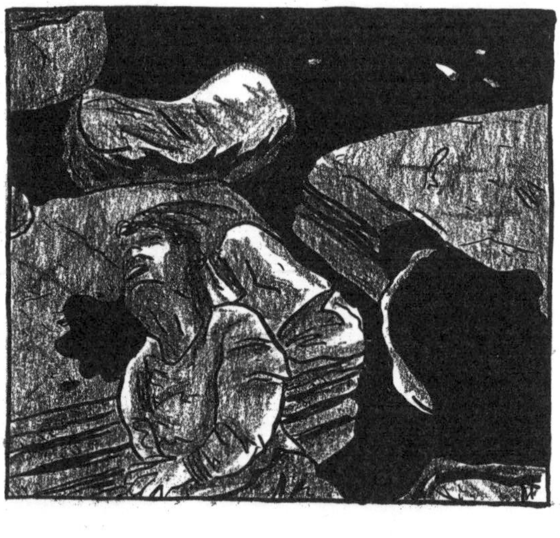

I SIT HERE, THIS SEPTEMBER 15, 2001, WITH A GRIEF TOO BIG TO EXPRESS. SOME FIVE THOUSAND OR MORE AMERICANS KILLED SENSELESSLY. PEOPLE OF EVERY CONCEIVABLE ETHNICITY, CREED, AND IDEOLOGY - TAKEN FROM US WITHOUT REASON. AND YET, I CANNOT FORGET THE SOFT FIELDS OF UPSTATE NEW YORK, OF BELTSVILLE. I CANNOT FORGET THE WAY THE WAY THE WALLS OF ATTICA LOOM OVER THE TINY STREETS OF THE TOWN THAT BEARS ITS NAME.

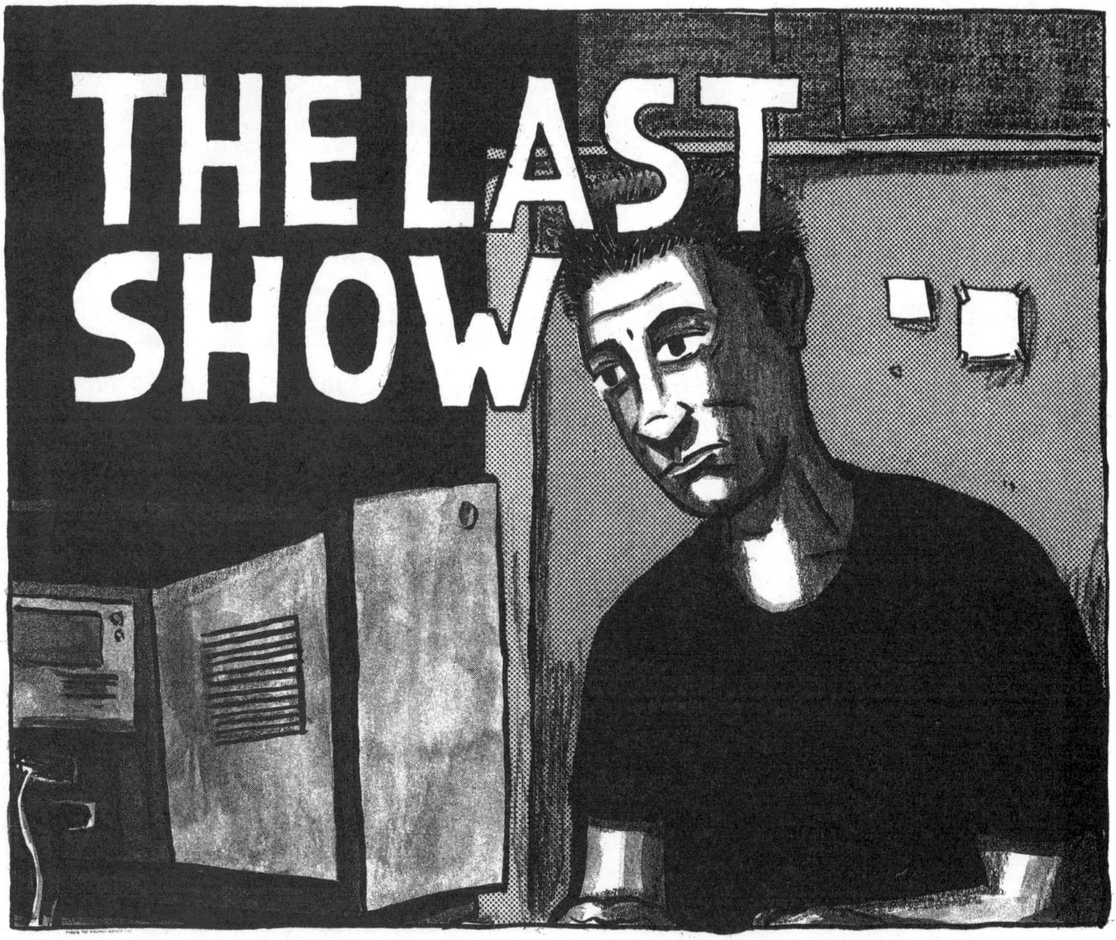
THE LAST SHOW

MY GRANDFATHER DIED FOUR YEARS AGO - TORN APART BY PANCREATIC CANCER, INOPERABLE FROM THE SCARS HE HAD SUFFERED SO MANY YEARS AGO.

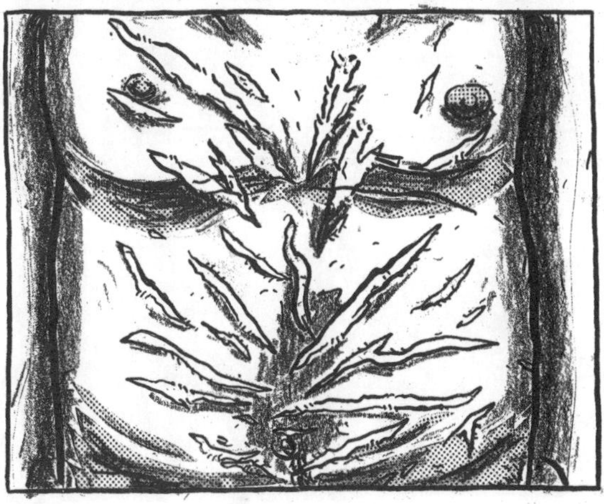

THOSE SCARS, INTERNAL AND EXTERNAL, THAT SEEMED TO THREATEN TO RIP MY FAMILY APART SO MANY TIMES.

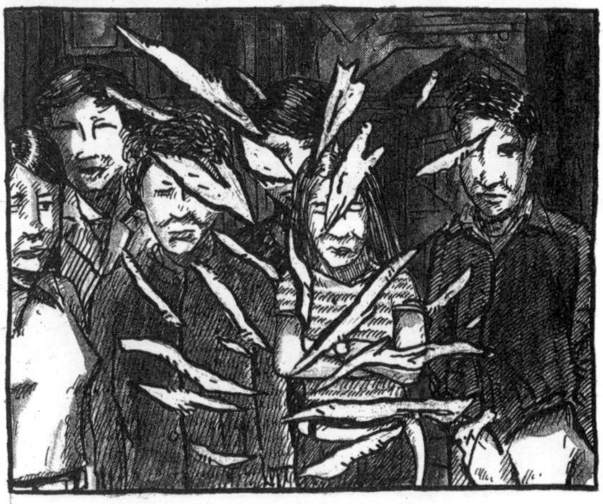

AND I AM THERE TOO, STILL SITTING IN MARLEY'S FUNERAL PARLOR, WATCHING AS THEY SPEAK HOLLOW WORDS OVER THE ASHES OF A FALLEN HERO.

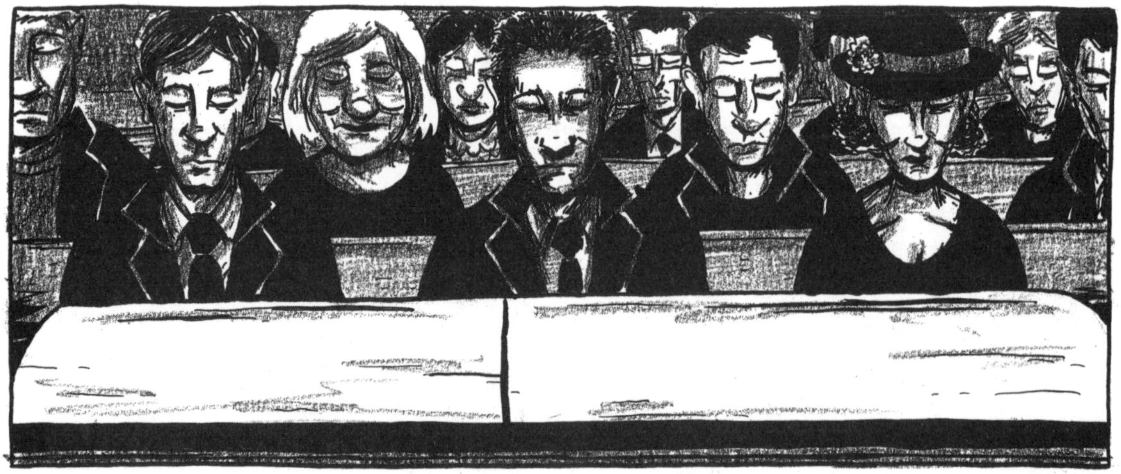

UNABLE TO LOOK ANY FURTHER AT DEAD THINGS, I LOOK UPON THE FLOWERS THAT ORNAMENT THAT PLACE. MY UNCLE, AN ATTICA GUARD HIMSELF, WHO SUFFERED SO DEEPLY AT THE MEMORIES HIS FATHER HELD, POINTS ME TO A PARTICULAR ARRANGEMENT.

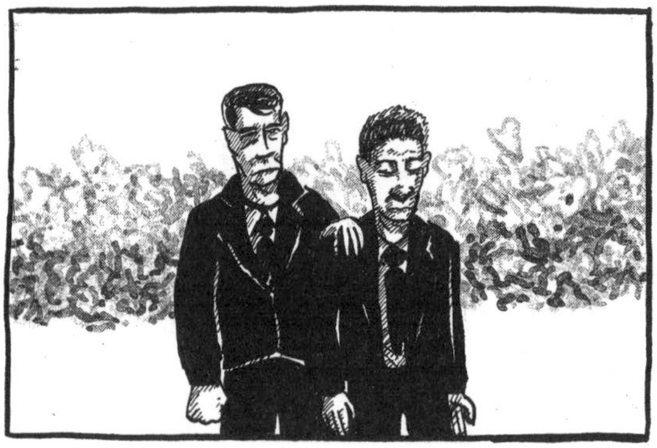

THERE, AMONG THE WELL-WISHES OF THE PEOPLE OF ATTICA, ARE FLOWERS FROM INMATES. ONE STANDS OUT; FROM A MAN SENTENCED TO LIFE FOR THE MURDER OF HIS WIFE AND HER ILLICIT LOVER.

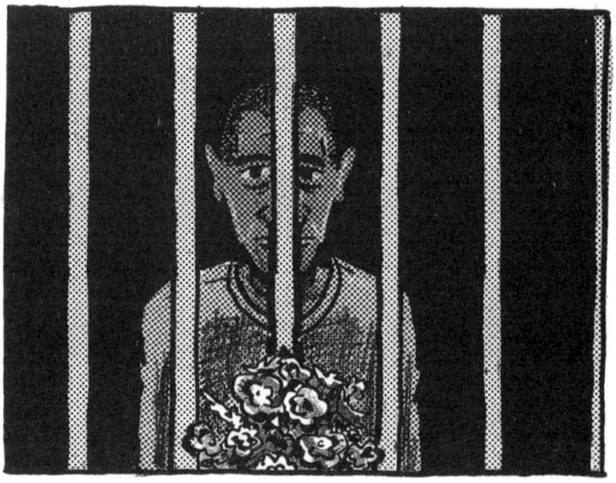

"ARTHUR, I'LL SEE YOU AT THE NEXT SHOW."

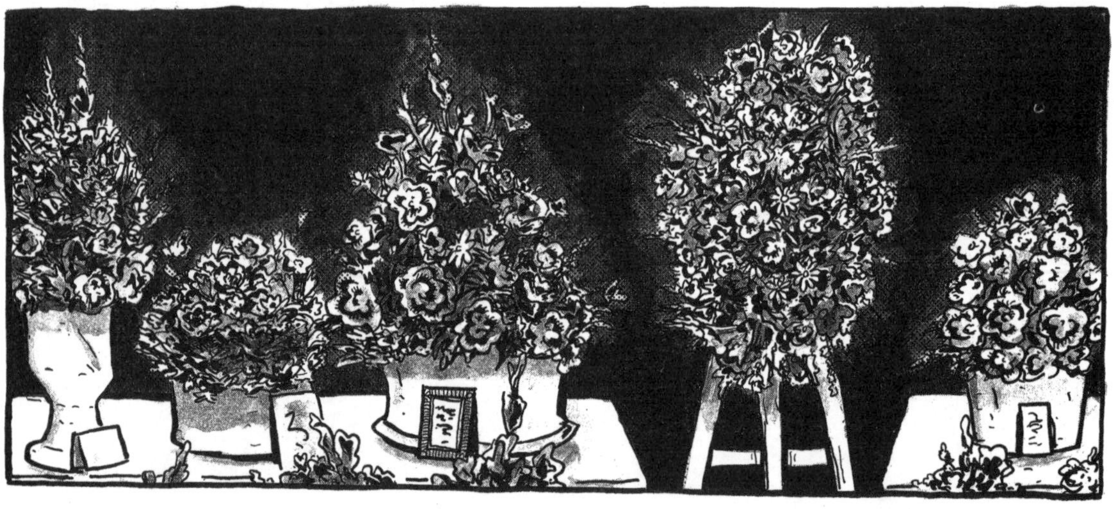

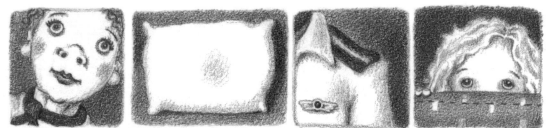

On the night of September 10, 2001 we flew home from Copenhagen to Newark.

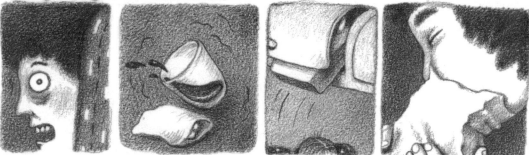

The flight was really rough. Severe turbulence. Screaming passengers. Nausea.

Then it smoothed out and the sky was perfectly clear. The city looked sparkly and happy from up there.

That view of the Twin Towers was the most beautiful I'd ever seen.

Renée French

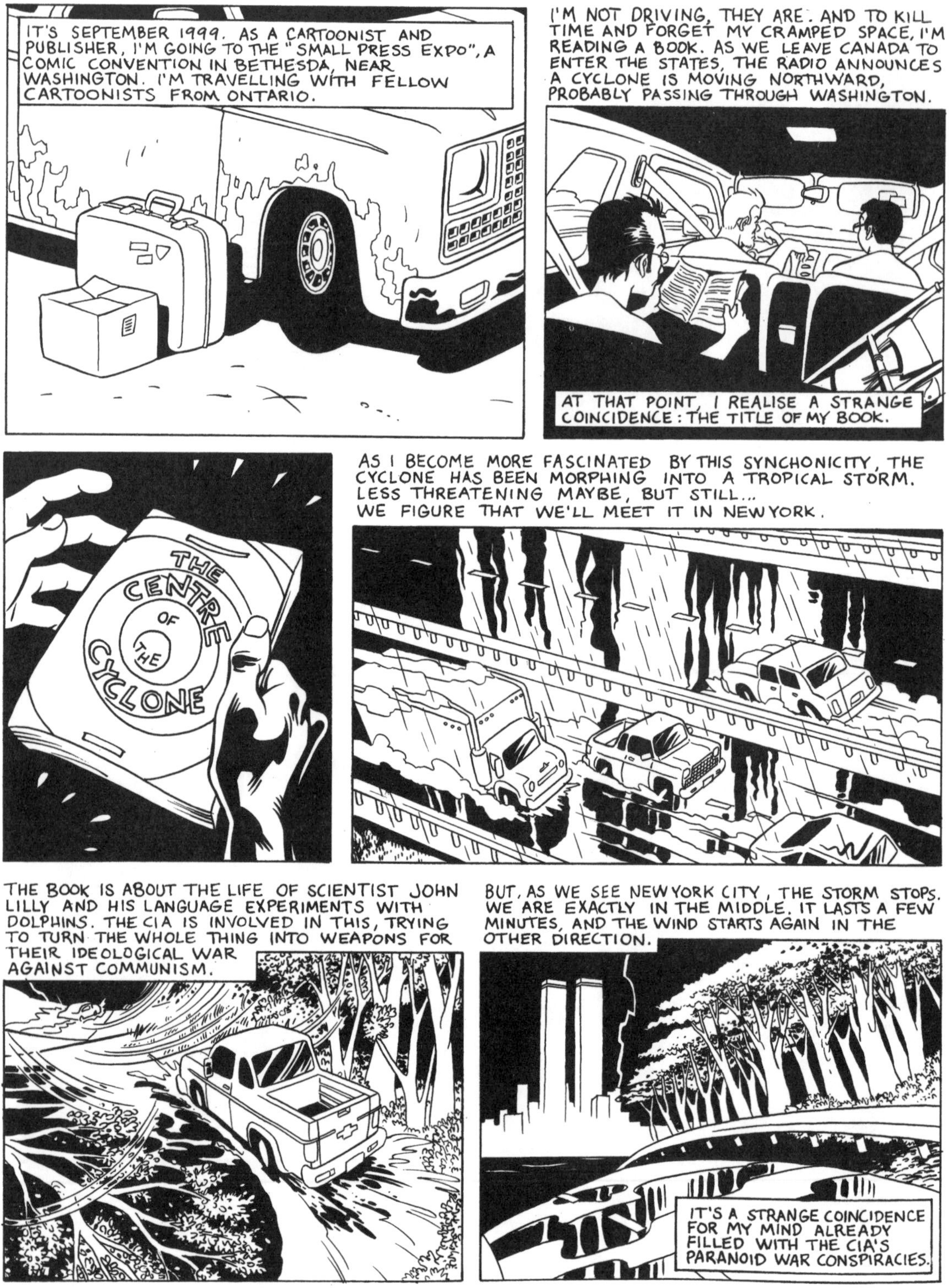
IT'S SEPTEMBER 1999. AS A CARTOONIST AND PUBLISHER, I'M GOING TO THE "SMALL PRESS EXPO", A COMIC CONVENTION IN BETHESDA, NEAR WASHINGTON. I'M TRAVELLING WITH FELLOW CARTOONISTS FROM ONTARIO.
I'M NOT DRIVING, THEY ARE. AND TO KILL TIME AND FORGET MY CRAMPED SPACE, I'M READING A BOOK. AS WE LEAVE CANADA TO ENTER THE STATES, THE RADIO ANNOUNCES A CYCLONE IS MOVING NORTHWARD, PROBABLY PASSING THROUGH WASHINGTON.
AT THAT POINT, I REALISE A STRANGE COINCIDENCE: THE TITLE OF MY BOOK.
THE CENTRE OF THE CYCLONE
AS I BECOME MORE FASCINATED BY THIS SYNCHONICITY, THE CYCLONE HAS BEEN MORPHING INTO A TROPICAL STORM. LESS THREATENING MAYBE, BUT STILL... WE FIGURE THAT WE'LL MEET IT IN NEW YORK.
THE BOOK IS ABOUT THE LIFE OF SCIENTIST JOHN LILLY AND HIS LANGUAGE EXPERIMENTS WITH DOLPHINS. THE CIA IS INVOLVED IN THIS, TRYING TO TURN THE WHOLE THING INTO WEAPONS FOR THEIR IDEOLOGICAL WAR AGAINST COMMUNISM.
BUT, AS WE SEE NEW YORK CITY, THE STORM STOPS. WE ARE EXACTLY IN THE MIDDLE. IT LASTS A FEW MINUTES, AND THE WIND STARTS AGAIN IN THE OTHER DIRECTION.
IT'S A STRANGE COINCIDENCE FOR MY MIND ALREADY FILLED WITH THE CIA'S PARANOID WAR CONSPIRACIES.

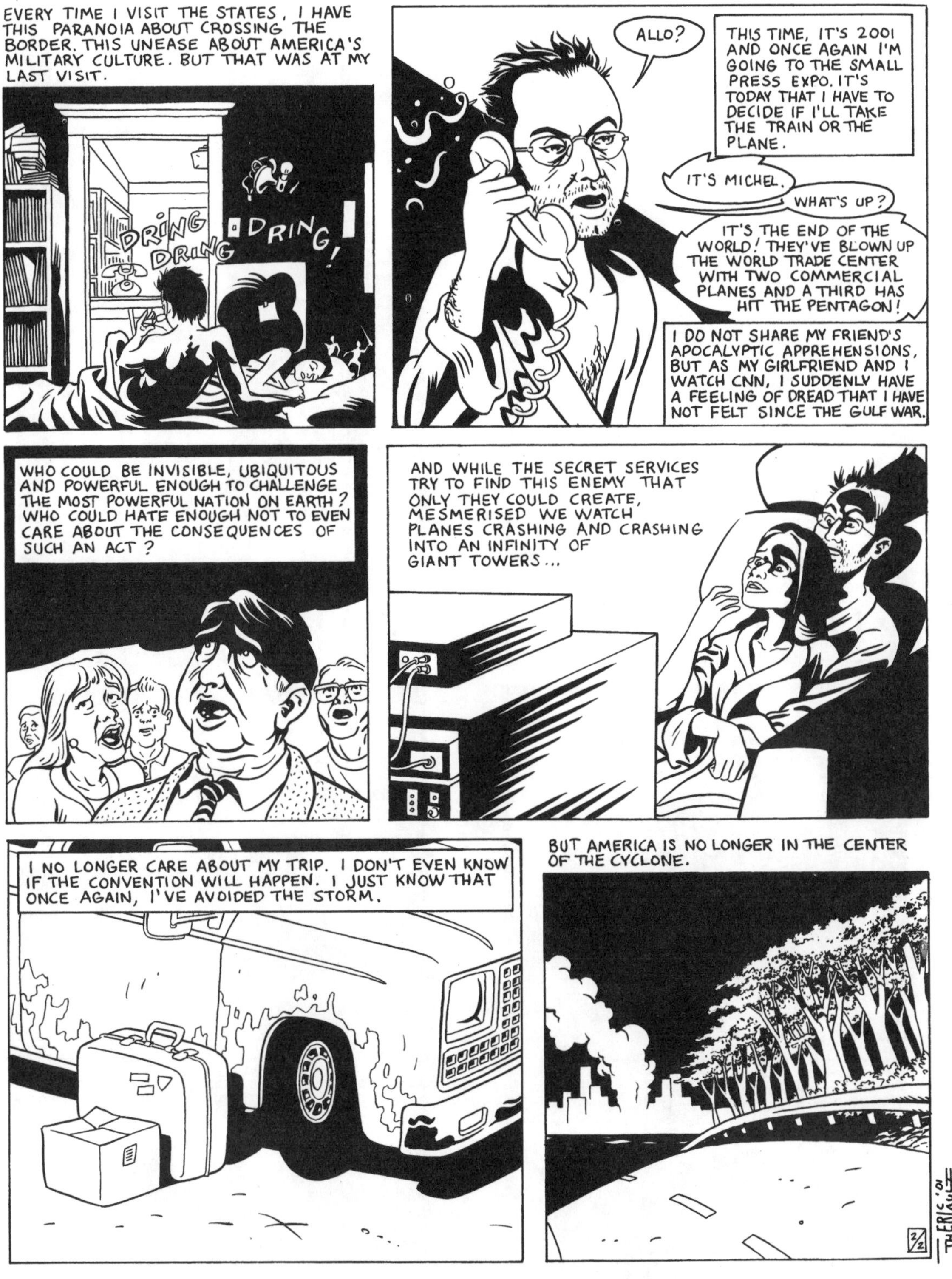

EVERY TIME I VISIT THE STATES, I HAVE THIS PARANOIA ABOUT CROSSING THE BORDER. THIS UNEASE ABOUT AMERICA'S MILITARY CULTURE. BUT THAT WAS AT MY LAST VISIT.
DRING DRING DRING!
ALLO?
THIS TIME, IT'S 2001 AND ONCE AGAIN I'M GOING TO THE SMALL PRESS EXPO. IT'S TODAY THAT I HAVE TO DECIDE IF I'LL TAKE THE TRAIN OR THE PLANE.
IT'S MICHEL.
WHAT'S UP?
IT'S THE END OF THE WORLD! THEY'VE BLOWN UP THE WORLD TRADE CENTER WITH TWO COMMERCIAL PLANES AND A THIRD HAS HIT THE PENTAGON!
I DO NOT SHARE MY FRIEND'S APOCALYPTIC APPREHENSIONS, BUT AS MY GIRLFRIEND AND I WATCH CNN, I SUDDENLY HAVE A FEELING OF DREAD THAT I HAVE NOT FELT SINCE THE GULF WAR.
WHO COULD BE INVISIBLE, UBIQUITOUS AND POWERFUL ENOUGH TO CHALLENGE THE MOST POWERFUL NATION ON EARTH? WHO COULD HATE ENOUGH NOT TO EVEN CARE ABOUT THE CONSEQUENCES OF SUCH AN ACT?
AND WHILE THE SECRET SERVICES TRY TO FIND THIS ENEMY THAT ONLY THEY COULD CREATE, MESMERISED WE WATCH PLANES CRASHING AND CRASHING INTO AN INFINITY OF GIANT TOWERS...
I NO LONGER CARE ABOUT MY TRIP. I DON'T EVEN KNOW IF THE CONVENTION WILL HAPPEN. I JUST KNOW THAT ONCE AGAIN, I'VE AVOIDED THE STORM.
BUT AMERICA IS NO LONGER IN THE CENTER OF THE CYCLONE.
2/2
ERIC '01
THERIAULT

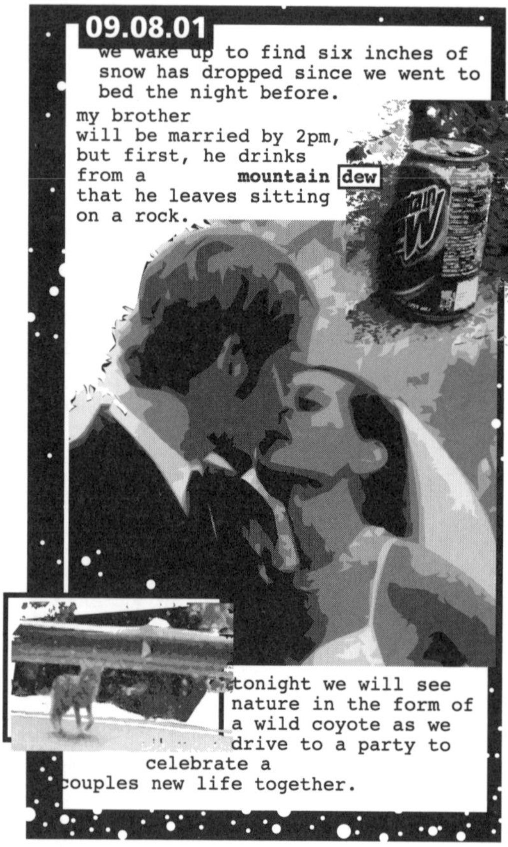
09.08.01
we wake up to find six inches of snow has dropped since we went to bed the night before.
my brother will be married by 2pm, but first, he drinks from a **mountain dew** that he leaves sitting on a rock.
tonight we will see nature in the form of a wild coyote as we drive to a party to celebrate a couples new life together.

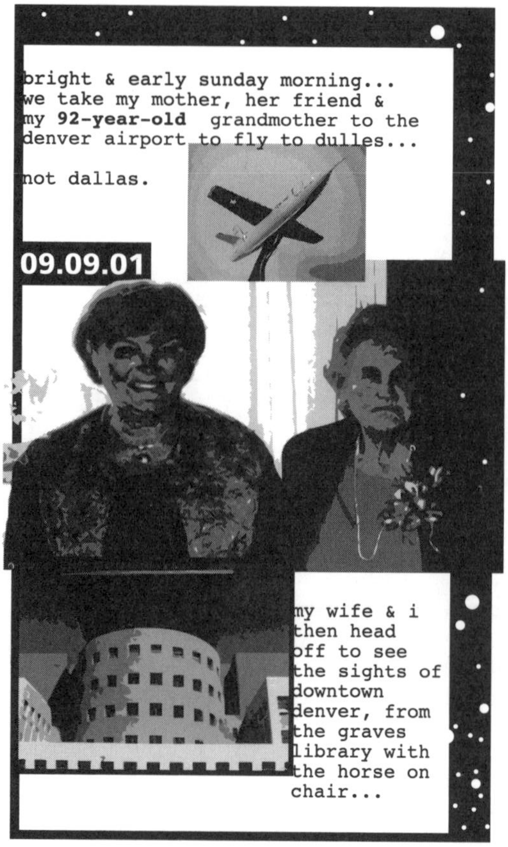
bright & early sunday morning... we take my mother, her friend & my **92-year-old** grandmother to the denver airport to fly to dulles...
not dallas.
09.09.01
my wife & i then head off to see the sights of downtown denver, from the graves library with the horse on chair...

Four Days in September

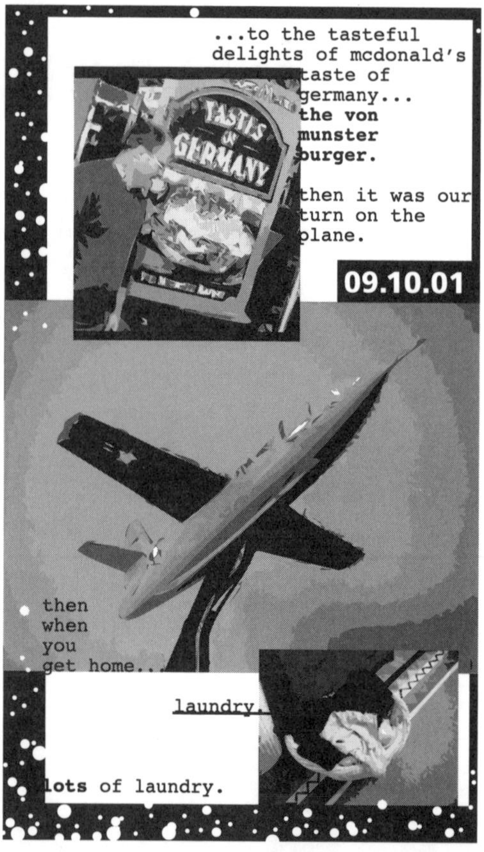
...to the tasteful delights of mcdonald's taste of germany... **the von munster burger.**
TASTES OF GERMANY
then it was our turn on the plane.
09.10.01
then when you get home...
laundry.
lots of laundry.

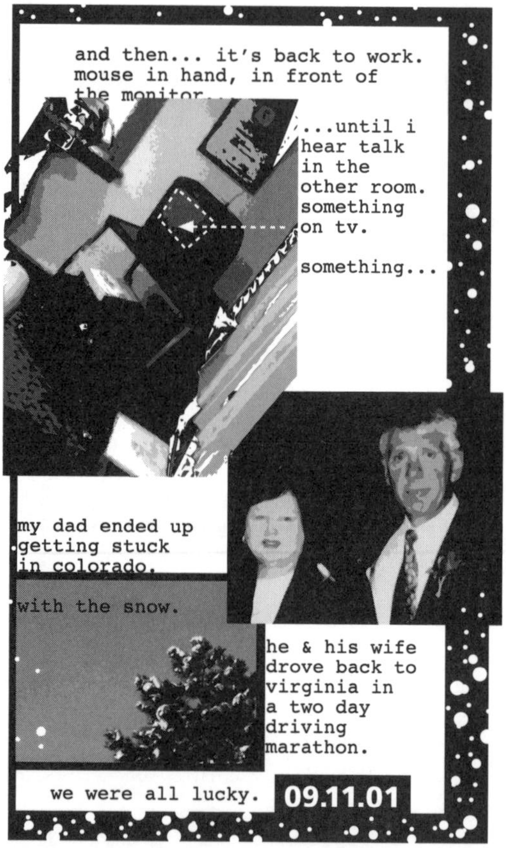
and then... it's back to work. mouse in hand, in front of the monitor...
...until i hear talk in the other room. something on tv.
something...
my dad ended up getting stuck in colorado.
with the snow.
he & his wife drove back to virginia in a two day driving marathon.
we were all lucky.
09.11.01

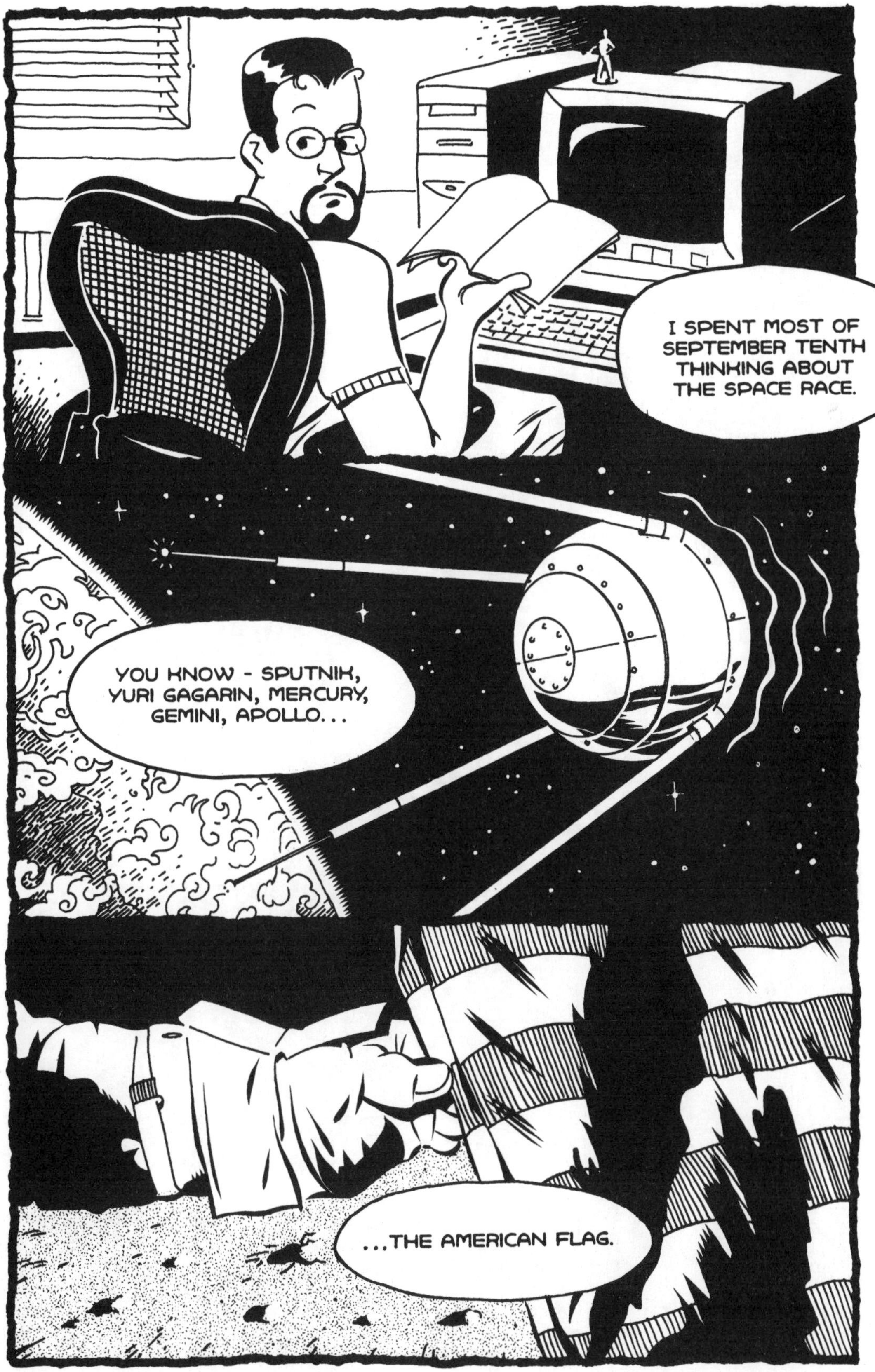
I SPENT MOST OF SEPTEMBER TENTH THINKING ABOUT THE SPACE RACE.
YOU KNOW - SPUTNIK, YURI GAGARIN, MERCURY, GEMINI, APOLLO...
...THE AMERICAN FLAG.

STORY AND ART : JIM HARRISON

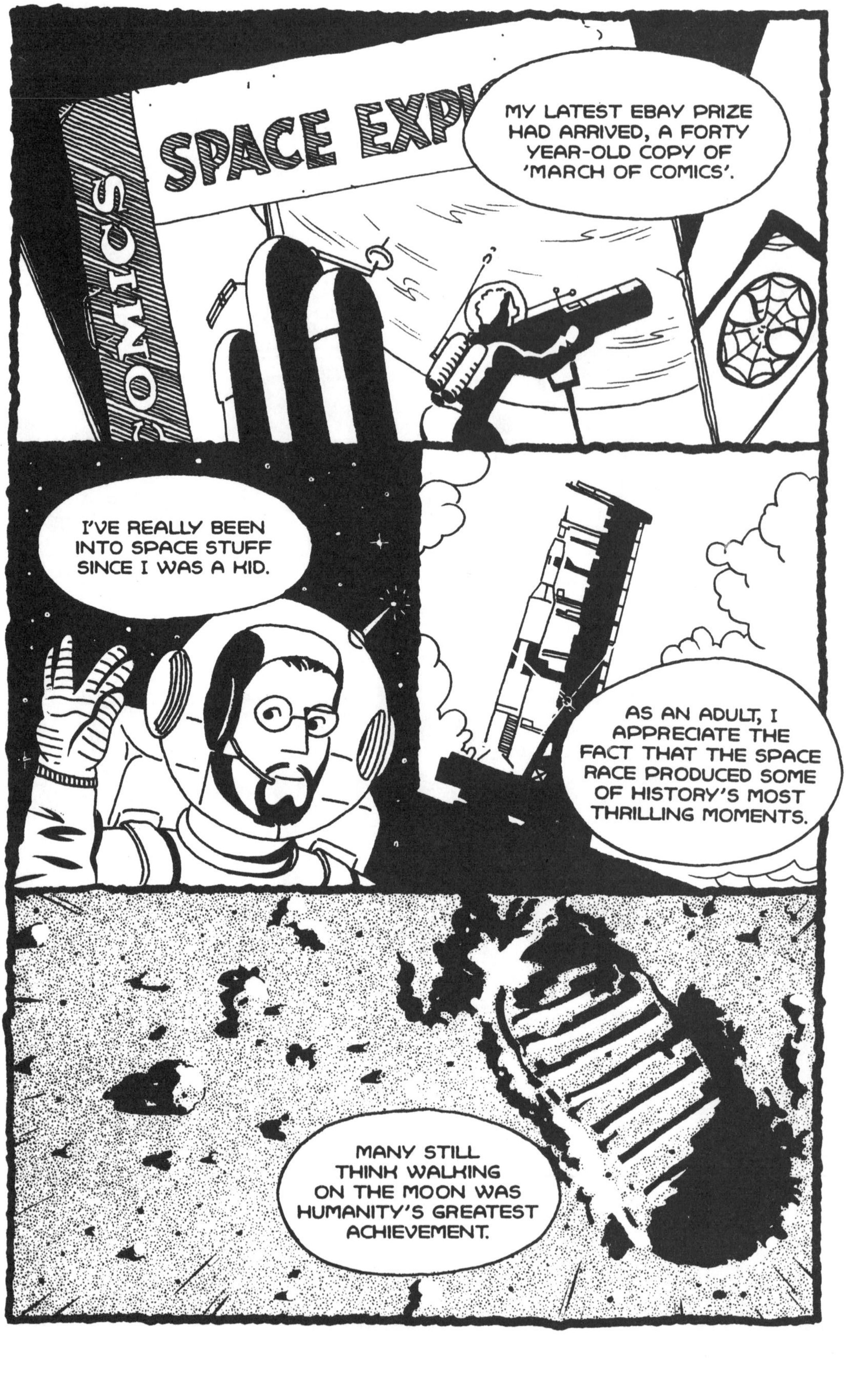
MY LATEST EBAY PRIZE HAD ARRIVED, A FORTY YEAR-OLD COPY OF 'MARCH OF COMICS'.
I'VE REALLY BEEN INTO SPACE STUFF SINCE I WAS A KID.
AS AN ADULT, I APPRECIATE THE FACT THAT THE SPACE RACE PRODUCED SOME OF HISTORY'S MOST THRILLING MOMENTS.
MANY STILL THINK WALKING ON THE MOON WAS HUMANITY'S GREATEST ACHIEVEMENT.

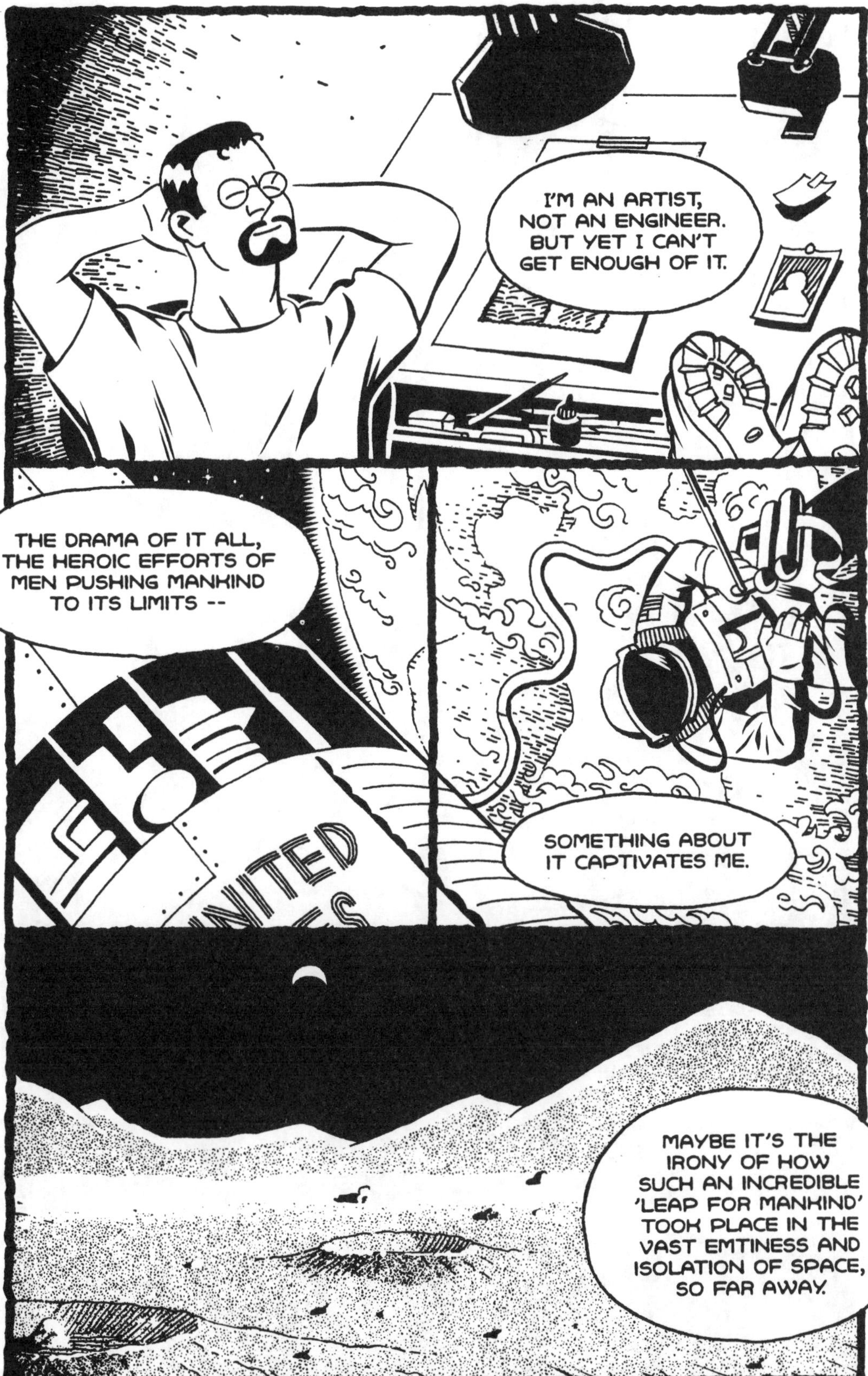
I'M AN ARTIST, NOT AN ENGINEER. BUT YET I CAN'T GET ENOUGH OF IT.
THE DRAMA OF IT ALL, THE HEROIC EFFORTS OF MEN PUSHING MANKIND TO ITS LIMITS --
NITED
SOMETHING ABOUT IT CAPTIVATES ME.
MAYBE IT'S THE IRONY OF HOW SUCH AN INCREDIBLE 'LEAP FOR MANKIND' TOOK PLACE IN THE VAST EMTINESS AND ISOLATION OF SPACE, SO FAR AWAY.

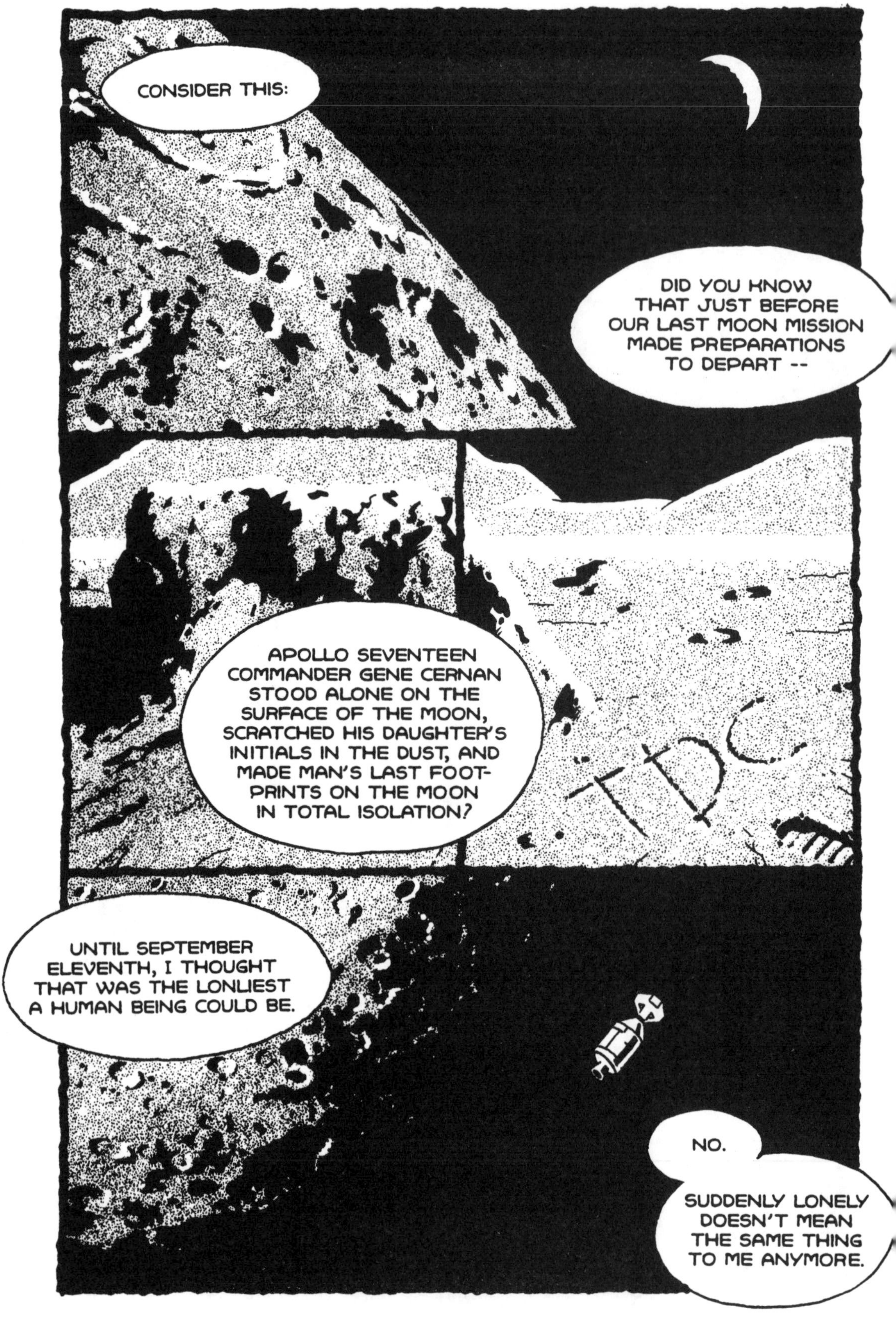
CONSIDER THIS:
DID YOU KNOW THAT JUST BEFORE OUR LAST MOON MISSION MADE PREPARATIONS TO DEPART --
APOLLO SEVENTEEN COMMANDER GENE CERNAN STOOD ALONE ON THE SURFACE OF THE MOON, SCRATCHED HIS DAUGHTER'S INITIALS IN THE DUST, AND MADE MAN'S LAST FOOT-PRINTS ON THE MOON IN TOTAL ISOLATION?
UNTIL SEPTEMBER ELEVENTH, I THOUGHT THAT WAS THE LONLIEST A HUMAN BEING COULD BE.
NO.
SUDDENLY LONELY DOESN'T MEAN THE SAME THING TO ME ANYMORE.

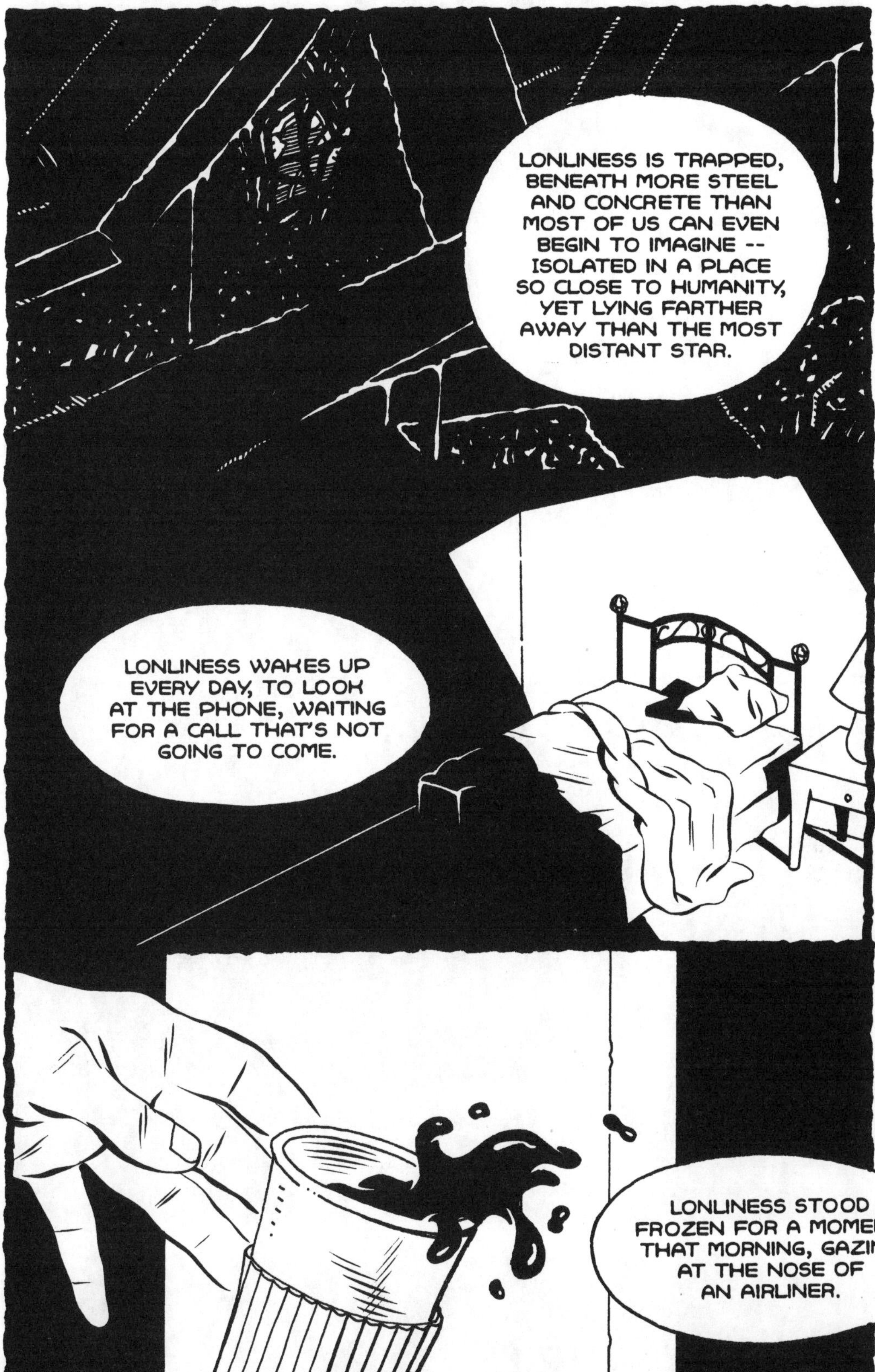
LONLINESS IS TRAPPED, BENEATH MORE STEEL AND CONCRETE THAN MOST OF US CAN EVEN BEGIN TO IMAGINE -- ISOLATED IN A PLACE SO CLOSE TO HUMANITY, YET LYING FARTHER AWAY THAN THE MOST DISTANT STAR.
LONLINESS WAKES UP EVERY DAY, TO LOOK AT THE PHONE, WAITING FOR A CALL THAT'S NOT GOING TO COME.
LONLINESS STOOD FROZEN FOR A MOMENT THAT MORNING, GAZING AT THE NOSE OF AN AIRLINER.

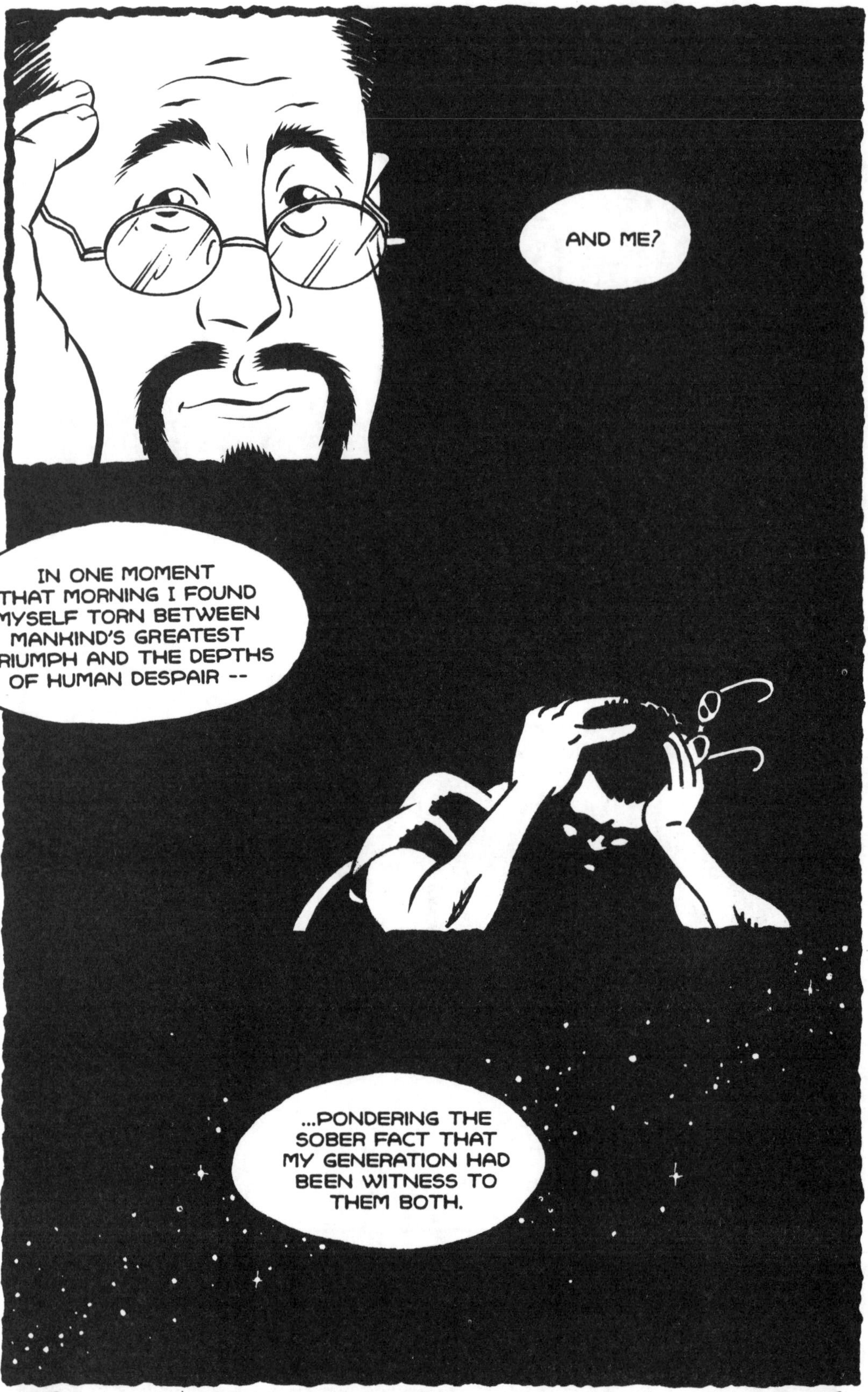
AND ME?
IN ONE MOMENT THAT MORNING I FOUND MYSELF TORN BETWEEN MANKIND'S GREATEST TRIUMPH AND THE DEPTHS OF HUMAN DESPAIR --
...PONDERING THE SOBER FACT THAT MY GENERATION HAD BEEN WITNESS TO THEM BOTH.
J.
9-11

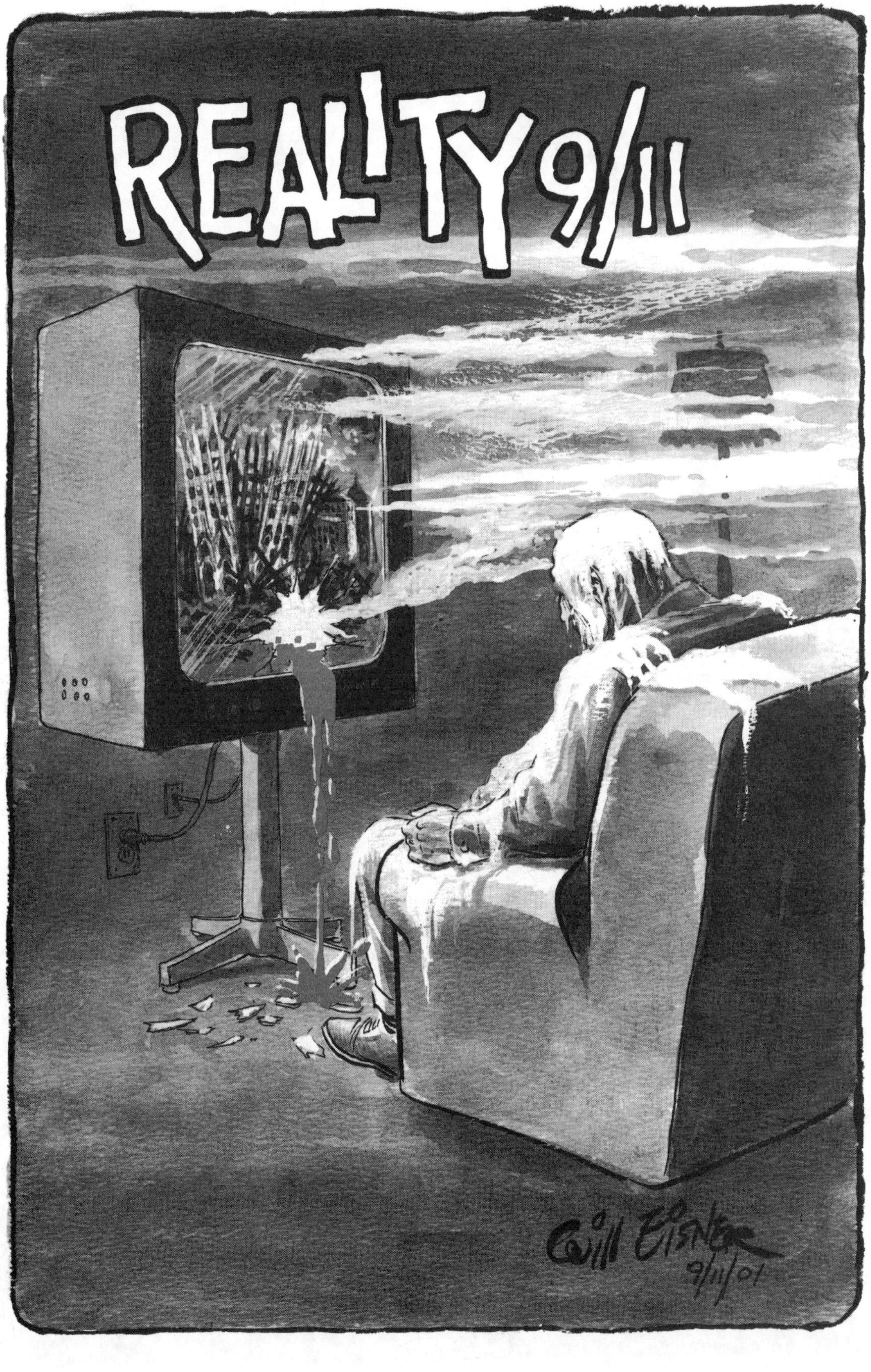
REALITY 9/11
Will Eisner
9/11/01

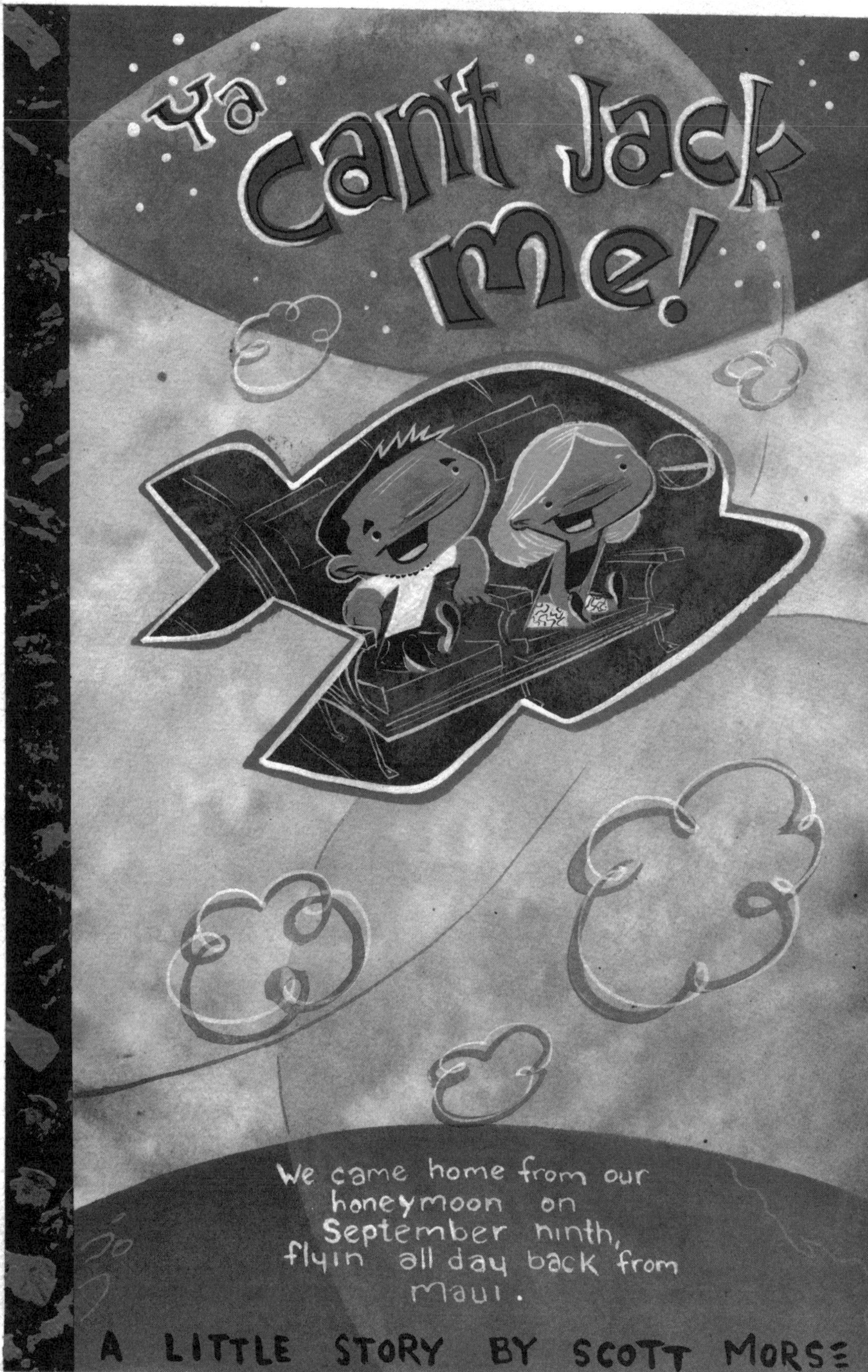
Ya Can't Jack Me!
We came home from our honeymoon on September ninth, flyin all day back from Maui.
A LITTLE STORY BY SCOTT MORSE

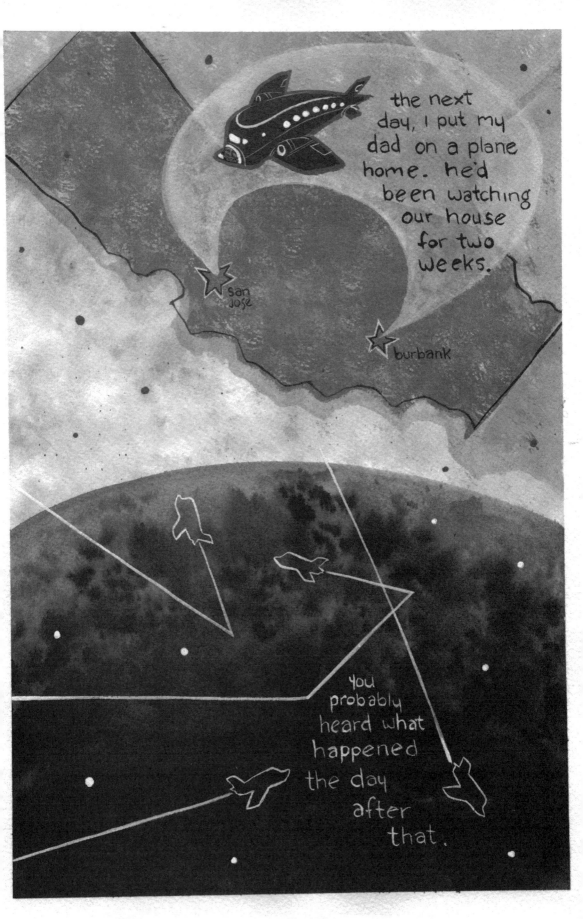

the next day, I put my dad on a plane home. he'd been watching our house for two weeks.

san jose

burbank

you probably heard what happened the day after that.

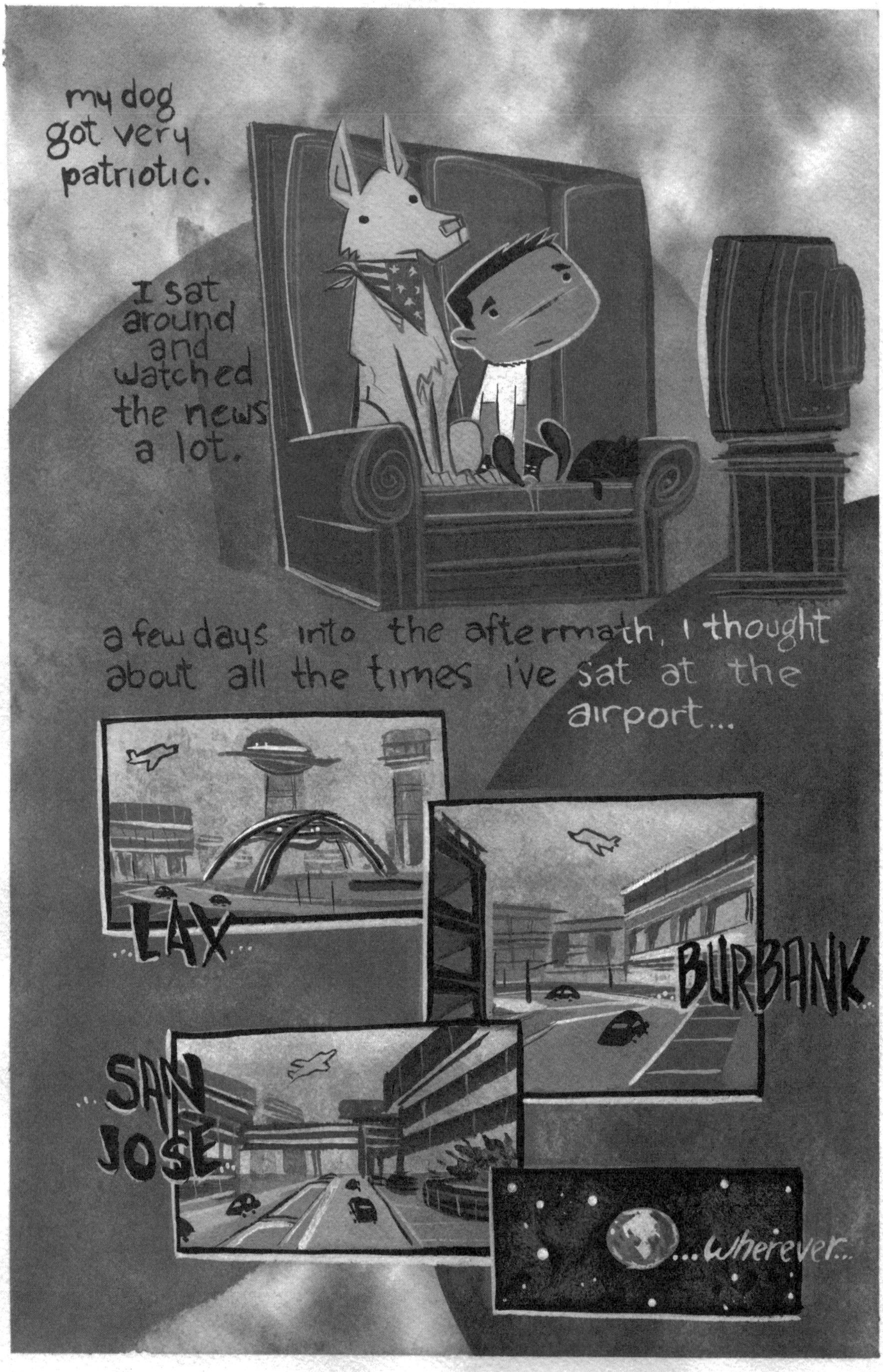
my dog got very patriotic.
I sat around and watched the news a lot.
a few days into the aftermath, I thought about all the times ive sat at the airport...
...LAX...
BURBANK...
...SAN JOSE...
...wherever...

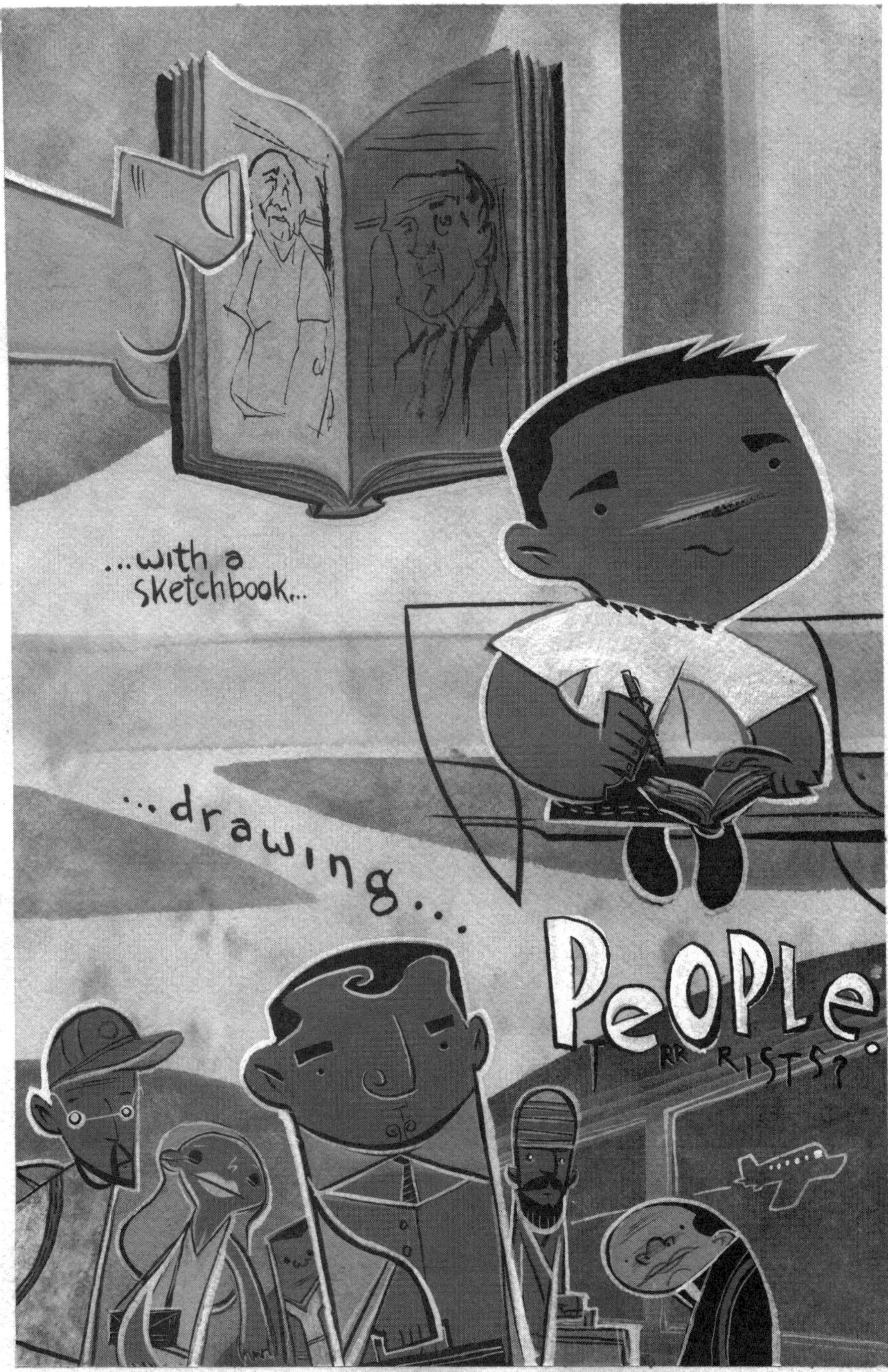

...with a sketchbook...
...drawing...
PeOPLe.
T RR RISTS?

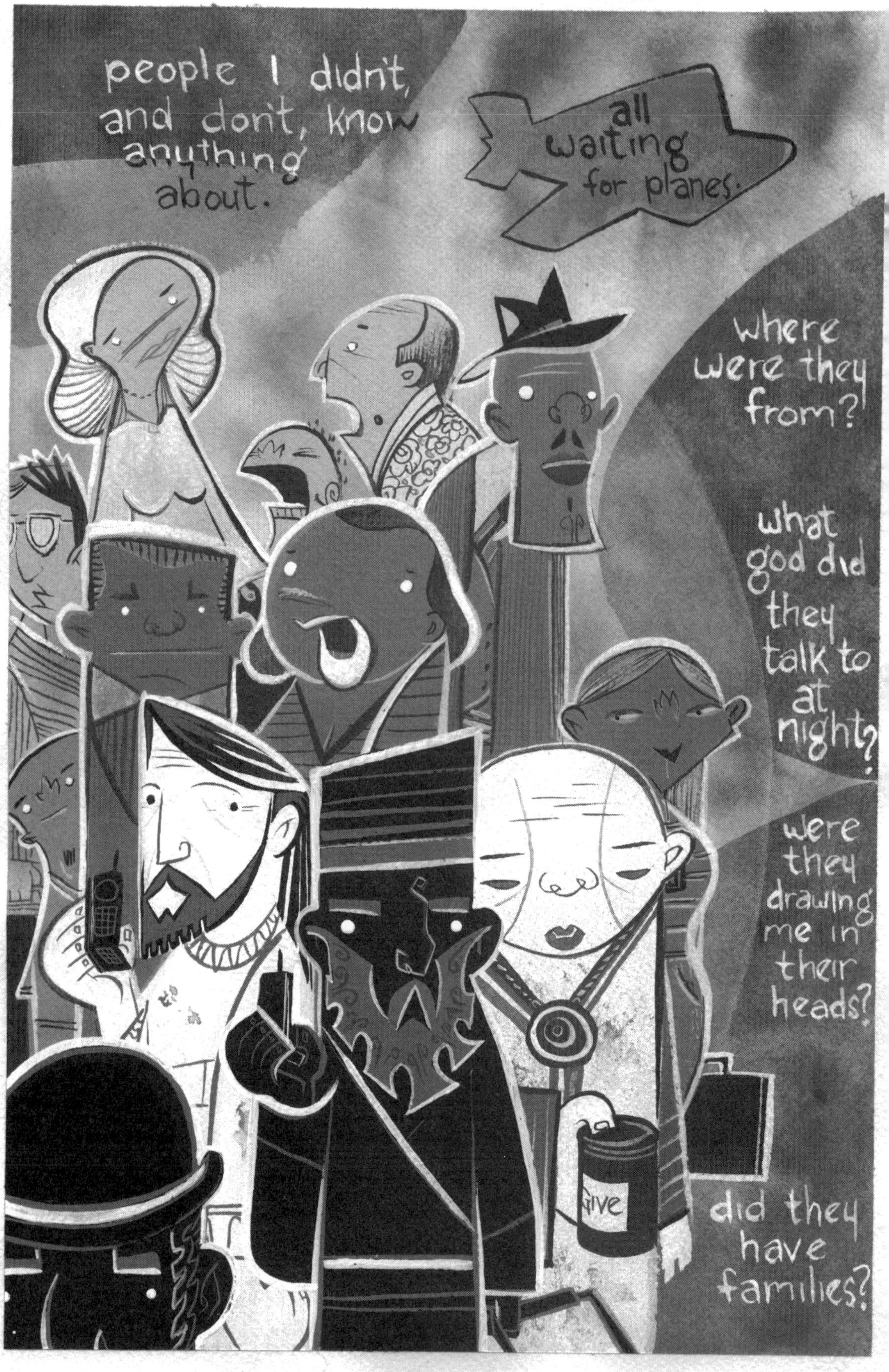
people I didn't, and don't, know anything about.
all waiting for planes.
where were they from?
what god did they talk to at night?
were they drawing me in their heads?
Give
did they have families?

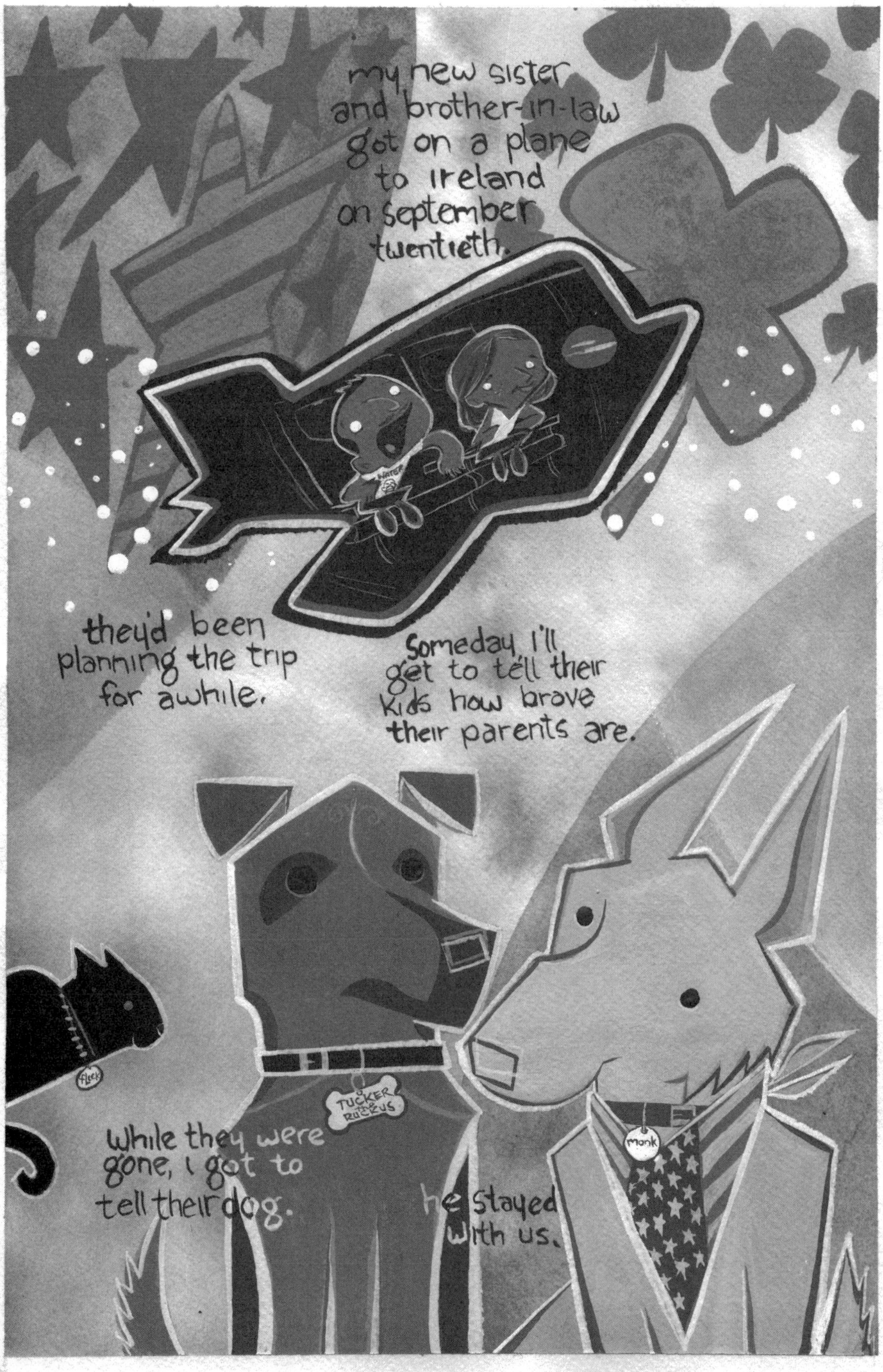
my new sister and brother-in-law got on a plane to ireland on september twentieth.
they'd been planning the trip for awhile.
Someday, I'll get to tell their kids how brave their parents are.
While they were gone, I got to tell their dog.
he stayed with us.
monk

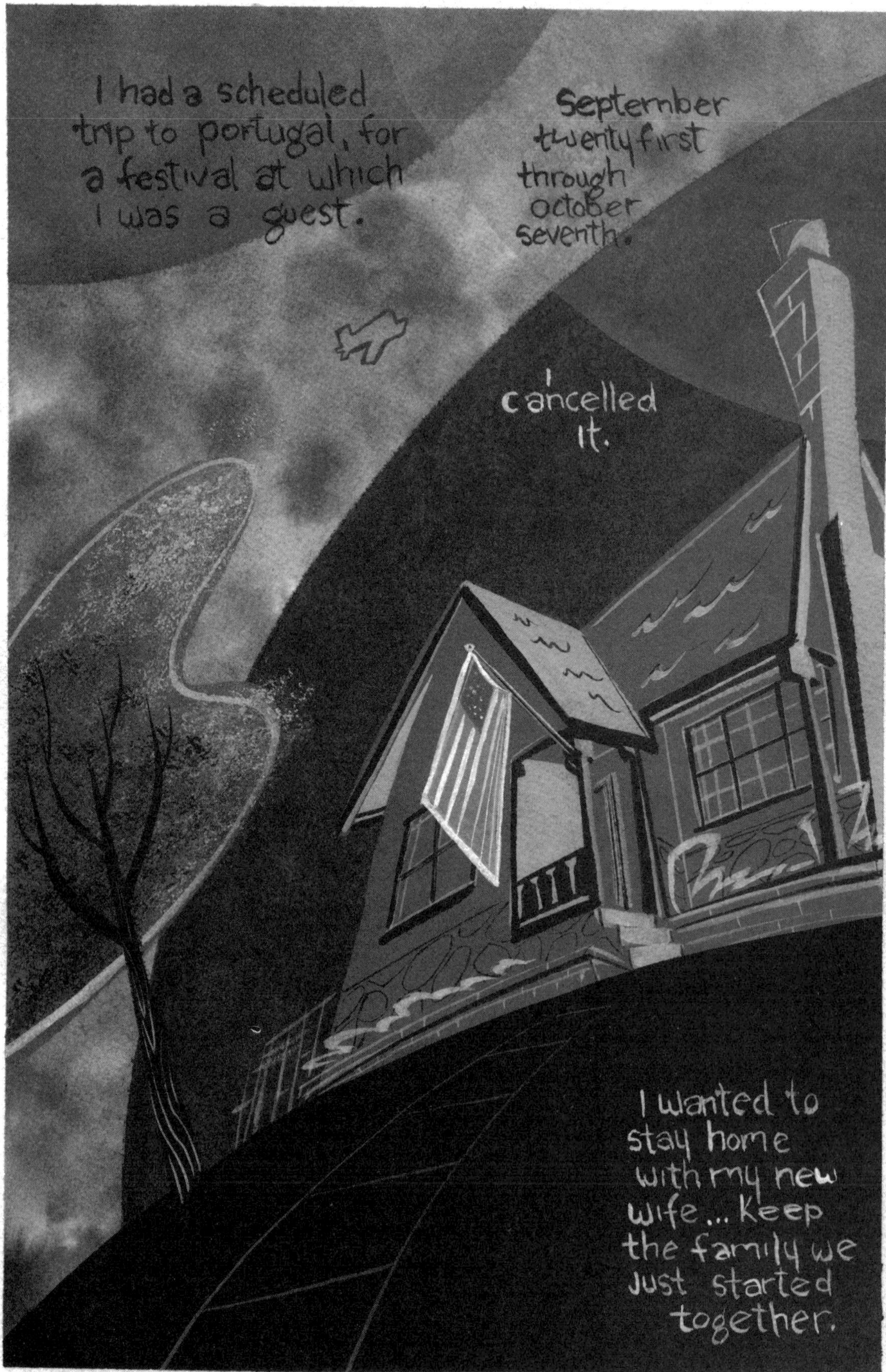

I had a scheduled trip to portugal, for a festival at which I was a guest.
September twenty first through october seventh.
I cancelled it.
I wanted to stay home with my new wife... keep the family we just started together.

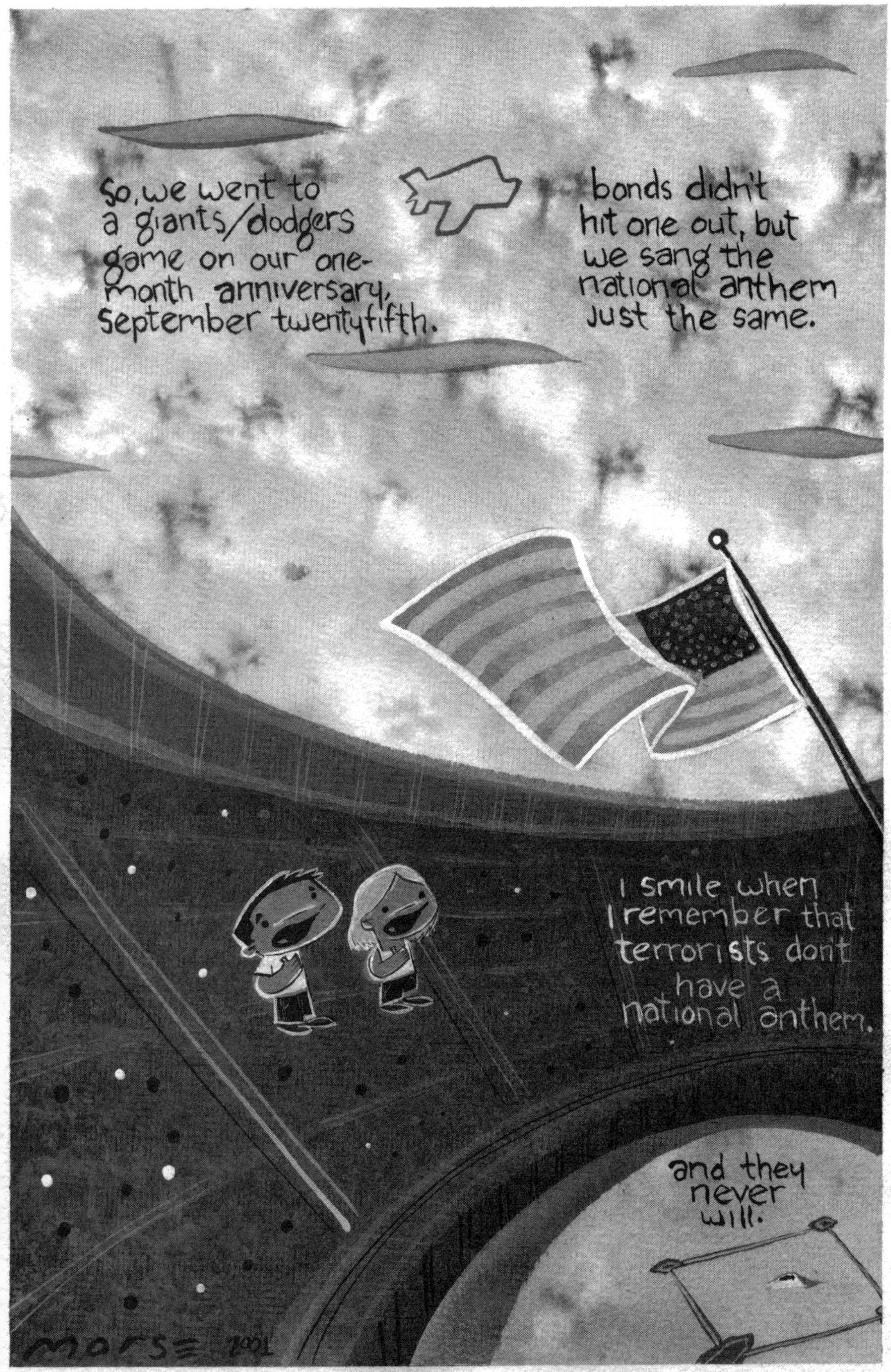
so, we went to a giants/dodgers game on our one-month anniversary, september twentyfifth.
bonds didn't hit one out, but we sang the national anthem just the same.
I smile when I remember that terrorists don't have a national anthem.
and they never will.
morse 2001

A DIFFERENT VIEW OF CANAL STREET

NICK ABADZIS 2001

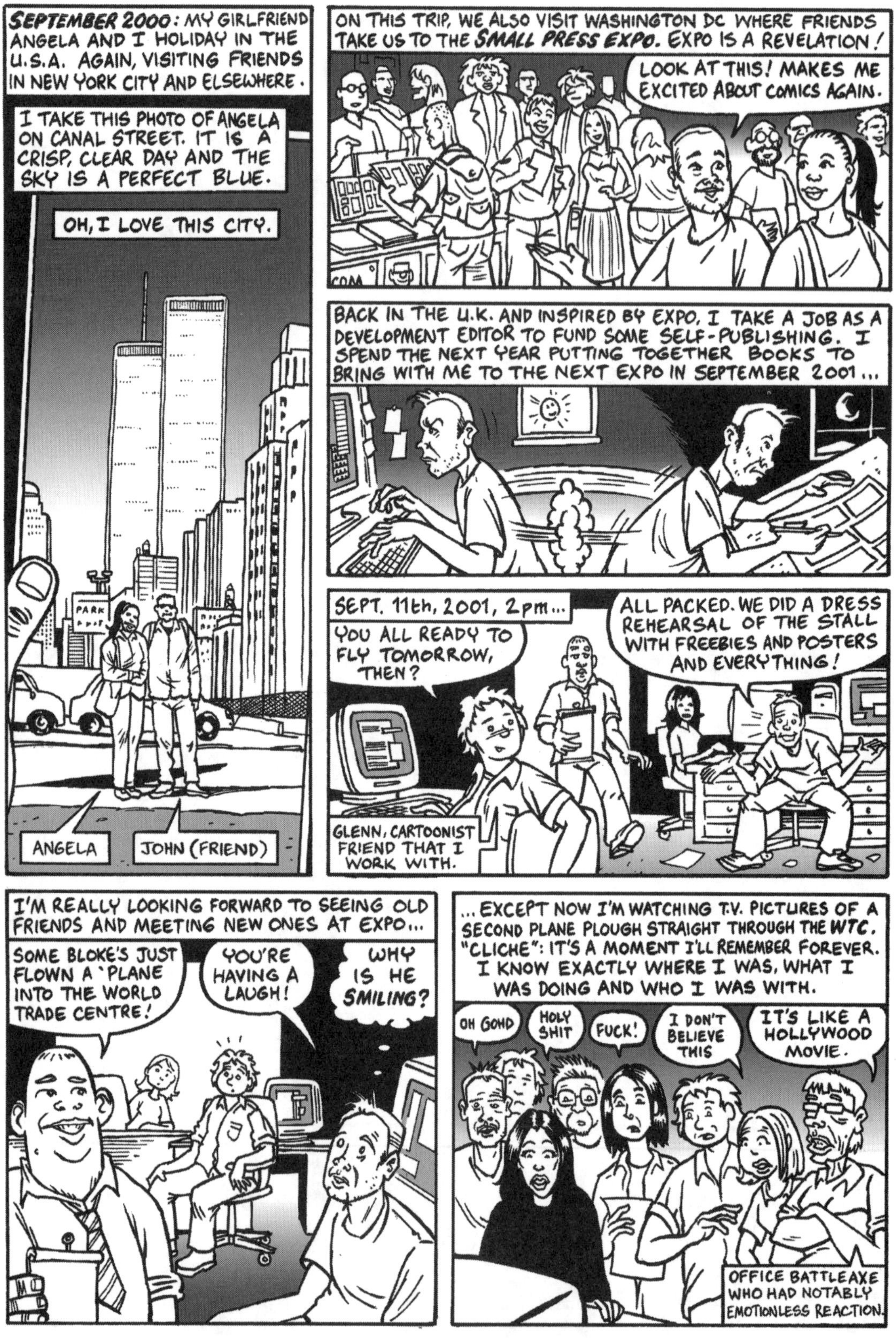

SEPTEMBER 2000: MY GIRLFRIEND ANGELA AND I HOLIDAY IN THE U.S.A. AGAIN, VISITING FRIENDS IN NEW YORK CITY AND ELSEWHERE.
I TAKE THIS PHOTO OF ANGELA ON CANAL STREET. IT IS A CRISP, CLEAR DAY AND THE SKY IS A PERFECT BLUE.
OH, I LOVE THIS CITY.
PARK
ANGELA
JOHN (FRIEND)
ON THIS TRIP, WE ALSO VISIT WASHINGTON DC WHERE FRIENDS TAKE US TO THE SMALL PRESS EXPO. EXPO IS A REVELATION!
LOOK AT THIS! MAKES ME EXCITED ABOUT COMICS AGAIN.
COM
BACK IN THE U.K. AND INSPIRED BY EXPO, I TAKE A JOB AS A DEVELOPMENT EDITOR TO FUND SOME SELF-PUBLISHING. I SPEND THE NEXT YEAR PUTTING TOGETHER BOOKS TO BRING WITH ME TO THE NEXT EXPO IN SEPTEMBER 2001...
SEPT. 11th, 2001, 2pm...
YOU ALL READY TO FLY TOMORROW, THEN?
ALL PACKED. WE DID A DRESS REHEARSAL OF THE STALL WITH FREEBIES AND POSTERS AND EVERYTHING!
GLENN, CARTOONIST FRIEND THAT I WORK WITH.
I'M REALLY LOOKING FORWARD TO SEEING OLD FRIENDS AND MEETING NEW ONES AT EXPO...
SOME BLOKE'S JUST FLOWN A 'PLANE INTO THE WORLD TRADE CENTRE!
YOU'RE HAVING A LAUGH!
WHY IS HE SMILING?
...EXCEPT NOW I'M WATCHING T.V. PICTURES OF A SECOND PLANE PLOUGH STRAIGHT THROUGH THE WTC. "CLICHE": IT'S A MOMENT I'LL REMEMBER FOREVER. I KNOW EXACTLY WHERE I WAS, WHAT I WAS DOING AND WHO I WAS WITH.
OH GOHD
HOLY SHIT
FUCK!
I DON'T BELIEVE THIS
IT'S LIKE A HOLLYWOOD MOVIE.
OFFICE BATTLEAXE WHO HAD NOTABLY EMOTIONLESS REACTION.

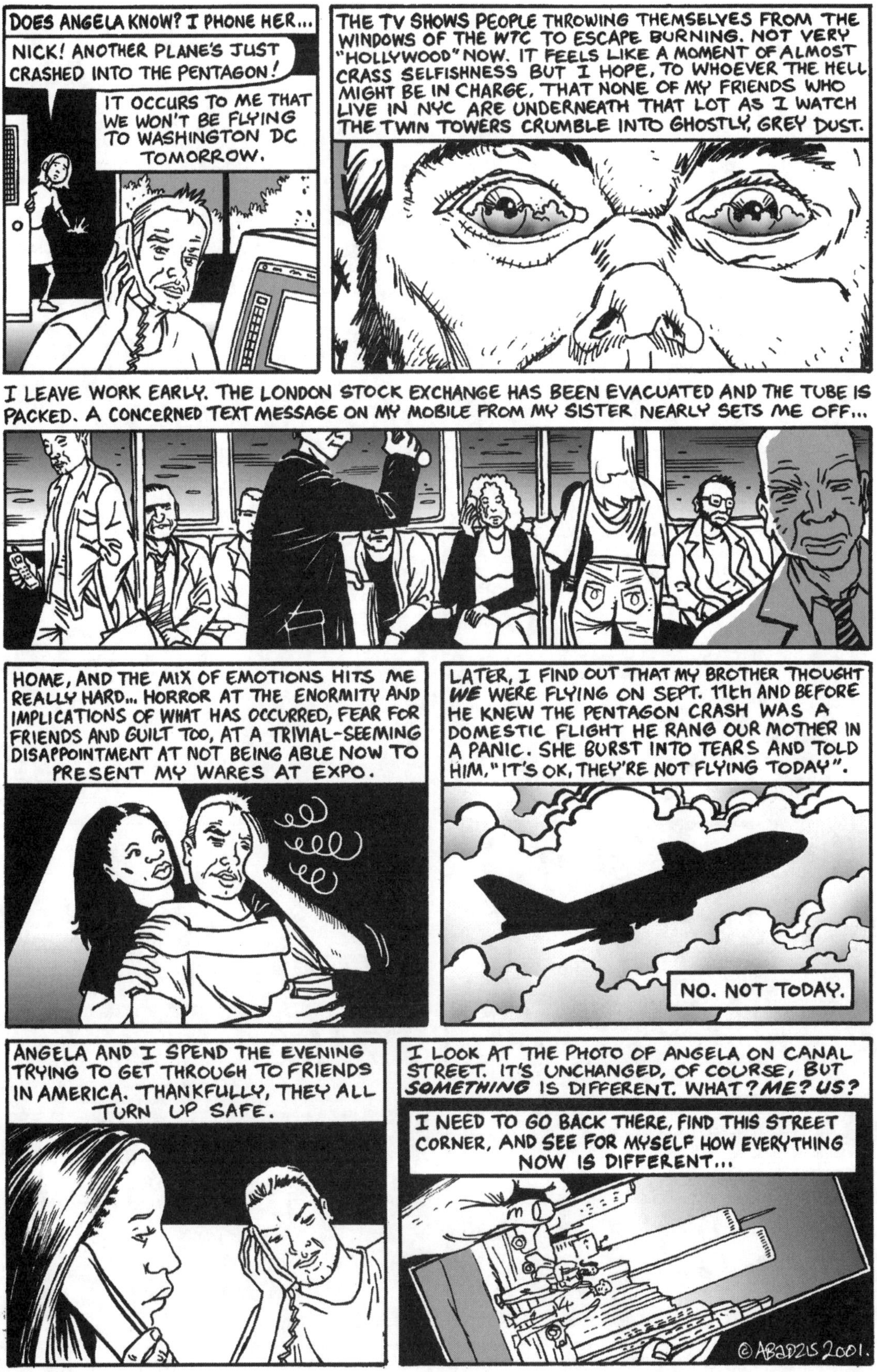
DOES ANGELA KNOW? I PHONE HER...
NICK! ANOTHER PLANE'S JUST CRASHED INTO THE PENTAGON!
IT OCCURS TO ME THAT WE WON'T BE FLYING TO WASHINGTON DC TOMORROW.
THE TV SHOWS PEOPLE THROWING THEMSELVES FROM THE WINDOWS OF THE WTC TO ESCAPE BURNING. NOT VERY "HOLLYWOOD" NOW. IT FEELS LIKE A MOMENT OF ALMOST CRASS SELFISHNESS BUT I HOPE, TO WHOEVER THE HELL MIGHT BE IN CHARGE, THAT NONE OF MY FRIENDS WHO LIVE IN NYC ARE UNDERNEATH THAT LOT AS I WATCH THE TWIN TOWERS CRUMBLE INTO GHOSTLY, GREY DUST.
I LEAVE WORK EARLY. THE LONDON STOCK EXCHANGE HAS BEEN EVACUATED AND THE TUBE IS PACKED. A CONCERNED TEXT MESSAGE ON MY MOBILE FROM MY SISTER NEARLY SETS ME OFF...
HOME, AND THE MIX OF EMOTIONS HITS ME REALLY HARD... HORROR AT THE ENORMITY AND IMPLICATIONS OF WHAT HAS OCCURRED, FEAR FOR FRIENDS AND GUILT TOO, AT A TRIVIAL-SEEMING DISAPPOINTMENT AT NOT BEING ABLE NOW TO PRESENT MY WARES AT EXPO.
LATER, I FIND OUT THAT MY BROTHER THOUGHT **WE** WERE FLYING ON SEPT. 11th AND BEFORE HE KNEW THE PENTAGON CRASH WAS A DOMESTIC FLIGHT HE RANG OUR MOTHER IN A PANIC. SHE BURST INTO TEARS AND TOLD HIM, "IT'S OK, THEY'RE NOT FLYING TODAY".
NO. NOT TODAY.
ANGELA AND I SPEND THE EVENING TRYING TO GET THROUGH TO FRIENDS IN AMERICA. THANKFULLY, THEY ALL TURN UP SAFE.
I LOOK AT THE PHOTO OF ANGELA ON CANAL STREET. IT'S UNCHANGED, OF COURSE, BUT **SOMETHING** IS DIFFERENT. WHAT? **ME? US?**
I NEED TO GO BACK THERE, FIND THIS STREET CORNER, AND SEE FOR MYSELF HOW EVERYTHING NOW IS DIFFERENT...
© ABADZIS 2001.

TWO YEARS' GRACE

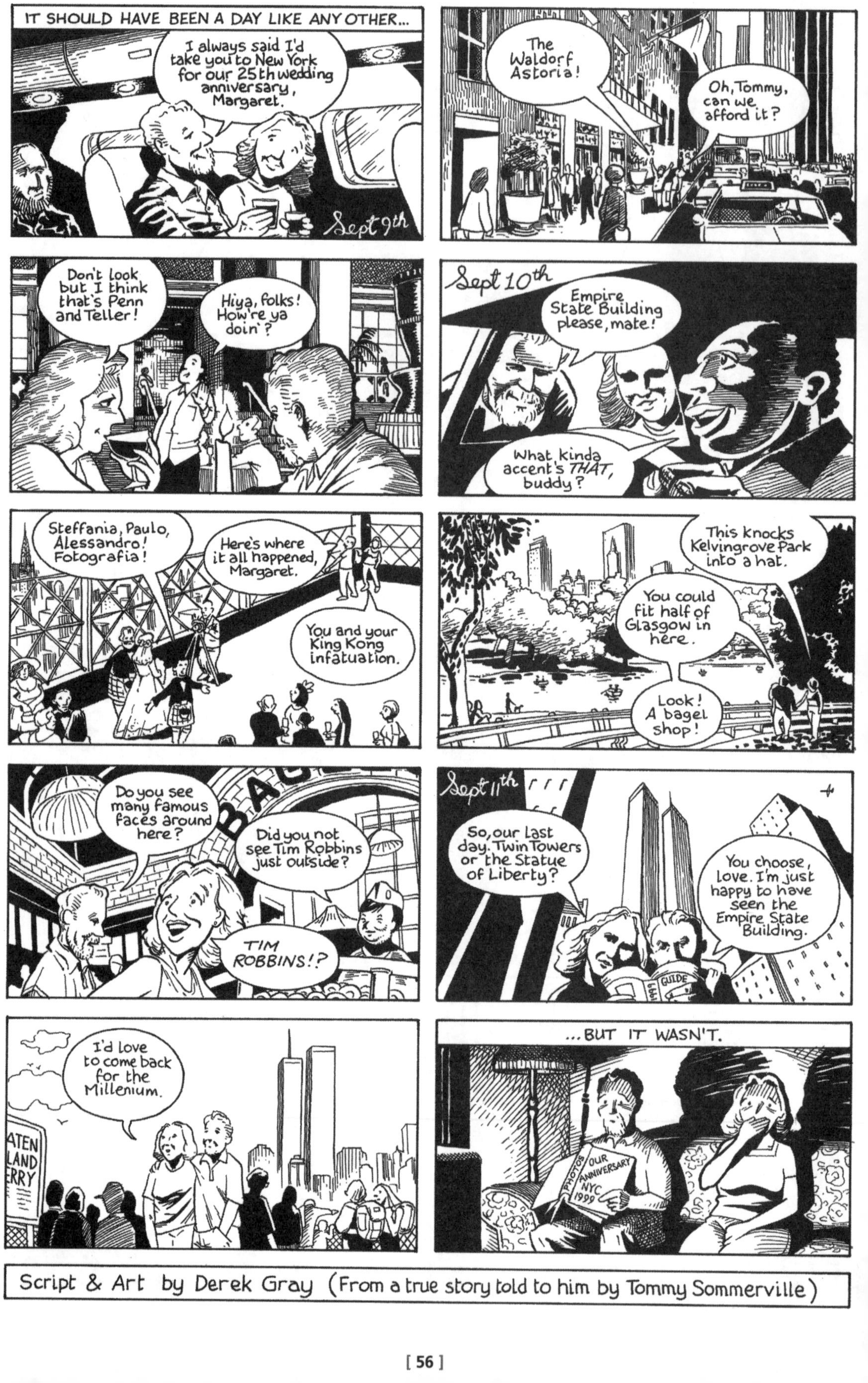

IT SHOULD HAVE BEEN A DAY LIKE ANY OTHER...
I always said I'd take you to New York for our 25th wedding anniversary, Margaret.
Sept 9th
The Waldorf Astoria!
Oh, Tommy, can we afford it?
Don't look but I think that's Penn and Teller!
Hiya, folks! How're ya doin'?
Sept 10th
Empire State Building please, mate!
What kinda accent's *THAT*, buddy?
Steffania, Paulo, Alessandro! Fotografia!
Here's where it all happened, Margaret.
You and your King Kong infatuation.
This knocks Kelvingrove Park into a hat.
You could fit half of Glasgow in here.
Look! A bagel shop!
Do you see many famous faces around here?
Did you not see Tim Robbins just outside?
TIM ROBBINS!?
Sept 11th
So, our last day. Twin Towers or the Statue of Liberty?
You choose, love. I'm just happy to have seen the Empire State Building.
GUIDE
1999
I'd love to come back for the Millenium.
ATEN
LAND
ERRY
...BUT IT WASN'T.
PHOTOS OUR ANNIVERSARY NYC 1999

Script & Art by Derek Gray (From a true story told to him by Tommy Sommerville)

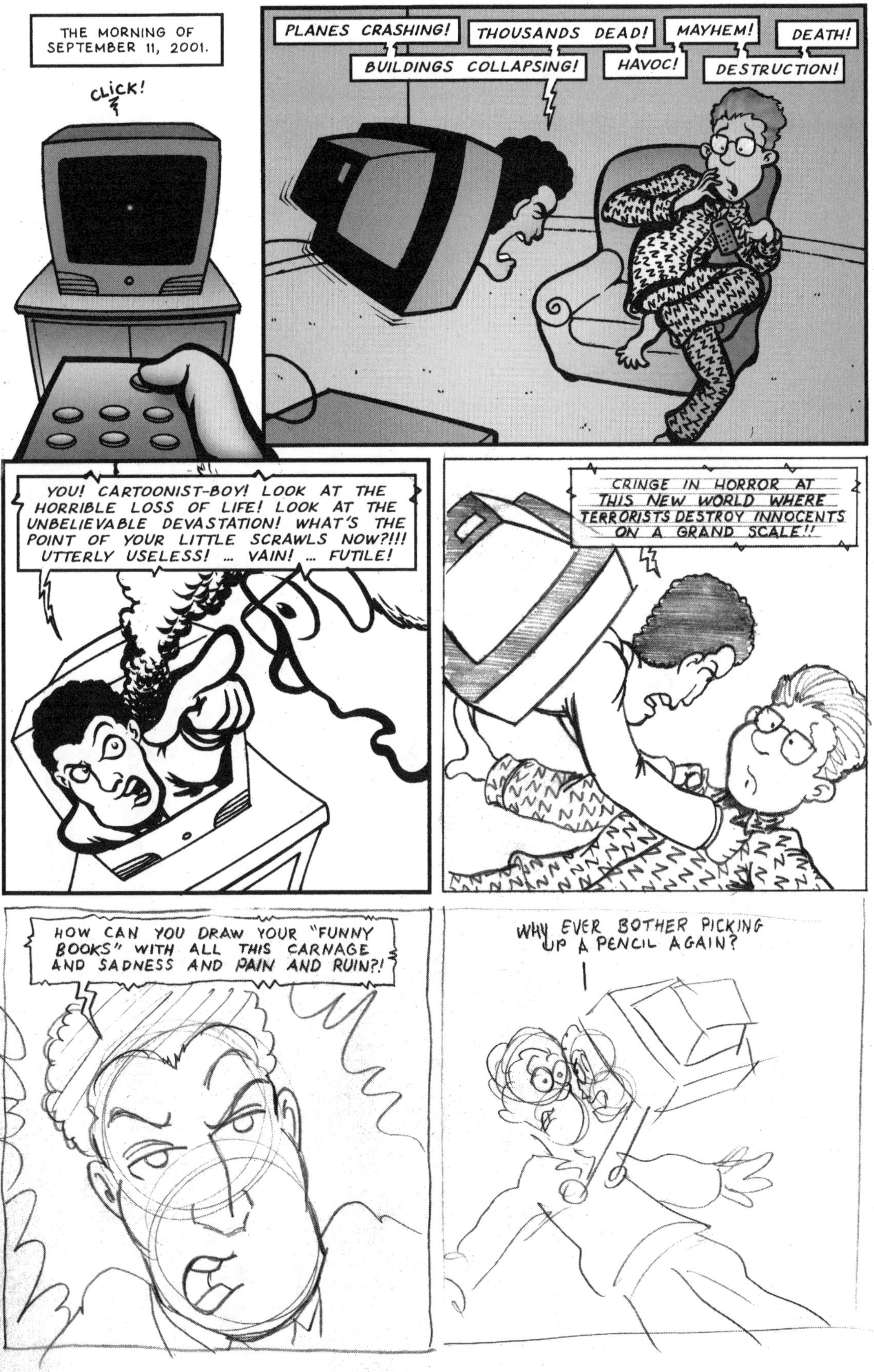
THE MORNING OF SEPTEMBER 11, 2001.
CLICK!
PLANES CRASHING!
THOUSANDS DEAD!
MAYHEM!
DEATH!
BUILDINGS COLLAPSING!
HAVOC!
DESTRUCTION!
YOU! CARTOONIST-BOY! LOOK AT THE HORRIBLE LOSS OF LIFE! LOOK AT THE UNBELIEVABLE DEVASTATION! WHAT'S THE POINT OF YOUR LITTLE SCRAWLS NOW?!!! UTTERLY USELESS! ... VAIN! ... FUTILE!
CRINGE IN HORROR AT THIS NEW WORLD WHERE TERRORISTS DESTROY INNOCENTS ON A GRAND SCALE!!
HOW CAN YOU DRAW YOUR "FUNNY BOOKS" WITH ALL THIS CARNAGE AND SADNESS AND PAIN AND RUIN?!
WHY EVER BOTHER PICKING UP A PENCIL AGAIN?

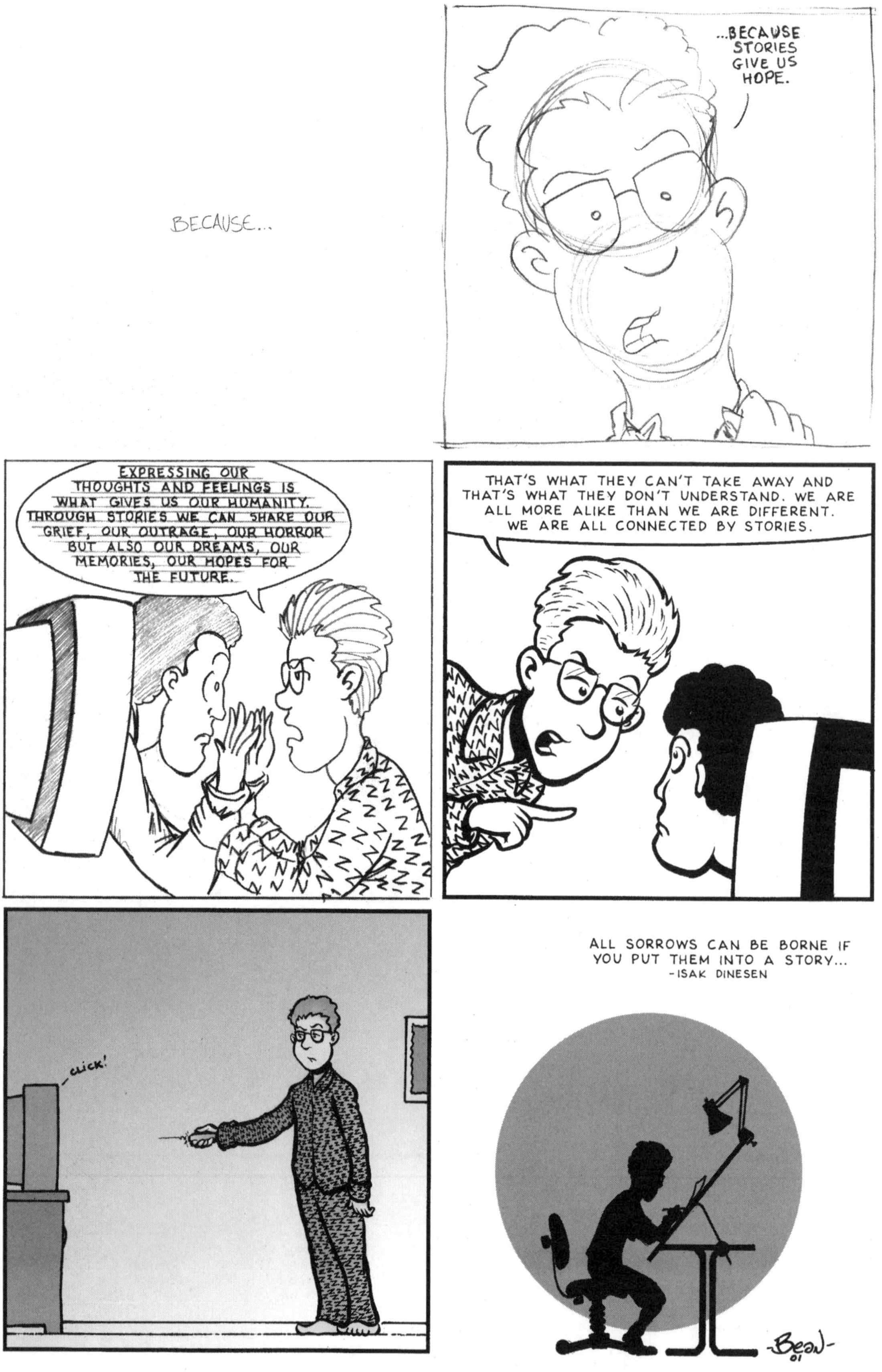
BECAUSE...
...BECAUSE STORIES GIVE US HOPE.
EXPRESSING OUR THOUGHTS AND FEELINGS IS WHAT GIVES US OUR HUMANITY. THROUGH STORIES WE CAN SHARE OUR GRIEF, OUR OUTRAGE, OUR HORROR BUT ALSO OUR DREAMS, OUR MEMORIES, OUR HOPES FOR THE FUTURE.
THAT'S WHAT THEY CAN'T TAKE AWAY AND THAT'S WHAT THEY DON'T UNDERSTAND. WE ARE ALL MORE ALIKE THAN WE ARE DIFFERENT. WE ARE ALL CONNECTED BY STORIES.
CLICK!
ALL SORROWS CAN BE BORNE IF YOU PUT THEM INTO A STORY...
-ISAK DINESEN
BEAN 01

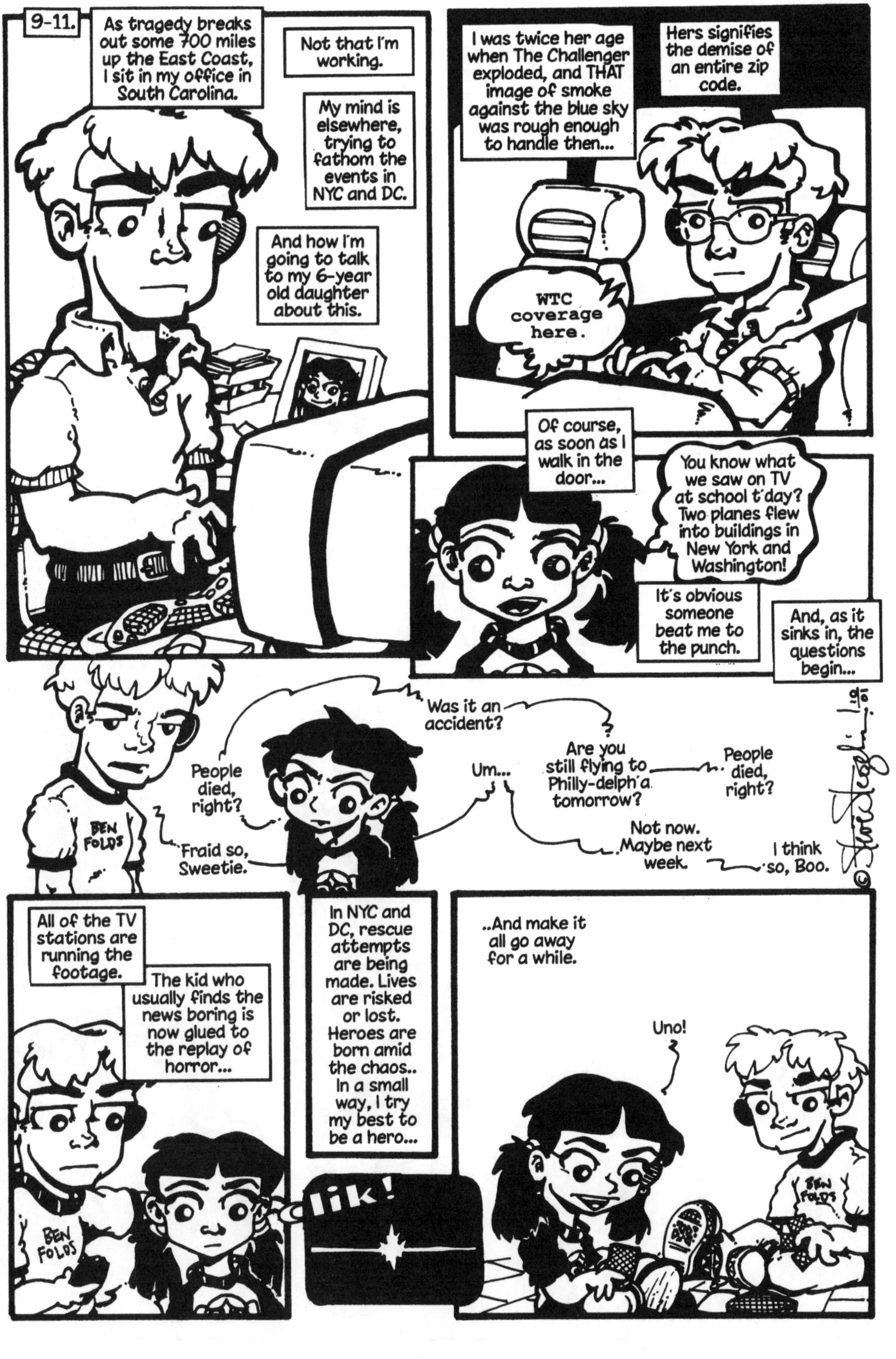
9-11.
As tragedy breaks out some 700 miles up the East Coast, I sit in my office in South Carolina.
Not that I'm working.
My mind is elsewhere, trying to fathom the events in NYC and DC.
And how I'm going to talk to my 6-year old daughter about this.
I was twice her age when The Challenger exploded, and THAT image of smoke against the blue sky was rough enough to handle then...
Hers signifies the demise of an entire zip code.
WTC coverage here.
Of course, as soon as I walk in the door...
You know what we saw on TV at school t'day? Two planes flew into buildings in New York and Washington!
It's obvious someone beat me to the punch.
And, as it sinks in, the questions begin...
People died, right?
'Fraid so, Sweetie.
Was it an accident?
Um...
Are you still flying to Philly-delph'a tomorrow?
Not now. Maybe next week.
People died, right?
I think so, Boo.
All of the TV stations are running the footage.
The kid who usually finds the news boring is now glued to the replay of horror...
In NYC and DC, rescue attempts are being made. Lives are risked or lost. Heroes are born amid the chaos.. In a small way, I try my best to be a hero...
Clik!
..And make it all go away for a while.
Uno!

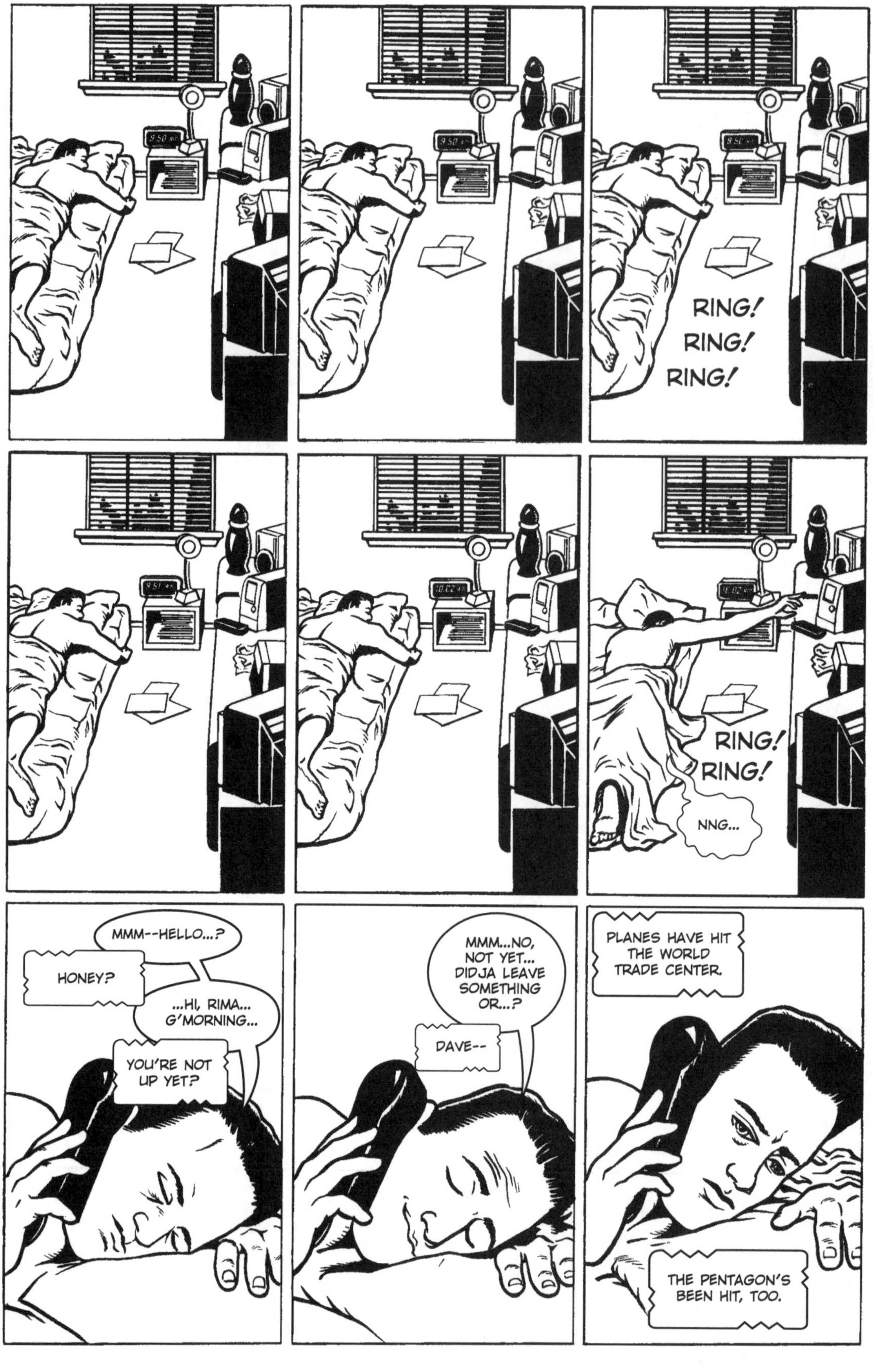
RING! RING! RING!
RING! RING!
NNG...
MMM--HELLO...?
HONEY?
...HI, RIMA... G'MORNING...
YOU'RE NOT UP YET?
MMM...NO, NOT YET... DIDJA LEAVE SOMETHING OR...?
DAVE--
PLANES HAVE HIT THE WORLD TRADE CENTER.
THE PENTAGON'S BEEN HIT, TOO.

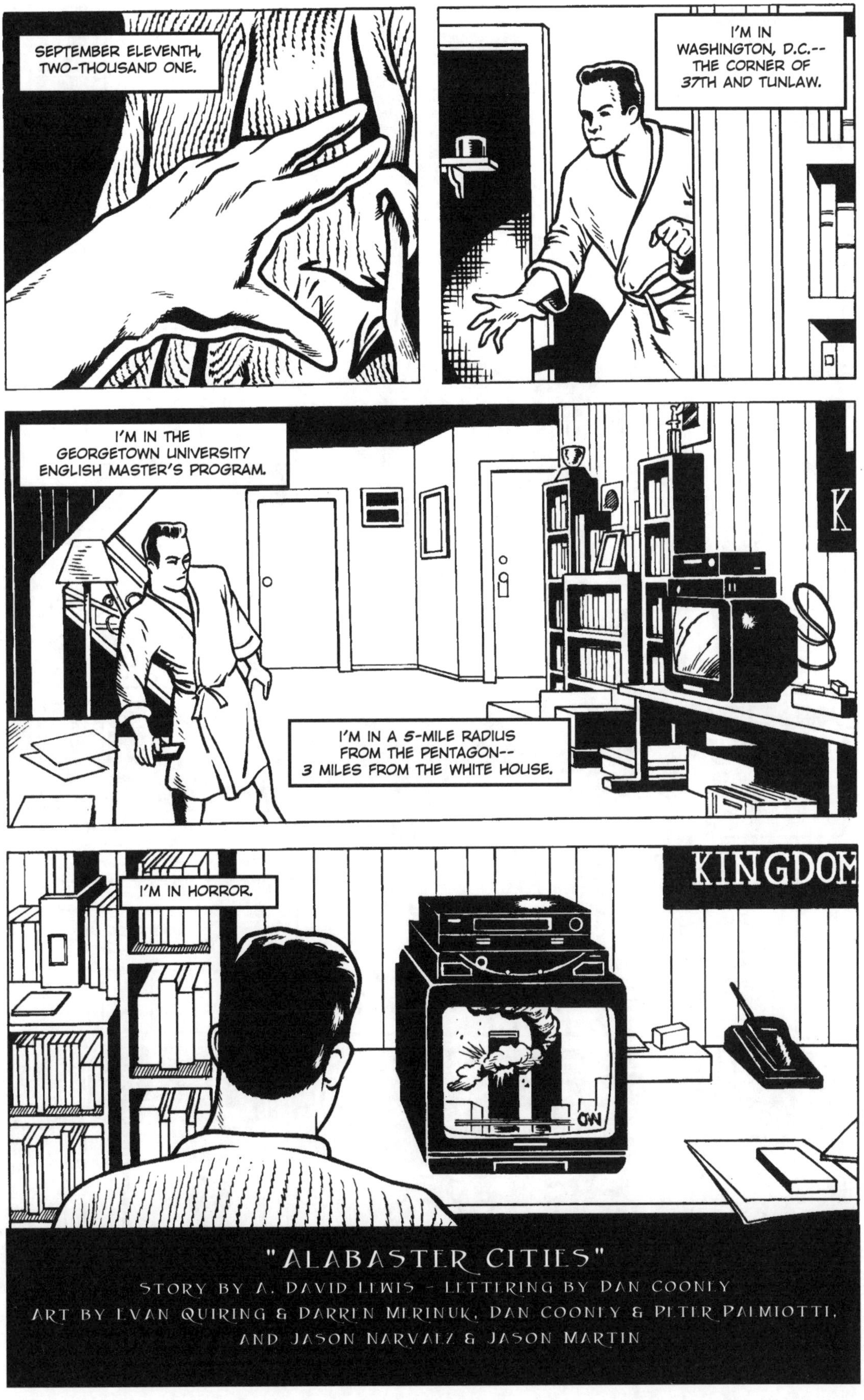
SEPTEMBER ELEVENTH, TWO-THOUSAND ONE.
I'M IN WASHINGTON, D.C.-- THE CORNER OF 37TH AND TUNLAW.
I'M IN THE GEORGETOWN UNIVERSITY ENGLISH MASTER'S PROGRAM.
I'M IN A 5-MILE RADIUS FROM THE PENTAGON-- 3 MILES FROM THE WHITE HOUSE.
I'M IN HORROR.
KINGDOM
"ALABASTER CITIES"
STORY BY A. DAVID LEWIS - LETTERING BY DAN COONEY
ART BY EVAN QUIRING & DARREN MERINUK, DAN COONEY & PETER PALMIOTTI, AND JASON NARVAEZ & JASON MARTIN

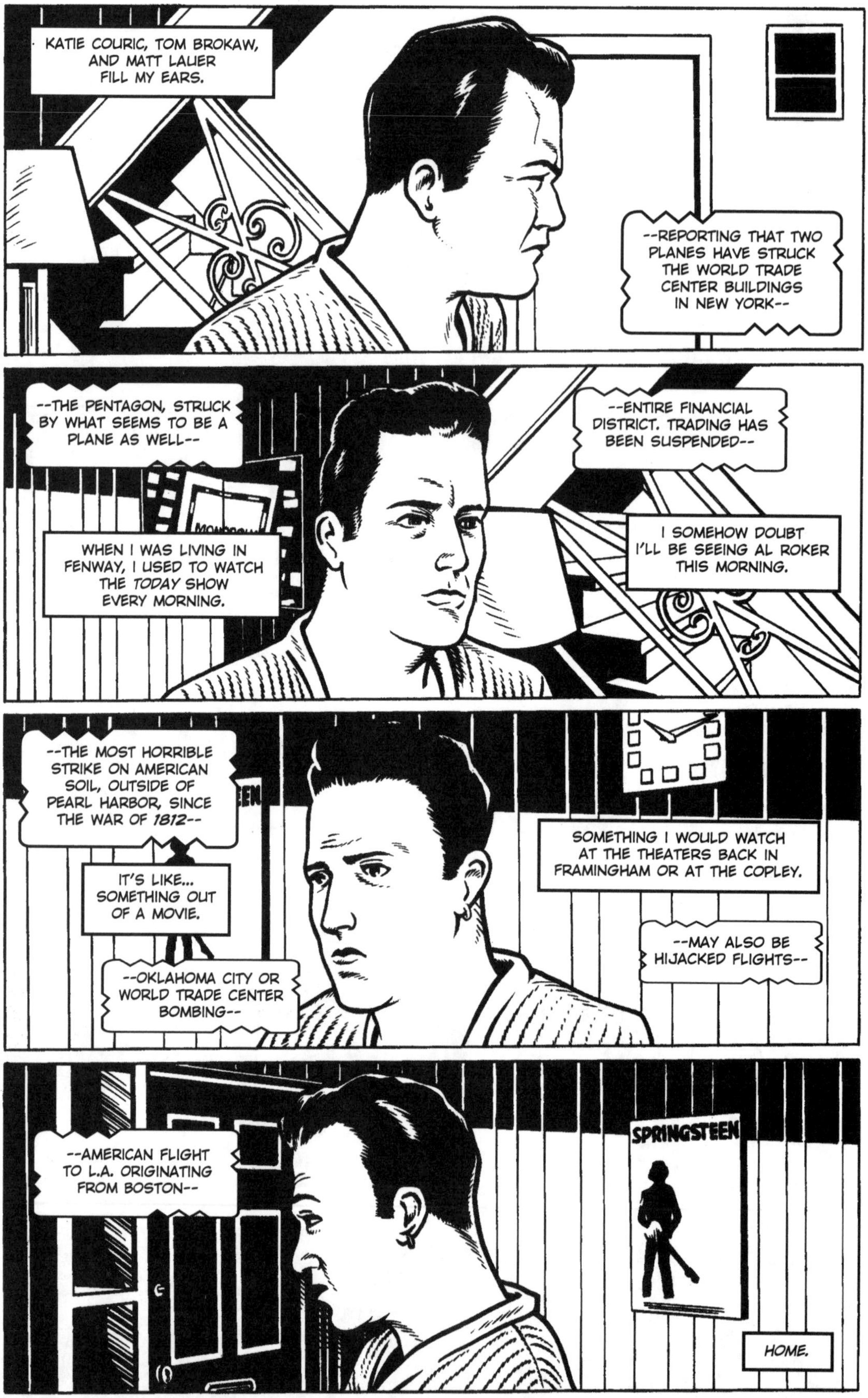
KATIE COURIC, TOM BROKAW, AND MATT LAUER FILL MY EARS.
--REPORTING THAT TWO PLANES HAVE STRUCK THE WORLD TRADE CENTER BUILDINGS IN NEW YORK--
--THE PENTAGON, STRUCK BY WHAT SEEMS TO BE A PLANE AS WELL--
WHEN I WAS LIVING IN FENWAY, I USED TO WATCH THE *TODAY* SHOW EVERY MORNING.
--ENTIRE FINANCIAL DISTRICT. TRADING HAS BEEN SUSPENDED--
I SOMEHOW DOUBT I'LL BE SEEING AL ROKER THIS MORNING.
--THE MOST HORRIBLE STRIKE ON AMERICAN SOIL, OUTSIDE OF PEARL HARBOR, SINCE THE WAR OF *1812*--
IT'S LIKE... SOMETHING OUT OF A MOVIE.
--OKLAHOMA CITY OR WORLD TRADE CENTER BOMBING--
SOMETHING I WOULD WATCH AT THE THEATERS BACK IN FRAMINGHAM OR AT THE COPLEY.
--MAY ALSO BE HIJACKED FLIGHTS--
--AMERICAN FLIGHT TO L.A. ORIGINATING FROM BOSTON--
SPRINGSTEEN
HOME.

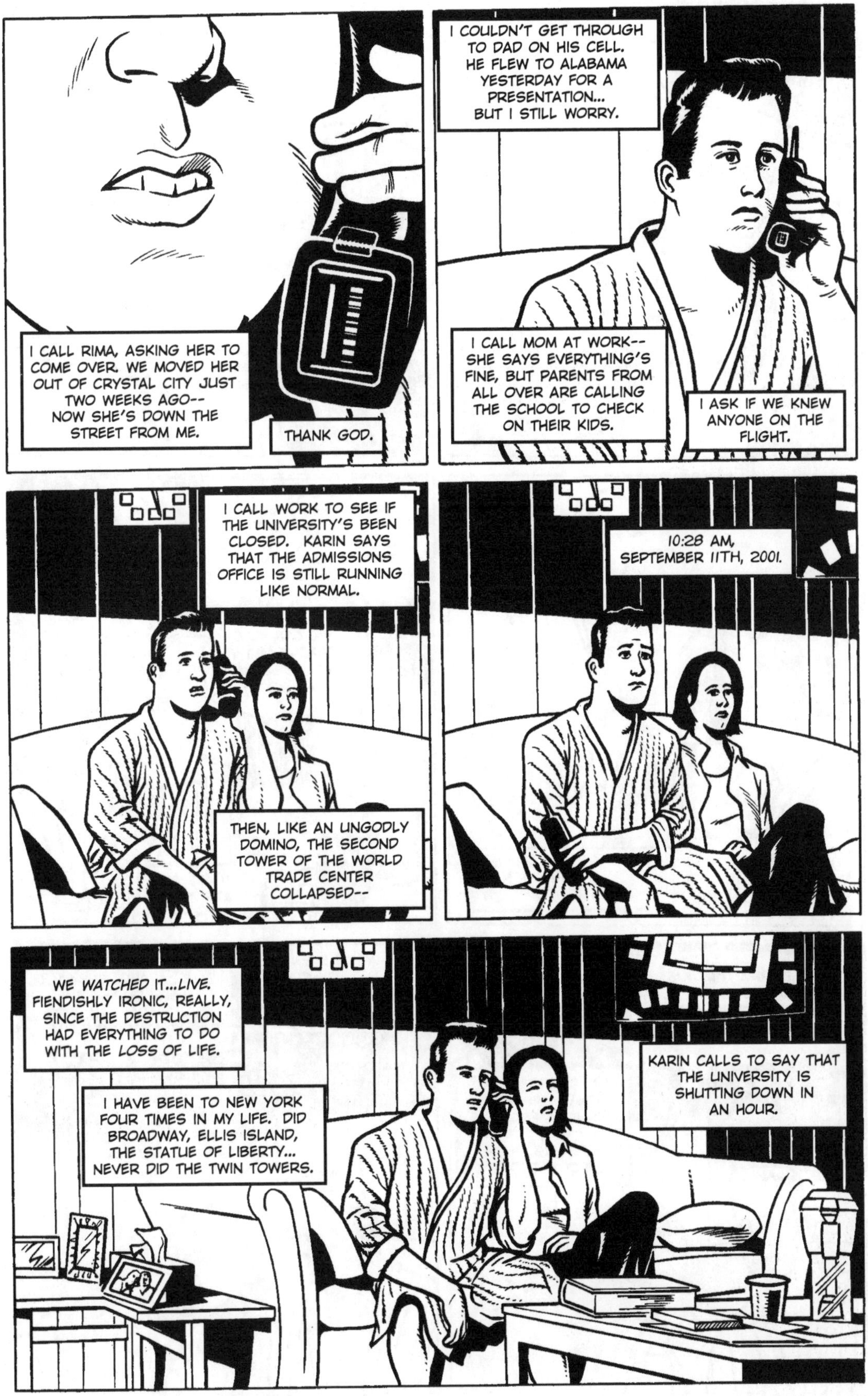
I CALL RIMA, ASKING HER TO COME OVER. WE MOVED HER OUT OF CRYSTAL CITY JUST TWO WEEKS AGO-- NOW SHE'S DOWN THE STREET FROM ME.
THANK GOD.
I COULDN'T GET THROUGH TO DAD ON HIS CELL. HE FLEW TO ALABAMA YESTERDAY FOR A PRESENTATION... BUT I STILL WORRY.
I CALL MOM AT WORK-- SHE SAYS EVERYTHING'S FINE, BUT PARENTS FROM ALL OVER ARE CALLING THE SCHOOL TO CHECK ON THEIR KIDS.
I ASK IF WE KNEW ANYONE ON THE FLIGHT.
I CALL WORK TO SEE IF THE UNIVERSITY'S BEEN CLOSED. KARIN SAYS THAT THE ADMISSIONS OFFICE IS STILL RUNNING LIKE NORMAL.
THEN, LIKE AN UNGODLY DOMINO, THE SECOND TOWER OF THE WORLD TRADE CENTER COLLAPSED--
10:28 AM, SEPTEMBER 11TH, 2001.
WE *WATCHED* IT...*LIVE.* FIENDISHLY IRONIC, REALLY, SINCE THE DESTRUCTION HAD EVERYTHING TO DO WITH THE *LOSS* OF LIFE.
I HAVE BEEN TO NEW YORK FOUR TIMES IN MY LIFE. DID BROADWAY, ELLIS ISLAND, THE STATUE OF LIBERTY... NEVER DID THE TWIN TOWERS.
KARIN CALLS TO SAY THAT THE UNIVERSITY IS SHUTTING DOWN IN AN HOUR.

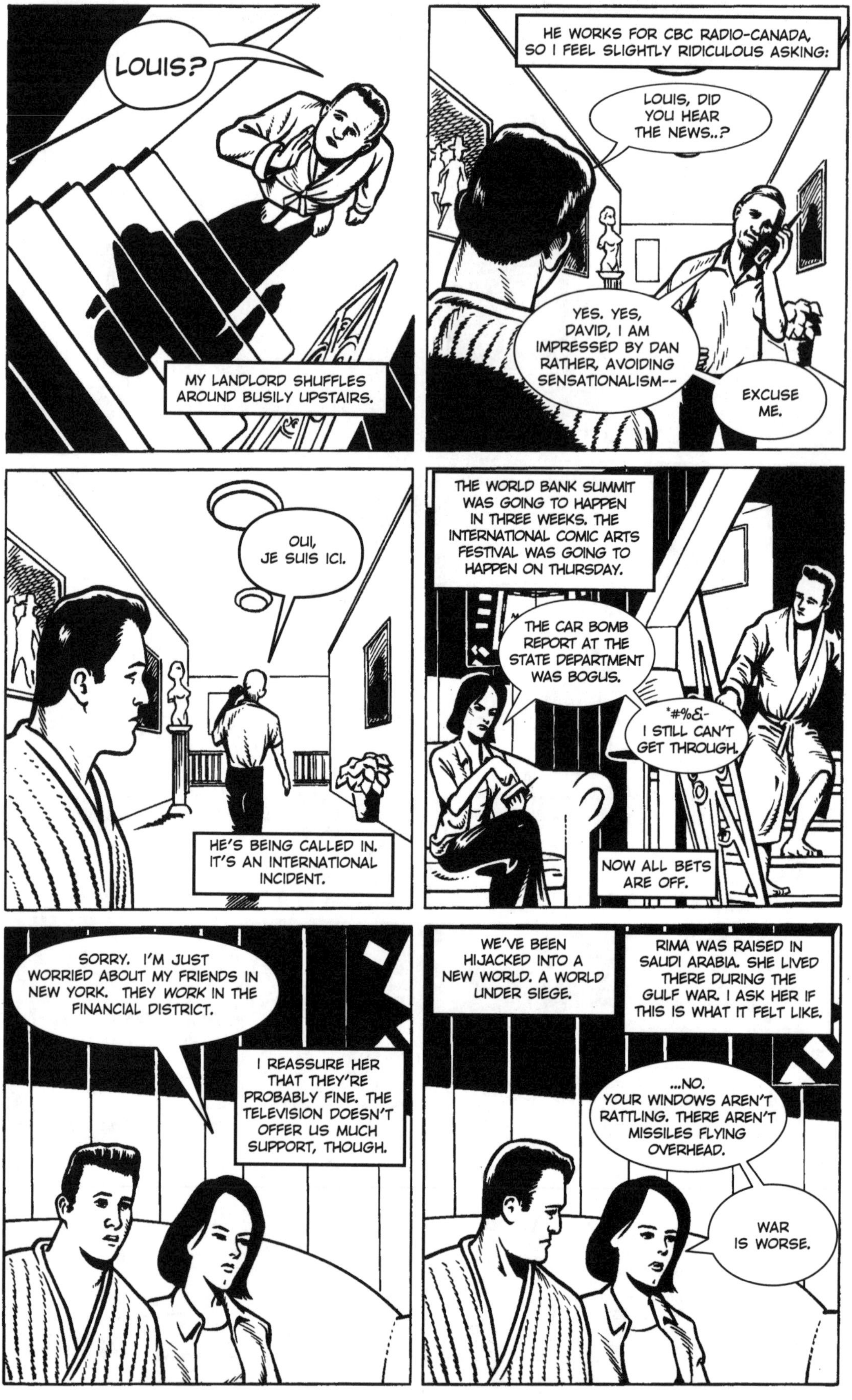
LOUIS?
MY LANDLORD SHUFFLES AROUND BUSILY UPSTAIRS.
HE WORKS FOR CBC RADIO-CANADA, SO I FEEL SLIGHTLY RIDICULOUS ASKING:
LOUIS, DID YOU HEAR THE NEWS..?
YES. YES, DAVID, I AM IMPRESSED BY DAN RATHER, AVOIDING SENSATIONALISM--
EXCUSE ME.
OUI, JE SUIS ICI.
HE'S BEING CALLED IN. IT'S AN INTERNATIONAL INCIDENT.
THE WORLD BANK SUMMIT WAS GOING TO HAPPEN IN THREE WEEKS. THE INTERNATIONAL COMIC ARTS FESTIVAL WAS GOING TO HAPPEN ON THURSDAY.
THE CAR BOMB REPORT AT THE STATE DEPARTMENT WAS BOGUS.
*#%&- I STILL CAN'T GET THROUGH.
NOW ALL BETS ARE OFF.
SORRY. I'M JUST WORRIED ABOUT MY FRIENDS IN NEW YORK. THEY *WORK* IN THE FINANCIAL DISTRICT.
I REASSURE HER THAT THEY'RE PROBABLY FINE. THE TELEVISION DOESN'T OFFER US MUCH SUPPORT, THOUGH.
WE'VE BEEN HIJACKED INTO A NEW WORLD. A WORLD UNDER SIEGE.
RIMA WAS RAISED IN SAUDI ARABIA. SHE LIVED THERE DURING THE GULF WAR. I ASK HER IF THIS IS WHAT IT FELT LIKE.
...NO. YOUR WINDOWS AREN'T RATTLING. THERE AREN'T MISSILES FLYING OVERHEAD.
WAR IS WORSE.

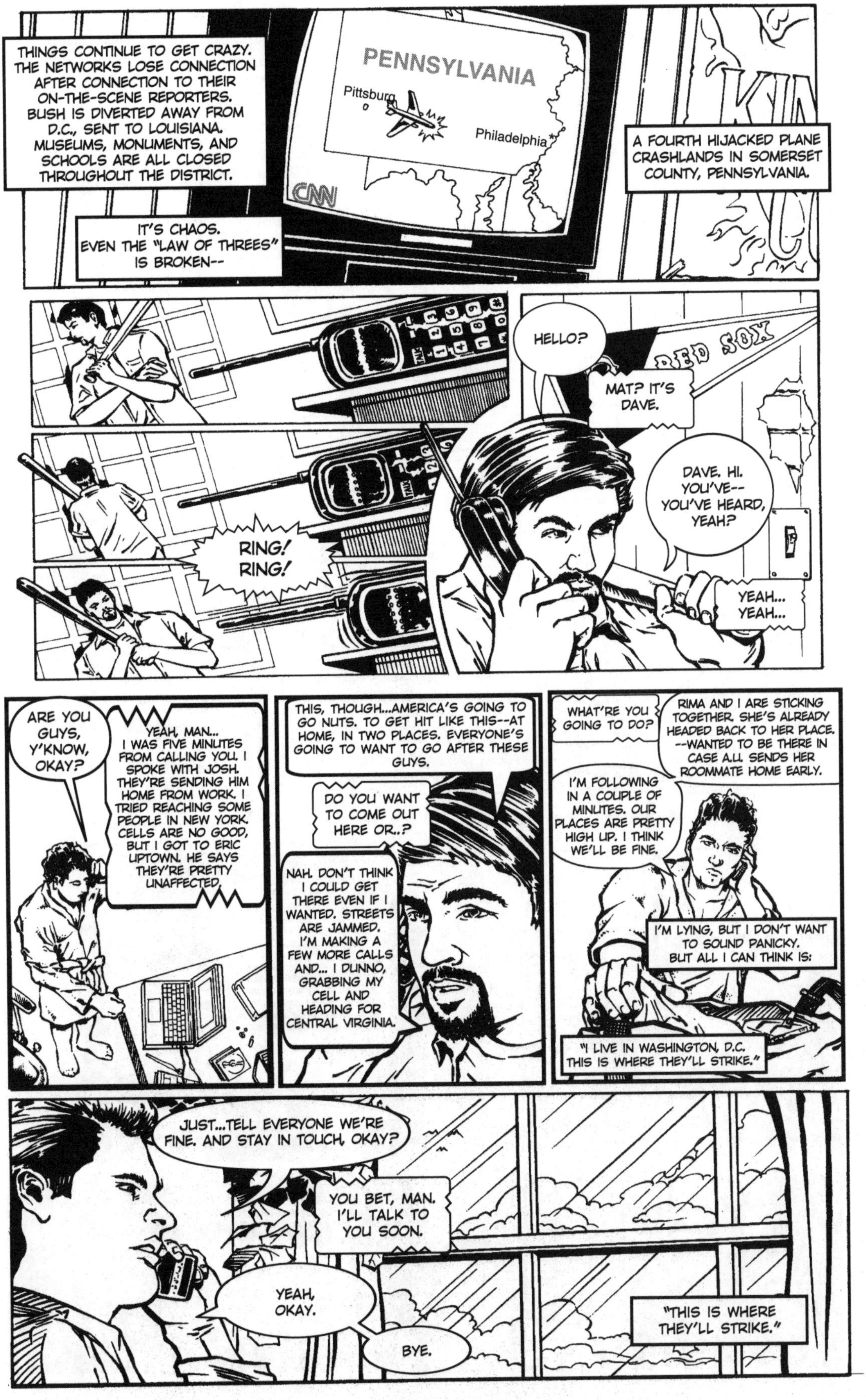
THINGS CONTINUE TO GET CRAZY. THE NETWORKS LOSE CONNECTION AFTER CONNECTION TO THEIR ON-THE-SCENE REPORTERS. BUSH IS DIVERTED AWAY FROM D.C., SENT TO LOUISIANA. MUSEUMS, MONUMENTS, AND SCHOOLS ARE ALL CLOSED THROUGHOUT THE DISTRICT.
PENNSYLVANIA
Pittsburg
Philadelphia
CNN
IT'S CHAOS. EVEN THE "LAW OF THREES" IS BROKEN--
A FOURTH HIJACKED PLANE CRASHLANDS IN SOMERSET COUNTY, PENNSYLVANIA.
RING! RING!
HELLO?
RED SOX
MAT? IT'S DAVE.
DAVE. HI. YOU'VE-- YOU'VE HEARD, YEAH?
YEAH... YEAH...
ARE YOU GUYS, Y'KNOW, OKAY?
YEAH, MAN... I WAS FIVE MINUTES FROM CALLING YOU. I SPOKE WITH JOSH. THEY'RE SENDING HIM HOME FROM WORK. I TRIED REACHING SOME PEOPLE IN NEW YORK. CELLS ARE NO GOOD, BUT I GOT TO ERIC UPTOWN. HE SAYS THEY'RE PRETTY UNAFFECTED.
THIS, THOUGH...AMERICA'S GOING TO GO NUTS. TO GET HIT LIKE THIS--AT HOME, IN TWO PLACES. EVERYONE'S GOING TO WANT TO GO AFTER THESE GUYS.
DO YOU WANT TO COME OUT HERE OR..?
NAH. DON'T THINK I COULD GET THERE EVEN IF I WANTED. STREETS ARE JAMMED. I'M MAKING A FEW MORE CALLS AND... I DUNNO, GRABBING MY CELL AND HEADING FOR CENTRAL VIRGINIA.
WHAT'RE YOU GOING TO DO?
RIMA AND I ARE STICKING TOGETHER. SHE'S ALREADY HEADED BACK TO HER PLACE. --WANTED TO BE THERE IN CASE A.U. SENDS HER ROOMMATE HOME EARLY.
I'M FOLLOWING IN A COUPLE OF MINUTES. OUR PLACES ARE PRETTY HIGH UP. I THINK WE'LL BE FINE.
I'M LYING, BUT I DON'T WANT TO SOUND PANICKY. BUT ALL I CAN THINK IS:
"I LIVE IN WASHINGTON, D.C. THIS IS WHERE THEY'LL STRIKE."
JUST...TELL EVERYONE WE'RE FINE. AND STAY IN TOUCH, OKAY?
YOU BET, MAN. I'LL TALK TO YOU SOON.
YEAH, OKAY.
BYE.
"THIS IS WHERE THEY'LL STRIKE."

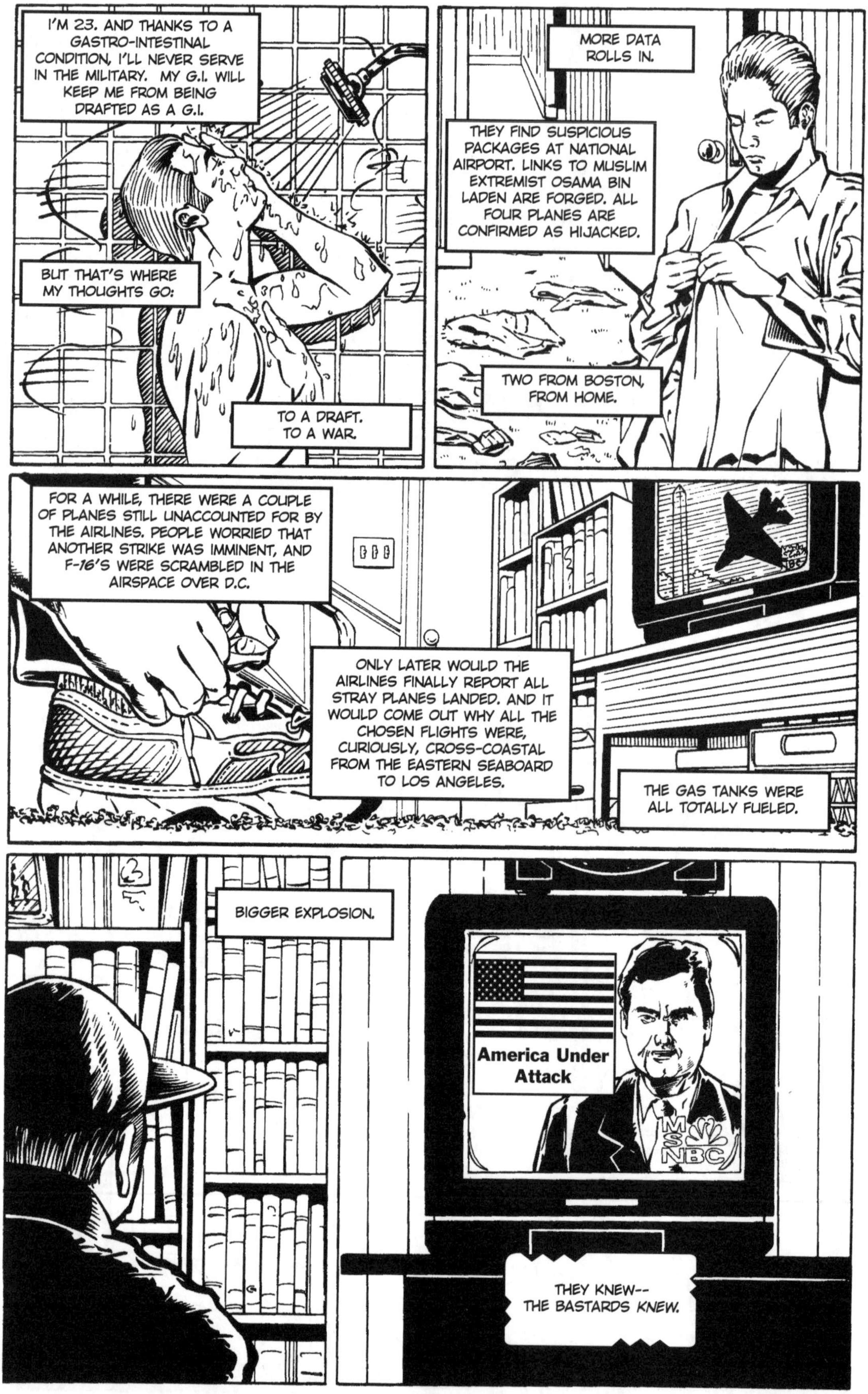
I'M 23. AND THANKS TO A GASTRO-INTESTINAL CONDITION, I'LL NEVER SERVE IN THE MILITARY. MY G.I. WILL KEEP ME FROM BEING DRAFTED AS A G.I.
BUT THAT'S WHERE MY THOUGHTS GO:
TO A DRAFT. TO A WAR.
MORE DATA ROLLS IN.
THEY FIND SUSPICIOUS PACKAGES AT NATIONAL AIRPORT. LINKS TO MUSLIM EXTREMIST OSAMA BIN LADEN ARE FORGED. ALL FOUR PLANES ARE CONFIRMED AS HIJACKED.
TWO FROM BOSTON, FROM HOME.
FOR A WHILE, THERE WERE A COUPLE OF PLANES STILL UNACCOUNTED FOR BY THE AIRLINES. PEOPLE WORRIED THAT ANOTHER STRIKE WAS IMMINENT, AND F-16'S WERE SCRAMBLED IN THE AIRSPACE OVER D.C.
ONLY LATER WOULD THE AIRLINES FINALLY REPORT ALL STRAY PLANES LANDED. AND IT WOULD COME OUT WHY ALL THE CHOSEN FLIGHTS WERE, CURIOUSLY, CROSS-COASTAL FROM THE EASTERN SEABOARD TO LOS ANGELES.
THE GAS TANKS WERE ALL TOTALLY FUELED.
BIGGER EXPLOSION.
America Under Attack
MSNBC
THEY KNEW-- THE BASTARDS KNEW.

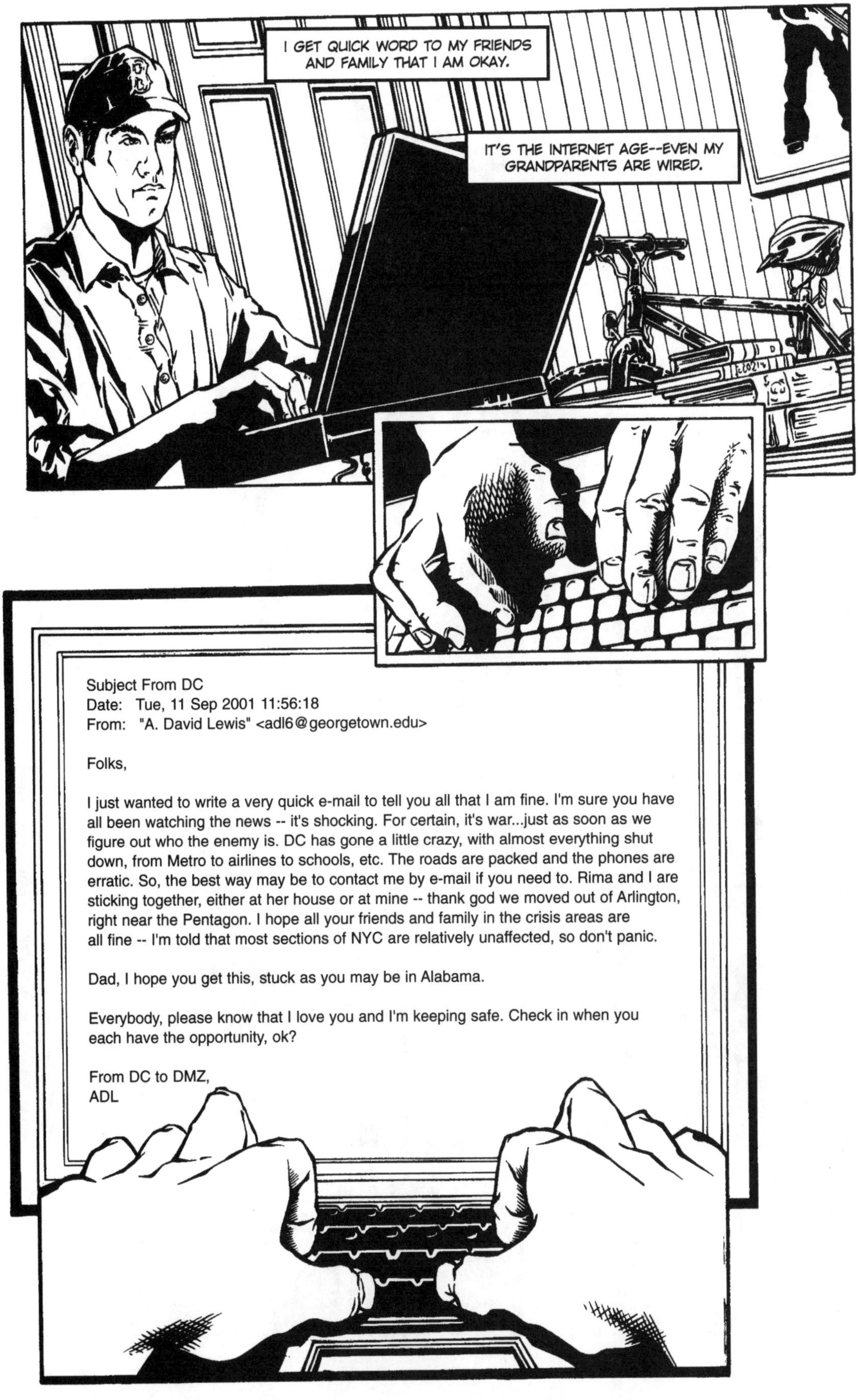

I GET QUICK WORD TO MY FRIENDS AND FAMILY THAT I AM OKAY.
IT'S THE INTERNET AGE--EVEN MY GRANDPARENTS ARE WIRED.
Subject From DC
Date: Tue, 11 Sep 2001 11:56:18
From: "A. David Lewis" <adl6@georgetown.edu>
Folks,
I just wanted to write a very quick e-mail to tell you all that I am fine. I'm sure you have all been watching the news -- it's shocking. For certain, it's war...just as soon as we figure out who the enemy is. DC has gone a little crazy, with almost everything shut down, from Metro to airlines to schools, etc. The roads are packed and the phones are erratic. So, the best way may be to contact me by e-mail if you need to. Rima and I are sticking together, either at her house or at mine -- thank god we moved out of Arlington, right near the Pentagon. I hope all your friends and family in the crisis areas are all fine -- I'm told that most sections of NYC are relatively unaffected, so don't panic.
Dad, I hope you get this, stuck as you may be in Alabama.
Everybody, please know that I love you and I'm keeping safe. Check in when you each have the opportunity, ok?
From DC to DMZ,
ADL

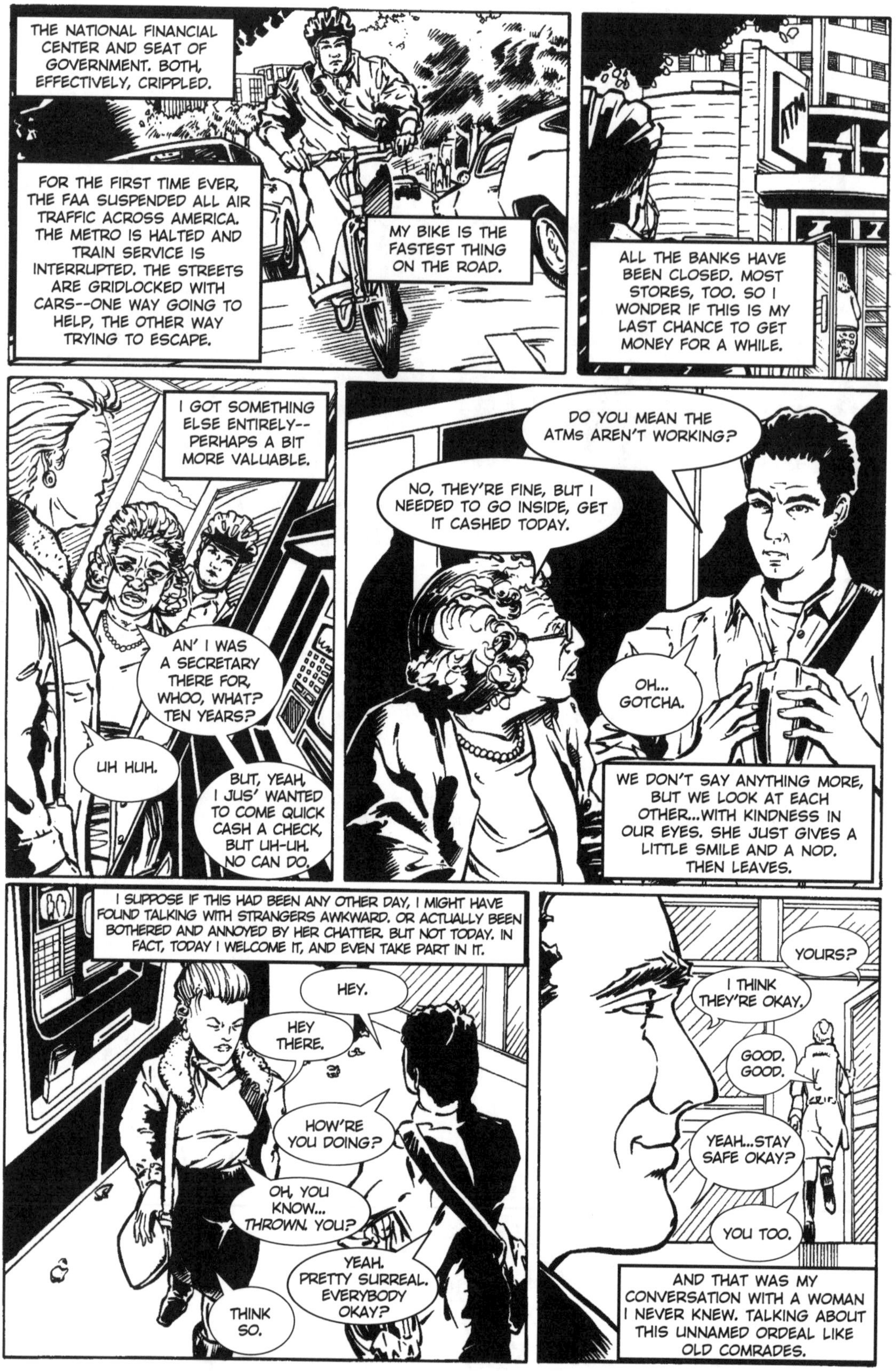
THE NATIONAL FINANCIAL CENTER AND SEAT OF GOVERNMENT. BOTH, EFFECTIVELY, CRIPPLED.
FOR THE FIRST TIME EVER, THE FAA SUSPENDED ALL AIR TRAFFIC ACROSS AMERICA. THE METRO IS HALTED AND TRAIN SERVICE IS INTERRUPTED. THE STREETS ARE GRIDLOCKED WITH CARS--ONE WAY GOING TO HELP, THE OTHER WAY TRYING TO ESCAPE.
MY BIKE IS THE FASTEST THING ON THE ROAD.
ALL THE BANKS HAVE BEEN CLOSED. MOST STORES, TOO. SO I WONDER IF THIS IS MY LAST CHANCE TO GET MONEY FOR A WHILE.
I GOT SOMETHING ELSE ENTIRELY-- PERHAPS A BIT MORE VALUABLE.
AN' I WAS A SECRETARY THERE FOR, WHOO, WHAT? TEN YEARS?
UH HUH.
BUT, YEAH, I JUS' WANTED TO COME QUICK CASH A CHECK, BUT UH-UH. NO CAN DO.
DO YOU MEAN THE ATMS AREN'T WORKING?
NO, THEY'RE FINE, BUT I NEEDED TO GO INSIDE, GET IT CASHED TODAY.
OH... GOTCHA.
WE DON'T SAY ANYTHING MORE, BUT WE LOOK AT EACH OTHER...WITH KINDNESS IN OUR EYES. SHE JUST GIVES A LITTLE SMILE AND A NOD. THEN LEAVES.
I SUPPOSE IF THIS HAD BEEN ANY OTHER DAY, I MIGHT HAVE FOUND TALKING WITH STRANGERS AWKWARD. OR ACTUALLY BEEN BOTHERED AND ANNOYED BY HER CHATTER. BUT NOT TODAY. IN FACT, TODAY I WELCOME IT, AND EVEN TAKE PART IN IT.
HEY.
HEY THERE.
HOW'RE YOU DOING?
OH, YOU KNOW... THROWN. YOU?
YEAH. PRETTY SURREAL. EVERYBODY OKAY?
THINK SO.
YOURS?
I THINK THEY'RE OKAY.
GOOD. GOOD.
YEAH...STAY SAFE OKAY?
YOU TOO.
AND THAT WAS MY CONVERSATION WITH A WOMAN I NEVER KNEW. TALKING ABOUT THIS UNNAMED ORDEAL LIKE OLD COMRADES.

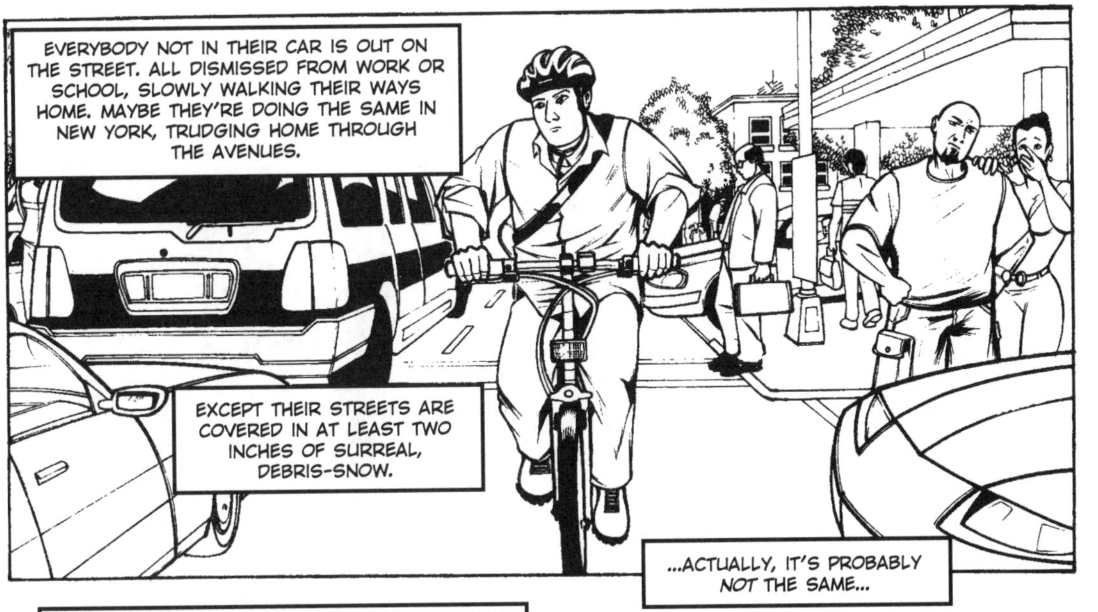
EVERYBODY NOT IN THEIR CAR IS OUT ON THE STREET. ALL DISMISSED FROM WORK OR SCHOOL, SLOWLY WALKING THEIR WAYS HOME. MAYBE THEY'RE DOING THE SAME IN NEW YORK, TRUDGING HOME THROUGH THE AVENUES.
EXCEPT THEIR STREETS ARE COVERED IN AT LEAST TWO INCHES OF SURREAL, DEBRIS-SNOW.
...ACTUALLY, IT'S PROBABLY *NOT* THE SAME...

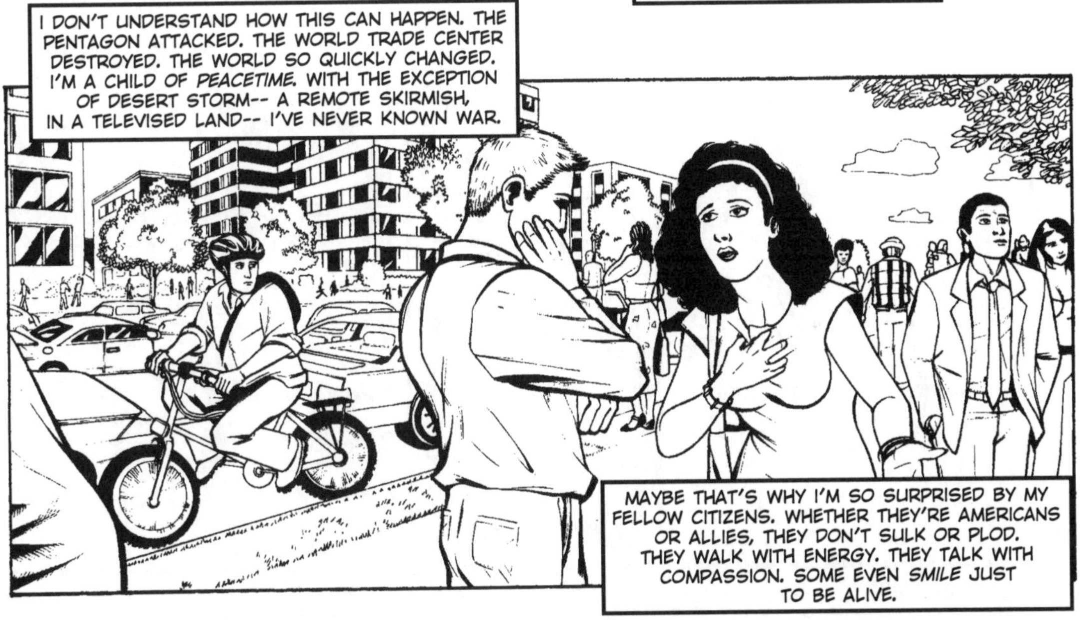
I DON'T UNDERSTAND HOW THIS CAN HAPPEN. THE PENTAGON ATTACKED. THE WORLD TRADE CENTER DESTROYED. THE WORLD SO QUICKLY CHANGED. I'M A CHILD OF *PEACETIME.* WITH THE EXCEPTION OF DESERT STORM-- A REMOTE SKIRMISH, IN A TELEVISED LAND-- I'VE NEVER KNOWN WAR.
MAYBE THAT'S WHY I'M SO SURPRISED BY MY FELLOW CITIZENS. WHETHER THEY'RE AMERICANS OR ALLIES, THEY DON'T SULK OR PLOD. THEY WALK WITH ENERGY. THEY TALK WITH COMPASSION. SOME EVEN *SMILE* JUST TO BE ALIVE.

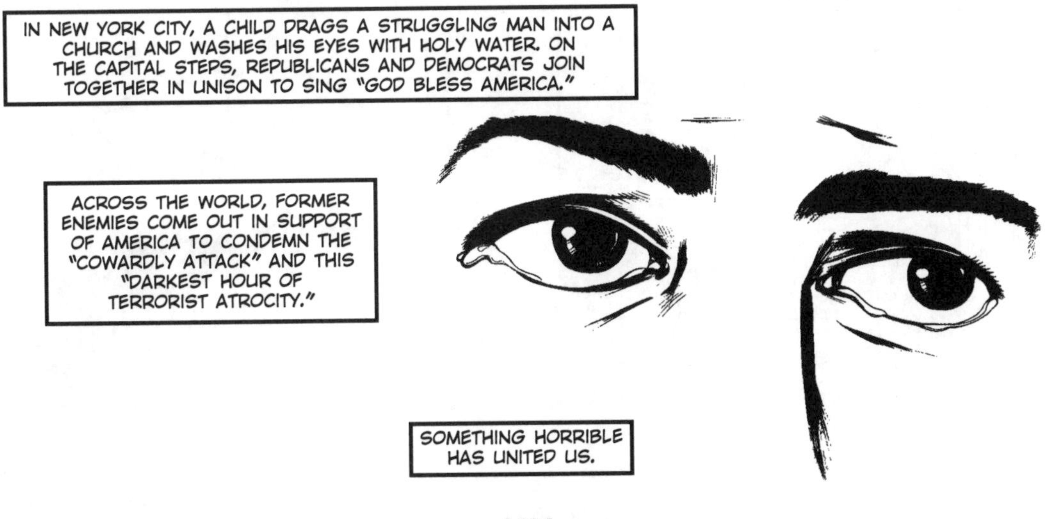
IN NEW YORK CITY, A CHILD DRAGS A STRUGGLING MAN INTO A CHURCH AND WASHES HIS EYES WITH HOLY WATER. ON THE CAPITAL STEPS, REPUBLICANS AND DEMOCRATS JOIN TOGETHER IN UNISON TO SING "GOD BLESS AMERICA."
ACROSS THE WORLD, FORMER ENEMIES COME OUT IN SUPPORT OF AMERICA TO CONDEMN THE "COWARDLY ATTACK" AND THIS "DARKEST HOUR OF TERRORIST ATROCITY."
SOMETHING HORRIBLE HAS UNITED US.

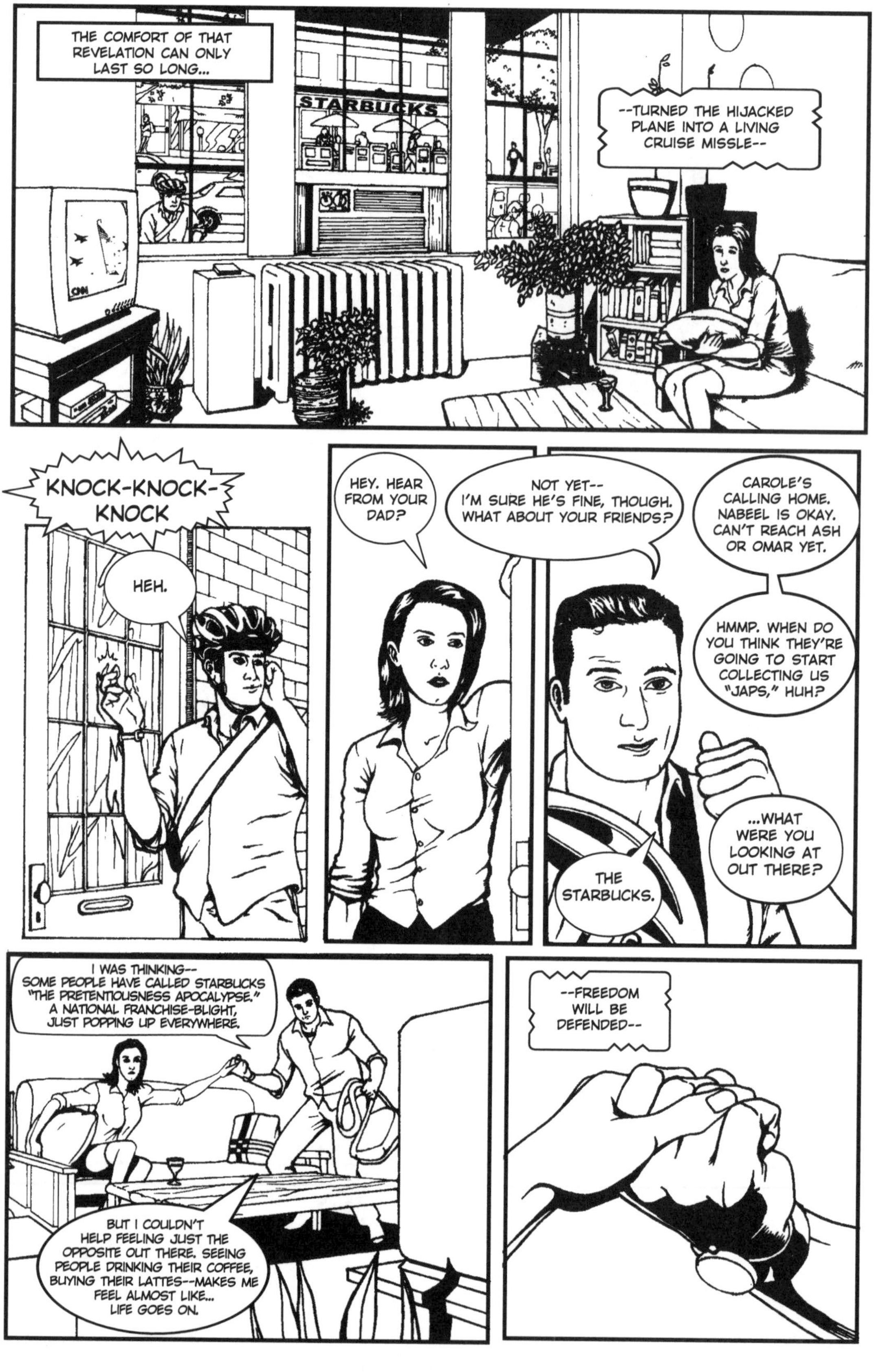
THE COMFORT OF THAT REVELATION CAN ONLY LAST SO LONG...
STARBUCKS
--TURNED THE HIJACKED PLANE INTO A LIVING CRUISE MISSLE--
KNOCK-KNOCK-KNOCK
HEH.
HEY. HEAR FROM YOUR DAD?
NOT YET-- I'M SURE HE'S FINE, THOUGH. WHAT ABOUT YOUR FRIENDS?
CAROLE'S CALLING HOME. NABEEL IS OKAY. CAN'T REACH ASH OR OMAR YET.
HMMP. WHEN DO YOU THINK THEY'RE GOING TO START COLLECTING US "JAPS," HUH?
...WHAT WERE YOU LOOKING AT OUT THERE?
THE STARBUCKS.
I WAS THINKING-- SOME PEOPLE HAVE CALLED STARBUCKS "THE PRETENTIOUSNESS APOCALYPSE." A NATIONAL FRANCHISE-BLIGHT, JUST POPPING UP EVERYWHERE.
BUT I COULDN'T HELP FEELING JUST THE OPPOSITE OUT THERE. SEEING PEOPLE DRINKING THEIR COFFEE, BUYING THEIR LATTES--MAKES ME FEEL ALMOST LIKE... LIFE GOES ON.
--FREEDOM WILL BE DEFENDED--

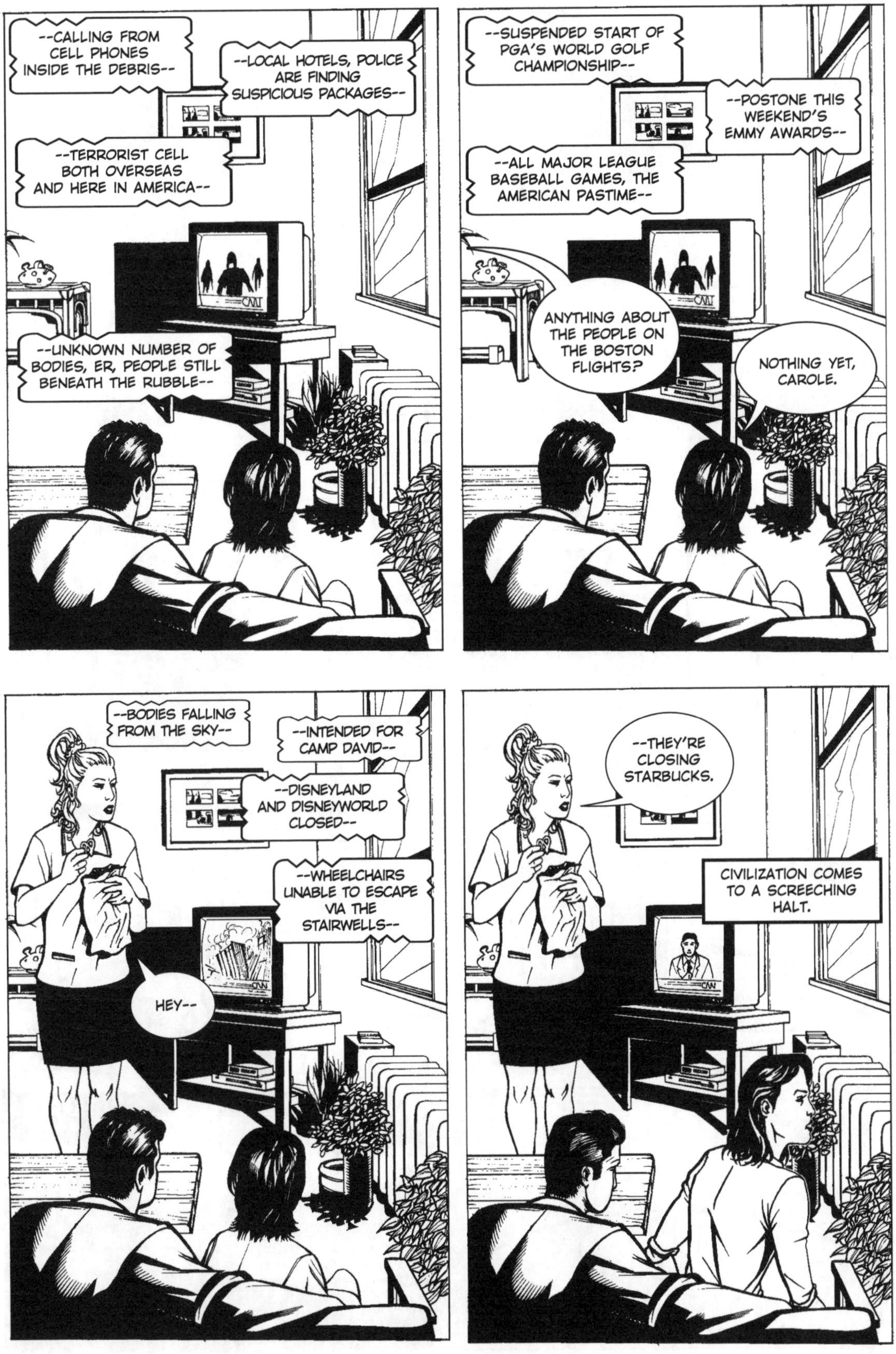
--CALLING FROM CELL PHONES INSIDE THE DEBRIS--
--LOCAL HOTELS, POLICE ARE FINDING SUSPICIOUS PACKAGES--
--TERRORIST CELL BOTH OVERSEAS AND HERE IN AMERICA--
--UNKNOWN NUMBER OF BODIES, ER, PEOPLE STILL BENEATH THE RUBBLE--
--SUSPENDED START OF PGA'S WORLD GOLF CHAMPIONSHIP--
--POSTONE THIS WEEKEND'S EMMY AWARDS--
--ALL MAJOR LEAGUE BASEBALL GAMES, THE AMERICAN PASTIME--
ANYTHING ABOUT THE PEOPLE ON THE BOSTON FLIGHTS?
NOTHING YET, CAROLE.
--BODIES FALLING FROM THE SKY--
--INTENDED FOR CAMP DAVID--
--DISNEYLAND AND DISNEYWORLD CLOSED--
--WHEELCHAIRS UNABLE TO ESCAPE VIA THE STAIRWELLS--
HEY--
--THEY'RE CLOSING STARBUCKS.
CIVILIZATION COMES TO A SCREECHING HALT.

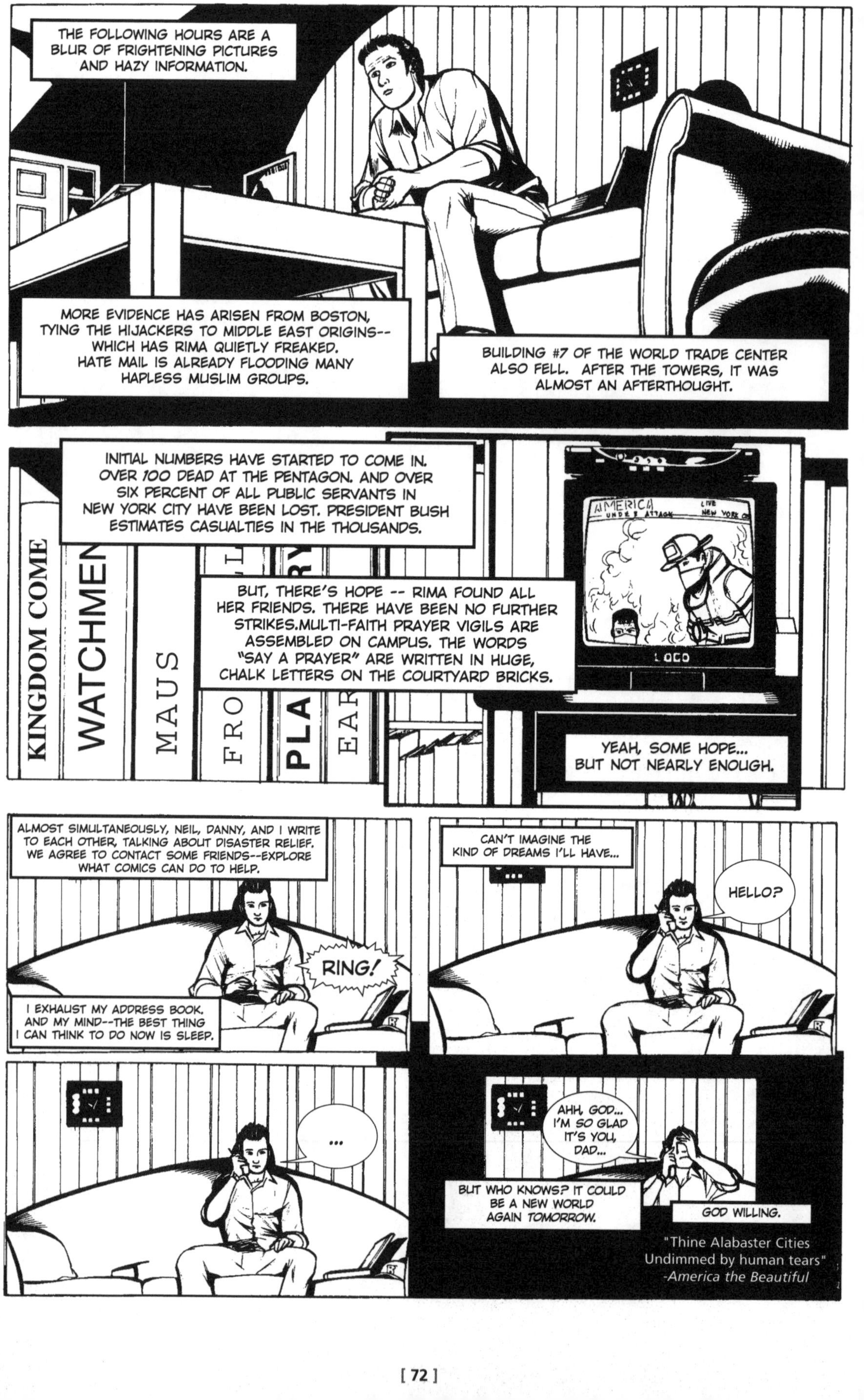
THE FOLLOWING HOURS ARE A BLUR OF FRIGHTENING PICTURES AND HAZY INFORMATION.
MORE EVIDENCE HAS ARISEN FROM BOSTON, TYING THE HIJACKERS TO MIDDLE EAST ORIGINS-- WHICH HAS RIMA QUIETLY FREAKED. HATE MAIL IS ALREADY FLOODING MANY HAPLESS MUSLIM GROUPS.
BUILDING #7 OF THE WORLD TRADE CENTER ALSO FELL. AFTER THE TOWERS, IT WAS ALMOST AN AFTERTHOUGHT.
INITIAL NUMBERS HAVE STARTED TO COME IN. OVER 100 DEAD AT THE PENTAGON. AND OVER SIX PERCENT OF ALL PUBLIC SERVANTS IN NEW YORK CITY HAVE BEEN LOST. PRESIDENT BUSH ESTIMATES CASUALTIES IN THE THOUSANDS.
KINGDOM COME
WATCHMEN
MAUS
BUT, THERE'S HOPE -- RIMA FOUND ALL HER FRIENDS. THERE HAVE BEEN NO FURTHER STRIKES.MULTI-FAITH PRAYER VIGILS ARE ASSEMBLED ON CAMPUS. THE WORDS "SAY A PRAYER" ARE WRITTEN IN HUGE, CHALK LETTERS ON THE COURTYARD BRICKS.
AMERICA
LIVE
LOGO
YEAH, SOME HOPE... BUT NOT NEARLY ENOUGH.
ALMOST SIMULTANEOUSLY, NEIL, DANNY, AND I WRITE TO EACH OTHER, TALKING ABOUT DISASTER RELIEF. WE AGREE TO CONTACT SOME FRIENDS--EXPLORE WHAT COMICS CAN DO TO HELP.
RING!
I EXHAUST MY ADDRESS BOOK. AND MY MIND--THE BEST THING I CAN THINK TO DO NOW IS SLEEP.
CAN'T IMAGINE THE KIND OF DREAMS I'LL HAVE...
HELLO?
...
AHH, GOD... I'M SO GLAD IT'S YOU, DAD...
BUT WHO KNOWS? IT COULD BE A NEW WORLD AGAIN TOMORROW.
GOD WILLING.
"Thine Alabaster Cities Undimmed by human tears"
-America the Beautiful

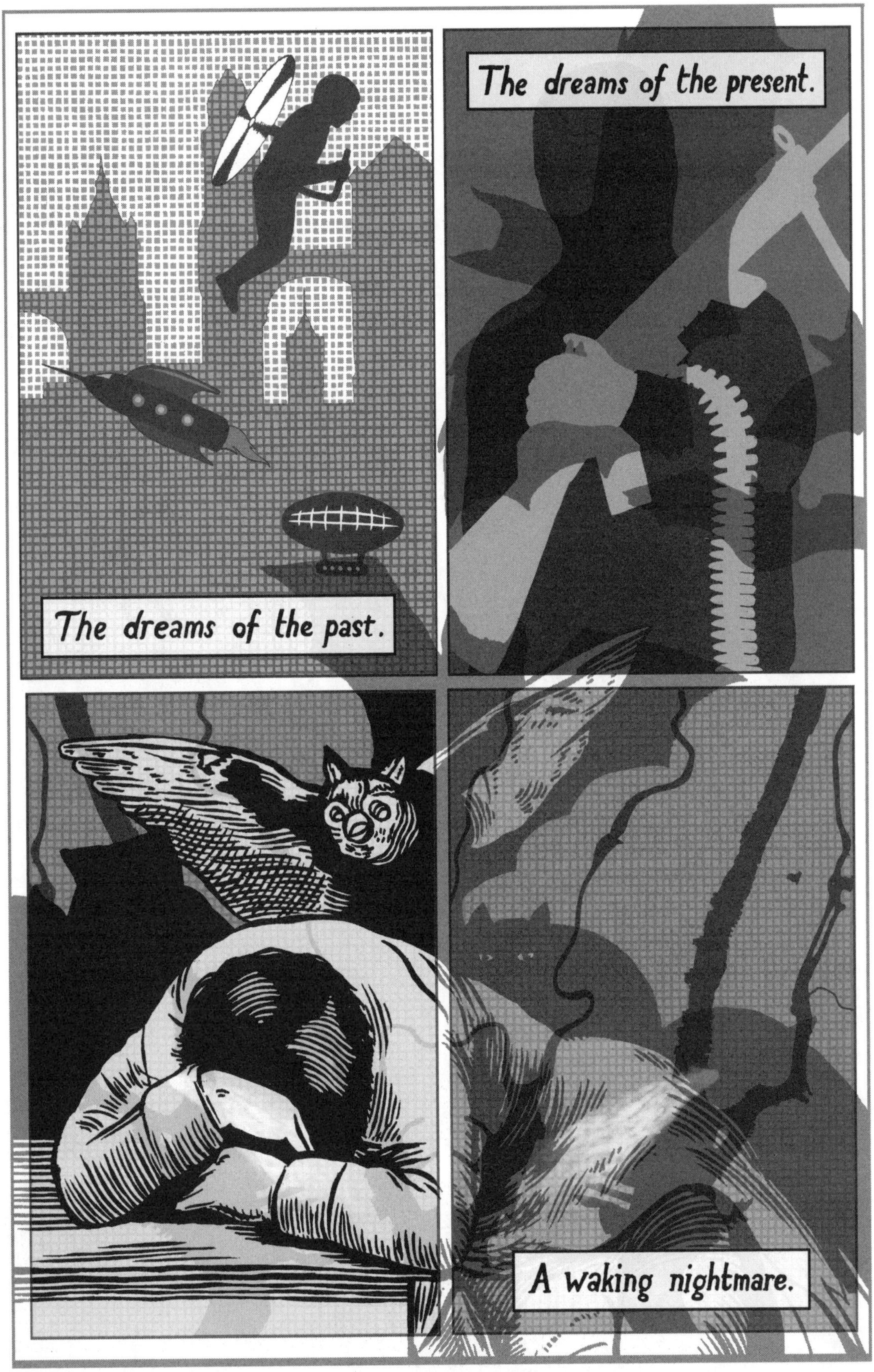

The dreams of the past.
The dreams of the present.
A waking nightmare.

SEPT 11TH
I WALKED INTO
MY LIVING
SEE A PLANE
STUCK IN THE
SIDE OF THE
WORLD TRADE
CENTRE,
FUCKING HELL.

MY WIFE
SAID IT WAS
COULD BE
TERRORISTS,
I THOUGHT
NO WAY, THEN
ANOTHER PLANE
HIT THE OTHER
TOWER...

MY 13
MONTH OLD
BABY
WATCHED

I FELT AS
THOUGH I WAS
IN A FUCKED
CHARLES BRONSON
FLICK...

MY WIFE
IS PREGNANT
WITH MY
SECOND SON,
I FEEL LIKE
CRAP FOR
THEM...

I WISH I
LIVED ON
MARS, MAYBE
THAT PLACE IS
REAL...

SECOND
SON

THEY KEEP
SHOWING THE
PLANES HITTING,
CNN FUCKERS,
THATS PEOPLES
CHILDREN DYING,
AND THEY REPLAY
IT LIKE A HOMERUN...

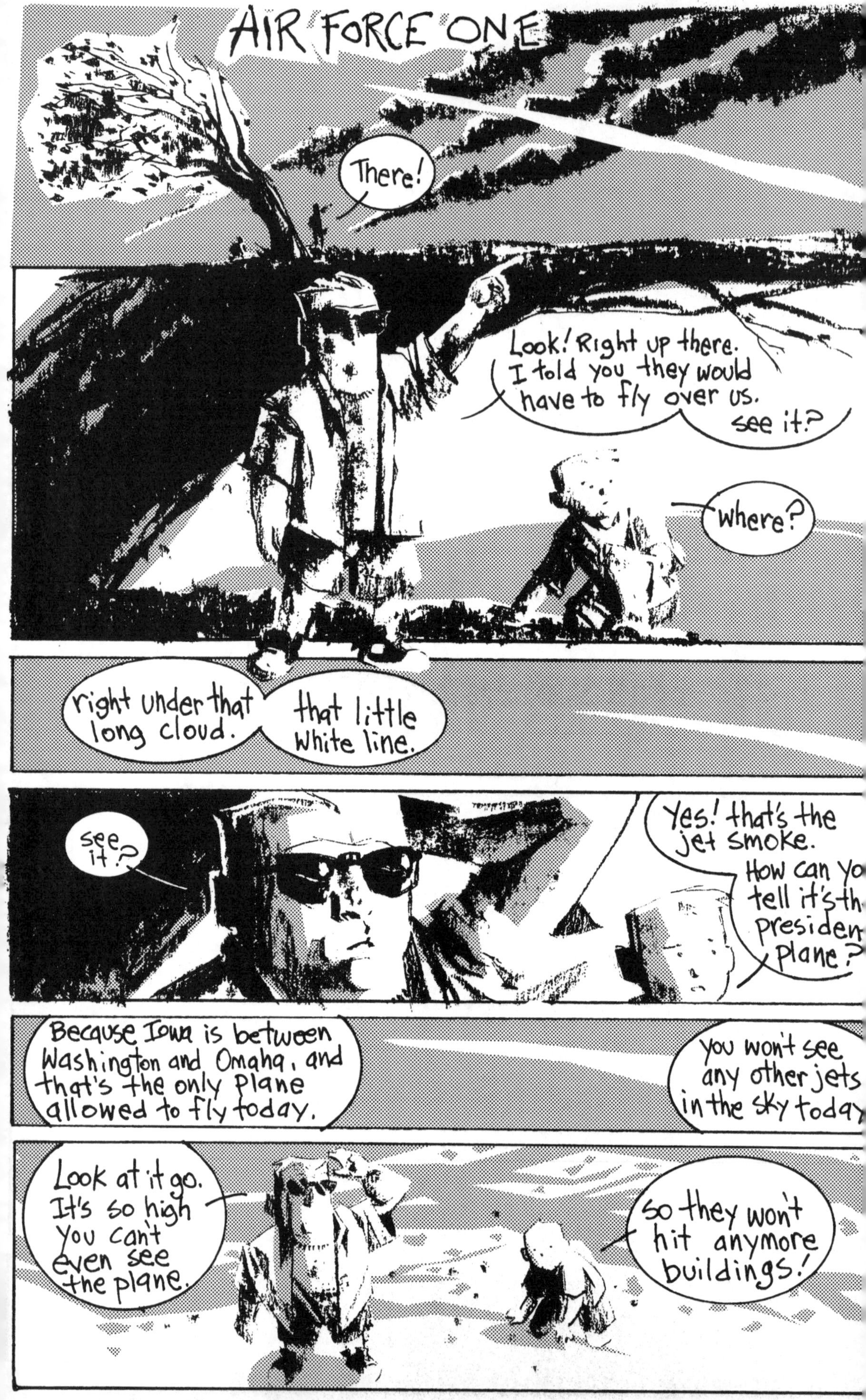
AIR FORCE ONE
There!
Look! Right up there. I told you they would have to fly over us. see it?
where?
right under that long cloud.
that little white line.
see it?
Yes! that's the jet smoke. How can yo tell it's th presiden plane?
Because Iowa is between Washington and Omaha, and that's the only plane allowed to fly today.
you won't see any other jets in the sky toda
Look at it go. It's so high you can't even see the plane.
So they won't hit anymore buildings!

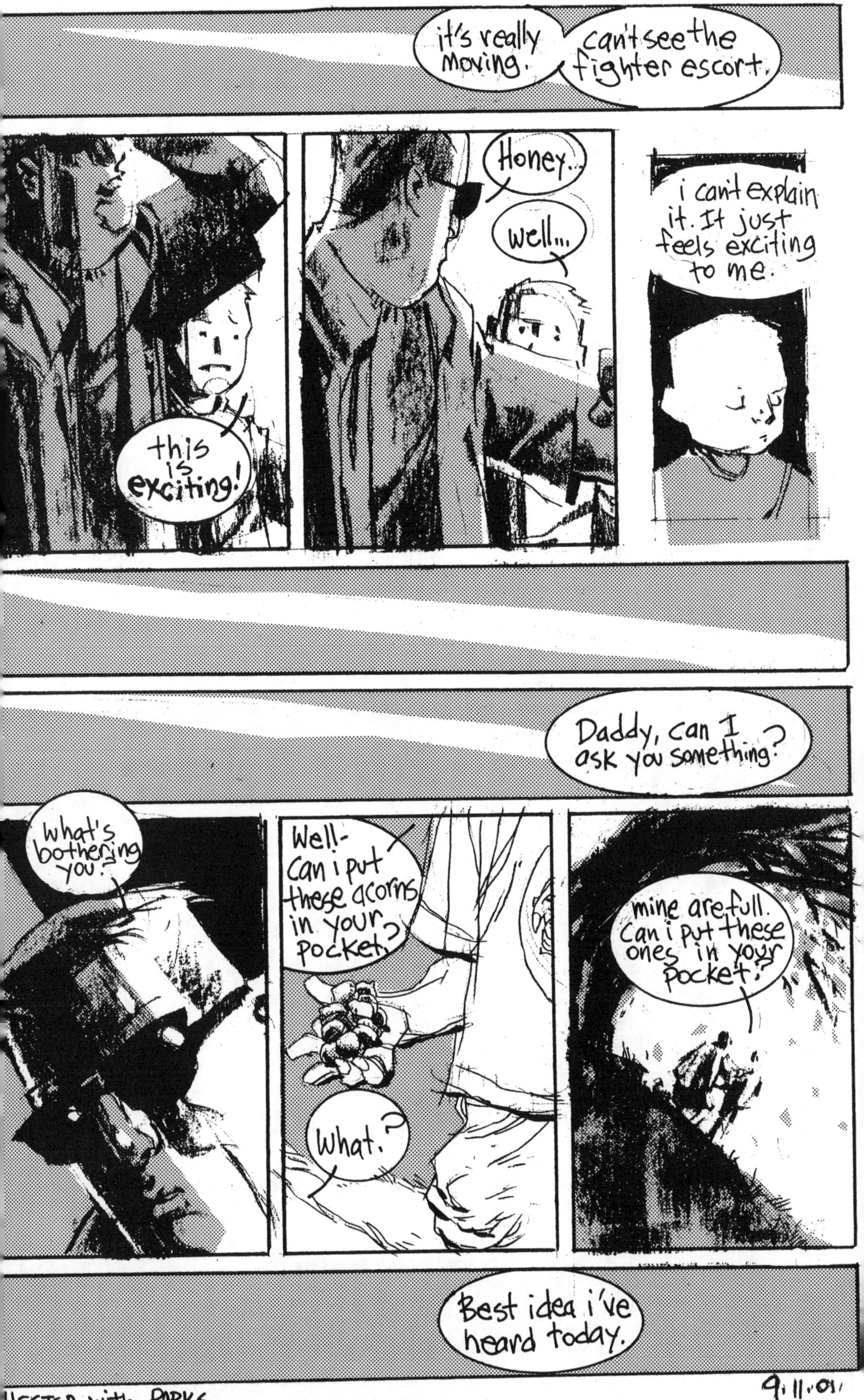
it's really moving.
can't see the fighter escort.
this is exciting!
Honey...
well...
i can't explain it. It just feels exciting to me.
Daddy, can I ask you something?
what's bothering you?
Well- can i put these acorns in your pocket?
What?
mine are full. Can i put these ones in your pocket?
Best idea i've heard today.

HESTER with PARKS 9.11.01.

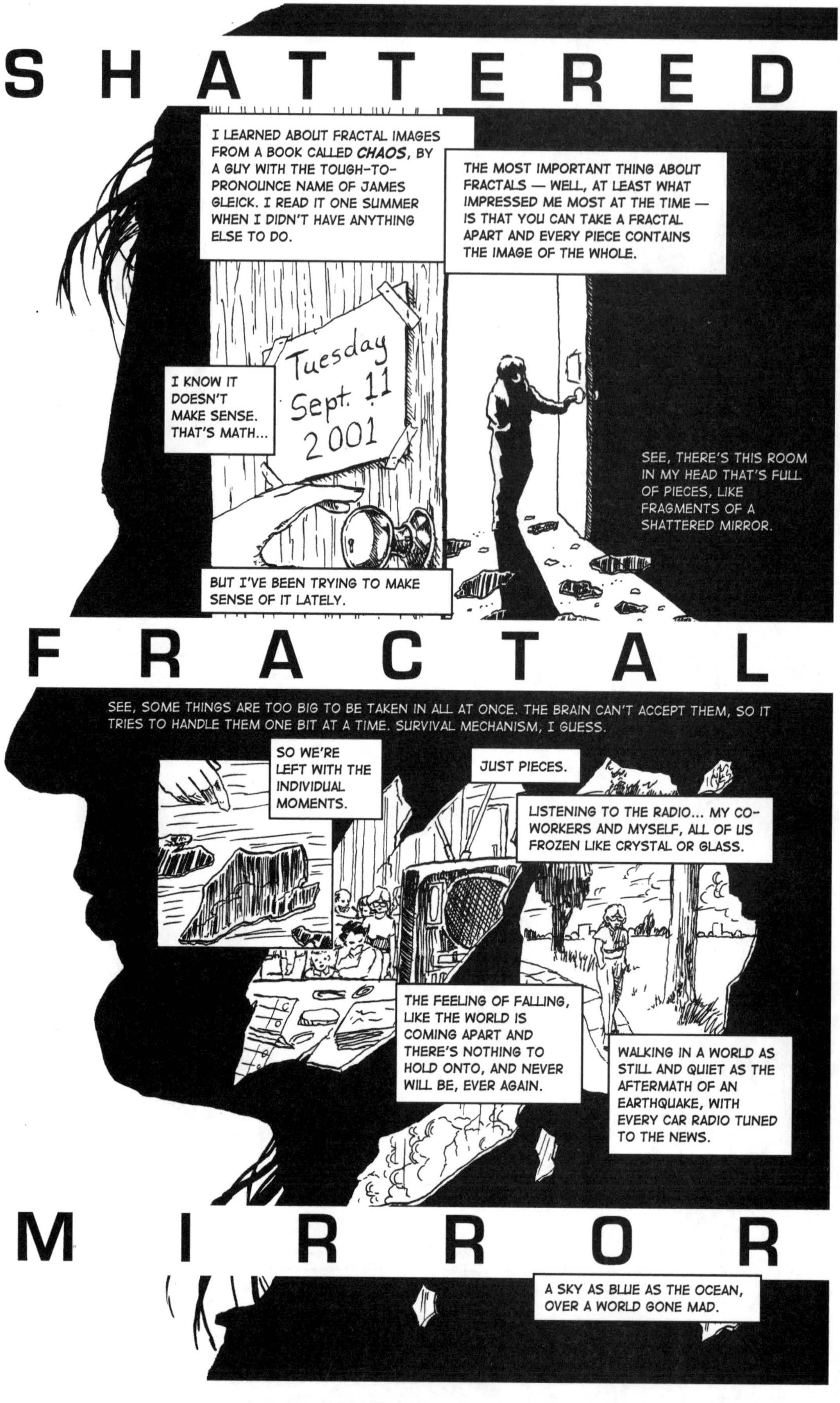
SHATTERED
I LEARNED ABOUT FRACTAL IMAGES FROM A BOOK CALLED *CHAOS*, BY A GUY WITH THE TOUGH-TO-PRONOUNCE NAME OF JAMES GLEICK. I READ IT ONE SUMMER WHEN I DIDN'T HAVE ANYTHING ELSE TO DO.
THE MOST IMPORTANT THING ABOUT FRACTALS — WELL, AT LEAST WHAT IMPRESSED ME MOST AT THE TIME — IS THAT YOU CAN TAKE A FRACTAL APART AND EVERY PIECE CONTAINS THE IMAGE OF THE WHOLE.
I KNOW IT DOESN'T MAKE SENSE. THAT'S MATH...
Tuesday Sept. 11 2001
BUT I'VE BEEN TRYING TO MAKE SENSE OF IT LATELY.
SEE, THERE'S THIS ROOM IN MY HEAD THAT'S FULL OF PIECES, LIKE FRAGMENTS OF A SHATTERED MIRROR.
FRACTAL
SEE, SOME THINGS ARE TOO BIG TO BE TAKEN IN ALL AT ONCE. THE BRAIN CAN'T ACCEPT THEM, SO IT TRIES TO HANDLE THEM ONE BIT AT A TIME. SURVIVAL MECHANISM, I GUESS.
SO WE'RE LEFT WITH THE INDIVIDUAL MOMENTS.
JUST PIECES.
LISTENING TO THE RADIO... MY CO-WORKERS AND MYSELF, ALL OF US FROZEN LIKE CRYSTAL OR GLASS.
THE FEELING OF FALLING, LIKE THE WORLD IS COMING APART AND THERE'S NOTHING TO HOLD ONTO, AND NEVER WILL BE, EVER AGAIN.
WALKING IN A WORLD AS STILL AND QUIET AS THE AFTERMATH OF AN EARTHQUAKE, WITH EVERY CAR RADIO TUNED TO THE NEWS.
MIRROR
A SKY AS BLUE AS THE OCEAN, OVER A WORLD GONE MAD.

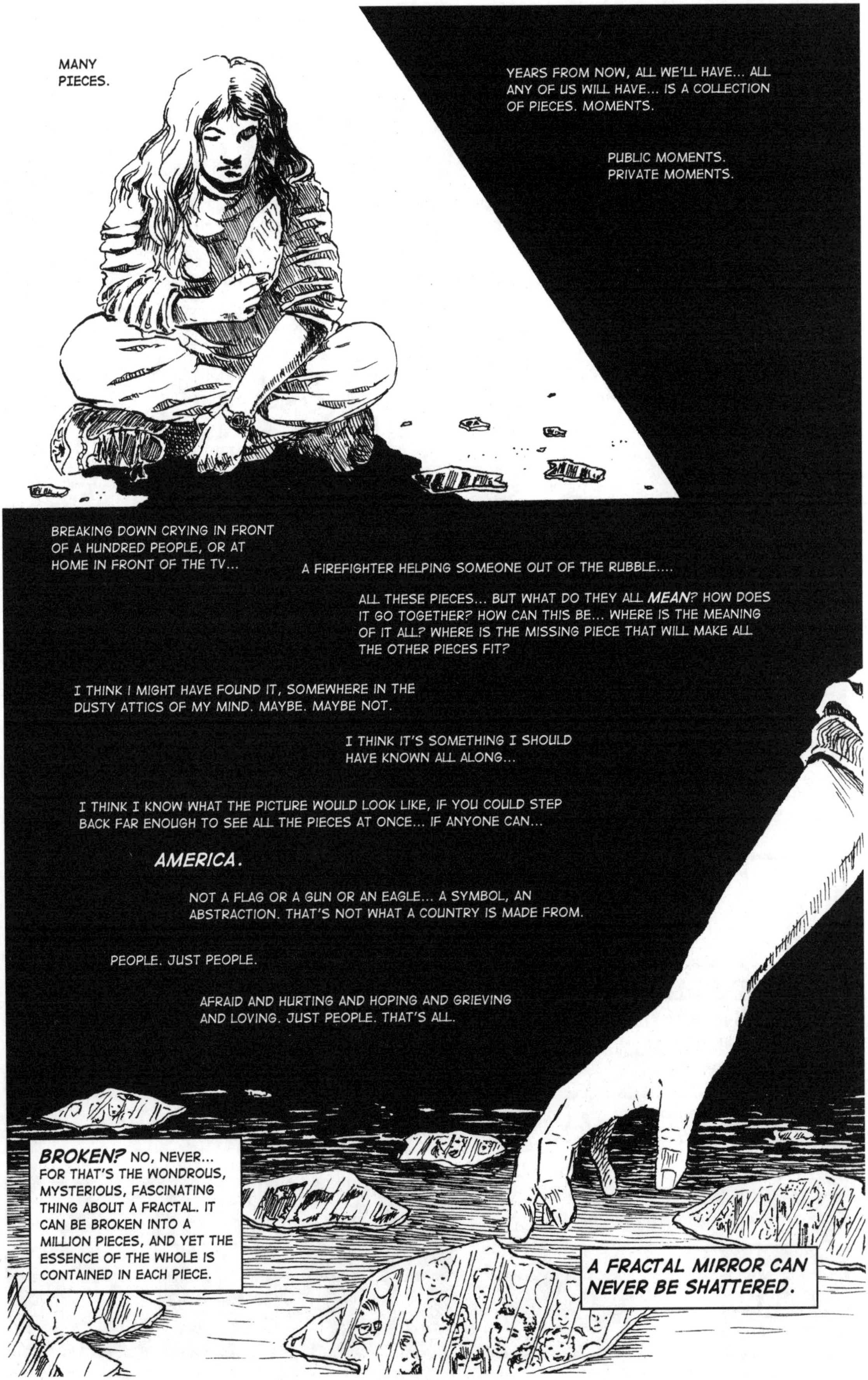

MANY PIECES.
YEARS FROM NOW, ALL WE'LL HAVE... ALL ANY OF US WILL HAVE... IS A COLLECTION OF PIECES. MOMENTS.
PUBLIC MOMENTS. PRIVATE MOMENTS.
BREAKING DOWN CRYING IN FRONT OF A HUNDRED PEOPLE, OR AT HOME IN FRONT OF THE TV...
A FIREFIGHTER HELPING SOMEONE OUT OF THE RUBBLE....
ALL THESE PIECES... BUT WHAT DO THEY ALL *MEAN*? HOW DOES IT GO TOGETHER? HOW CAN THIS BE... WHERE IS THE MEANING OF IT ALL? WHERE IS THE MISSING PIECE THAT WILL MAKE ALL THE OTHER PIECES FIT?
I THINK I MIGHT HAVE FOUND IT, SOMEWHERE IN THE DUSTY ATTICS OF MY MIND. MAYBE. MAYBE NOT.
I THINK IT'S SOMETHING I SHOULD HAVE KNOWN ALL ALONG...
I THINK I KNOW WHAT THE PICTURE WOULD LOOK LIKE, IF YOU COULD STEP BACK FAR ENOUGH TO SEE ALL THE PIECES AT ONCE... IF ANYONE CAN...
AMERICA.
NOT A FLAG OR A GUN OR AN EAGLE... A SYMBOL, AN ABSTRACTION. THAT'S NOT WHAT A COUNTRY IS MADE FROM.
PEOPLE. JUST PEOPLE.
AFRAID AND HURTING AND HOPING AND GRIEVING AND LOVING. JUST PEOPLE. THAT'S ALL.
BROKEN? NO, NEVER... FOR THAT'S THE WONDROUS, MYSTERIOUS, FASCINATING THING ABOUT A FRACTAL. IT CAN BE BROKEN INTO A MILLION PIECES, AND YET THE ESSENCE OF THE WHOLE IS CONTAINED IN EACH PIECE.
A FRACTAL MIRROR CAN NEVER BE SHATTERED.

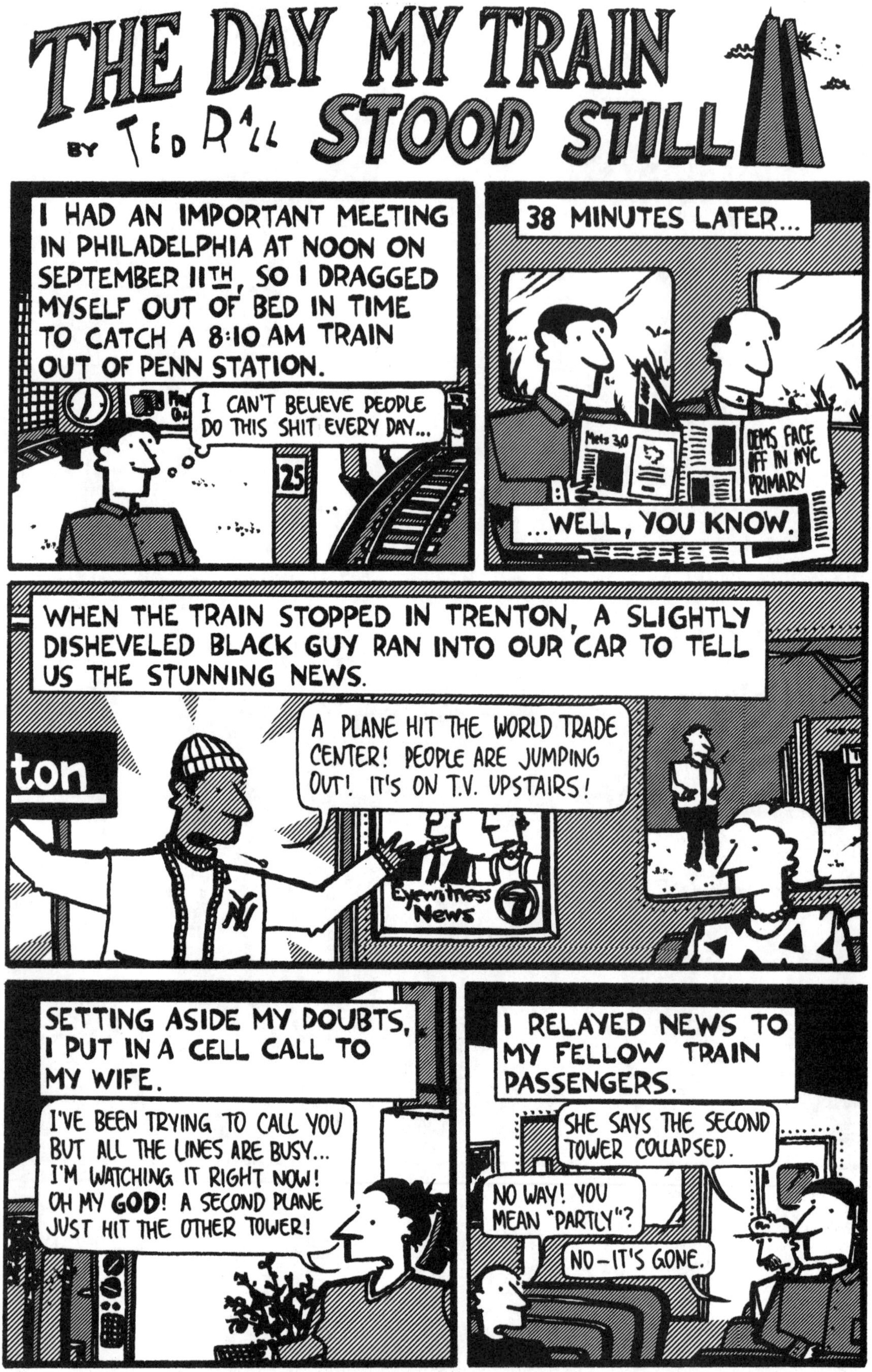
THE DAY MY TRAIN STOOD STILL
BY TED RALL
I HAD AN IMPORTANT MEETING IN PHILADELPHIA AT NOON ON SEPTEMBER 11TH, SO I DRAGGED MYSELF OUT OF BED IN TIME TO CATCH A 8:10 AM TRAIN OUT OF PENN STATION.
I CAN'T BELIEVE PEOPLE DO THIS SHIT EVERY DAY...
125
38 MINUTES LATER...
DEMS FACE OFF IN NYC PRIMARY
...WELL, YOU KNOW.
WHEN THE TRAIN STOPPED IN TRENTON, A SLIGHTLY DISHEVELED BLACK GUY RAN INTO OUR CAR TO TELL US THE STUNNING NEWS.
ton
A PLANE HIT THE WORLD TRADE CENTER! PEOPLE ARE JUMPING OUT! IT'S ON T.V. UPSTAIRS!
Eyewitness News 7
SETTING ASIDE MY DOUBTS, I PUT IN A CELL CALL TO MY WIFE.
I'VE BEEN TRYING TO CALL YOU BUT ALL THE LINES ARE BUSY... I'M WATCHING IT RIGHT NOW! OH MY GOD! A SECOND PLANE JUST HIT THE OTHER TOWER!
I RELAYED NEWS TO MY FELLOW TRAIN PASSENGERS.
SHE SAYS THE SECOND TOWER COLLAPSED.
NO WAY! YOU MEAN "PARTLY"?
NO—IT'S GONE.

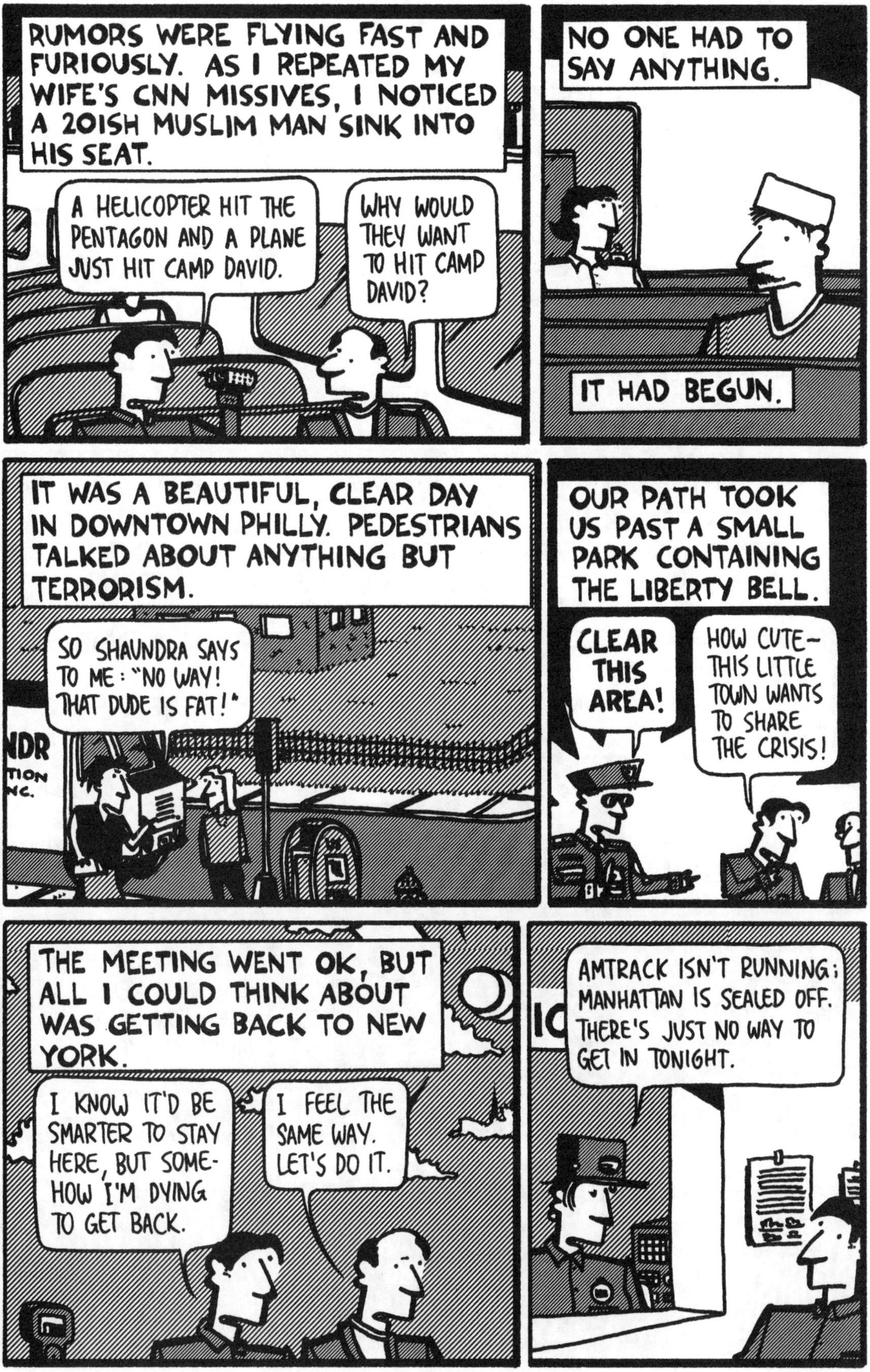
RUMORS WERE FLYING FAST AND FURIOUSLY. AS I REPEATED MY WIFE'S CNN MISSIVES, I NOTICED A 20ISH MUSLIM MAN SINK INTO HIS SEAT.
A HELICOPTER HIT THE PENTAGON AND A PLANE JUST HIT CAMP DAVID.
WHY WOULD THEY WANT TO HIT CAMP DAVID?
NO ONE HAD TO SAY ANYTHING.
IT HAD BEGUN.
IT WAS A BEAUTIFUL, CLEAR DAY IN DOWNTOWN PHILLY. PEDESTRIANS TALKED ABOUT ANYTHING BUT TERRORISM.
SO SHAUNDRA SAYS TO ME: "NO WAY! THAT DUDE IS FAT!"
OUR PATH TOOK US PAST A SMALL PARK CONTAINING THE LIBERTY BELL.
CLEAR THIS AREA!
HOW CUTE– THIS LITTLE TOWN WANTS TO SHARE THE CRISIS!
THE MEETING WENT OK, BUT ALL I COULD THINK ABOUT WAS GETTING BACK TO NEW YORK.
I KNOW IT'D BE SMARTER TO STAY HERE, BUT SOMEHOW I'M DYING TO GET BACK.
I FEEL THE SAME WAY. LET'S DO IT.
AMTRACK ISN'T RUNNING; MANHATTAN IS SEALED OFF. THERE'S JUST NO WAY TO GET IN TONIGHT.

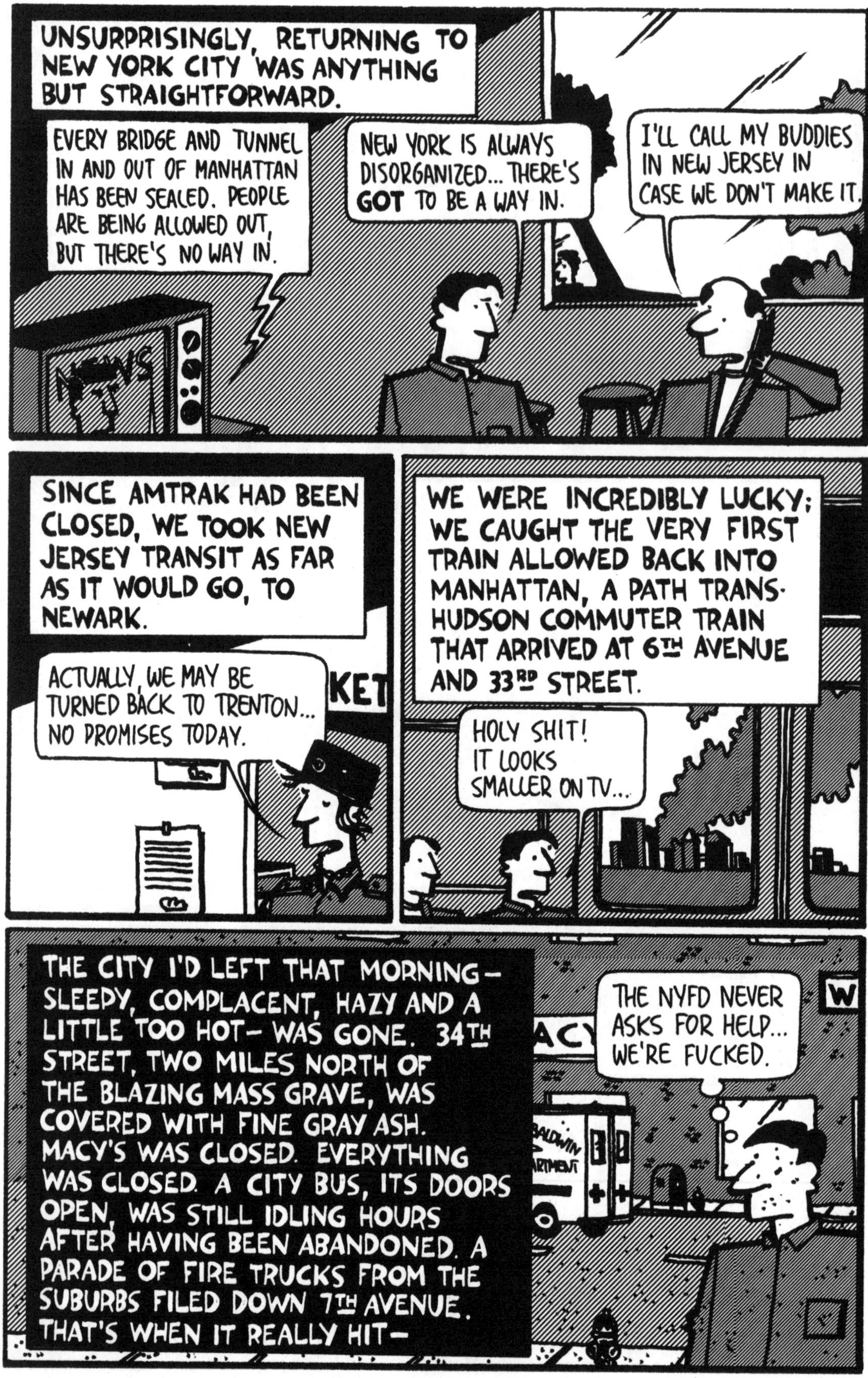
UNSURPRISINGLY, RETURNING TO NEW YORK CITY WAS ANYTHING BUT STRAIGHTFORWARD.
EVERY BRIDGE AND TUNNEL IN AND OUT OF MANHATTAN HAS BEEN SEALED. PEOPLE ARE BEING ALLOWED OUT, BUT THERE'S NO WAY IN.
NEWS
NEW YORK IS ALWAYS DISORGANIZED... THERE'S **GOT** TO BE A WAY IN.
I'LL CALL MY BUDDIES IN NEW JERSEY IN CASE WE DON'T MAKE IT.
SINCE AMTRAK HAD BEEN CLOSED, WE TOOK NEW JERSEY TRANSIT AS FAR AS IT WOULD GO, TO NEWARK.
ACTUALLY, WE MAY BE TURNED BACK TO TRENTON... NO PROMISES TODAY.
KET
WE WERE INCREDIBLY LUCKY; WE CAUGHT THE VERY FIRST TRAIN ALLOWED BACK INTO MANHATTAN, A PATH TRANS-HUDSON COMMUTER TRAIN THAT ARRIVED AT 6TH AVENUE AND 33RD STREET.
HOLY SHIT! IT LOOKS SMALLER ON TV...
THE CITY I'D LEFT THAT MORNING— SLEEPY, COMPLACENT, HAZY AND A LITTLE TOO HOT— WAS GONE. 34TH STREET, TWO MILES NORTH OF THE BLAZING MASS GRAVE, WAS COVERED WITH FINE GRAY ASH. MACY'S WAS CLOSED. EVERYTHING WAS CLOSED. A CITY BUS, ITS DOORS OPEN, WAS STILL IDLING HOURS AFTER HAVING BEEN ABANDONED. A PARADE OF FIRE TRUCKS FROM THE SUBURBS FILED DOWN 7TH AVENUE. THAT'S WHEN IT REALLY HIT—
ACY
W
THE NYFD NEVER ASKS FOR HELP... WE'RE FUCKED.
BALDWIN
ARTMENT

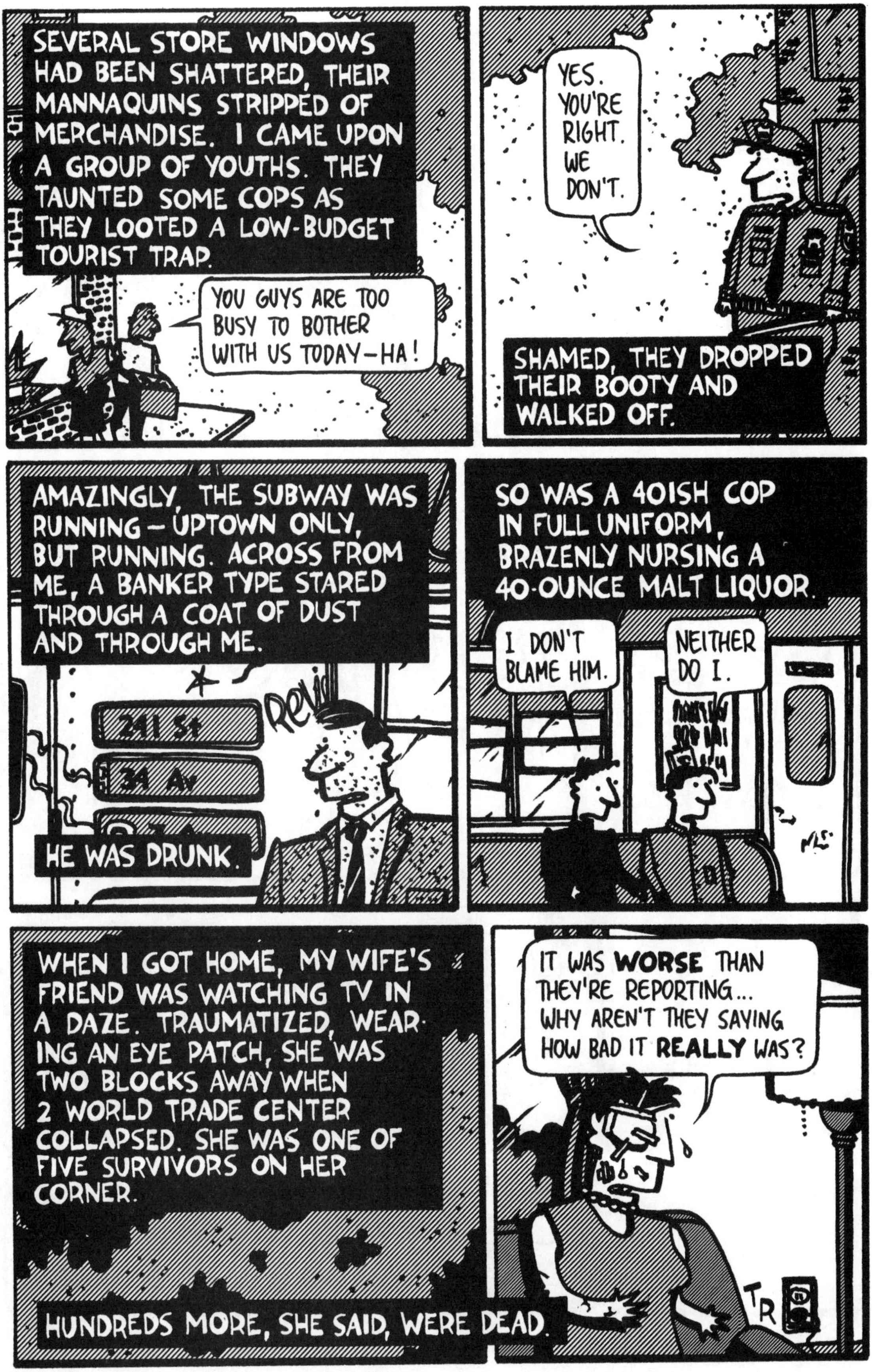
SEVERAL STORE WINDOWS HAD BEEN SHATTERED, THEIR MANNAQUINS STRIPPED OF MERCHANDISE. I CAME UPON A GROUP OF YOUTHS. THEY TAUNTED SOME COPS AS THEY LOOTED A LOW-BUDGET TOURIST TRAP.
YOU GUYS ARE TOO BUSY TO BOTHER WITH US TODAY—HA!
YES. YOU'RE RIGHT. WE DON'T.
SHAMED, THEY DROPPED THEIR BOOTY AND WALKED OFF.
AMAZINGLY, THE SUBWAY WAS RUNNING—UPTOWN ONLY, BUT RUNNING. ACROSS FROM ME, A BANKER TYPE STARED THROUGH A COAT OF DUST AND THROUGH ME.
241 St
34 Av
HE WAS DRUNK.
SO WAS A 40ISH COP IN FULL UNIFORM, BRAZENLY NURSING A 40-OUNCE MALT LIQUOR.
I DON'T BLAME HIM.
NEITHER DO I.
WHEN I GOT HOME, MY WIFE'S FRIEND WAS WATCHING TV IN A DAZE. TRAUMATIZED, WEARING AN EYE PATCH, SHE WAS TWO BLOCKS AWAY WHEN 2 WORLD TRADE CENTER COLLAPSED. SHE WAS ONE OF FIVE SURVIVORS ON HER CORNER.
IT WAS **WORSE** THAN THEY'RE REPORTING... WHY AREN'T THEY SAYING HOW BAD IT **REALLY** WAS?
HUNDREDS MORE, SHE SAID, WERE DEAD.
TR

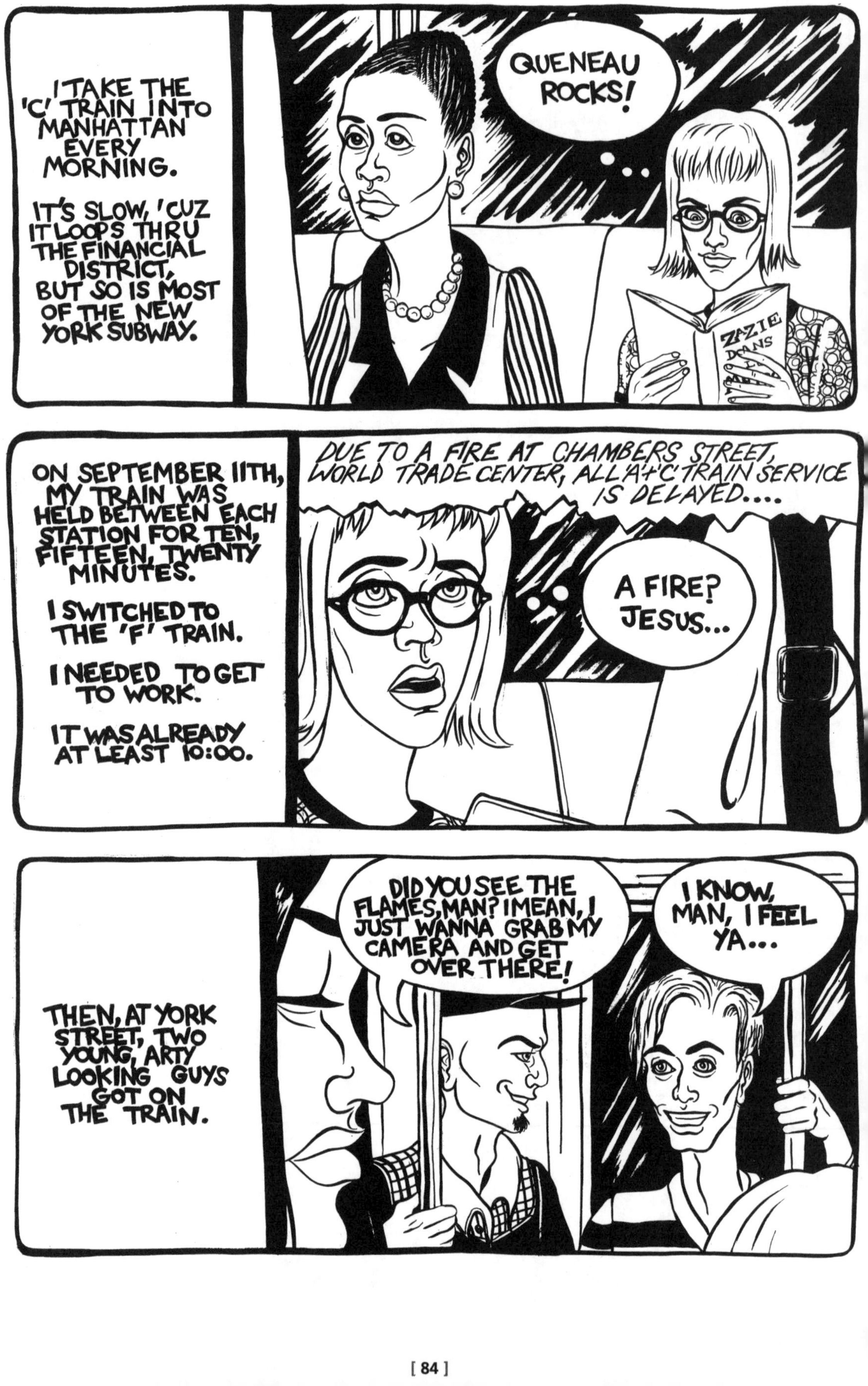
I TAKE THE 'C' TRAIN INTO MANHATTAN EVERY MORNING.
IT'S SLOW, 'CUZ IT LOOPS THRU THE FINANCIAL DISTRICT, BUT SO IS MOST OF THE NEW YORK SUBWAY.
QUENEAU ROCKS!
ZAZIE DANS
ON SEPTEMBER 11TH, MY TRAIN WAS HELD BETWEEN EACH STATION FOR TEN, FIFTEEN, TWENTY MINUTES.
I SWITCHED TO THE 'F' TRAIN.
I NEEDED TO GET TO WORK.
IT WAS ALREADY AT LEAST 10:00.
DUE TO A FIRE AT CHAMBERS STREET, WORLD TRADE CENTER, ALL 'A'+'C' TRAIN SERVICE IS DELAYED....
A FIRE? JESUS...
THEN, AT YORK STREET, TWO YOUNG, ARTY LOOKING GUYS GOT ON THE TRAIN.
DID YOU SEE THE FLAMES, MAN? I MEAN, I JUST WANNA GRAB MY CAMERA AND GET OVER THERE!
I KNOW, MAN, I FEEL YA...

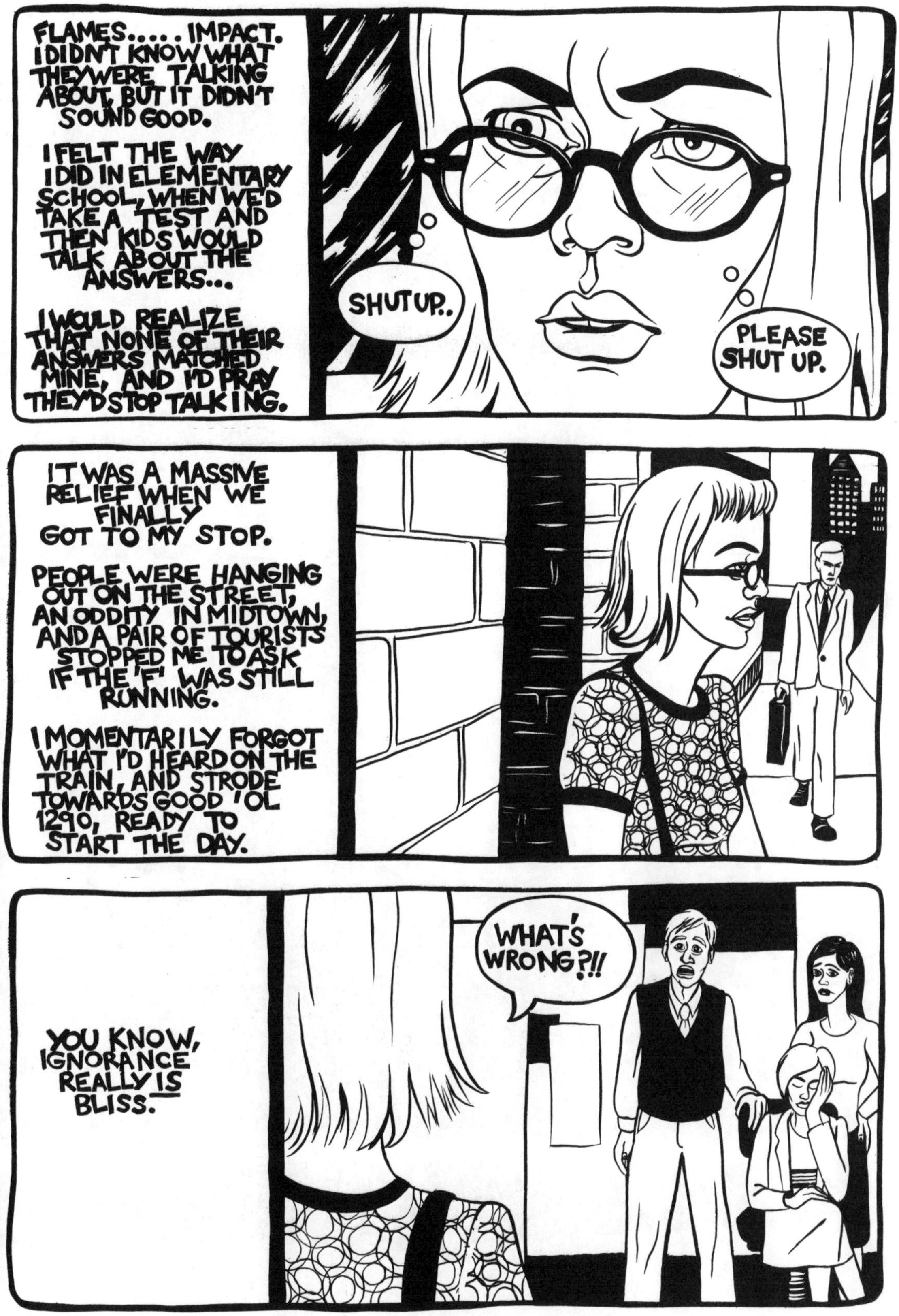

FLAMES..... IMPACT. I DIDN'T KNOW WHAT THEY WERE TALKING ABOUT, BUT IT DIDN'T SOUND GOOD.
I FELT THE WAY I DID IN ELEMENTARY SCHOOL, WHEN WE'D TAKE A TEST AND THEN KIDS WOULD TALK ABOUT THE ANSWERS...
I WOULD REALIZE THAT NONE OF THEIR ANSWERS MATCHED MINE, AND I'D PRAY THEY'D STOP TALKING.
SHUT UP..
PLEASE SHUT UP.
IT WAS A MASSIVE RELIEF WHEN WE FINALLY GOT TO MY STOP.
PEOPLE WERE HANGING OUT ON THE STREET, AN ODDITY IN MIDTOWN, AND A PAIR OF TOURISTS STOPPED ME TO ASK IF THE 'F' WAS STILL RUNNING.
I MOMENTARILY FORGOT WHAT I'D HEARD ON THE TRAIN, AND STRODE TOWARDS GOOD 'OL 1290, READY TO START THE DAY.
YOU KNOW, IGNORANCE REALLY IS BLISS.
WHAT'S WRONG?!!

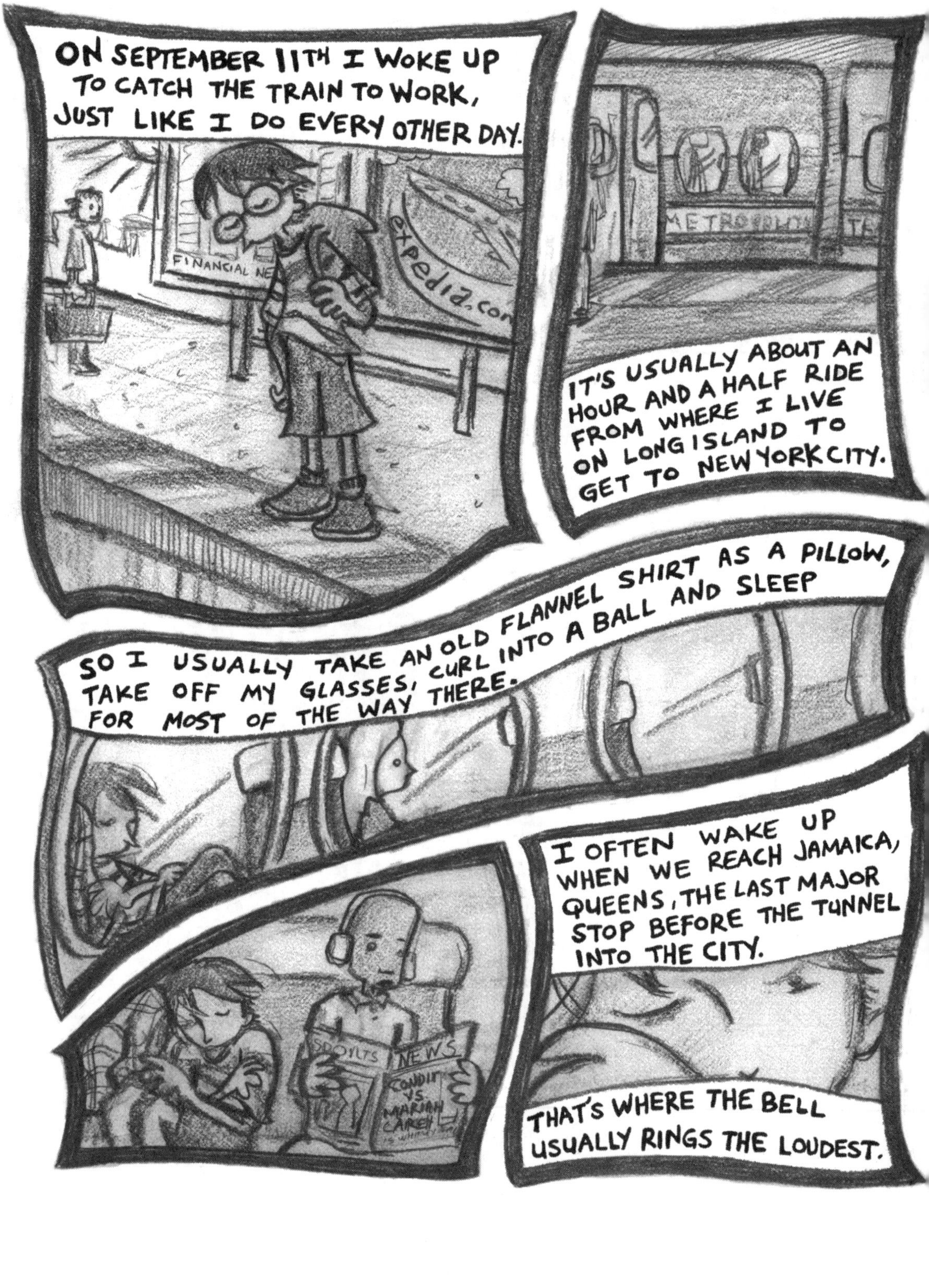
ON SEPTEMBER 11TH I WOKE UP TO CATCH THE TRAIN TO WORK, JUST LIKE I DO EVERY OTHER DAY.
FINANCIAL NE
expedia.com
METROPOLITAN
IT'S USUALLY ABOUT AN HOUR AND A HALF RIDE FROM WHERE I LIVE ON LONG ISLAND TO GET TO NEW YORK CITY.
SO I USUALLY TAKE AN OLD FLANNEL SHIRT AS A PILLOW, TAKE OFF MY GLASSES, CURL INTO A BALL AND SLEEP FOR MOST OF THE WAY THERE.
I OFTEN WAKE UP WHEN WE REACH JAMAICA, QUEENS, THE LAST MAJOR STOP BEFORE THE TUNNEL INTO THE CITY.
SPORTS
NEWS
CONDIT VS. MARIAH CAREY
THAT'S WHERE THE BELL USUALLY RINGS THE LOUDEST.

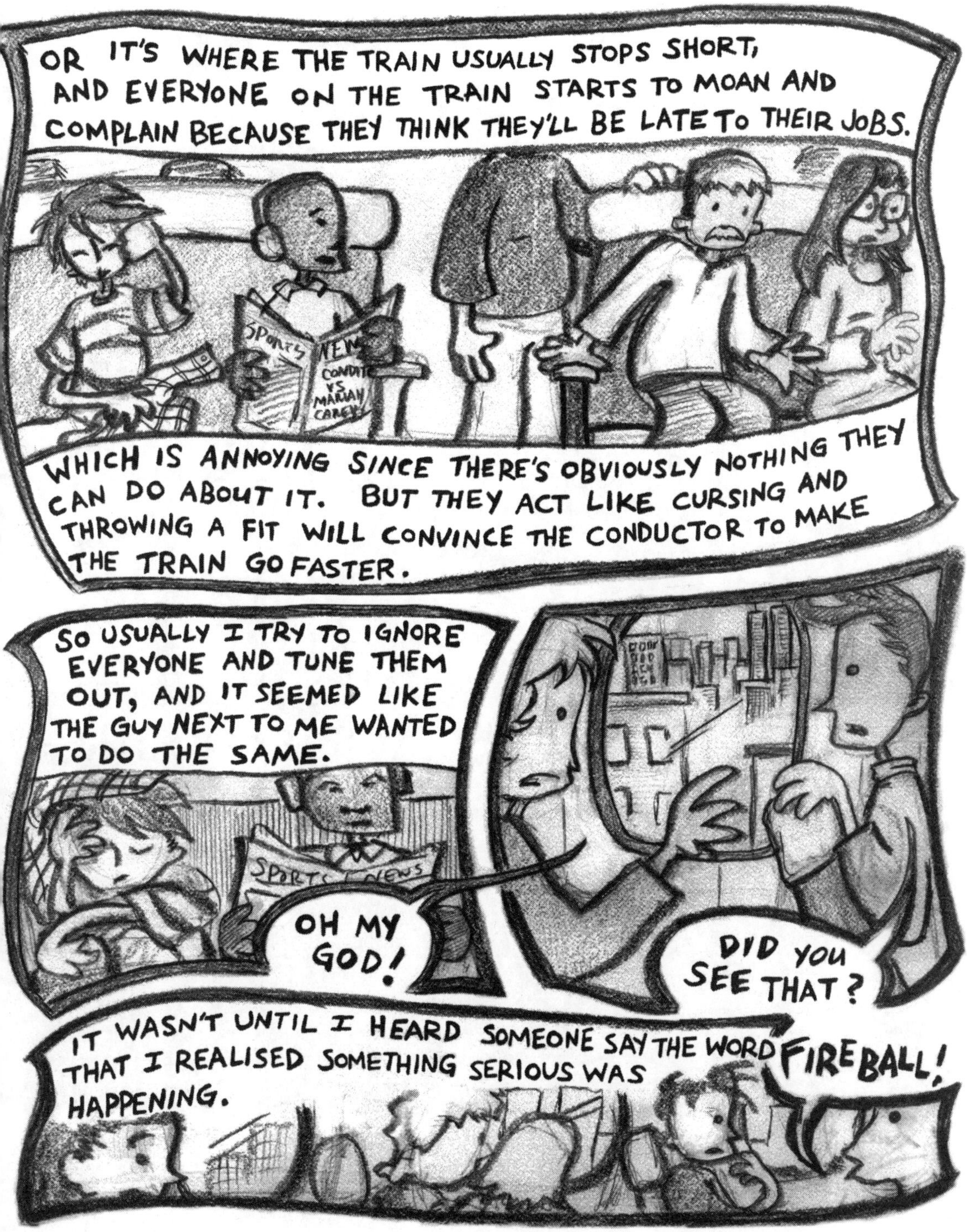
OR IT'S WHERE THE TRAIN USUALLY STOPS SHORT, AND EVERYONE ON THE TRAIN STARTS TO MOAN AND COMPLAIN BECAUSE THEY THINK THEY'LL BE LATE TO THEIR JOBS.
SPORTS NEWS
WHICH IS ANNOYING SINCE THERE'S OBVIOUSLY NOTHING THEY CAN DO ABOUT IT. BUT THEY ACT LIKE CURSING AND THROWING A FIT WILL CONVINCE THE CONDUCTOR TO MAKE THE TRAIN GO FASTER.
SO USUALLY I TRY TO IGNORE EVERYONE AND TUNE THEM OUT, AND IT SEEMED LIKE THE GUY NEXT TO ME WANTED TO DO THE SAME.
SPORTS NEWS
OH MY GOD!
DID YOU SEE THAT?
IT WASN'T UNTIL I HEARD SOMEONE SAY THE WORD FIREBALL! THAT I REALISED SOMETHING SERIOUS WAS HAPPENING.

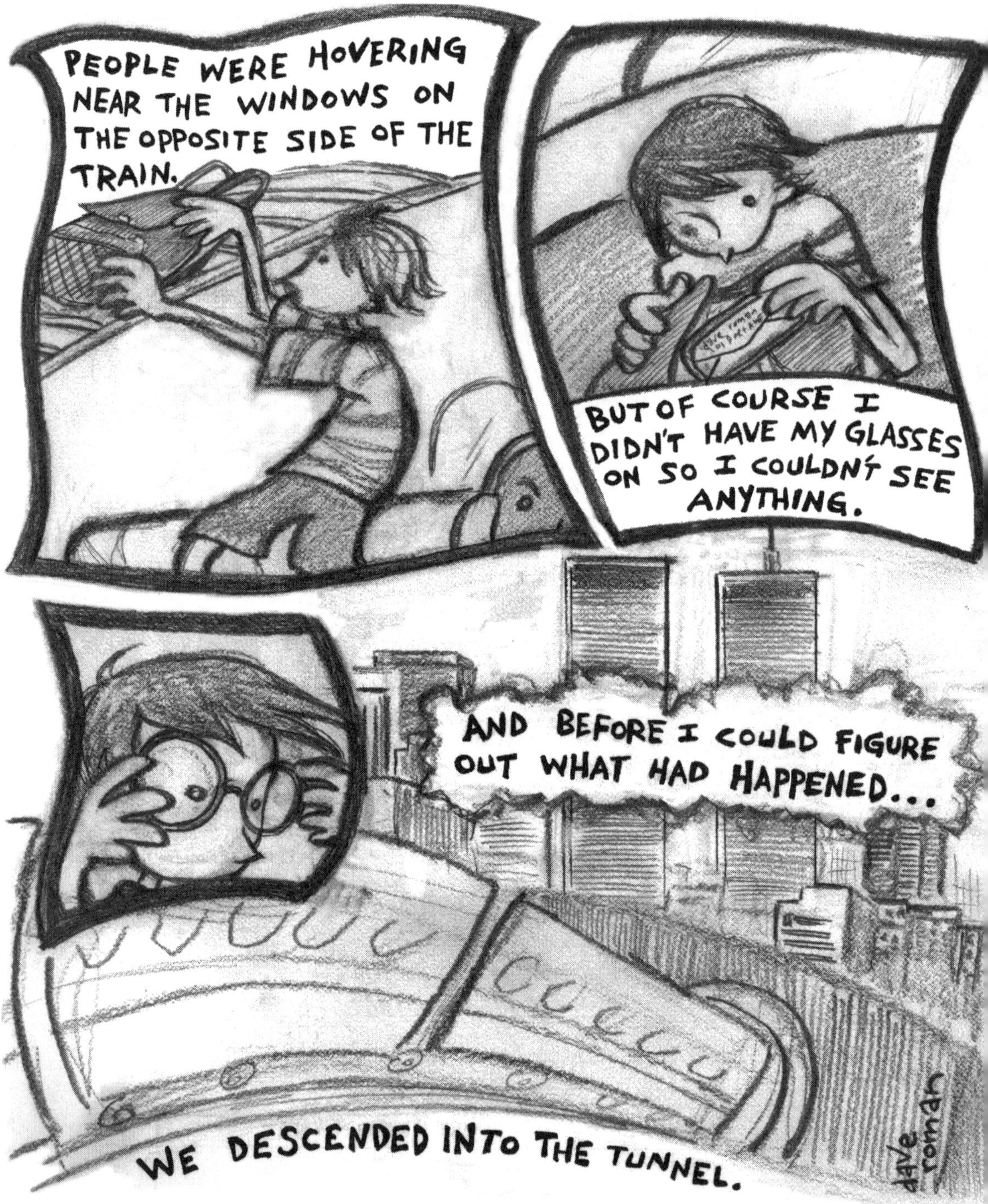
PEOPLE WERE HOVERING NEAR THE WINDOWS ON THE OPPOSITE SIDE OF THE TRAIN.
BUT OF COURSE I DIDN'T HAVE MY GLASSES ON SO I COULDN'T SEE ANYTHING.
AND BEFORE I COULD FIGURE OUT WHAT HAD HAPPENED...
WE DESCENDED INTO THE TUNNEL.
dave roman

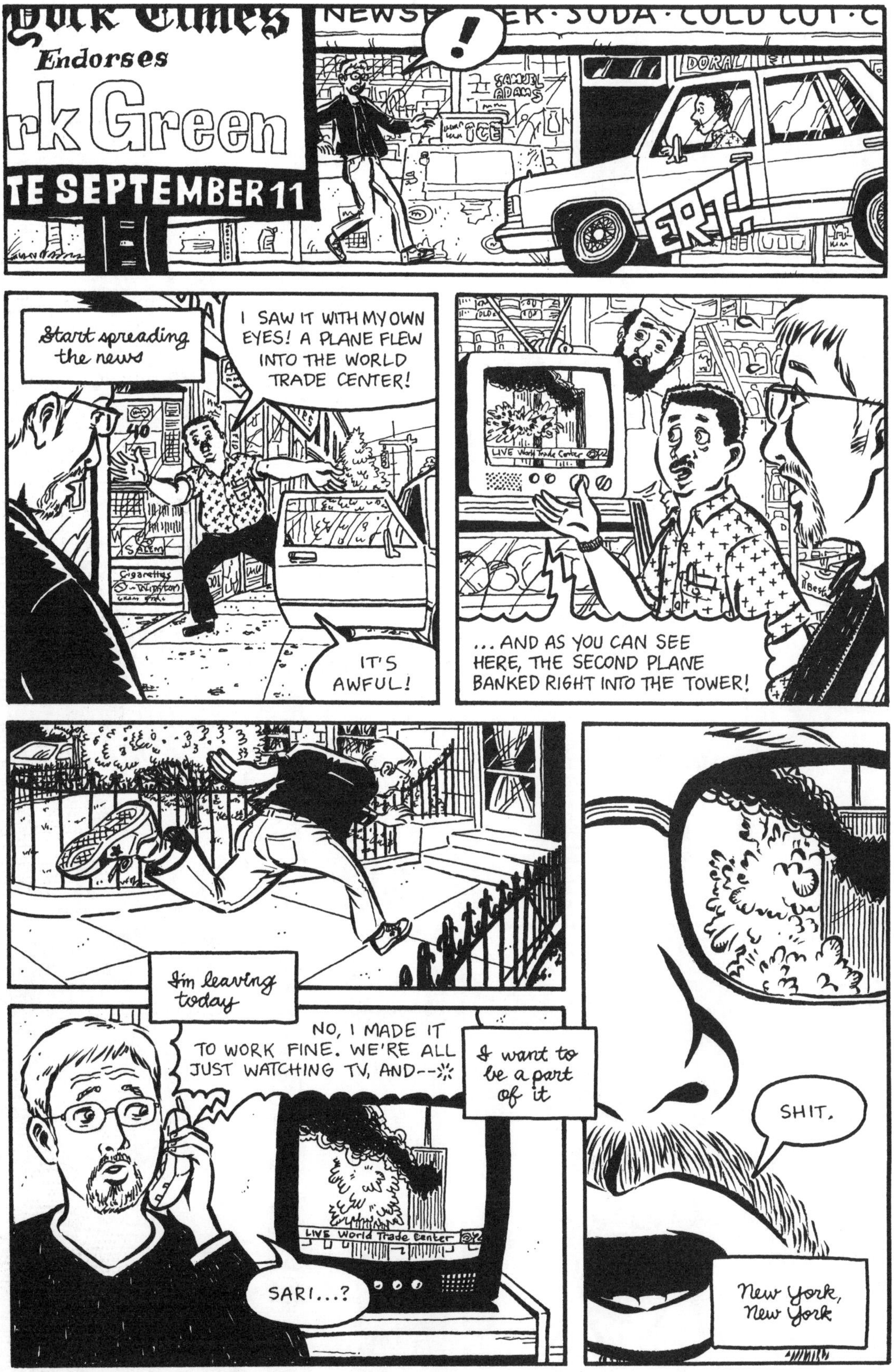
York Times
Endorses
rk Green
TE SEPTEMBER 11
NEWS ER · SODA · COLD CUT · C
!
DORAL
SAMUEL ADAMS
ICE
ERT!
Start spreading the news
I SAW IT WITH MY OWN EYES! A PLANE FLEW INTO THE WORLD TRADE CENTER!
IT'S AWFUL!
LIVE World Trade Center
... AND AS YOU CAN SEE HERE, THE SECOND PLANE BANKED RIGHT INTO THE TOWER!
I'm leaving today
NO, I MADE IT TO WORK FINE. WE'RE ALL JUST WATCHING TV, AND--
LIVE World Trade Center
SARI...?
I want to be a part of it
SHIT.
New York, New York

©2001 Josh Neufeld

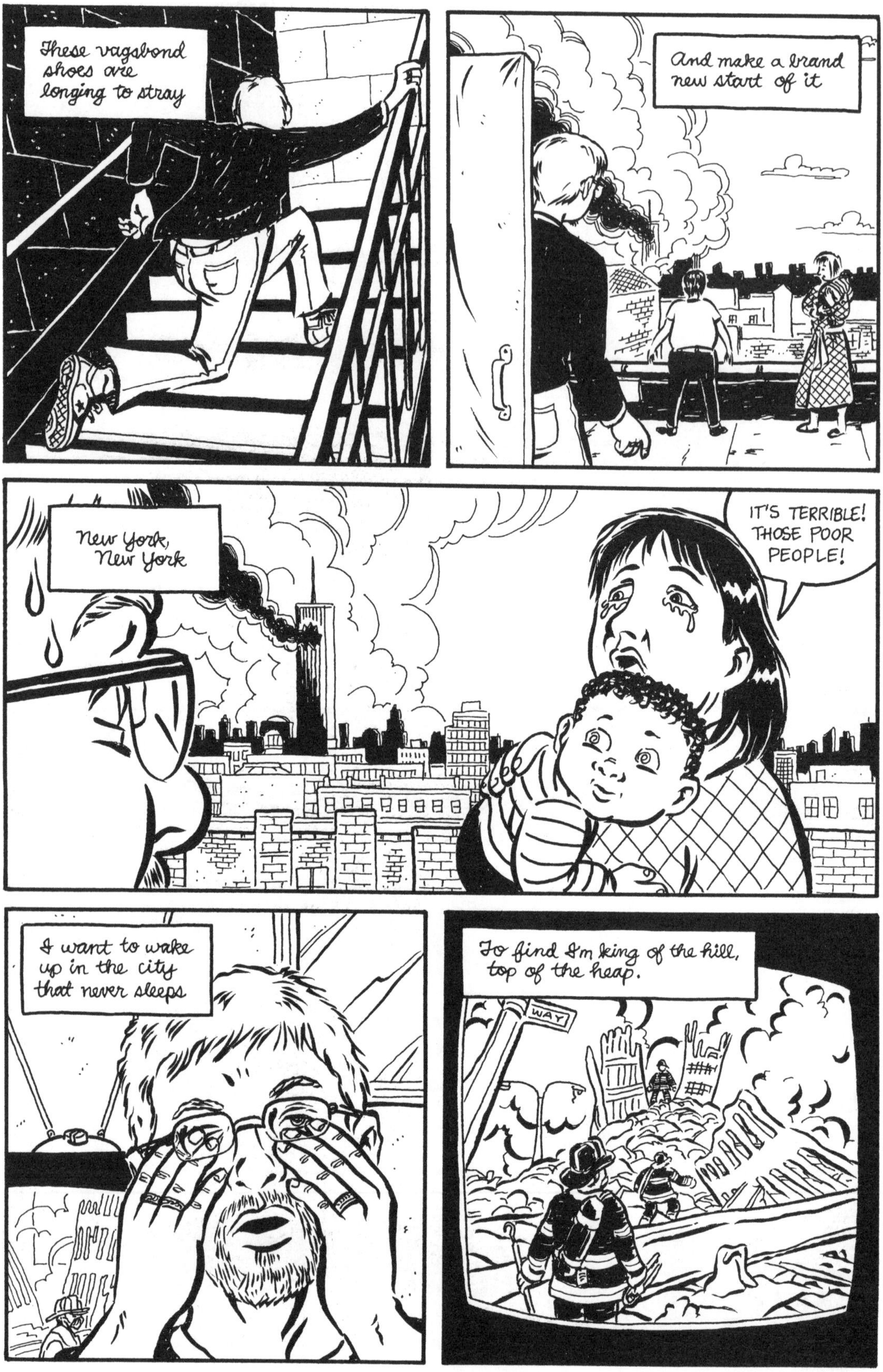
These vagabond shoes are longing to stray
And make a brand new start of it
New York, New York
IT'S TERRIBLE! THOSE POOR PEOPLE!
I want to wake up in the city that never sleeps
To find I'm king of the hill, top of the heap.
WAY

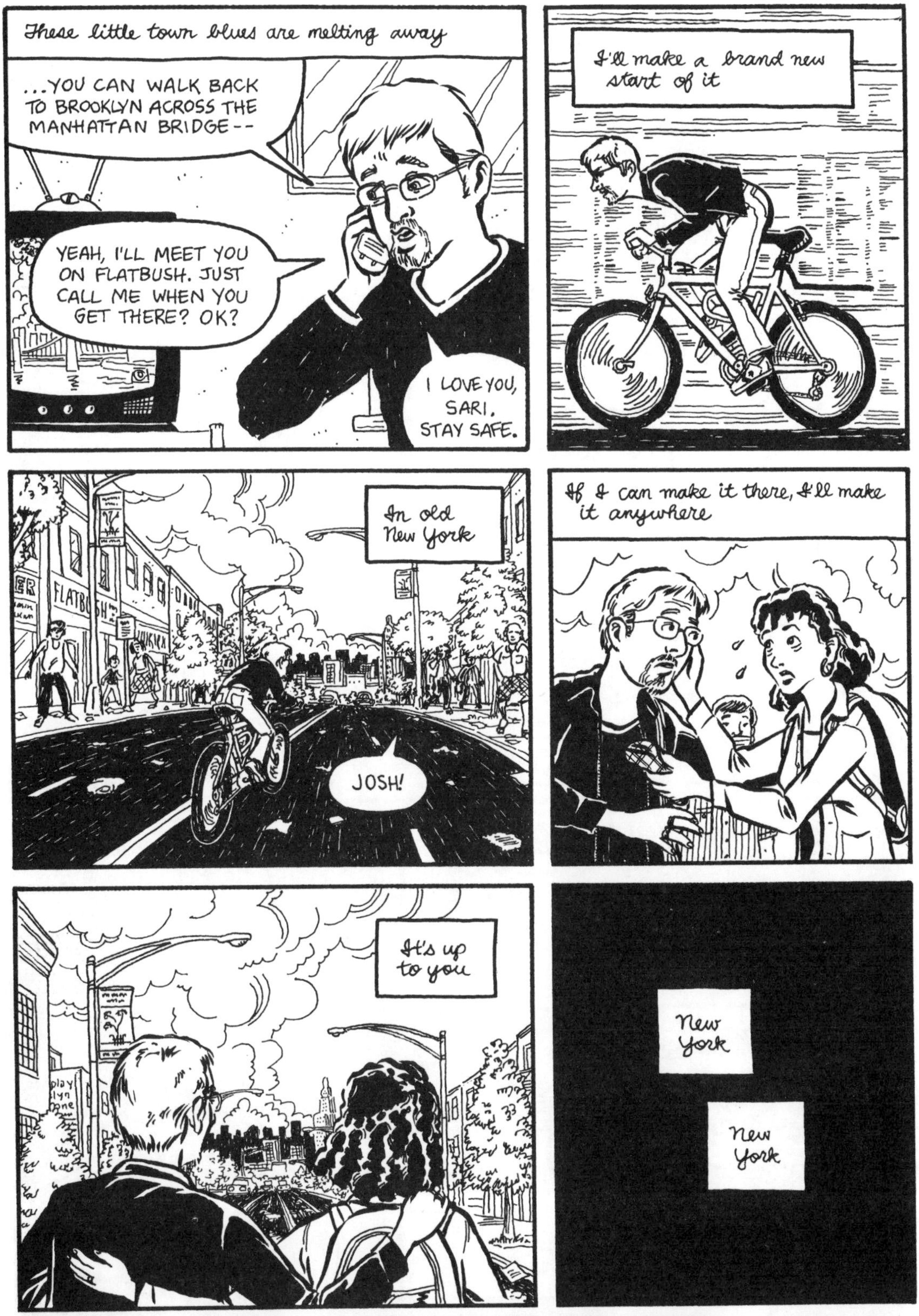
These little town blues are melting away
...YOU CAN WALK BACK TO BROOKLYN ACROSS THE MANHATTAN BRIDGE--
YEAH, I'LL MEET YOU ON FLATBUSH. JUST CALL ME WHEN YOU GET THERE? OK?
I LOVE YOU, SARI. STAY SAFE.
I'll make a brand new start of it
In old New York
FLATBUSH
JOSH!
If I can make it there, I'll make it anywhere
It's up to you
New York
New York

SONG FOR SEPTEMBER 11TH

by JOSH '01
Lyrics by
JOHN KANDER &
FRED EBB

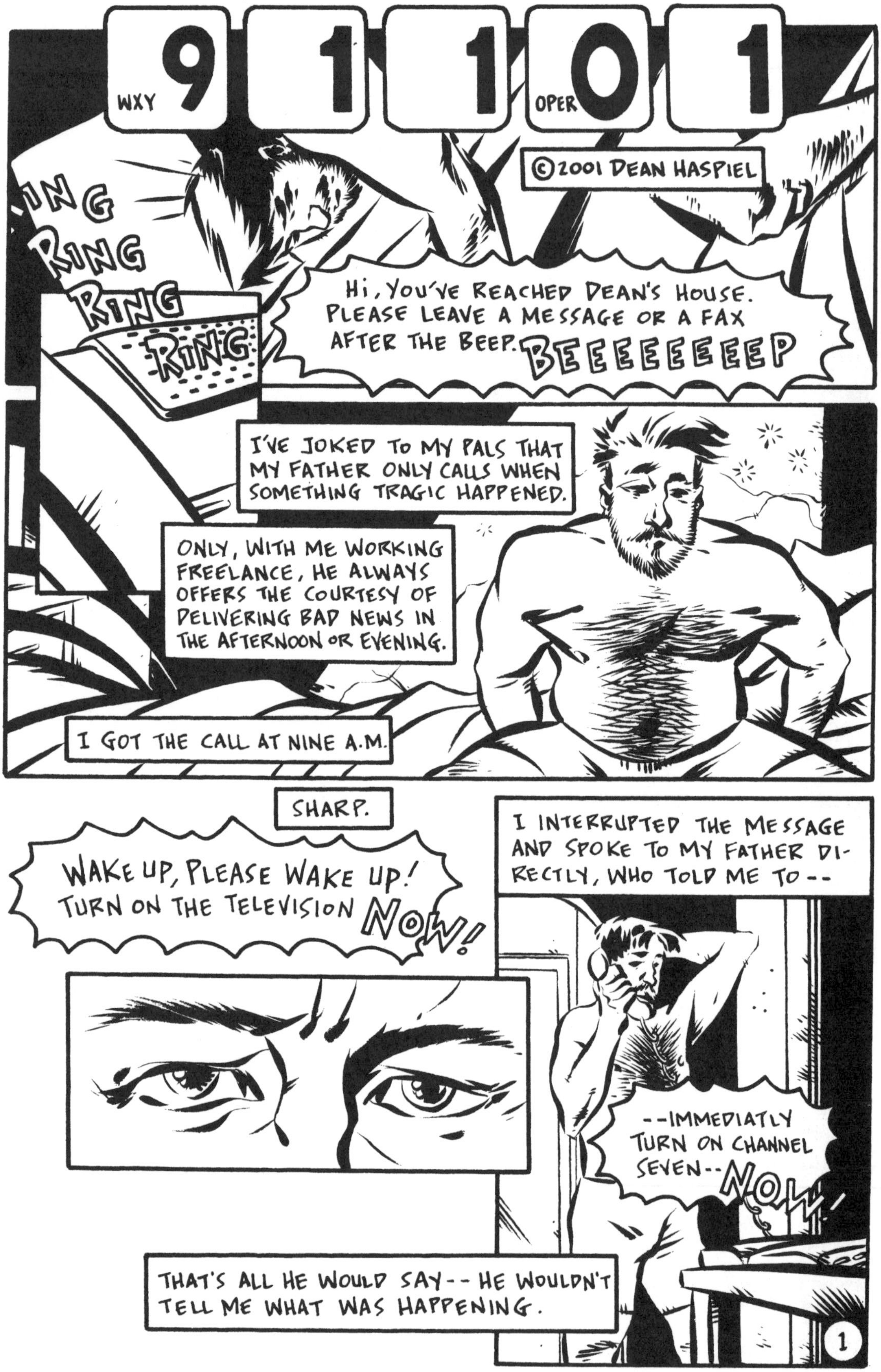

WXY 9 1 1 OPER 0 1
©2001 DEAN HASPIEL
...NG RING RING RING
Hi, YOU'VE REACHED DEAN'S HOUSE. PLEASE LEAVE A MESSAGE OR A FAX AFTER THE BEEP. BEEEEEEEEP
I'VE JOKED TO MY PALS THAT MY FATHER ONLY CALLS WHEN SOMETHING TRAGIC HAPPENED.
ONLY, WITH ME WORKING FREELANCE, HE ALWAYS OFFERS THE COURTESY OF DELIVERING BAD NEWS IN THE AFTERNOON OR EVENING.
I GOT THE CALL AT NINE A.M.
SHARP.
WAKE UP, PLEASE WAKE UP! TURN ON THE TELEVISION NOW!
I INTERRUPTED THE MESSAGE AND SPOKE TO MY FATHER DIRECTLY, WHO TOLD ME TO --
--IMMEDIATLY TURN ON CHANNEL SEVEN--NOW!
THAT'S ALL HE WOULD SAY-- HE WOULDN'T TELL ME WHAT WAS HAPPENING.
1

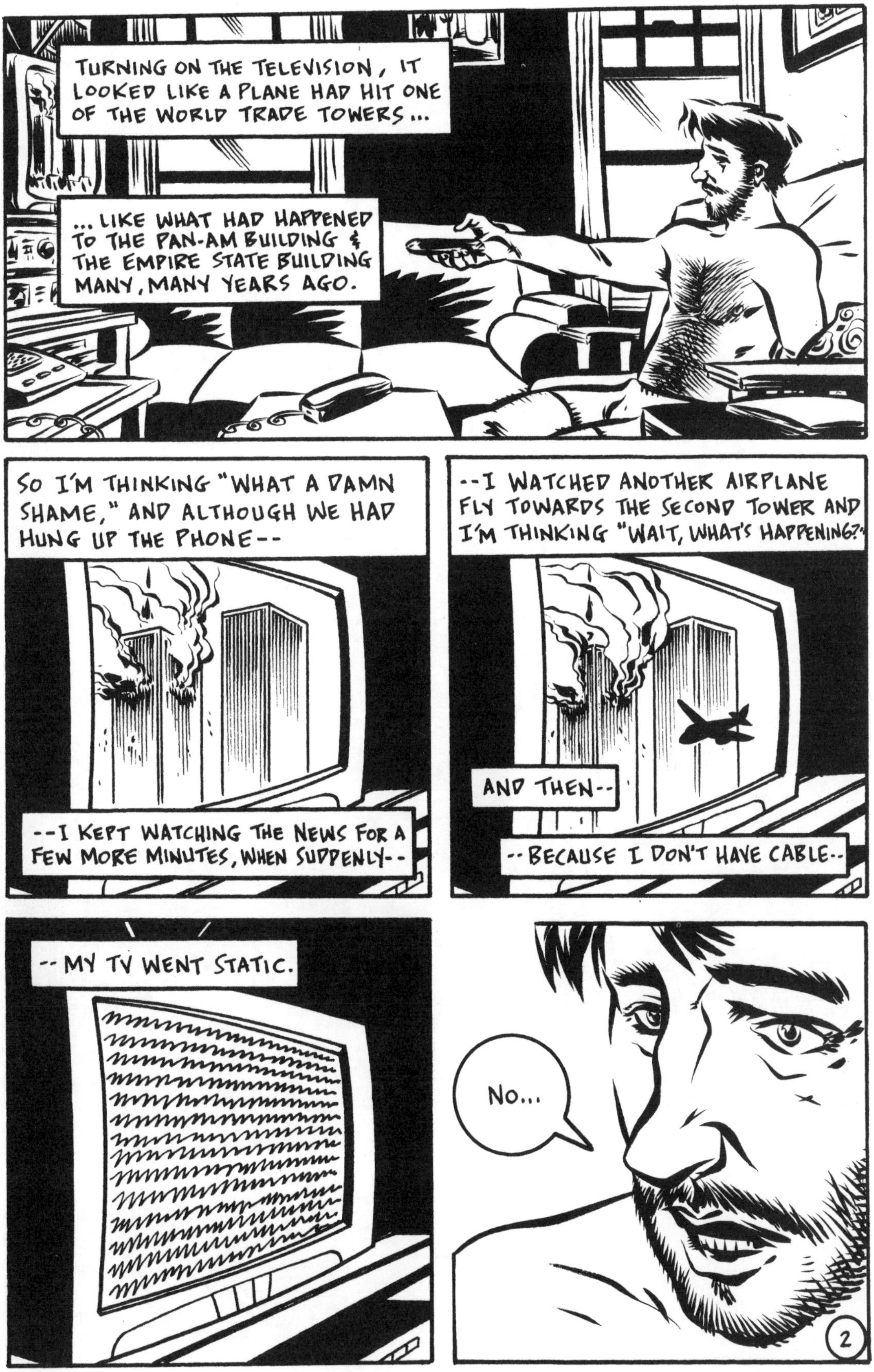
TURNING ON THE TELEVISION, IT LOOKED LIKE A PLANE HAD HIT ONE OF THE WORLD TRADE TOWERS...
...LIKE WHAT HAD HAPPENED TO THE PAN-AM BUILDING & THE EMPIRE STATE BUILDING MANY, MANY YEARS AGO.
SO I'M THINKING "WHAT A DAMN SHAME," AND ALTHOUGH WE HAD HUNG UP THE PHONE--
--I KEPT WATCHING THE NEWS FOR A FEW MORE MINUTES, WHEN SUDDENLY--
--I WATCHED ANOTHER AIRPLANE FLY TOWARDS THE SECOND TOWER AND I'M THINKING "WAIT, WHAT'S HAPPENING?"
AND THEN--
--BECAUSE I DON'T HAVE CABLE--
--MY TV WENT STATIC.
No...
2

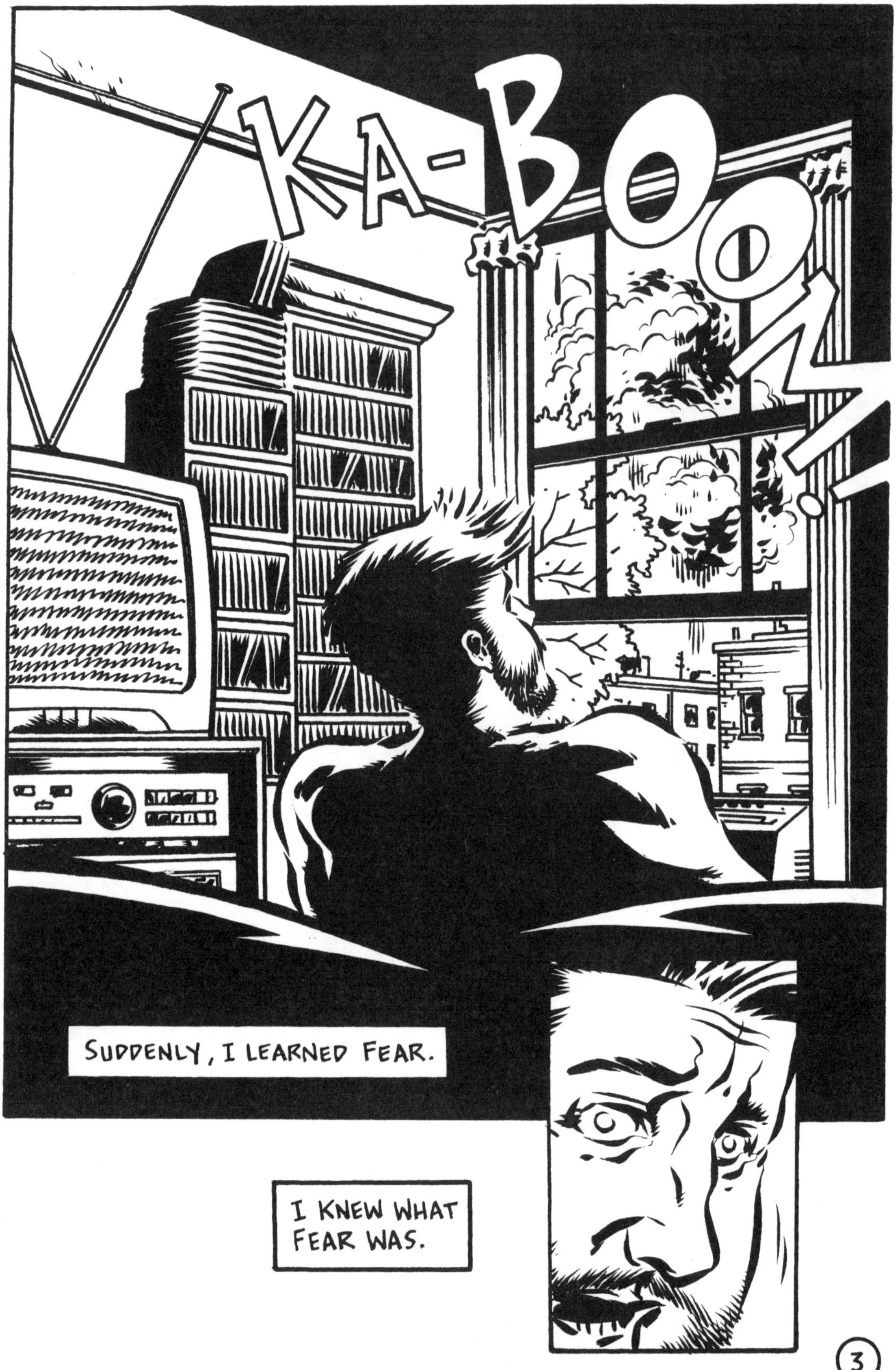
KA-BOOM!
SUDDENLY, I LEARNED FEAR.
I KNEW WHAT FEAR WAS.
3

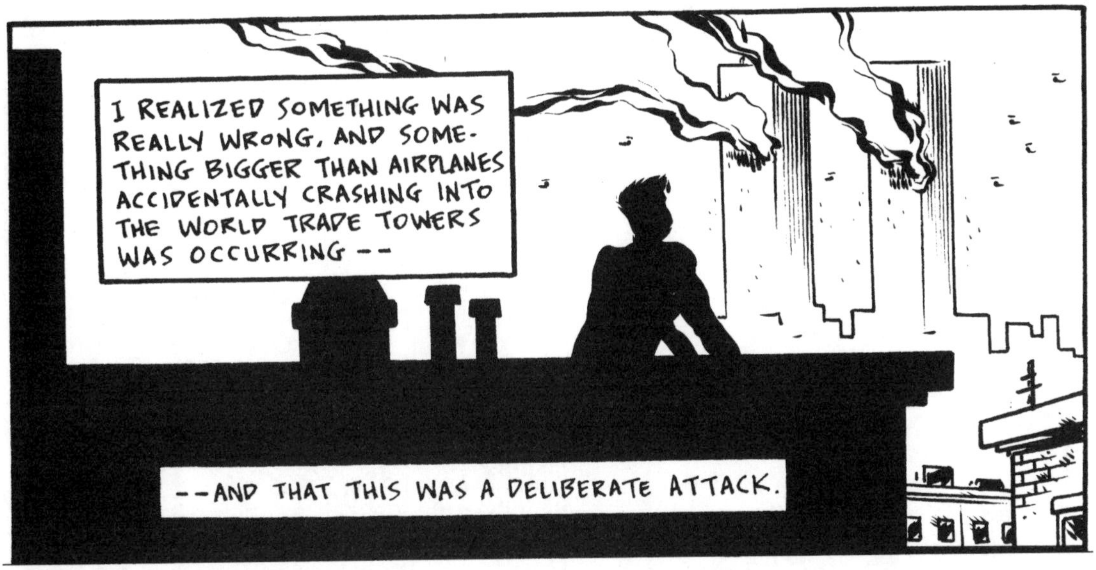
I REALIZED SOMETHING WAS REALLY WRONG, AND SOMETHING BIGGER THAN AIRPLANES ACCIDENTALLY CRASHING INTO THE WORLD TRADE TOWERS WAS OCCURRING --
--AND THAT THIS WAS A DELIBERATE ATTACK.

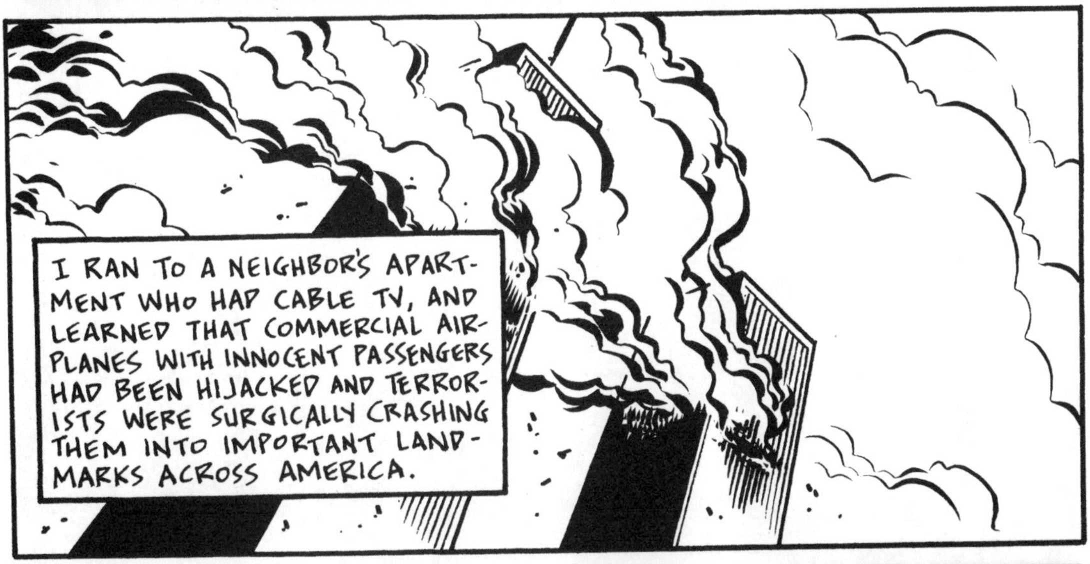
I RAN TO A NEIGHBOR'S APARTMENT WHO HAD CABLE TV, AND LEARNED THAT COMMERCIAL AIRPLANES WITH INNOCENT PASSENGERS HAD BEEN HIJACKED AND TERRORISTS WERE SURGICALLY CRASHING THEM INTO IMPORTANT LANDMARKS ACROSS AMERICA.

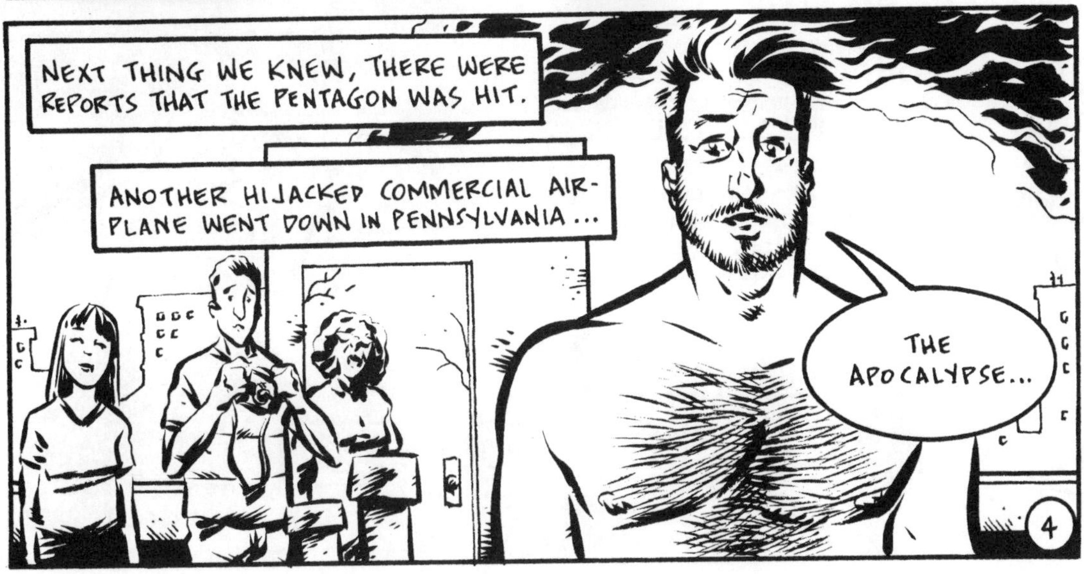
NEXT THING WE KNEW, THERE WERE REPORTS THAT THE PENTAGON WAS HIT.
ANOTHER HIJACKED COMMERCIAL AIRPLANE WENT DOWN IN PENNSYLVANIA...
THE APOCALYPSE...
4

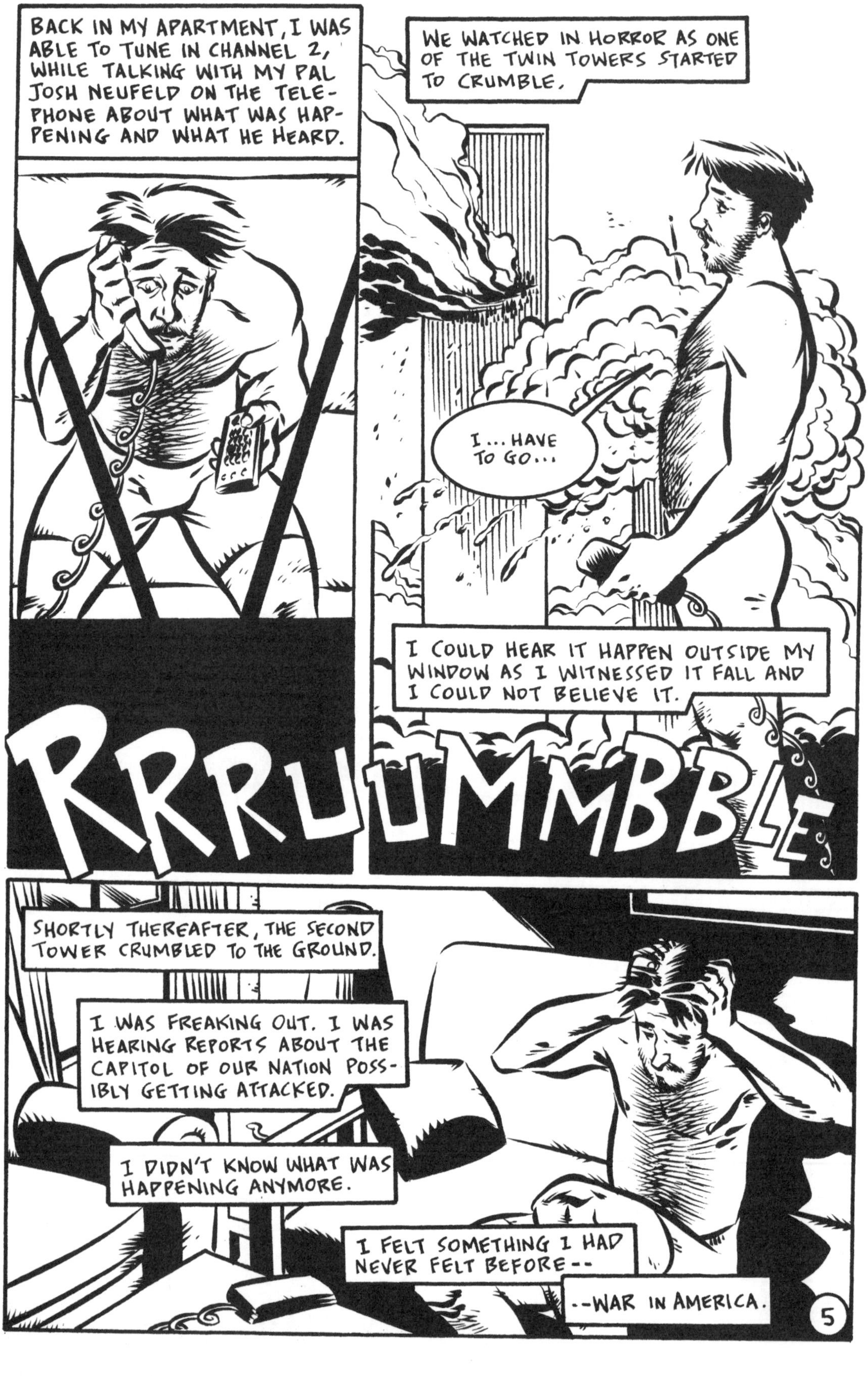
BACK IN MY APARTMENT, I WAS ABLE TO TUNE IN CHANNEL 2, WHILE TALKING WITH MY PAL JOSH NEUFELD ON THE TELEPHONE ABOUT WHAT WAS HAPPENING AND WHAT HE HEARD.
WE WATCHED IN HORROR AS ONE OF THE TWIN TOWERS STARTED TO CRUMBLE.
I... HAVE TO GO...
I COULD HEAR IT HAPPEN OUTSIDE MY WINDOW AS I WITNESSED IT FALL AND I COULD NOT BELIEVE IT.
RRRUUMMBBLE
SHORTLY THEREAFTER, THE SECOND TOWER CRUMBLED TO THE GROUND.
I WAS FREAKING OUT. I WAS HEARING REPORTS ABOUT THE CAPITOL OF OUR NATION POSSIBLY GETTING ATTACKED.
I DIDN'T KNOW WHAT WAS HAPPENING ANYMORE.
I FELT SOMETHING I HAD NEVER FELT BEFORE--
--WAR IN AMERICA.
5

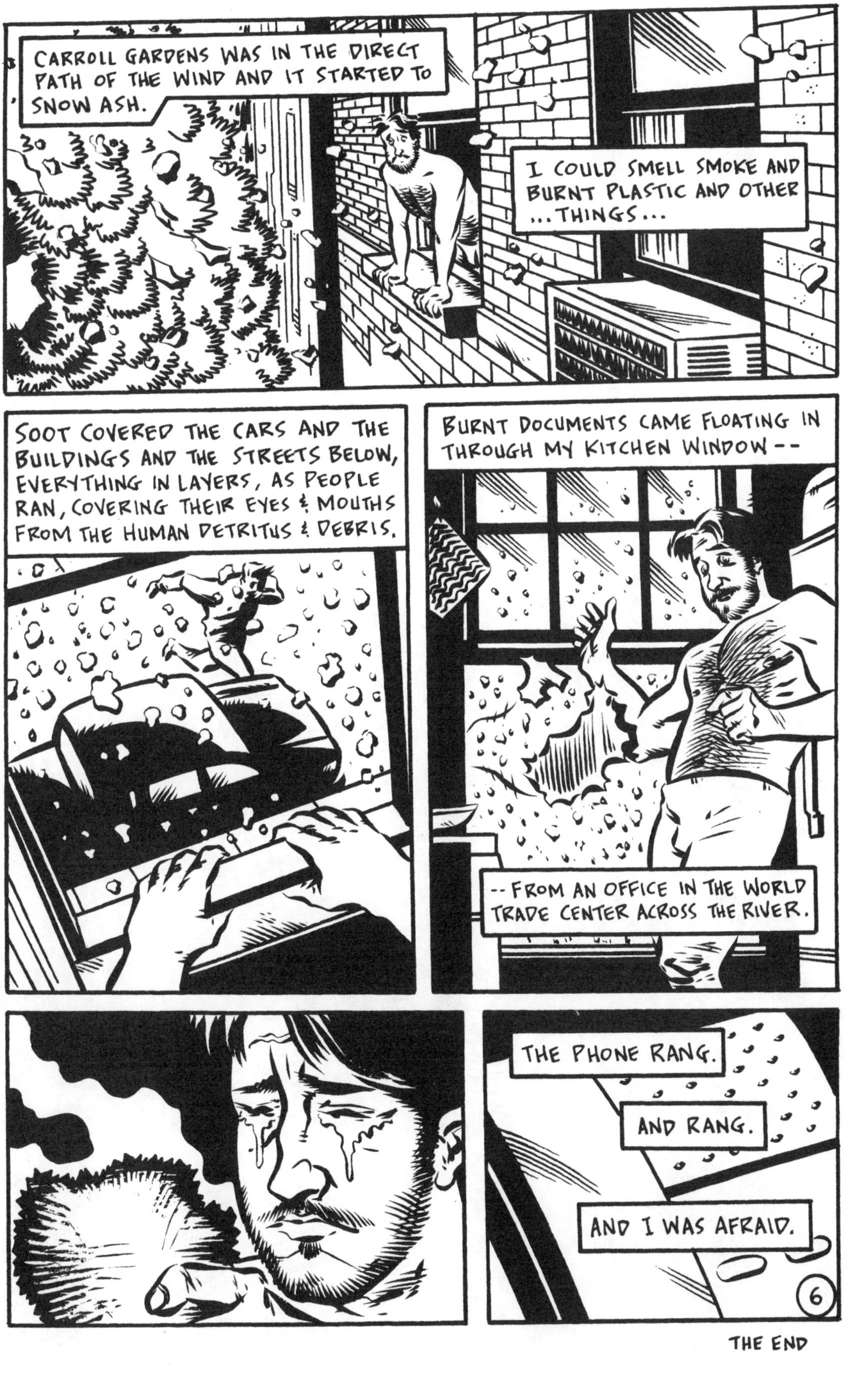
CARROLL GARDENS WAS IN THE DIRECT PATH OF THE WIND AND IT STARTED TO SNOW ASH.
I COULD SMELL SMOKE AND BURNT PLASTIC AND OTHER ...THINGS...
SOOT COVERED THE CARS AND THE BUILDINGS AND THE STREETS BELOW, EVERYTHING IN LAYERS, AS PEOPLE RAN, COVERING THEIR EYES & MOUTHS FROM THE HUMAN DETRITUS & DEBRIS.
BURNT DOCUMENTS CAME FLOATING IN THROUGH MY KITCHEN WINDOW --
-- FROM AN OFFICE IN THE WORLD TRADE CENTER ACROSS THE RIVER.
THE PHONE RANG.
AND RANG.
AND I WAS AFRAID.
6
THE END

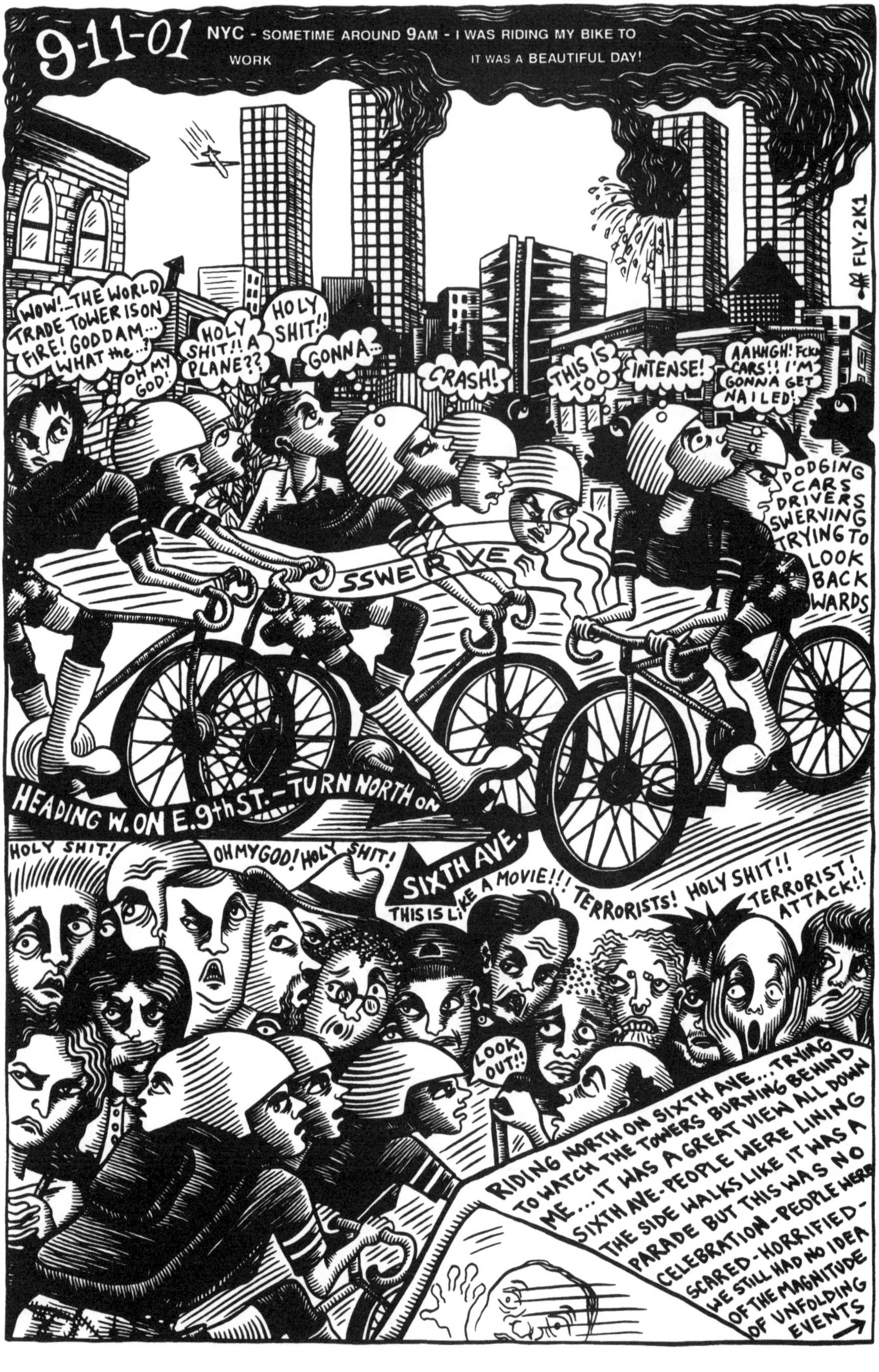
9-11-01
NYC - SOMETIME AROUND 9AM - I WAS RIDING MY BIKE TO WORK
IT WAS A BEAUTIFUL DAY!
WOW!..THE WORLD TRADE TOWER IS ON FIRE! GODDAM... WHAT the...?
OH MY GOD!
HOLY SHIT!! A PLANE??
HOLY SHIT!!
GONNA...
CRASH!
THIS IS TOO
INTENSE!
AAHHGH! FCKN CARS!! I'M GONNA GET NAILED!
FLY·2K1
DODGING CARS DRIVERS SWERVING TRYING TO LOOK BACK WARDS
SSWERVE
HEADING W. ON E. 9th ST. - TURN NORTH ON
SIXTH AVE.
HOLY SHIT!
OH MY GOD! HOLY SHIT!
THIS IS LIKE A MOVIE!!!
TERRORISTS!
HOLY SHIT!!
TERRORIST ATTACK!!
LOOK OUT!!
RIDING NORTH ON SIXTH AVE... TRYING TO WATCH THE TOWERS BURNING BEHIND ME... IT WAS A GREAT VIEW ALL DOWN SIXTH AVE - PEOPLE WERE LINING THE SIDE WALKS LIKE IT WAS A PARADE BUT THIS WAS NO CELEBRATION - PEOPLE WERE SCARED - HORRIFIED - WE STILL HAD NO IDEA OF THE MAGNITUDE OF UNFOLDING EVENTS

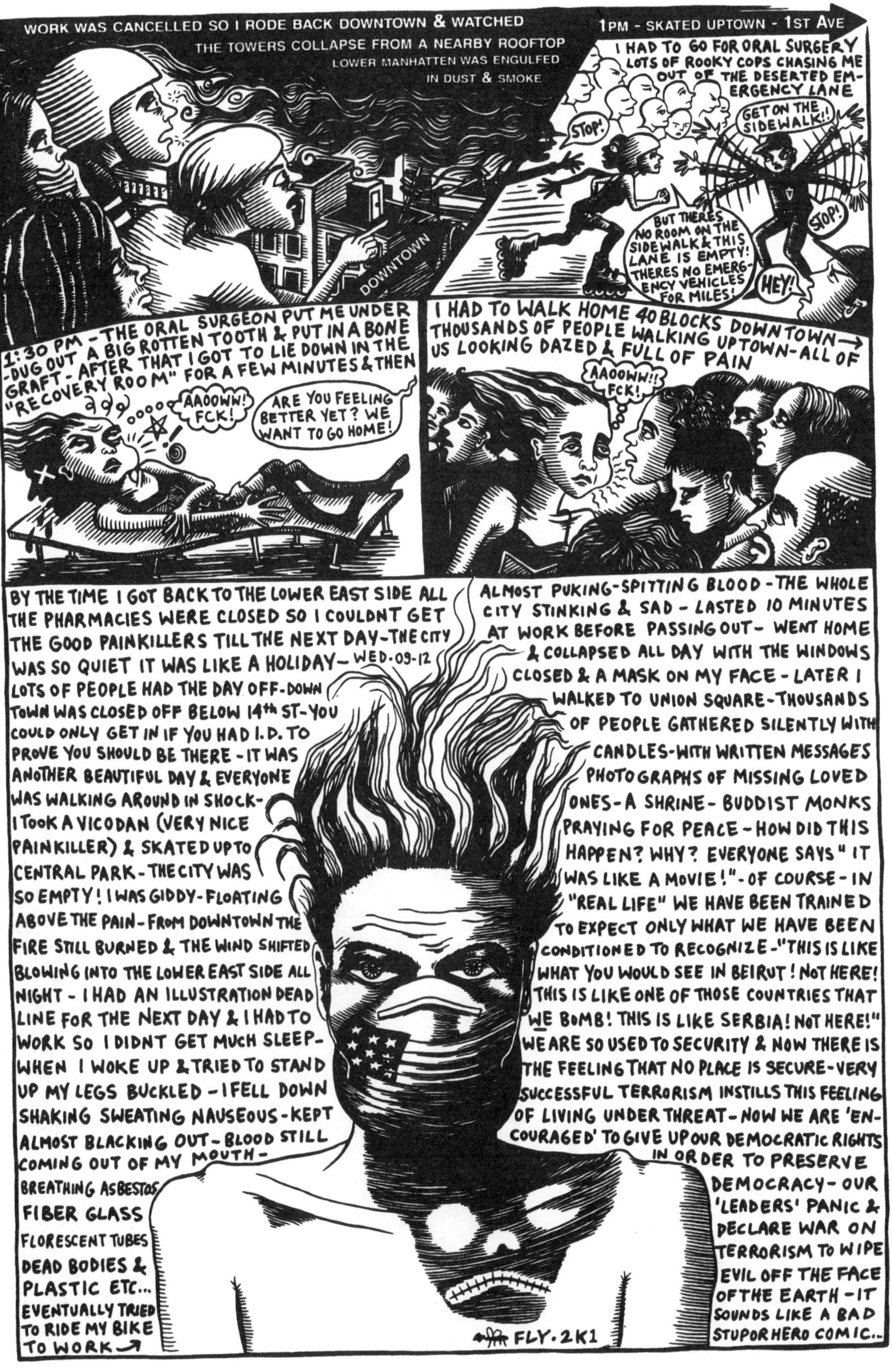
WORK WAS CANCELLED SO I RODE BACK DOWNTOWN & WATCHED
THE TOWERS COLLAPSE FROM A NEARBY ROOFTOP
LOWER MANHATTEN WAS ENGULFED
IN DUST & SMOKE
DOWNTOWN
1PM - SKATED UPTOWN - 1ST AVE
I HAD TO GO FOR ORAL SURGERY LOTS OF ROOKY COPS CHASING ME OUT OF THE DESERTED EMERGENCY LANE
STOP!
GET ON THE SIDEWALK!!
BUT THERES NO ROOM ON THE SIDEWALK & THIS LANE IS EMPTY! THERES NO EMERGENCY VEHICLES FOR MILES!
STOP!
HEY!
1:30 PM - THE ORAL SURGEON PUT ME UNDER - DUG OUT A BIG ROTTEN TOOTH & PUT IN A BONE GRAFT - AFTER THAT I GOT TO LIE DOWN IN THE "RECOVERY ROOM" FOR A FEW MINUTES & THEN
AAOOWW! FCK!
ARE YOU FEELING BETTER YET? WE WANT TO GO HOME!
I HAD TO WALK HOME 40 BLOCKS DOWNTOWN → THOUSANDS OF PEOPLE WALKING UPTOWN - ALL OF US LOOKING DAZED & FULL OF PAIN
AAOOWW!! FCK!
BY THE TIME I GOT BACK TO THE LOWER EAST SIDE ALL THE PHARMACIES WERE CLOSED SO I COULDNT GET THE GOOD PAINKILLERS TILL THE NEXT DAY - THE CITY WAS SO QUIET IT WAS LIKE A HOLIDAY - WED - 09 - 12 LOTS OF PEOPLE HAD THE DAY OFF - DOWN TOWN WAS CLOSED OFF BELOW 14th ST - YOU COULD ONLY GET IN IF YOU HAD I.D. TO PROVE YOU SHOULD BE THERE - IT WAS ANOTHER BEAUTIFUL DAY & EVERYONE WAS WALKING AROUND IN SHOCK - I TOOK A VICODAN (VERY NICE PAINKILLER) & SKATED UP TO CENTRAL PARK - THE CITY WAS SO EMPTY! I WAS GIDDY - FLOATING ABOVE THE PAIN - FROM DOWNTOWN THE FIRE STILL BURNED & THE WIND SHIFTED BLOWING INTO THE LOWER EAST SIDE ALL NIGHT - I HAD AN ILLUSTRATION DEAD LINE FOR THE NEXT DAY & I HAD TO WORK SO I DIDNT GET MUCH SLEEP - WHEN I WOKE UP & TRIED TO STAND UP MY LEGS BUCKLED - I FELL DOWN SHAKING SWEATING NAUSEOUS - KEPT ALMOST BLACKING OUT - BLOOD STILL COMING OUT OF MY MOUTH -
BREATHING ASBESTOS FIBER GLASS FLORESCENT TUBES DEAD BODIES & PLASTIC ETC... EVENTUALLY TRIED TO RIDE MY BIKE TO WORK →
ALMOST PUKING - SPITTING BLOOD - THE WHOLE CITY STINKING & SAD - LASTED 10 MINUTES AT WORK BEFORE PASSING OUT - WENT HOME & COLLAPSED ALL DAY WITH THE WINDOWS CLOSED & A MASK ON MY FACE - LATER I WALKED TO UNION SQUARE - THOUSANDS OF PEOPLE GATHERED SILENTLY WITH CANDLES - WITH WRITTEN MESSAGES PHOTOGRAPHS OF MISSING LOVED ONES - A SHRINE - BUDDIST MONKS PRAYING FOR PEACE - HOW DID THIS HAPPEN? WHY? EVERYONE SAYS " IT WAS LIKE A MOVIE!" - OF COURSE - IN "REAL LIFE" WE HAVE BEEN TRAINED TO EXPECT ONLY WHAT WE HAVE BEEN CONDITIONED TO RECOGNIZE - "THIS IS LIKE WHAT YOU WOULD SEE IN BEIRUT! NOT HERE! THIS IS LIKE ONE OF THOSE COUNTRIES THAT WE BOMB! THIS IS LIKE SERBIA! NOT HERE!" WE ARE SO USED TO SECURITY & NOW THERE IS THE FEELING THAT NO PLACE IS SECURE - VERY SUCCESSFUL TERRORISM INSTILLS THIS FEELING OF LIVING UNDER THREAT - NOW WE ARE 'ENCOURAGED' TO GIVE UP OUR DEMOCRATIC RIGHTS IN ORDER TO PRESERVE DEMOCRACY - OUR 'LEADERS' PANIC & DECLARE WAR ON TERRORISM TO WIPE EVIL OFF THE FACE OF THE EARTH - IT SOUNDS LIKE A BAD STUPOR HERO COMIC...
FLY • 2K1

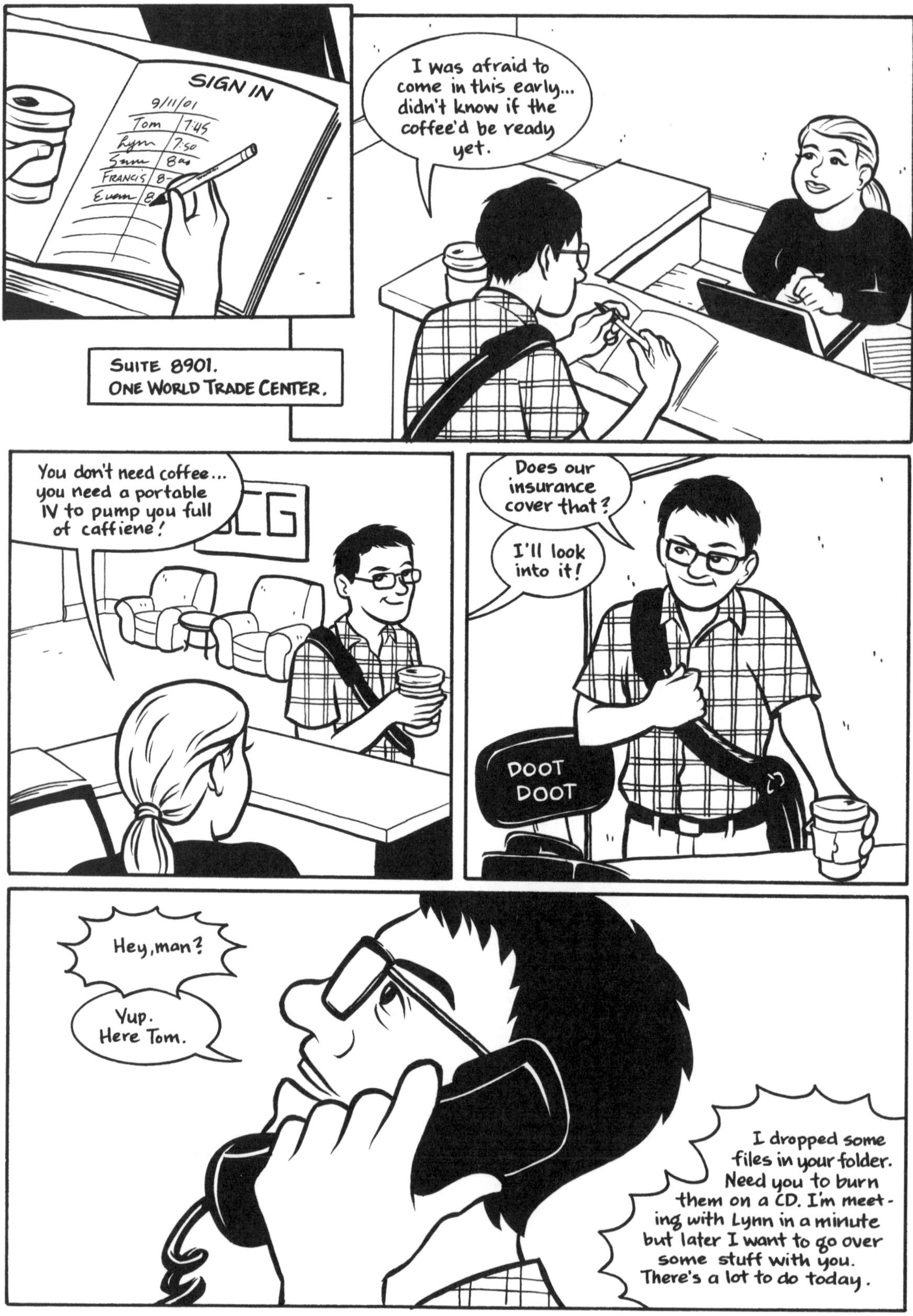
SIGN IN
9/11/01
Tom 7:45
Lynn 7:50
Sam 8:05
FRANCIS 8-
Evan 8
SUITE 8901.
ONE WORLD TRADE CENTER.
I was afraid to come in this early... didn't know if the coffee'd be ready yet.
You don't need coffee... you need a portable IV to pump you full of caffiene!
Does our insurance cover that?
I'll look into it!
DOOT DOOT
Hey, man?
Yup. Here Tom.
I dropped some files in your folder. Need you to burn them on a CD. I'm meet-ing with Lynn in a minute but later I want to go over some stuff with you. There's a lot to do today.

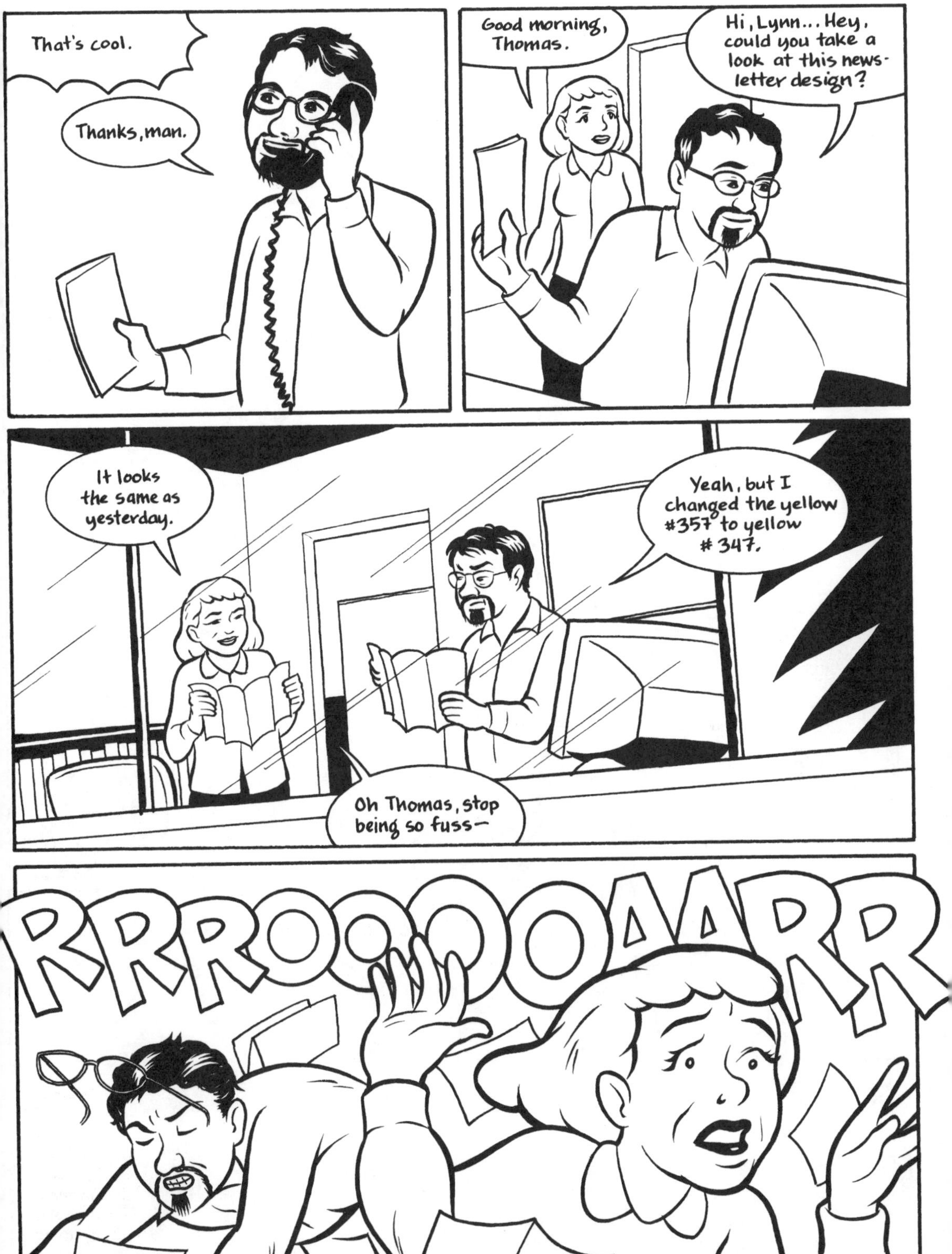
That's cool.
Thanks, man.
Good morning, Thomas.
Hi, Lynn... Hey, could you take a look at this news-letter design?
It looks the same as yesterday.
Yeah, but I changed the yellow #357 to yellow #347.
Oh Thomas, stop being so fuss—
RRROOOOAARR

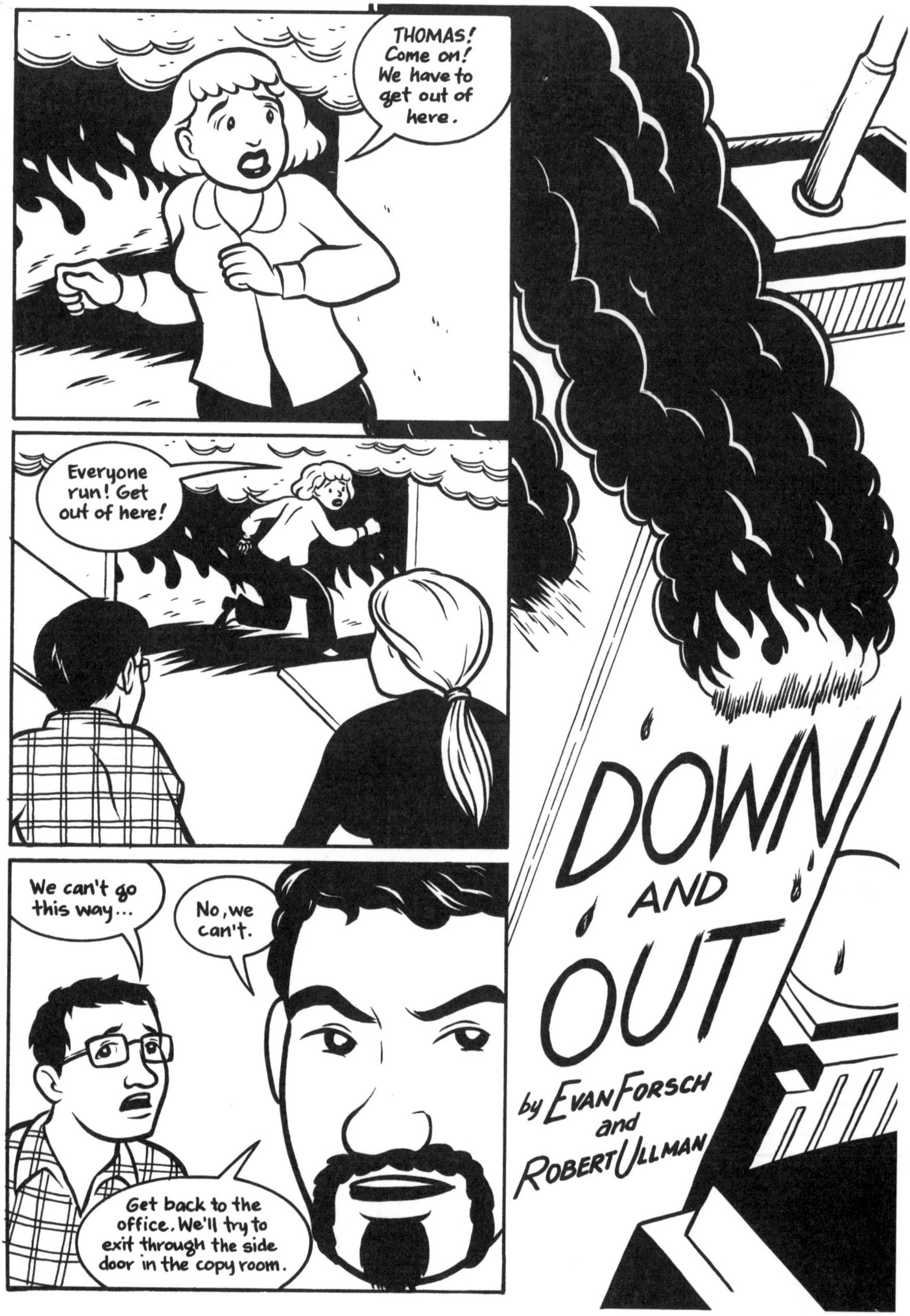
THOMAS! Come on! We have to get out of here.
Everyone run! Get out of here!
We can't go this way...
No, we can't.
Get back to the office. We'll try to exit through the side door in the copy room.
DOWN AND OUT
by EVAN FORSCH and ROBERT ULLMAN

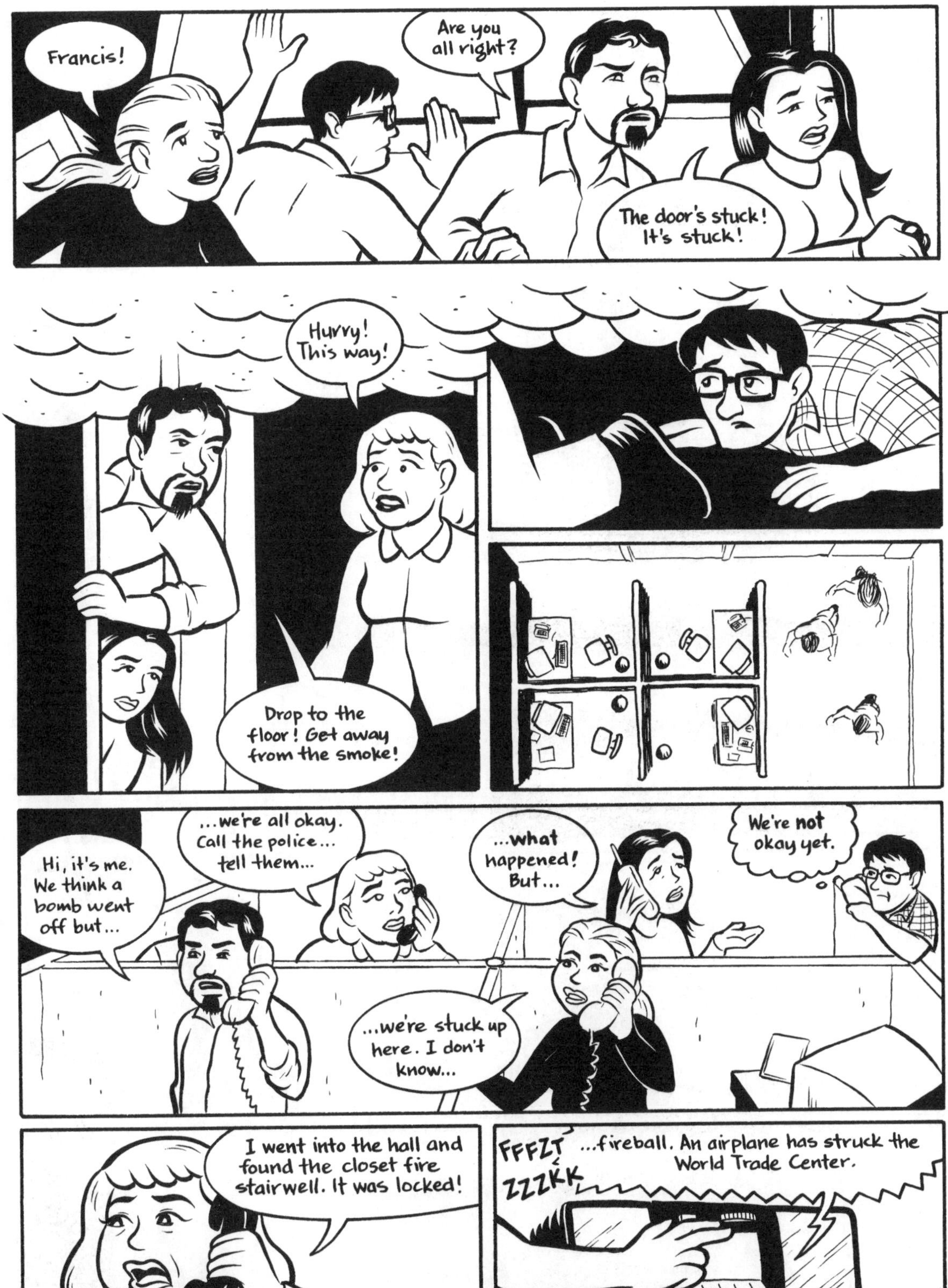
Francis!
Are you all right?
The door's stuck! It's stuck!
Hurry! This way!
Drop to the floor! Get away from the smoke!
Hi, it's me. We think a bomb went off but...
...we're all okay. Call the police... tell them...
...what happened! But...
We're not okay yet.
...we're stuck up here. I don't know...
I went into the hall and found the closet fire stairwell. It was locked!
FFFZT ZZZKK
...fireball. An airplane has struck the World Trade Center.

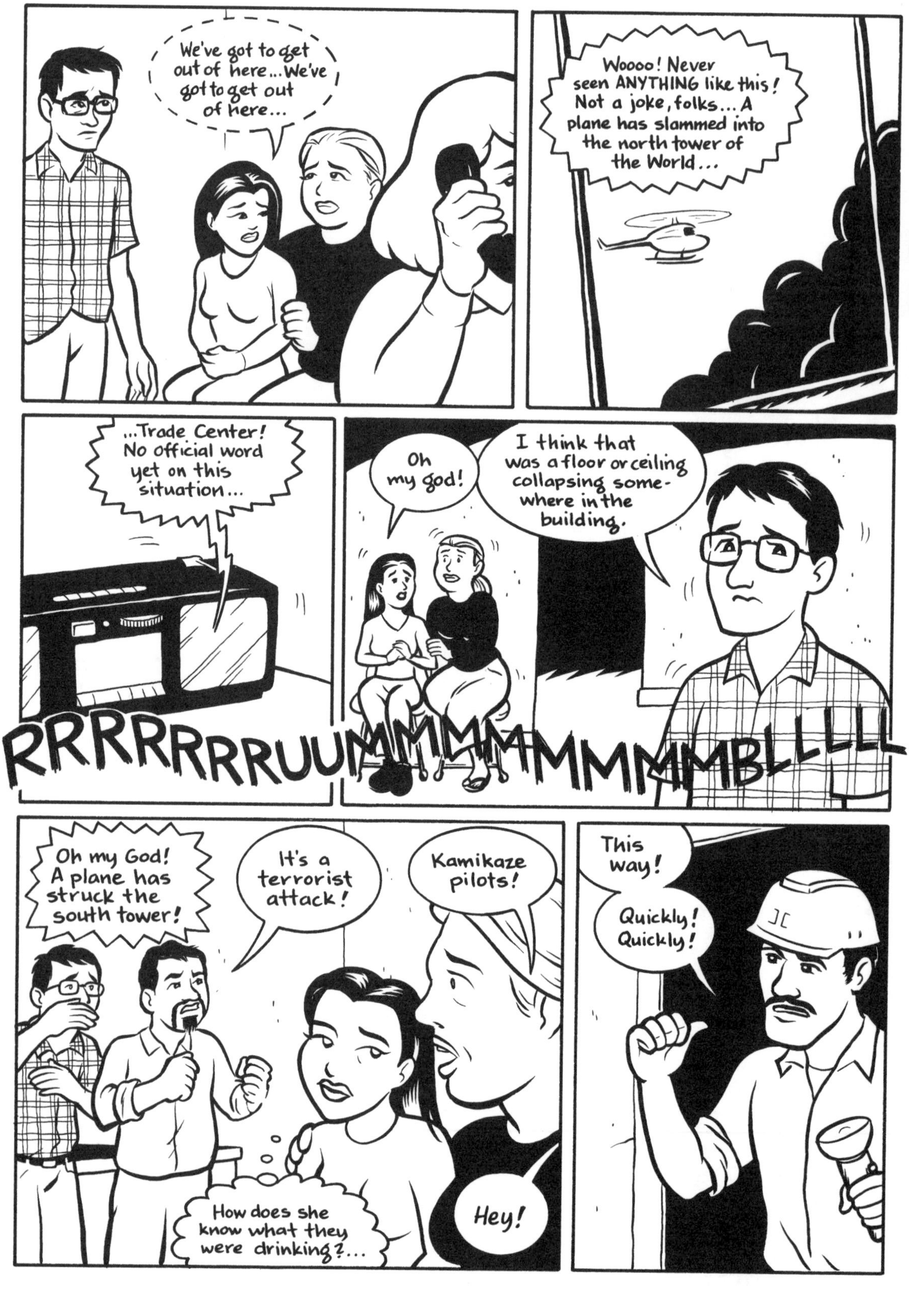
We've got to get out of here...We've got to get out of here...
Woooo! Never seen ANYTHING like this! Not a joke, folks... A plane has slammed into the north tower of the World...
...Trade Center! No official word yet on this situation...
Oh my god!
I think that was a floor or ceiling collapsing some-where in the building.
RRRRRRRUUMMMMMMMMMBLLLL
Oh my God! A plane has struck the south tower!
It's a terrorist attack!
Kamikaze pilots!
How does she know what they were drinking?...
Hey!
This way!
Quickly! Quickly!

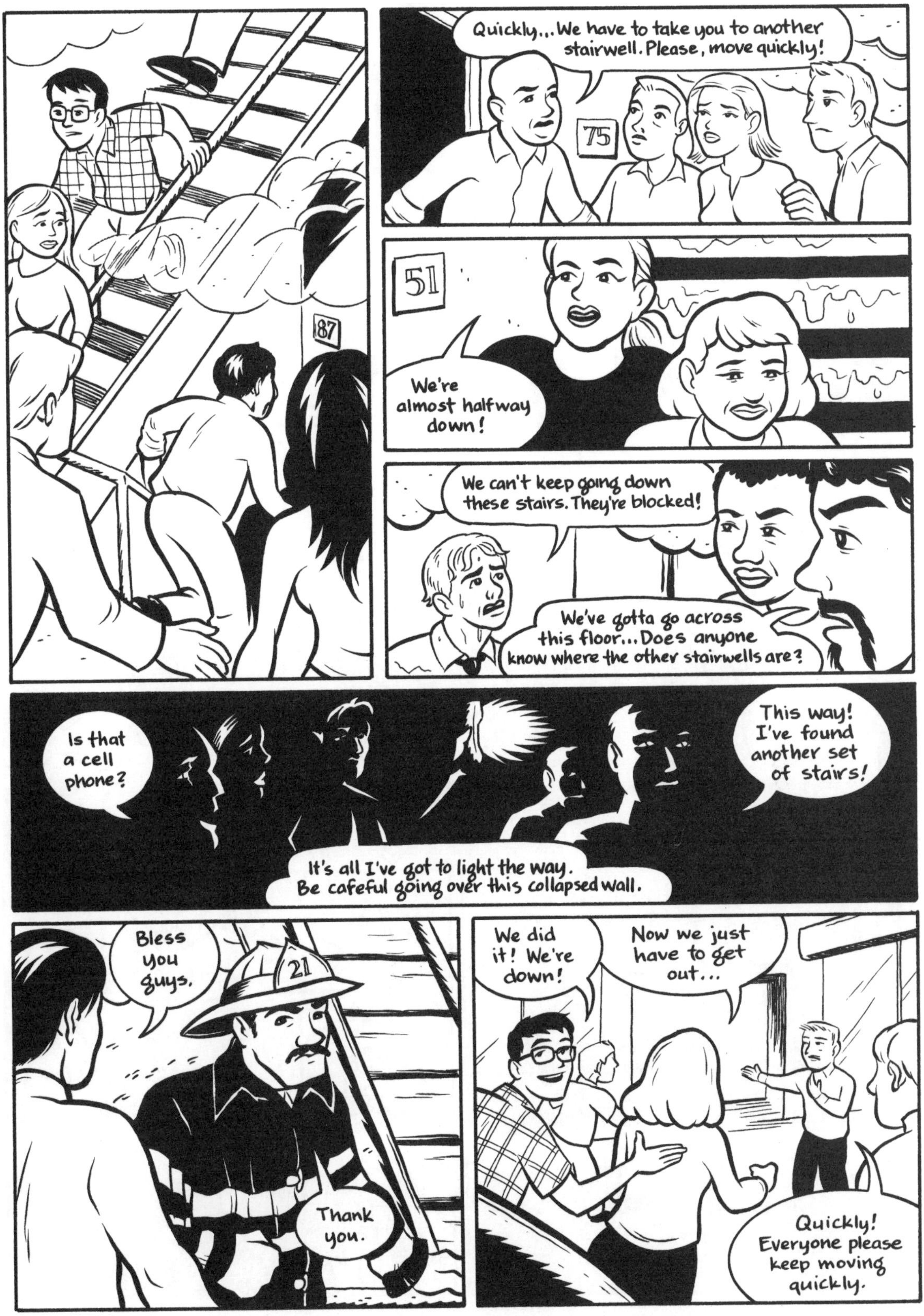
87
Quickly... We have to take you to another stairwell. Please, move quickly!
75
51
We're almost halfway down!
We can't keep going down these stairs. They're blocked!
We've gotta go across this floor... Does anyone know where the other stairwells are?
Is that a cell phone?
It's all I've got to light the way. Be cafeful going over this collapsed wall.
This way! I've found another set of stairs!
Bless you guys.
21
Thank you.
We did it! We're down!
Now we just have to get out...
Quickly! Everyone please keep moving quickly.

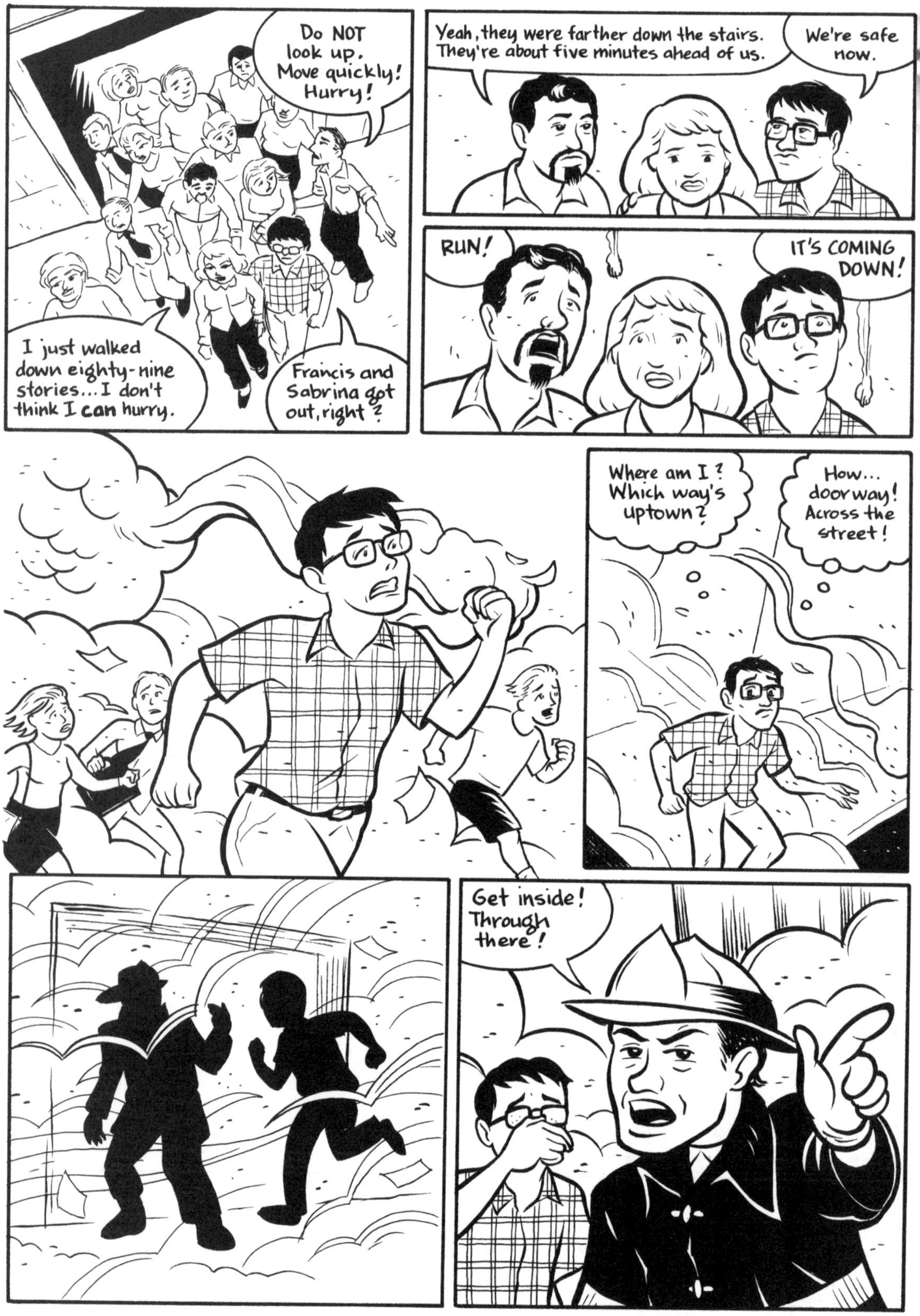

Do NOT look up. Move quickly! Hurry!
I just walked down eighty-nine stories... I don't think I **can** hurry.
Francis and Sabrina got out, right?
Yeah, they were farther down the stairs. They're about five minutes ahead of us.
We're safe now.
RUN!
IT'S COMING DOWN!
Where am I? Which way's uptown?
How... doorway! Across the street!
Get inside! Through there!

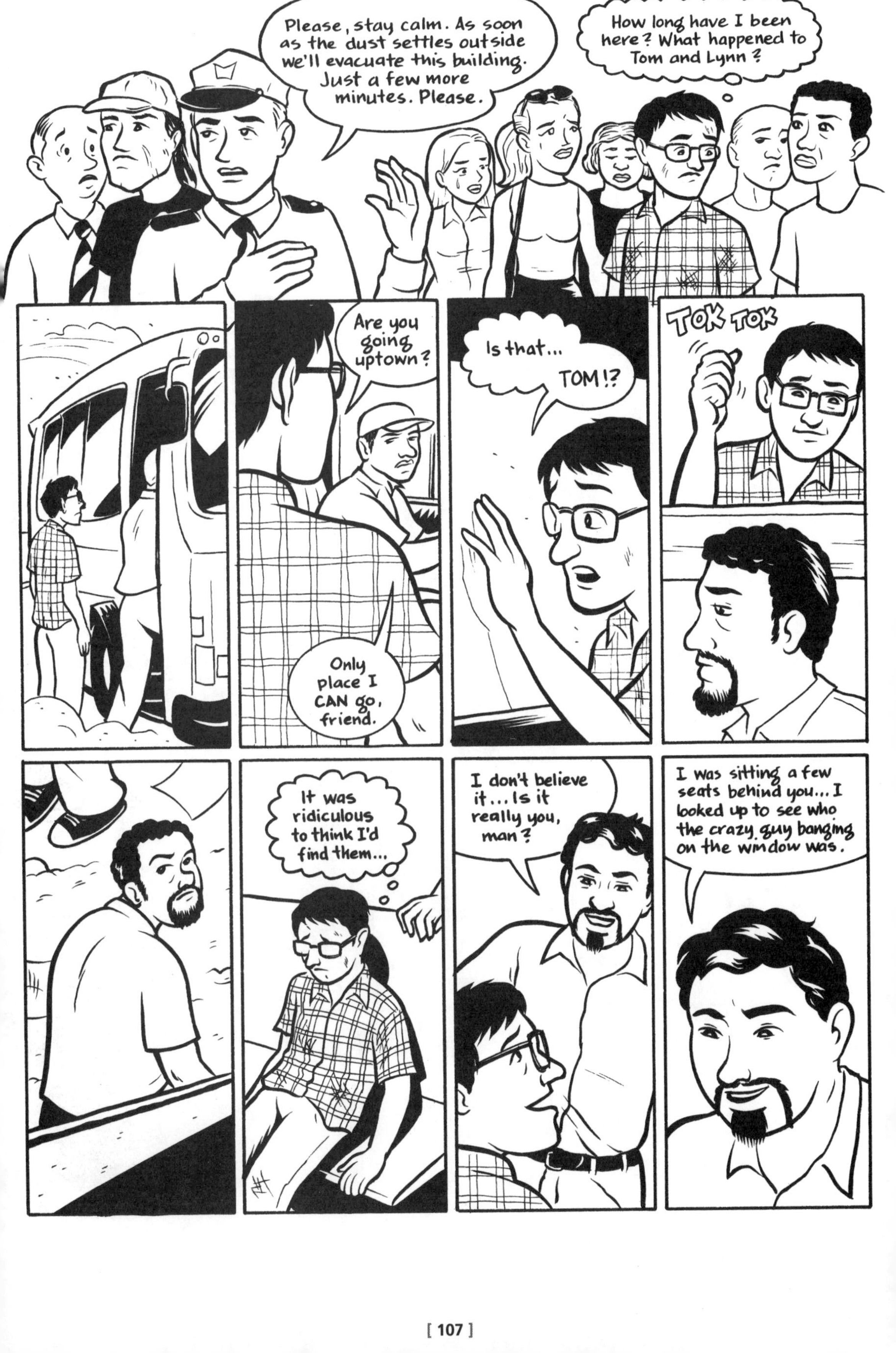
Please, stay calm. As soon as the dust settles outside we'll evacuate this building. Just a few more minutes. Please.
How long have I been here? What happened to Tom and Lynn?
Are you going uptown?
Only place I CAN go, friend.
Is that...
TOM!?
TOK TOK
It was ridiculous to think I'd find them...
I don't believe it... Is it really you, man?
I was sitting a few seats behind you... I looked up to see who the crazy guy banging on the window was.

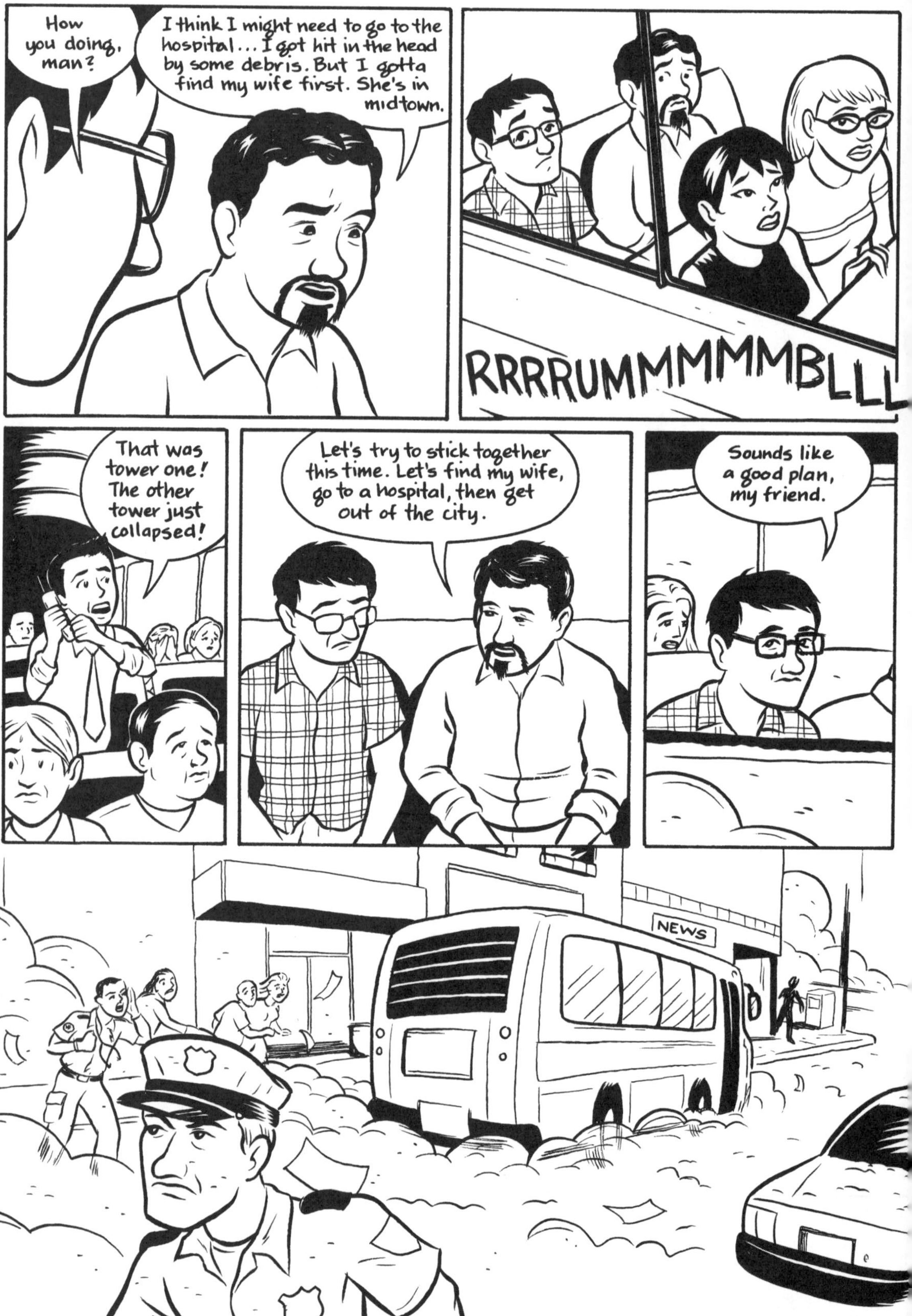
How you doing, man?
I think I might need to go to the hospital... I got hit in the head by some debris. But I gotta find my wife first. She's in midtown.
RRRRUMMMMMBLLL
That was tower one! The other tower just collapsed!
Let's try to stick together this time. Let's find my wife, go to a hospital, then get out of the city.
Sounds like a good plan, my friend.
NEWS

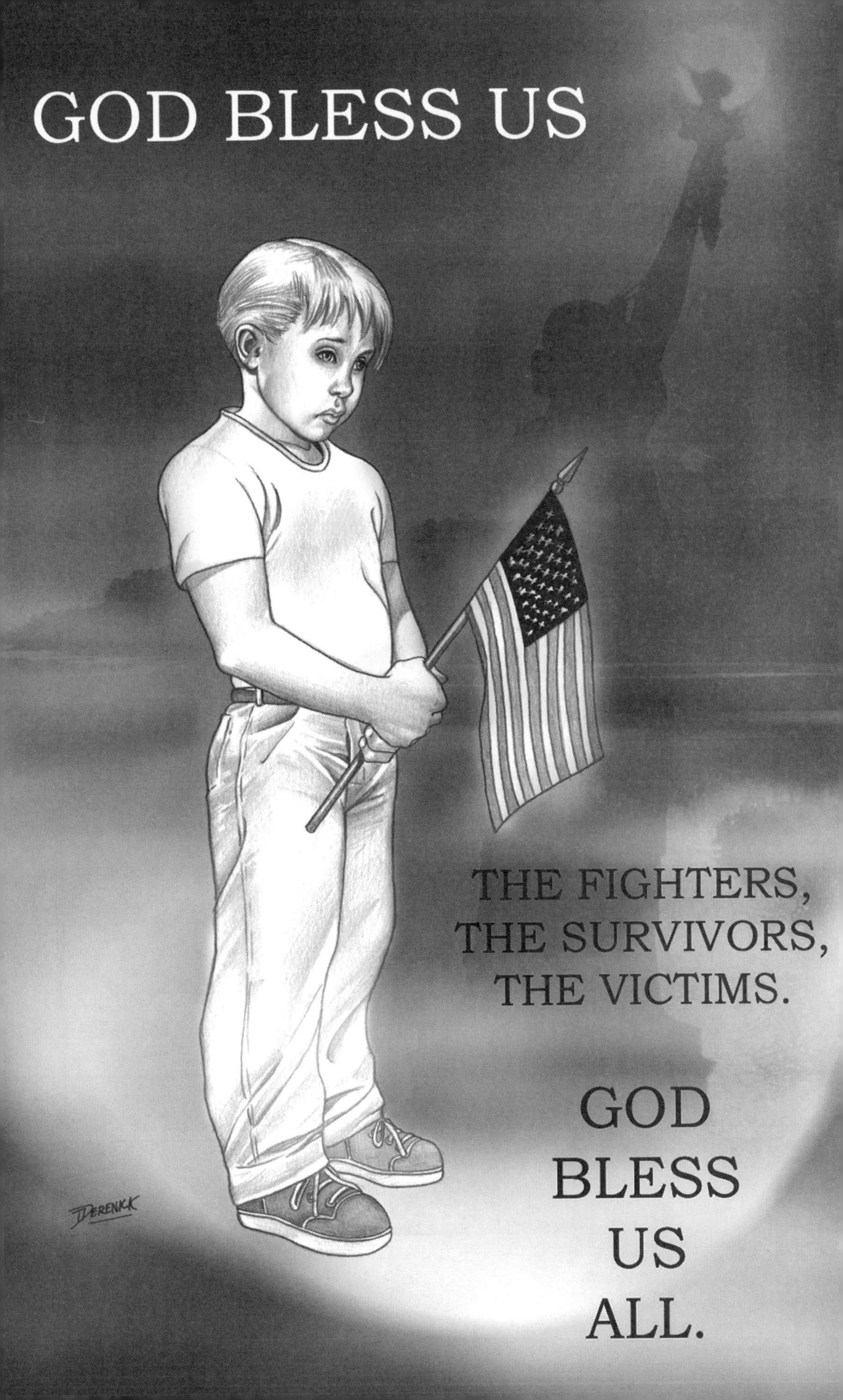
GOD BLESS US
THE FIGHTERS,
THE SURVIVORS,
THE VICTIMS.
GOD
BLESS
US
ALL.

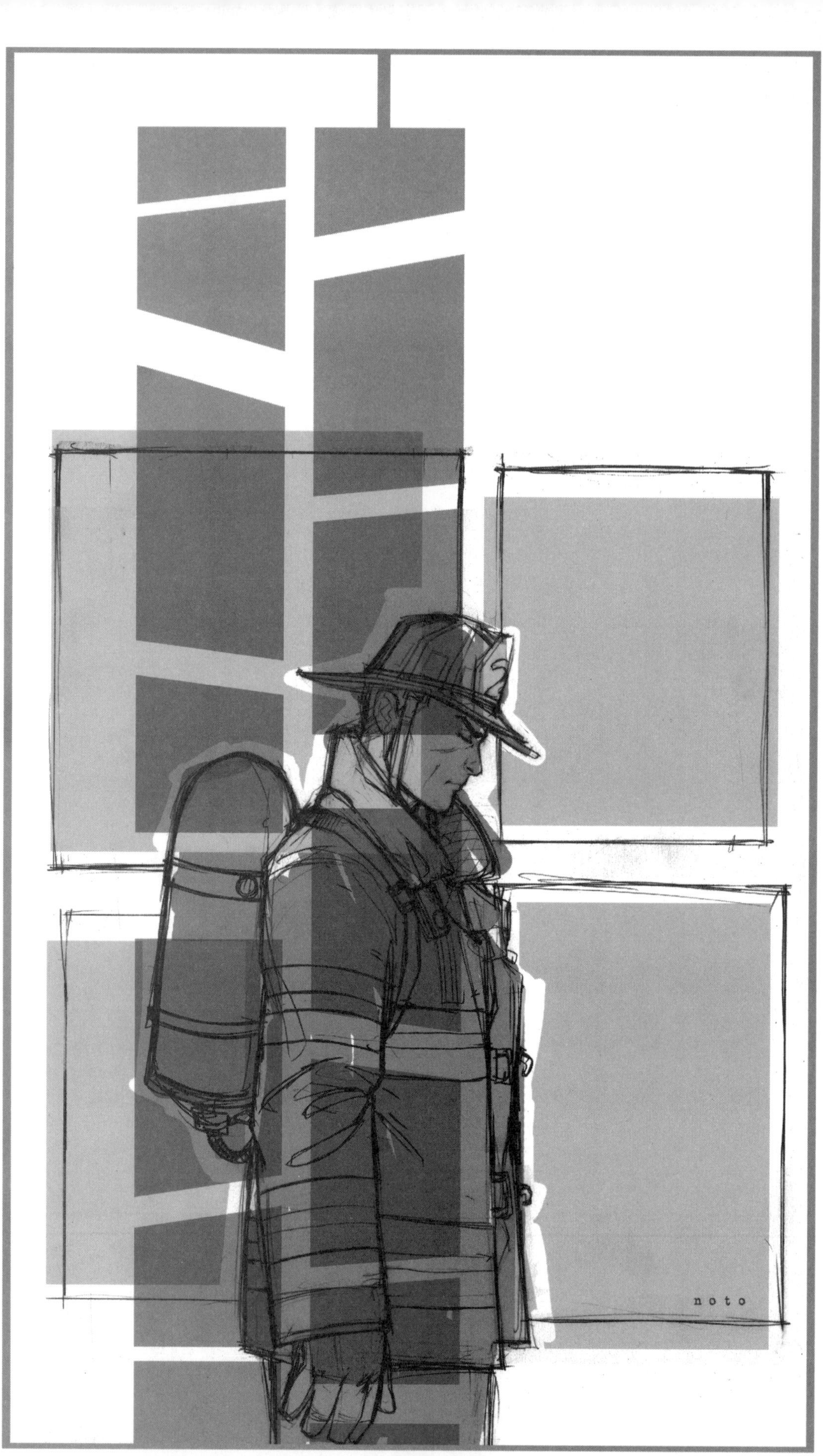
noto

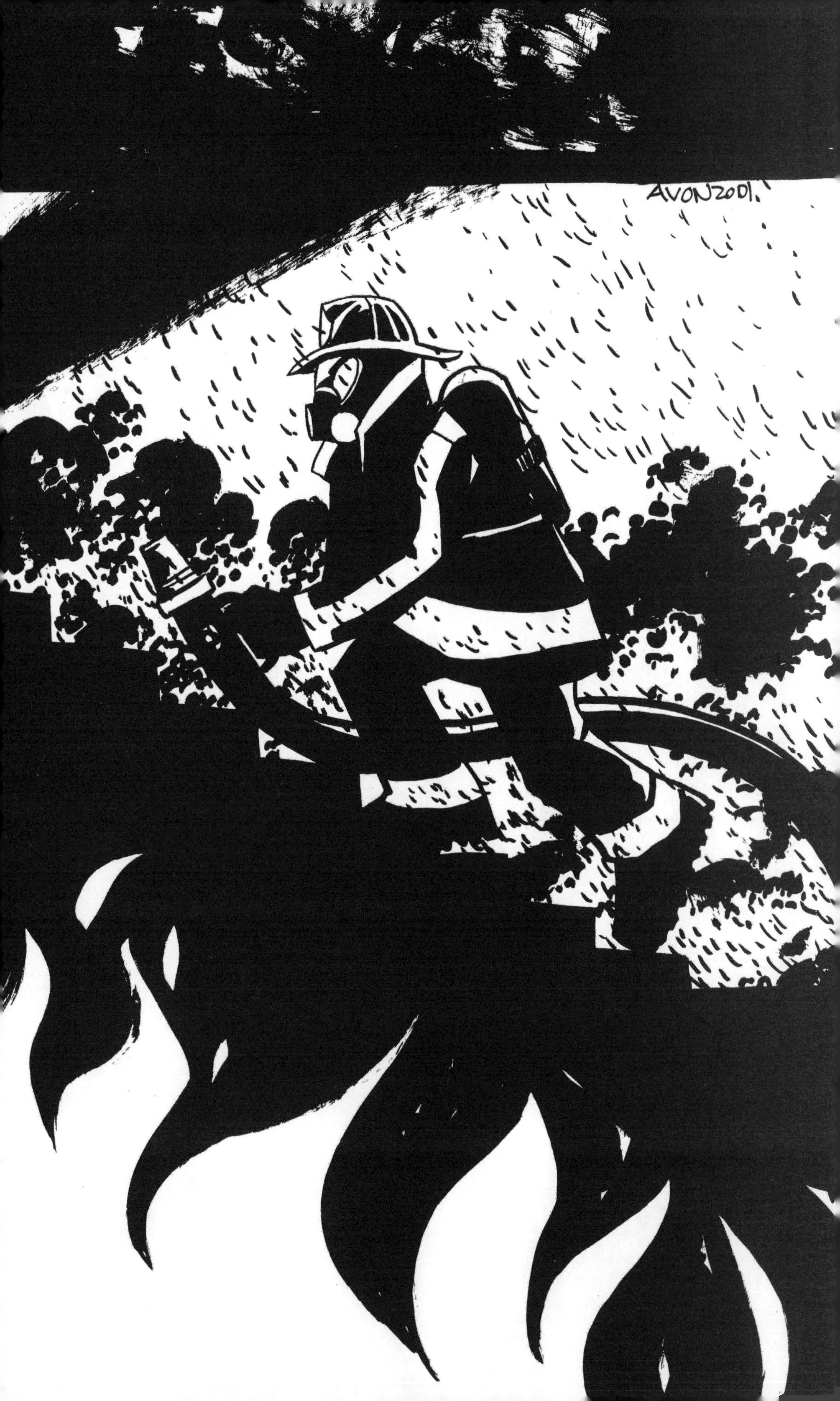
AVON2001.

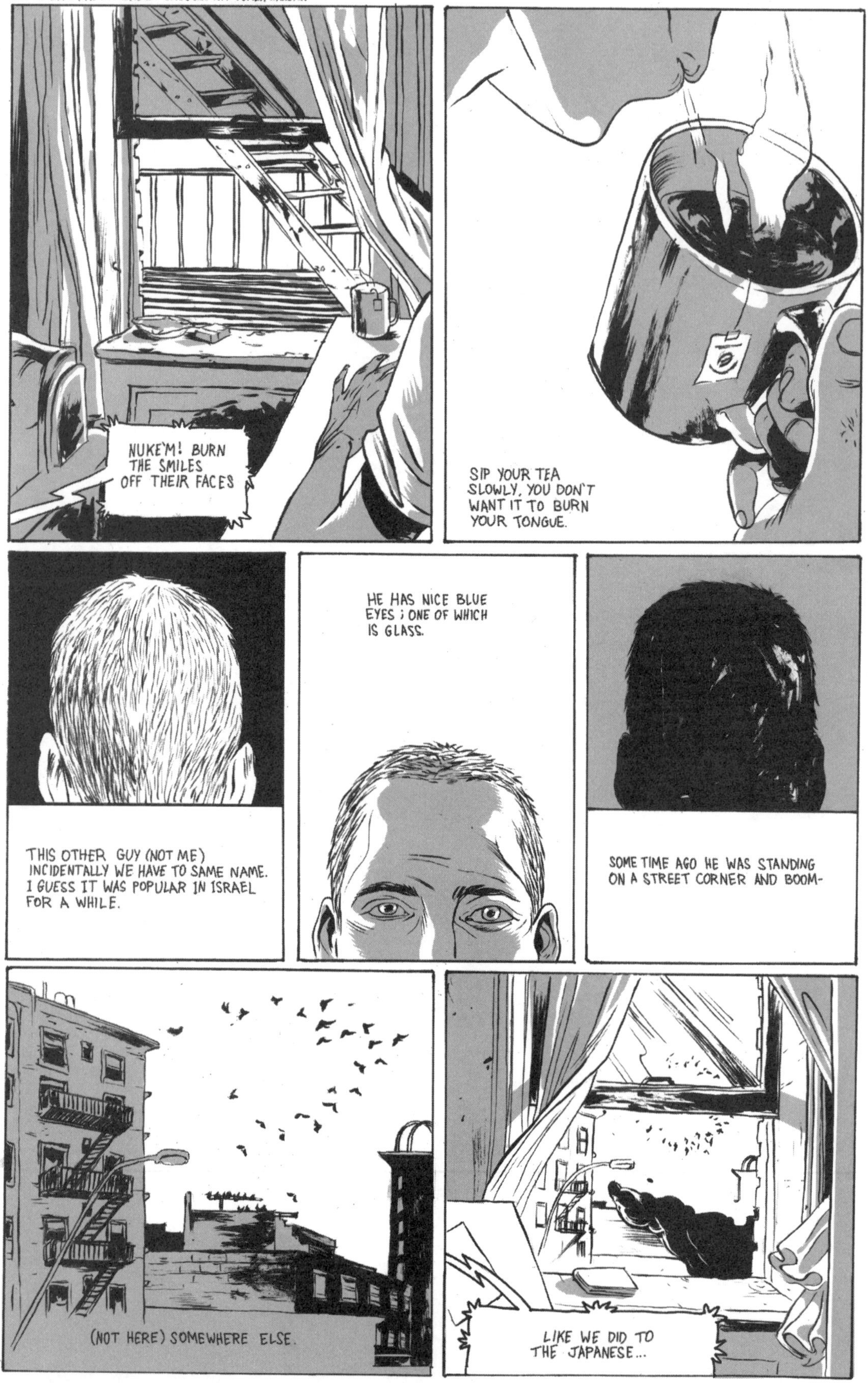
NUKE'M! BURN THE SMILES OFF THEIR FACES
SIP YOUR TEA SLOWLY. YOU DON'T WANT IT TO BURN YOUR TONGUE.
THIS OTHER GUY (NOT ME) INCIDENTALLY WE HAVE TO SAME NAME. I GUESS IT WAS POPULAR IN ISRAEL FOR A WHILE.
HE HAS NICE BLUE EYES ; ONE OF WHICH IS GLASS.
SOME TIME AGO HE WAS STANDING ON A STREET CORNER AND BOOM-
(NOT HERE) SOMEWHERE ELSE.
LIKE WE DID TO THE JAPANESE...

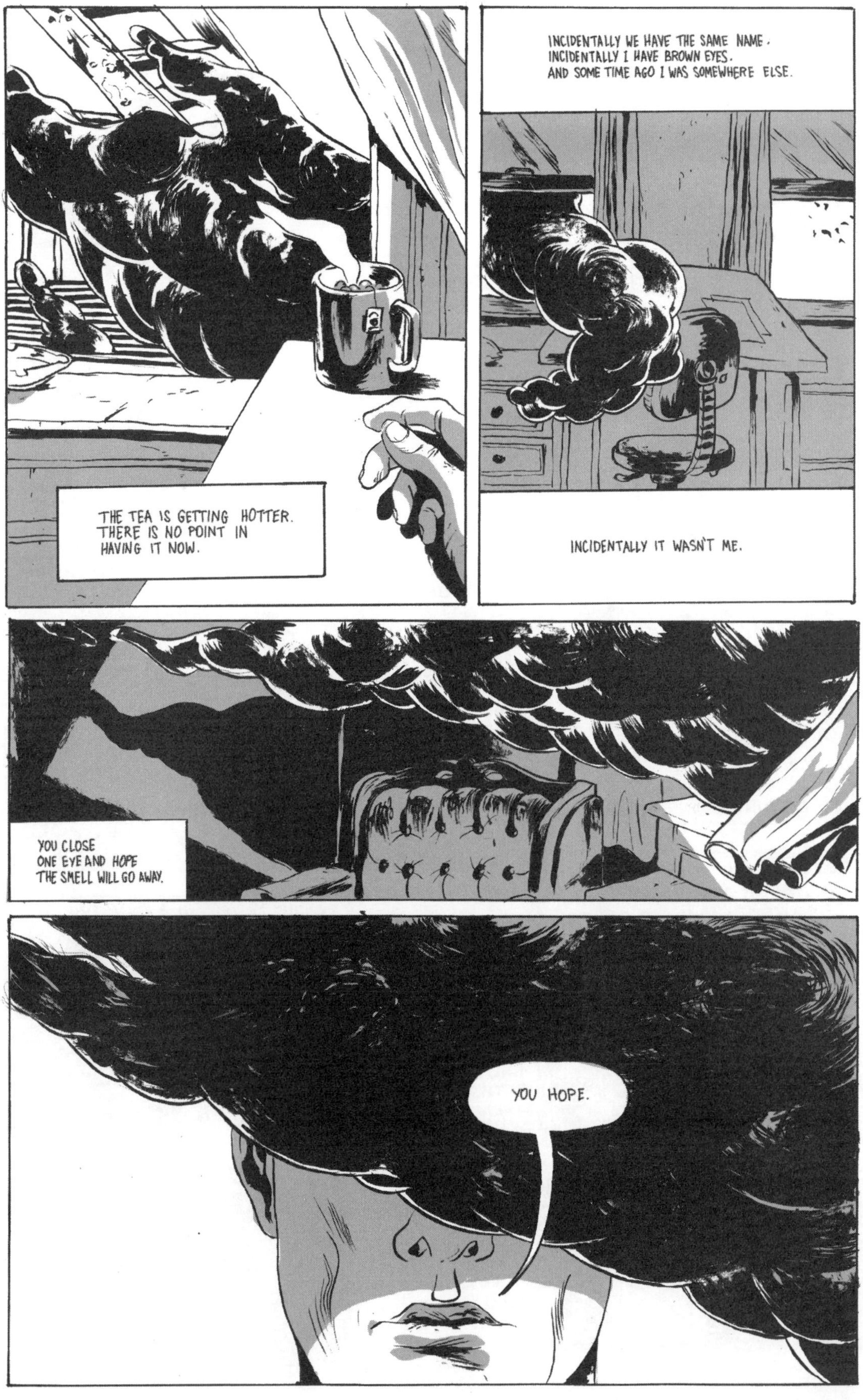
THE TEA IS GETTING HOTTER. THERE IS NO POINT IN HAVING IT NOW.
INCIDENTALLY WE HAVE THE SAME NAME. INCIDENTALLY I HAVE BROWN EYES. AND SOME TIME AGO I WAS SOMEWHERE ELSE.
INCIDENTALLY IT WASN'T ME.
YOU CLOSE ONE EYE AND HOPE THE SMELL WILL GO AWAY.
YOU HOPE.

COLLAPSE

BY JENNY GONZALEZ

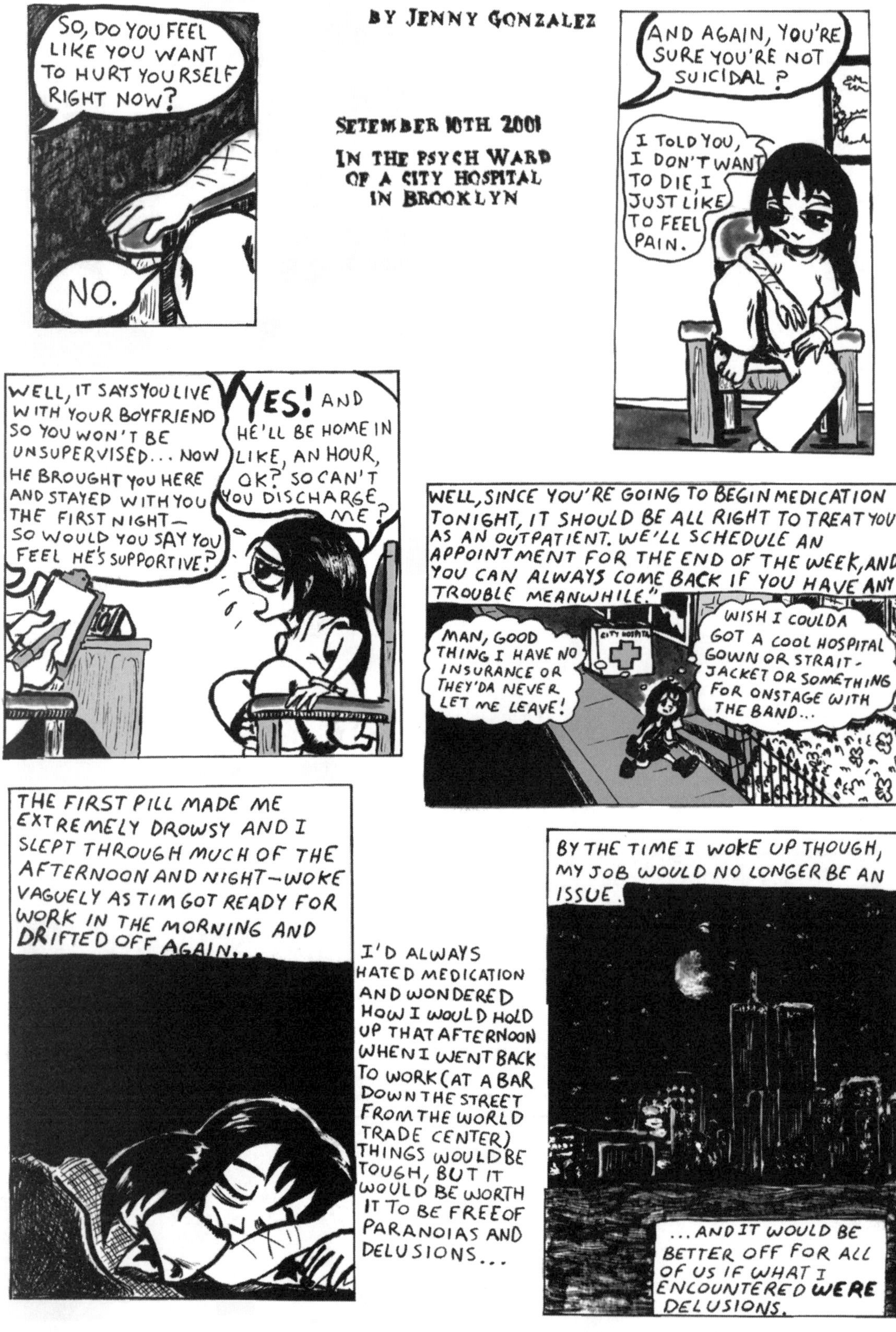

SO, DO YOU FEEL LIKE YOU WANT TO HURT YOURSELF RIGHT NOW?
NO.
SETEMBER 10TH 2001
IN THE PSYCH WARD OF A CITY HOSPITAL IN BROOKLYN
AND AGAIN, YOU'RE SURE YOU'RE NOT SUICIDAL?
I TOLD YOU, I DON'T WANT TO DIE, I JUST LIKE TO FEEL PAIN.
WELL, IT SAYS YOU LIVE WITH YOUR BOYFRIEND SO YOU WON'T BE UNSUPERVISED... NOW HE BROUGHT YOU HERE AND STAYED WITH YOU THE FIRST NIGHT— SO WOULD YOU SAY YOU FEEL HE'S SUPPORTIVE?
YES! AND HE'LL BE HOME IN LIKE, AN HOUR, OK? SO CAN'T YOU DISCHARGE ME?
WELL, SINCE YOU'RE GOING TO BEGIN MEDICATION TONIGHT, IT SHOULD BE ALL RIGHT TO TREAT YOU AS AN OUTPATIENT. WE'LL SCHEDULE AN APPOINTMENT FOR THE END OF THE WEEK, AND YOU CAN ALWAYS COME BACK IF YOU HAVE ANY TROUBLE MEANWHILE."
MAN, GOOD THING I HAVE NO INSURANCE OR THEY'DA NEVER LET ME LEAVE!
CITY HOSPITAL
WISH I COULDA GOT A COOL HOSPITAL GOWN OR STRAIT-JACKET OR SOMETHING FOR ONSTAGE WITH THE BAND...
THE FIRST PILL MADE ME EXTREMELY DROWSY AND I SLEPT THROUGH MUCH OF THE AFTERNOON AND NIGHT—WOKE VAGUELY AS TIM GOT READY FOR WORK IN THE MORNING AND DRIFTED OFF AGAIN...
I'D ALWAYS HATED MEDICATION AND WONDERED HOW I WOULD HOLD UP THAT AFTERNOON WHEN I WENT BACK TO WORK (AT A BAR DOWN THE STREET FROM THE WORLD TRADE CENTER) THINGS WOULD BE TOUGH, BUT IT WOULD BE WORTH IT TO BE FREE OF PARANOIAS AND DELUSIONS...
BY THE TIME I WOKE UP THOUGH, MY JOB WOULD NO LONGER BE AN ISSUE.
...AND IT WOULD BE BETTER OFF FOR ALL OF US IF WHAT I ENCOUNTERED WERE DELUSIONS.

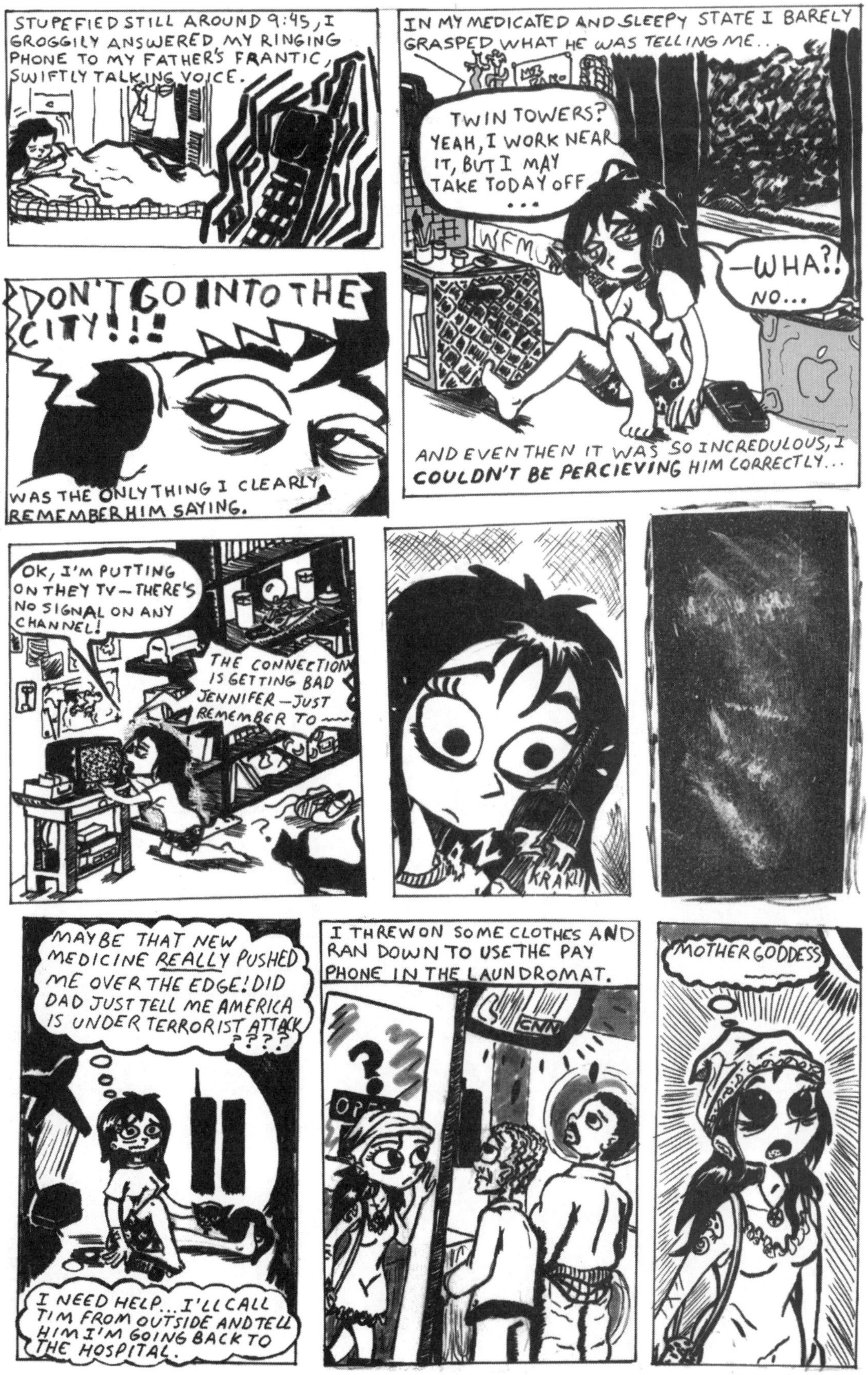
STUPEFIED STILL AROUND 9:45, I GROGGILY ANSWERED MY RINGING PHONE TO MY FATHER'S FRANTIC, SWIFTLY TALKING VOICE.
IN MY MEDICATED AND SLEEPY STATE I BARELY GRASPED WHAT HE WAS TELLING ME..
TWIN TOWERS? YEAH, I WORK NEAR IT, BUT I MAY TAKE TODAY OFF ...
WFMU
—WHA?! NO...
AND EVEN THEN IT WAS SO INCREDULOUS, I **COULDN'T BE PERCIEVING** HIM CORRECTLY...
DON'T GO INTO THE CITY!!!
WAS THE ONLY THING I CLEARLY REMEMBER HIM SAYING.
OK, I'M PUTTING ON THEY TV—THERE'S NO SIGNAL ON ANY CHANNEL!
THE CONNECTION IS GETTING BAD JENNIFER—JUST REMEMBER TO——
?
KRAK!
MAYBE THAT NEW MEDICINE REALLY PUSHED ME OVER THE EDGE! DID DAD JUST TELL ME AMERICA IS UNDER TERRORIST ATTACK ????
I NEED HELP... I'LL CALL TIM FROM OUTSIDE AND TELL HIM I'M GOING BACK TO THE HOSPITAL.
I THREW ON SOME CLOTHES AND RAN DOWN TO USE THE PAY PHONE IN THE LAUNDROMAT.
CNN
MOTHER GODDESS

THIS IS

ABERRATION ...

A DISTORTION

OF THE

CURRENT OF LIFE

IT WAS A HORRIFIC SIGHT

AND THEN SOMETHING THAT HAD NEVER OCCURED DURING ANY OF MY DELUSIONS OR PARANOIAS...

... EVERYONE ELSE WAS REACTING TO THE SAME THING I THOUGHT — I KNEW I SAW.

I GOTTA FIND OUT ABOUT MY SISTER — SHE WAS WORKING IN THE SECOND BUILDING!

OH, LORD JESUS

IT WAS REAL.

I MANAGED TO GET THROUGH TO TIM ON THE PAY PHONE. I REMEMBER THE FIRST THING HE SAID WHEN HE HEARD MY VOICE...

I LOVE YOU SWEETIE BUT I DON'T KNOW WHEN I CAN LEAVE THE CITY.

THAT FOR SOME REASON IS WHAT REALLY BROUGHT THE SITUATION HOME.

I LOVE YOU TOO — BUT I DON'T WANT YOU IN MANHATTAN — IT'S TOO DANGEROUS! I MEAN WHAT IF THE EMPIRE STATE IS NEXT???

DON'T THINK I DIDN'T THINK OF THAT. AND I DON'T WANT TO LEAVE YOU ALONE, BUT I'M STRANDED AT THE OFFICE.

BED-STUY WAS FAIRLY QUIET EXCEPT FOR THE LOW, REVERENTIAL TONES OF THE FEW PEOPLE OUT DISCUSSING THE DISASTER OR FUMBLING WITH SPORADICALLY WORKING CEL AND PAY PHONES.

BUT IN THE SILENCE I COULD HEAR THE CRIES OF THOUSANDS OF PASSING SOULS

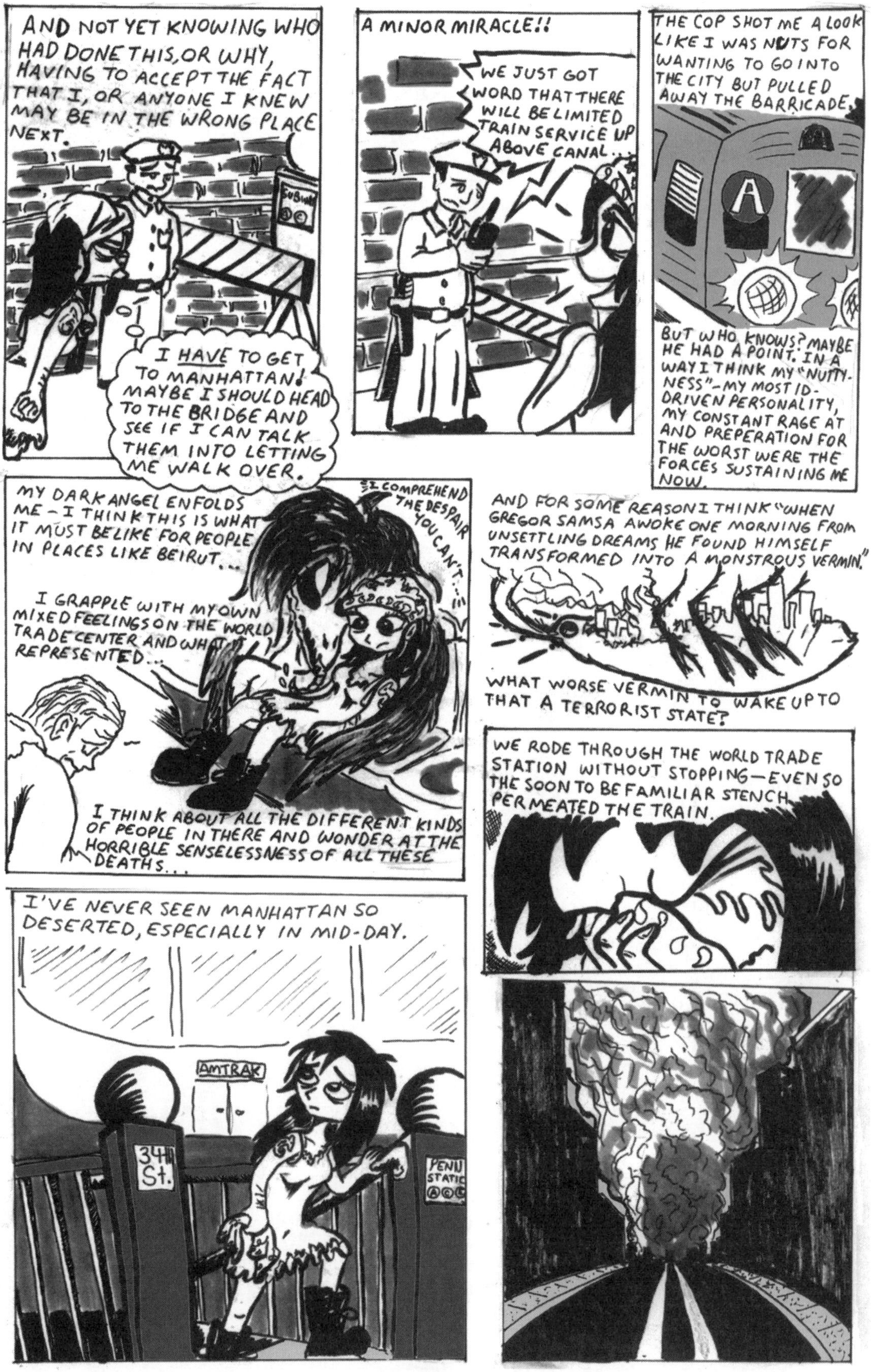
AND NOT YET KNOWING WHO HAD DONE THIS, OR WHY, HAVING TO ACCEPT THE FACT THAT I, OR ANYONE I KNEW MAY BE IN THE WRONG PLACE NEXT.
SUBWAY
I HAVE TO GET TO MANHATTAN! MAYBE I SHOULD HEAD TO THE BRIDGE AND SEE IF I CAN TALK THEM INTO LETTING ME WALK OVER.
A MINOR MIRACLE!!
WE JUST GOT WORD THAT THERE WILL BE LIMITED TRAIN SERVICE UP ABOVE CANAL...
THE COP SHOT ME A LOOK LIKE I WAS NUTS FOR WANTING TO GO INTO THE CITY BUT PULLED AWAY THE BARRICADE.
A
BUT WHO KNOWS? MAYBE HE HAD A POINT. IN A WAY I THINK MY "NUTTY-NESS"- MY MOST ID-DRIVEN PERSONALITY, MY CONSTANT RAGE AT AND PREPERATION FOR THE WORST WERE THE FORCES SUSTAINING ME NOW.
MY DARK ANGEL ENFOLDS ME - I THINK THIS IS WHAT IT MUST BE LIKE FOR PEOPLE IN PLACES LIKE BEIRUT...
I COMPREHEND THE DESPAIR YOU CAN'T...!!
I GRAPPLE WITH MY OWN MIXED FEELINGS ON THE WORLD TRADE CENTER AND WHAT IT REPRESENTED...
I THINK ABOUT ALL THE DIFFERENT KINDS OF PEOPLE IN THERE AND WONDER AT THE HORRIBLE SENSELESSNESS OF ALL THESE DEATHS...
AND FOR SOME REASON I THINK "WHEN GREGOR SAMSA AWOKE ONE MORNING FROM UNSETTLING DREAMS HE FOUND HIMSELF TRANSFORMED INTO A MONSTROUS VERMIN."
WHAT WORSE VERMIN TO WAKE UP TO THAT A TERRORIST STATE?
WE RODE THROUGH THE WORLD TRADE STATION WITHOUT STOPPING—EVEN SO THE SOON TO BE FAMILIAR STENCH PERMEATED THE TRAIN.
I'VE NEVER SEEN MANHATTAN SO DESERTED, ESPECIALLY IN MID-DAY.
AMTRAK
34th St.
PENN STATIO

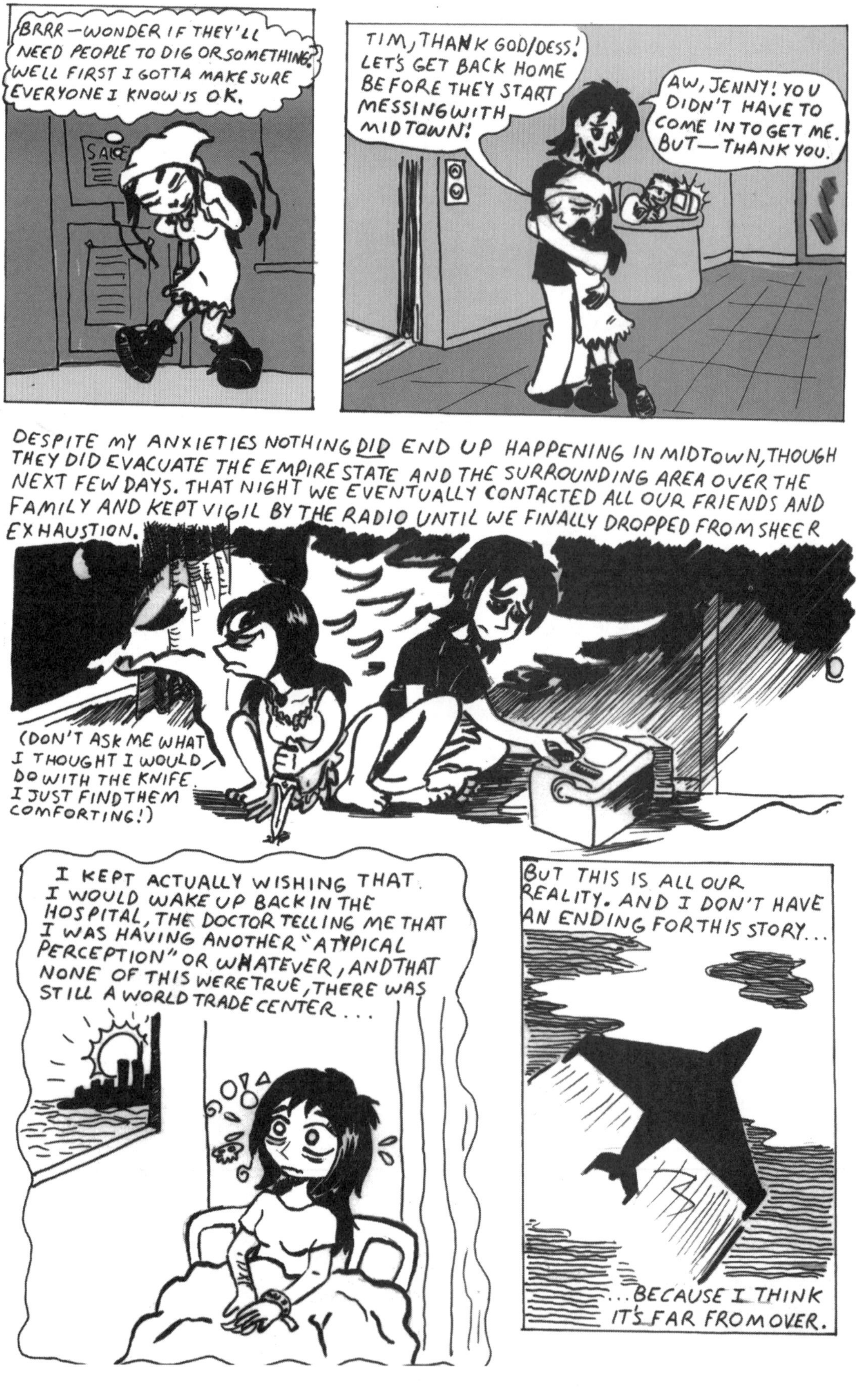
BRRR—WONDER IF THEY'LL NEED PEOPLE TO DIG OR SOMETHING. WELL FIRST I GOTTA MAKE SURE EVERYONE I KNOW IS OK.
TIM, THANK GOD/DESS! LET'S GET BACK HOME BEFORE THEY START MESSING WITH MIDTOWN!
AW, JENNY! YOU DIDN'T HAVE TO COME IN TO GET ME. BUT—THANK YOU.
DESPITE MY ANXIETIES NOTHING DID END UP HAPPENING IN MIDTOWN, THOUGH THEY DID EVACUATE THE EMPIRE STATE AND THE SURROUNDING AREA OVER THE NEXT FEW DAYS. THAT NIGHT WE EVENTUALLY CONTACTED ALL OUR FRIENDS AND FAMILY AND KEPT VIGIL BY THE RADIO UNTIL WE FINALLY DROPPED FROM SHEER EXHAUSTION.
(DON'T ASK ME WHAT I THOUGHT I WOULD DO WITH THE KNIFE. I JUST FIND THEM COMFORTING!)
I KEPT ACTUALLY WISHING THAT I WOULD WAKE UP BACK IN THE HOSPITAL, THE DOCTOR TELLING ME THAT I WAS HAVING ANOTHER "ATYPICAL PERCEPTION" OR WHATEVER, AND THAT NONE OF THIS WERE TRUE, THERE WAS STILL A WORLD TRADE CENTER...
BUT THIS IS ALL OUR REALITY. AND I DON'T HAVE AN ENDING FOR THIS STORY...
...BECAUSE I THINK IT'S FAR FROM OVER.

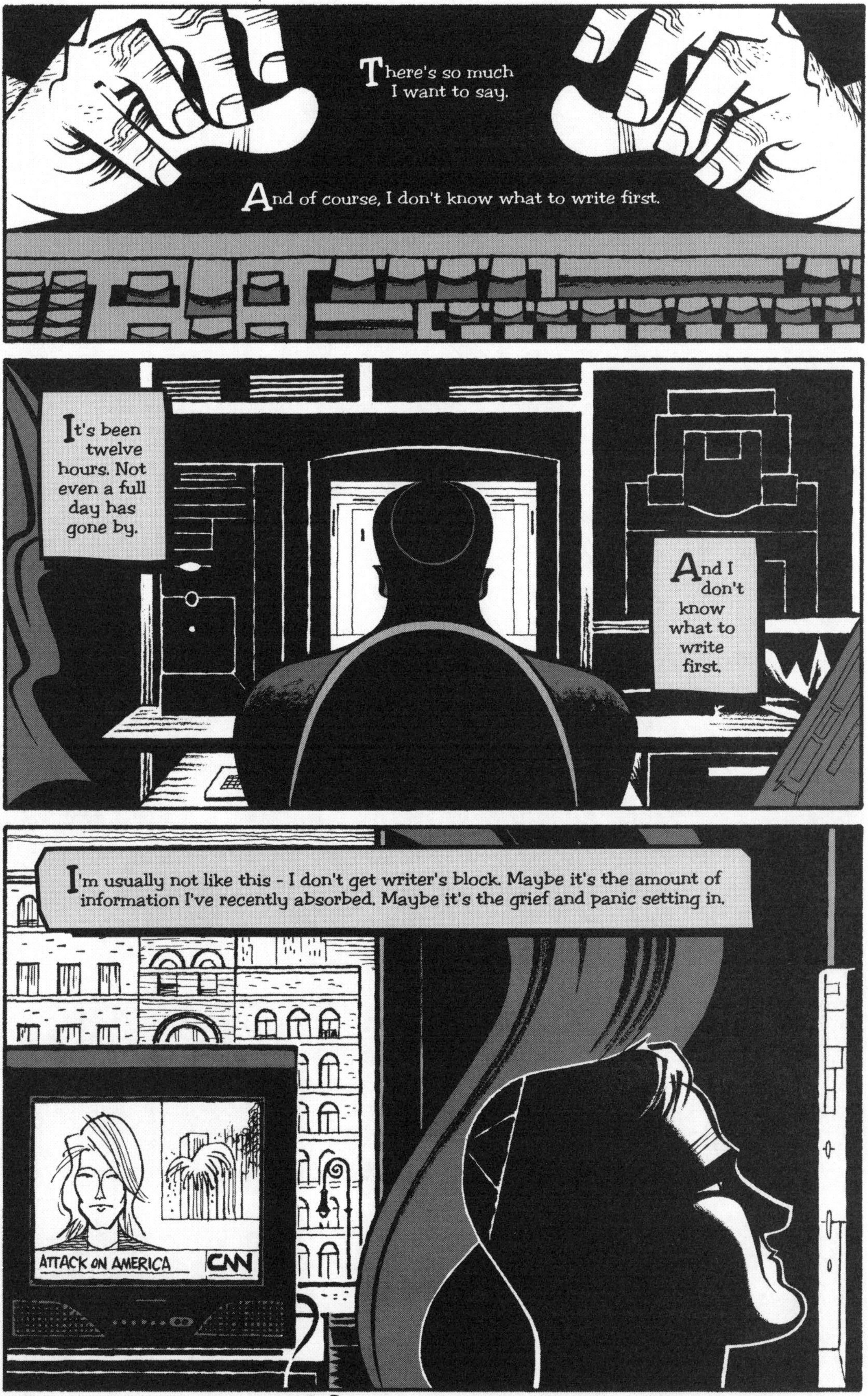
There's so much I want to say.
And of course, I don't know what to write first.
It's been twelve hours. Not even a full day has gone by.
And I don't know what to write first.
I'm usually not like this - I don't get writer's block. Maybe it's the amount of information I've recently absorbed. Maybe it's the grief and panic setting in.
ATTACK ON AMERICA
CNN
Maybe it's the tears — I don't know. But I really need to write this all down, and for that I need to know where to start.

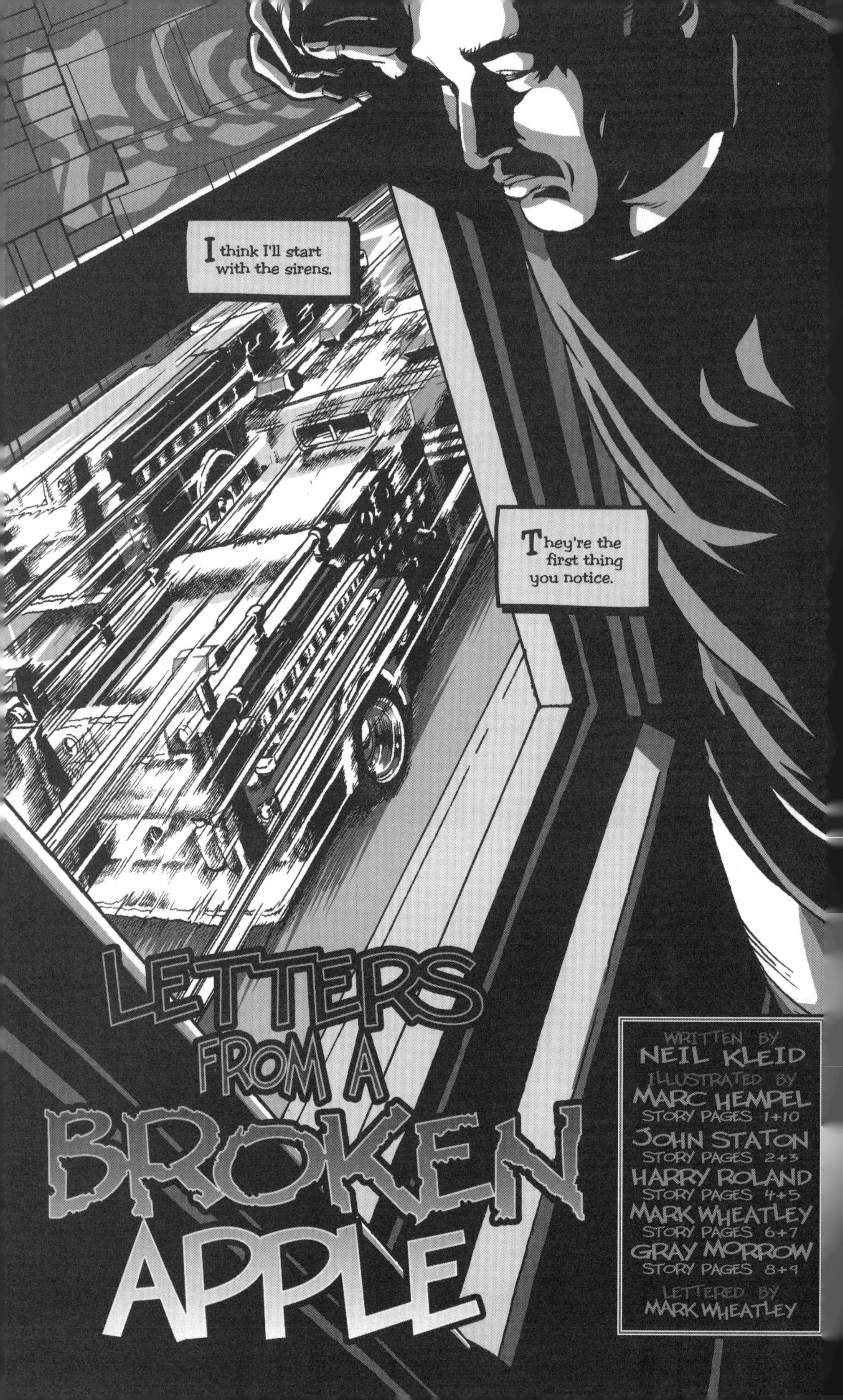
I think I'll start with the sirens.
They're the first thing you notice.
LETTERS FROM A BROKEN APPLE
WRITTEN BY NEIL KLEID
ILLUSTRATED BY MARC HEMPEL STORY PAGES 1+10
JOHN STATON STORY PAGES 2+3
HARRY ROLAND STORY PAGES 4+5
MARK WHEATLEY STORY PAGES 6+7
GRAY MORROW STORY PAGES 8+9
LETTERED BY MARK WHEATLEY

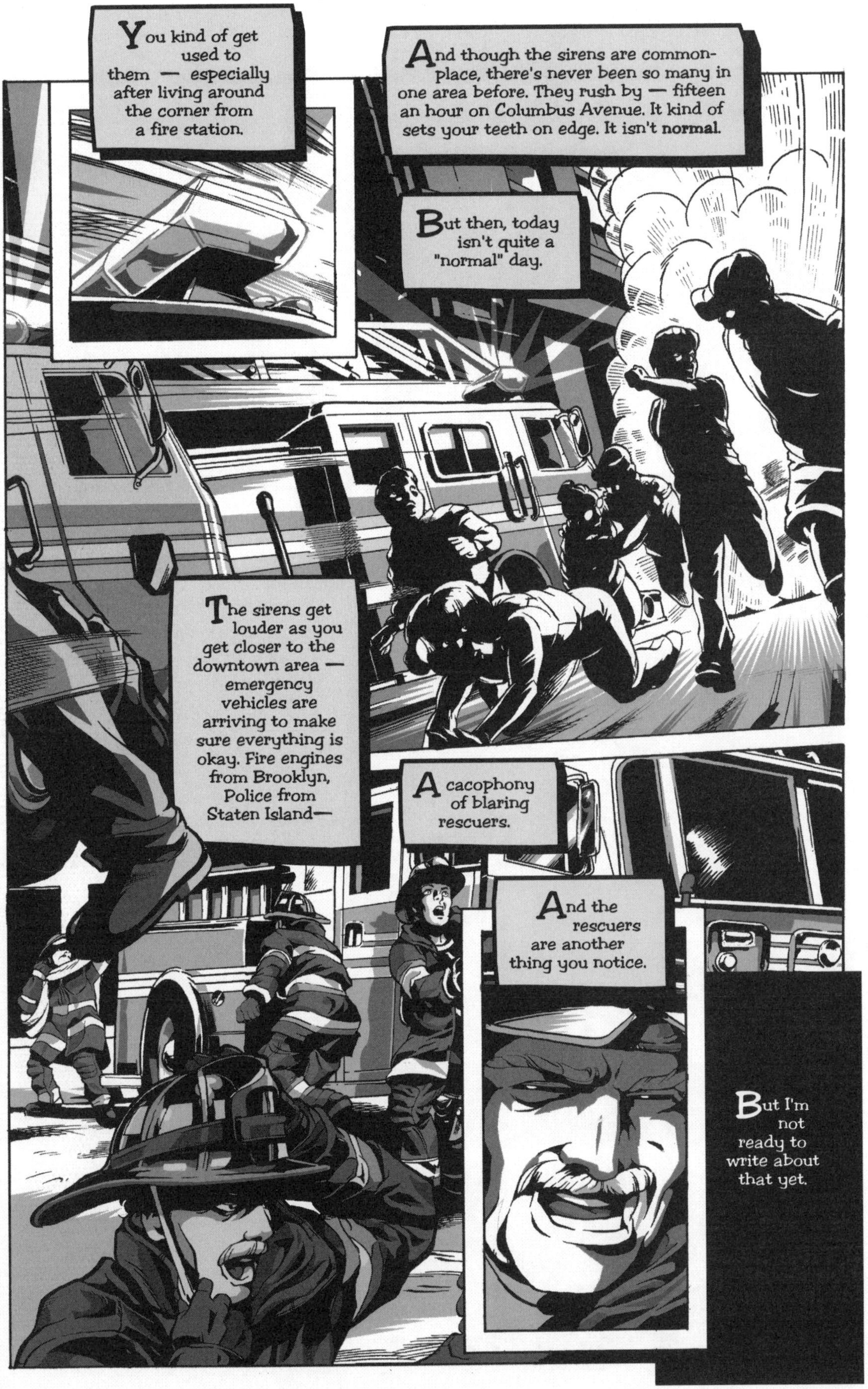
You kind of get used to them — especially after living around the corner from a fire station.
And though the sirens are commonplace, there's never been so many in one area before. They rush by — fifteen an hour on Columbus Avenue. It kind of sets your teeth on edge. It isn't **normal**.
But then, today isn't quite a "normal" day.
The sirens get louder as you get closer to the downtown area — emergency vehicles are arriving to make sure everything is okay. Fire engines from Brooklyn, Police from Staten Island—
A cacophony of blaring rescuers.
And the rescuers are another thing you notice.
But I'm not ready to write about that yet.

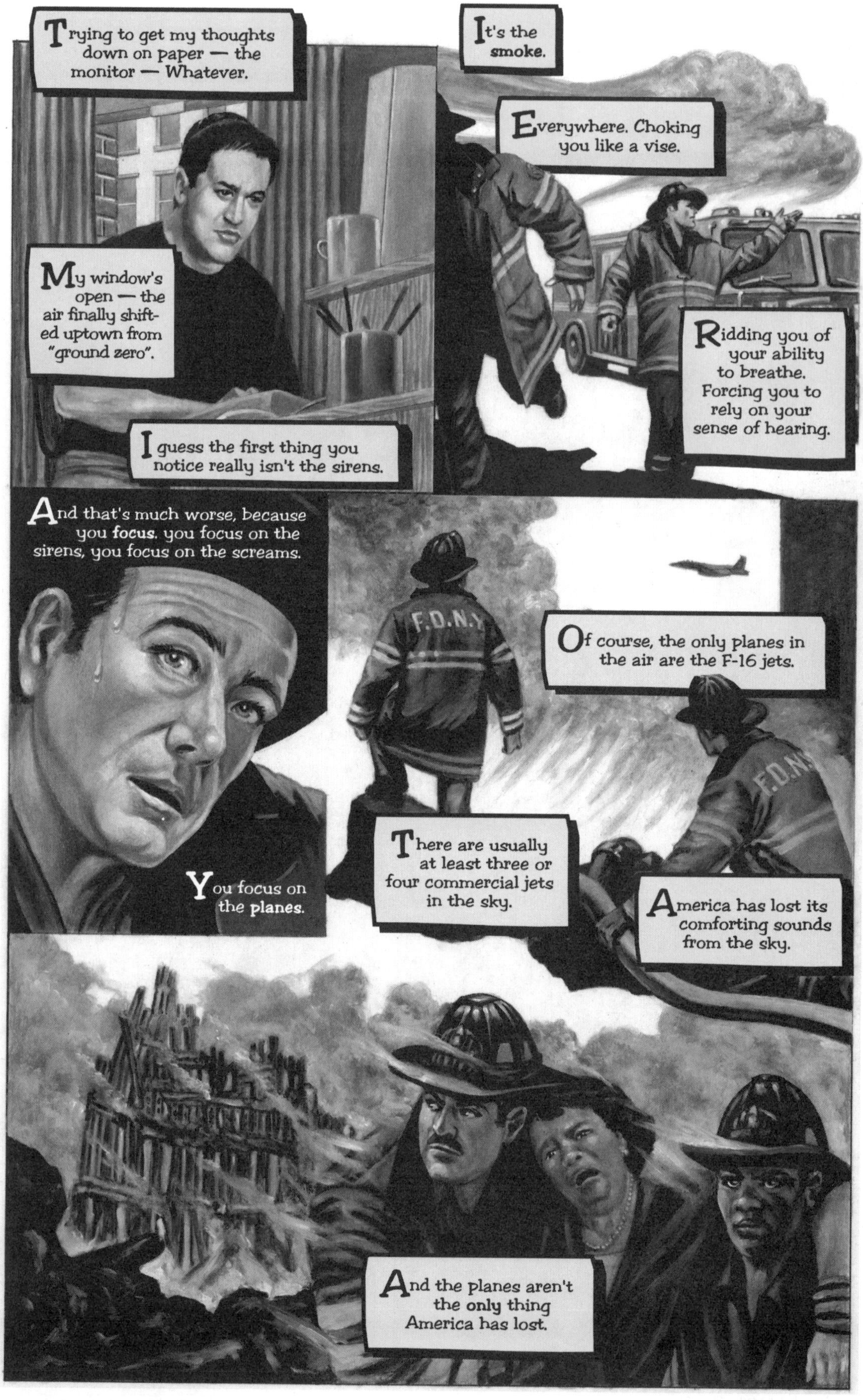
Trying to get my thoughts down on paper — the monitor — Whatever.
My window's open — the air finally shifted uptown from "ground zero".
I guess the first thing you notice really isn't the sirens.
It's the smoke.
Everywhere. Choking you like a vise.
Ridding you of your ability to breathe. Forcing you to rely on your sense of hearing.
And that's much worse, because you focus. you focus on the sirens, you focus on the screams.
You focus on the planes.
F.D.N.Y.
Of course, the only planes in the air are the F-16 jets.
F.D.N.
There are usually at least three or four commercial jets in the sky.
America has lost its comforting sounds from the sky.
And the planes aren't the only thing America has lost.

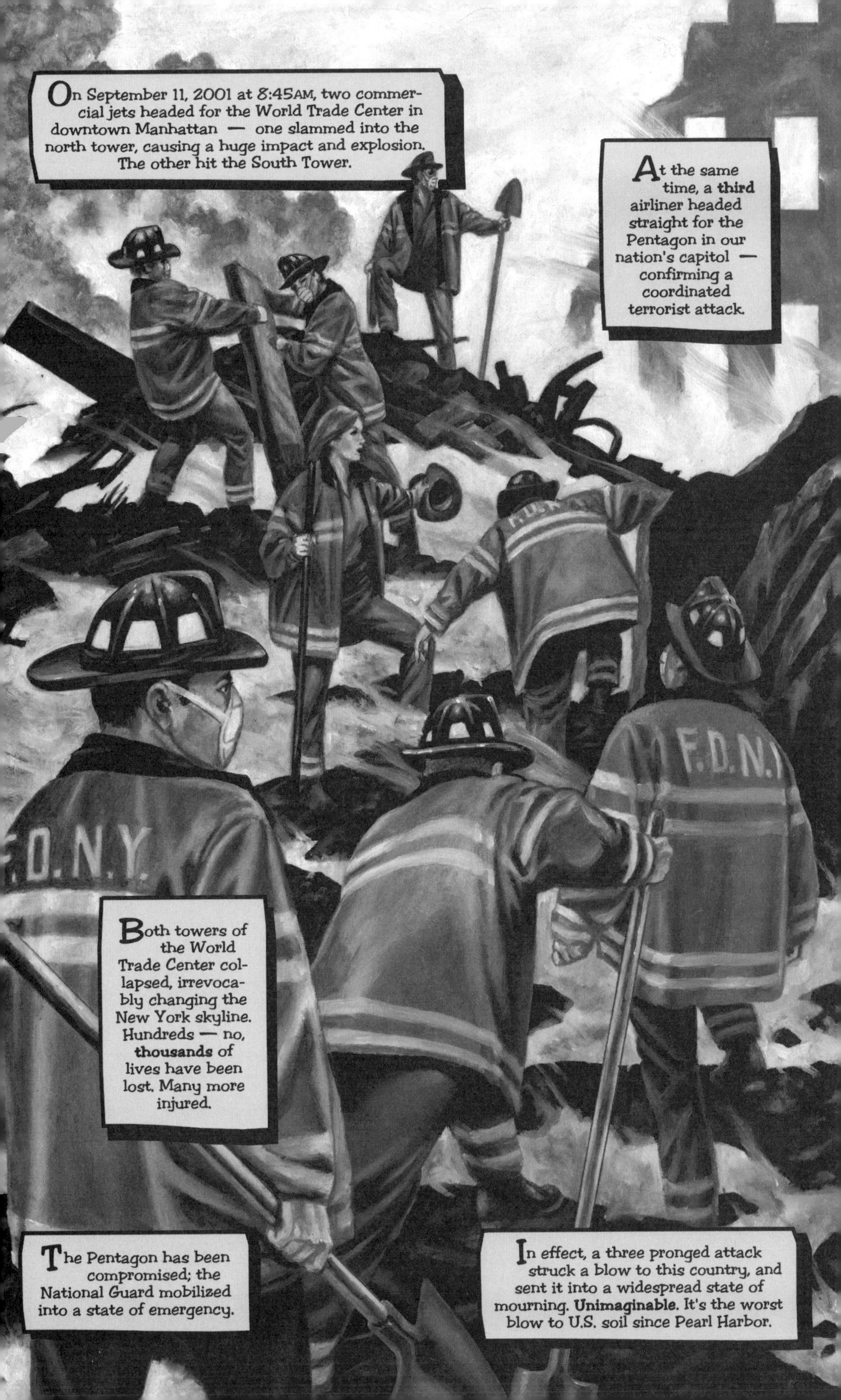
On September 11, 2001 at 8:45AM, two commercial jets headed for the World Trade Center in downtown Manhattan — one slammed into the north tower, causing a huge impact and explosion. The other hit the South Tower.
At the same time, a **third** airliner headed straight for the Pentagon in our nation's capitol — confirming a coordinated terrorist attack.
Both towers of the World Trade Center collapsed, irrevocably changing the New York skyline. Hundreds — no, **thousands** of lives have been lost. Many more injured.
The Pentagon has been compromised; the National Guard mobilized into a state of emergency.
In effect, a three pronged attack struck a blow to this country, and sent it into a widespread state of mourning. **Unimaginable.** It's the worst blow to U.S. soil since Pearl Harbor.
F.D.N.Y.
D.N.Y.
F.D.N.

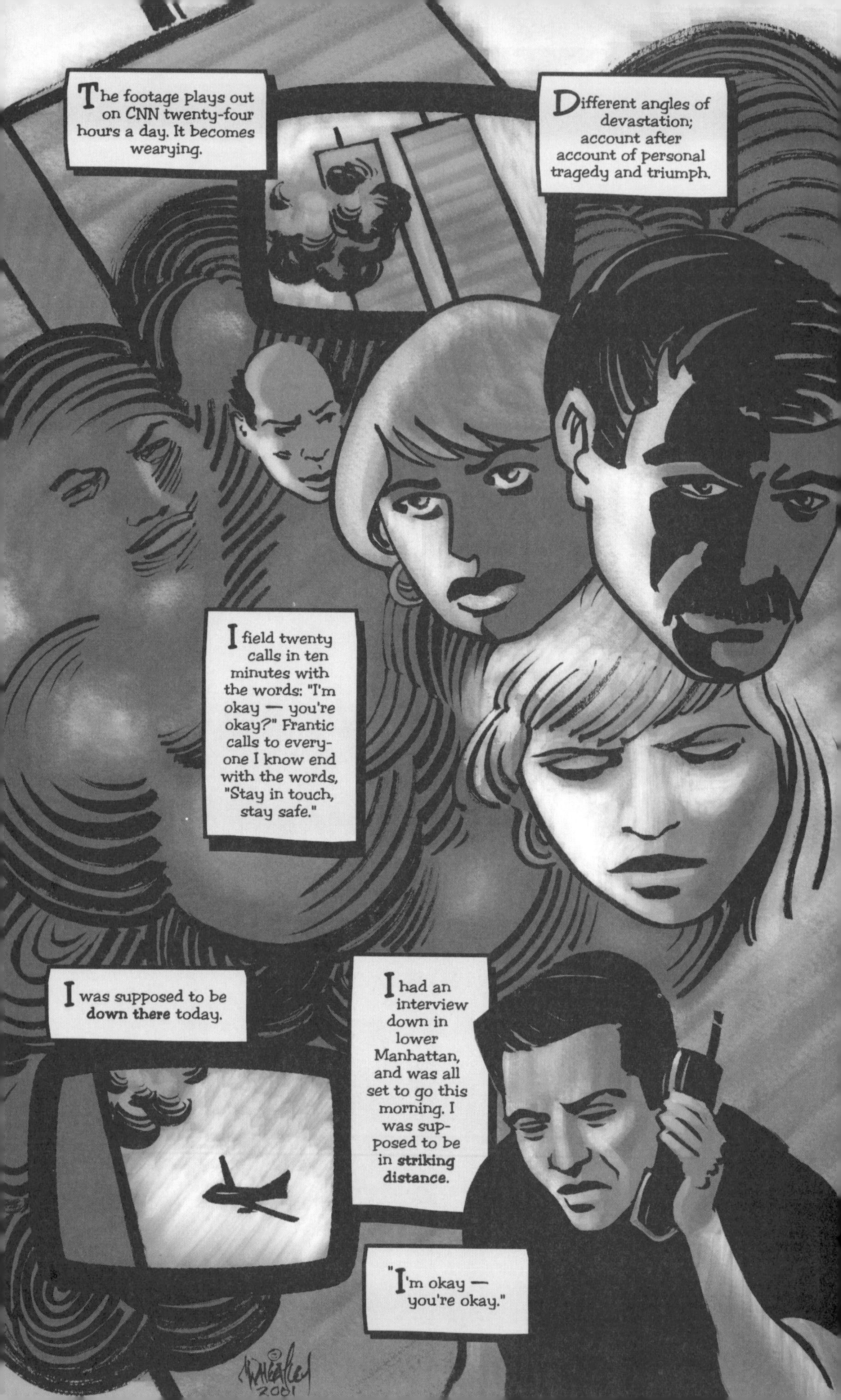
The footage plays out on CNN twenty-four hours a day. It becomes wearying.
Different angles of devastation; account after account of personal tragedy and triumph.
I field twenty calls in ten minutes with the words: "I'm okay — you're okay?" Frantic calls to everyone I know end with the words, "Stay in touch, stay safe."
I was supposed to be **down there** today.
I had an interview down in lower Manhattan, and was all set to go this morning. I was supposed to be in **striking distance**.
"I'm okay — you're okay."
2001

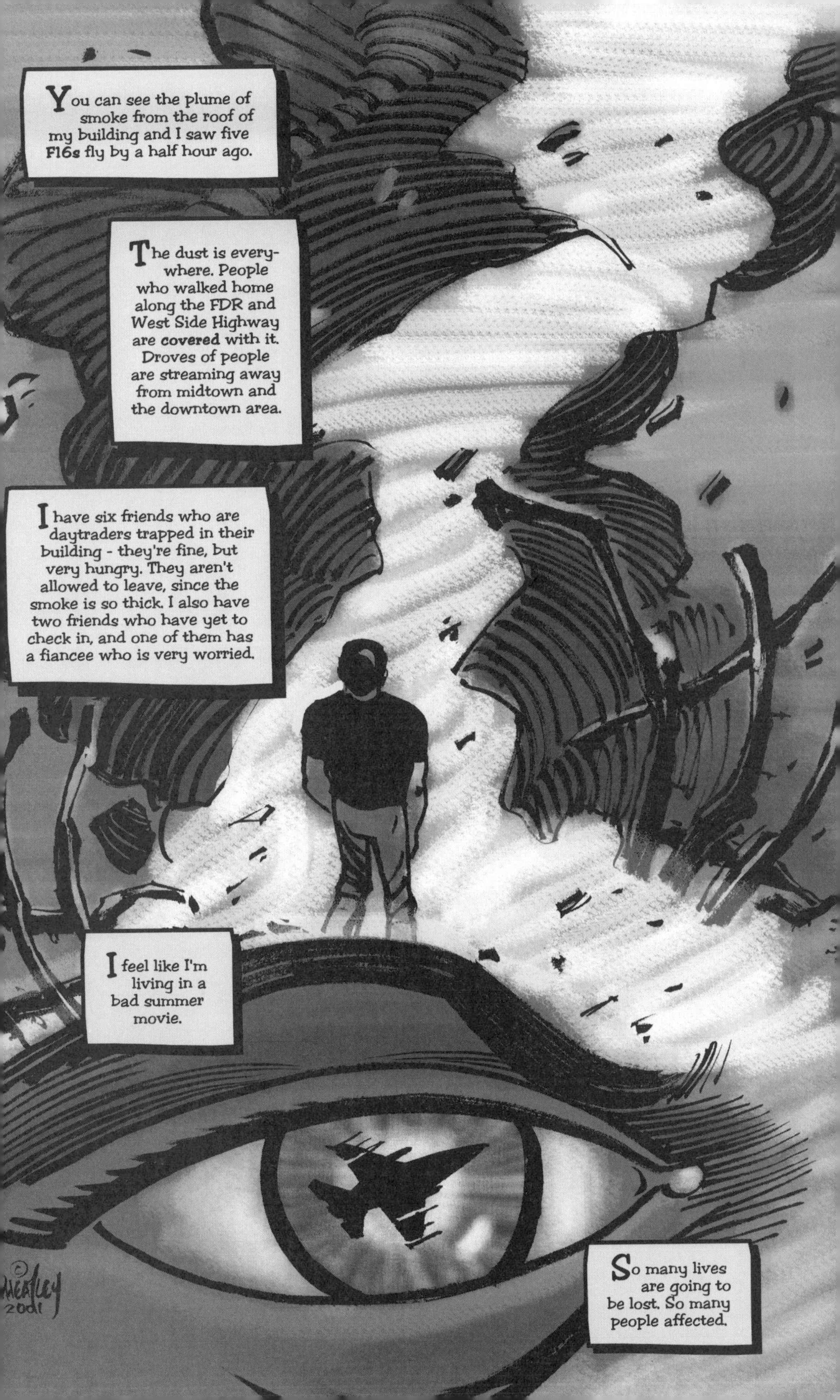
You can see the plume of smoke from the roof of my building and I saw five F16s fly by a half hour ago.
The dust is everywhere. People who walked home along the FDR and West Side Highway are covered with it. Droves of people are streaming away from midtown and the downtown area.
I have six friends who are daytraders trapped in their building - they're fine, but very hungry. They aren't allowed to leave, since the smoke is so thick. I also have two friends who have yet to check in, and one of them has a fiancee who is very worried.
I feel like I'm living in a bad summer movie.
So many lives are going to be lost. So many people affected.

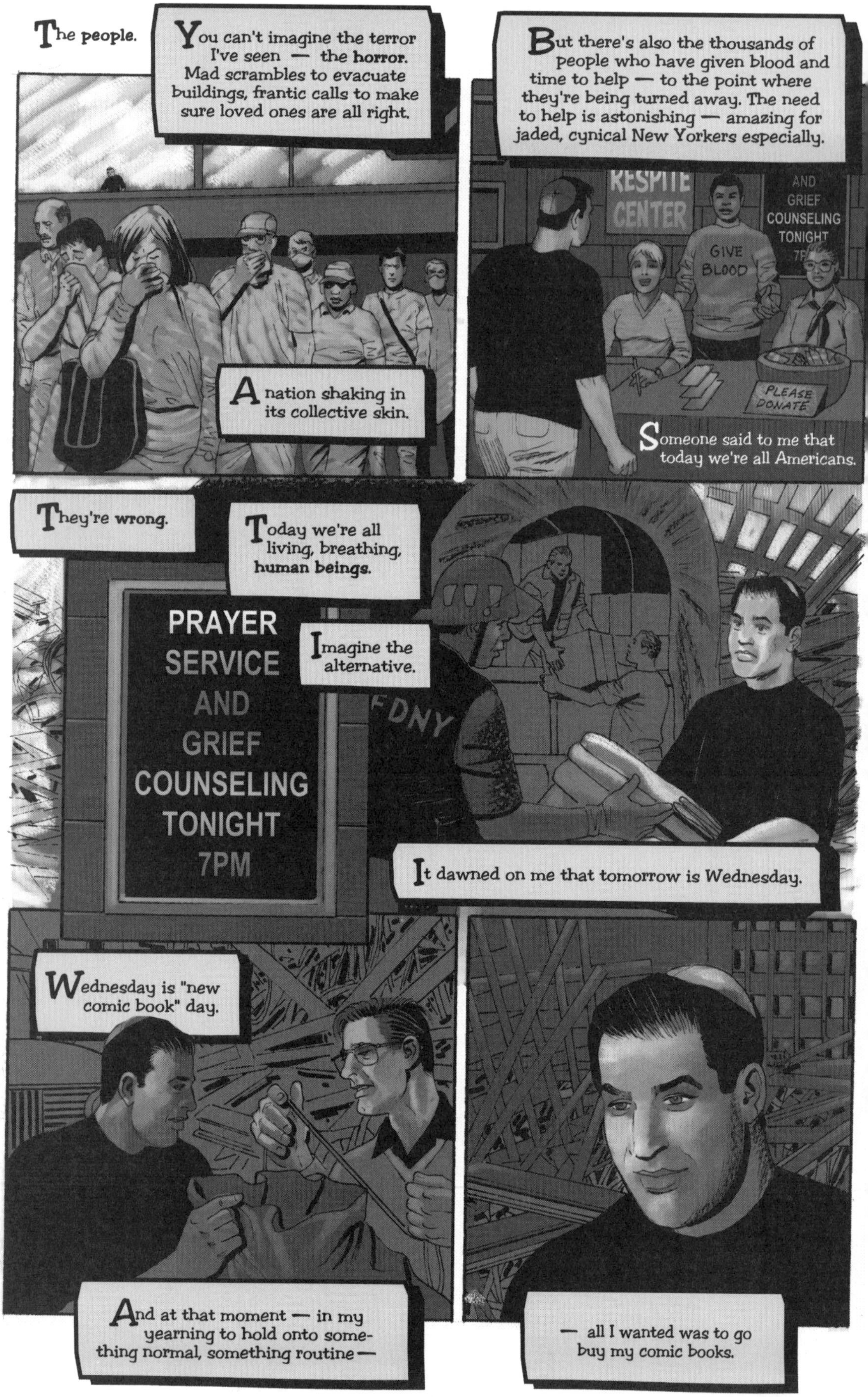
The people.
You can't imagine the terror I've seen — the **horror**. Mad scrambles to evacuate buildings, frantic calls to make sure loved ones are all right.
A nation shaking in its collective skin.
But there's also the thousands of people who have given blood and time to help — to the point where they're being turned away. The need to help is astonishing — amazing for jaded, cynical New Yorkers especially.
RESPITE CENTER
GIVE BLOOD
PLEASE DONATE
Someone said to me that today we're all Americans.
They're **wrong**.
Today we're all living, breathing, **human beings**.
PRAYER SERVICE AND GRIEF COUNSELING TONIGHT 7PM
Imagine the alternative.
FDNY
It dawned on me that tomorrow is Wednesday.
Wednesday is "new comic book" day.
And at that moment — in my yearning to hold onto something normal, something routine —
— all I wanted was to go buy my comic books.

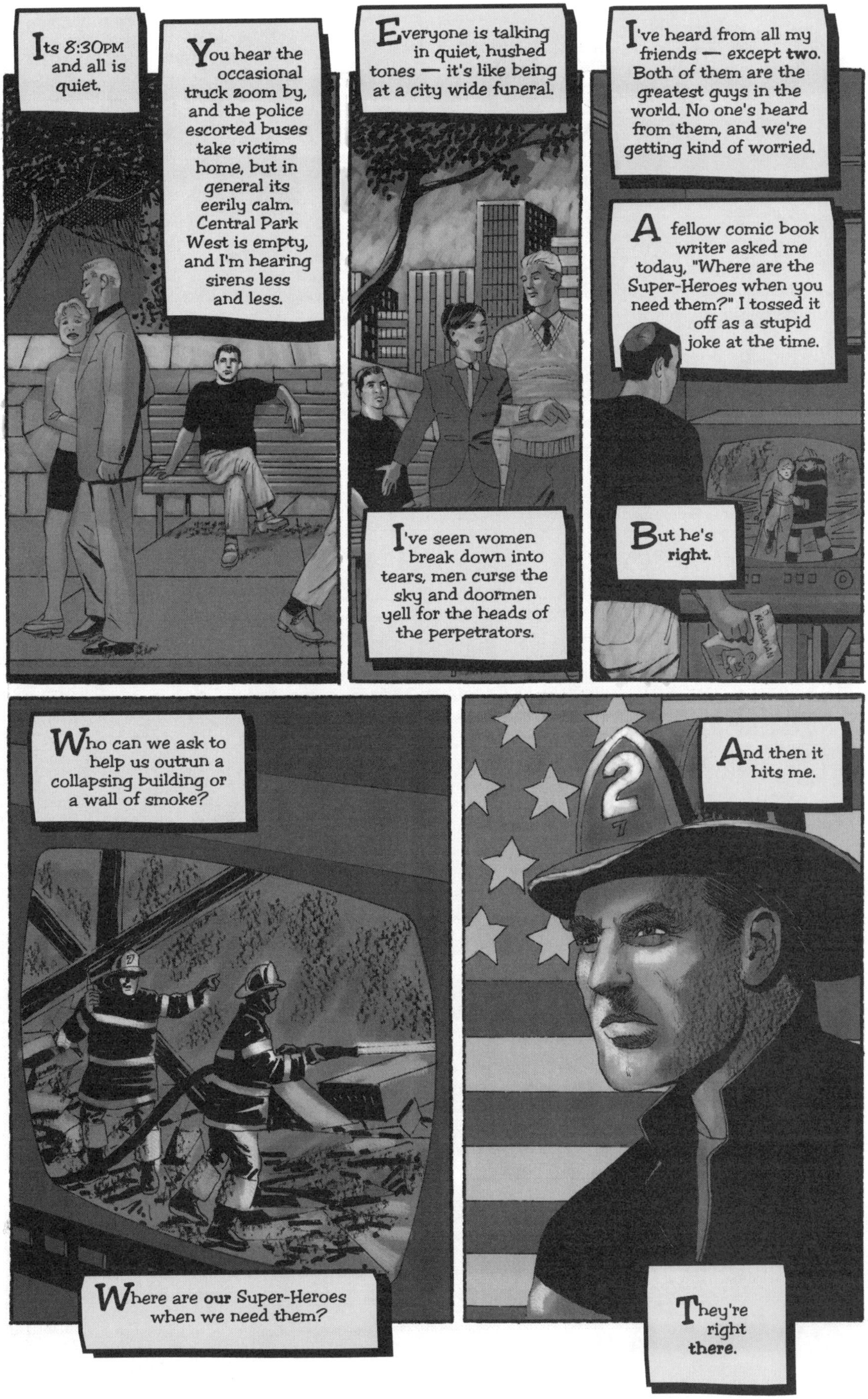

Its 8:30PM and all is quiet.
You hear the occasional truck zoom by, and the police escorted buses take victims home, but in general its eerily calm. Central Park West is empty, and I'm hearing sirens less and less.
Everyone is talking in quiet, hushed tones — it's like being at a city wide funeral.
I've seen women break down into tears, men curse the sky and doormen yell for the heads of the perpetrators.
I've heard from all my friends — except **two**. Both of them are the greatest guys in the world. No one's heard from them, and we're getting kind of worried.
A fellow comic book writer asked me today, "Where are the Super-Heroes when you need them?" I tossed it off as a stupid joke at the time.
But he's **right**.
Who can we ask to help us outrun a collapsing building or a wall of smoke?
Where are **our** Super-Heroes when we need them?
And then it hits me.
They're right **there**.

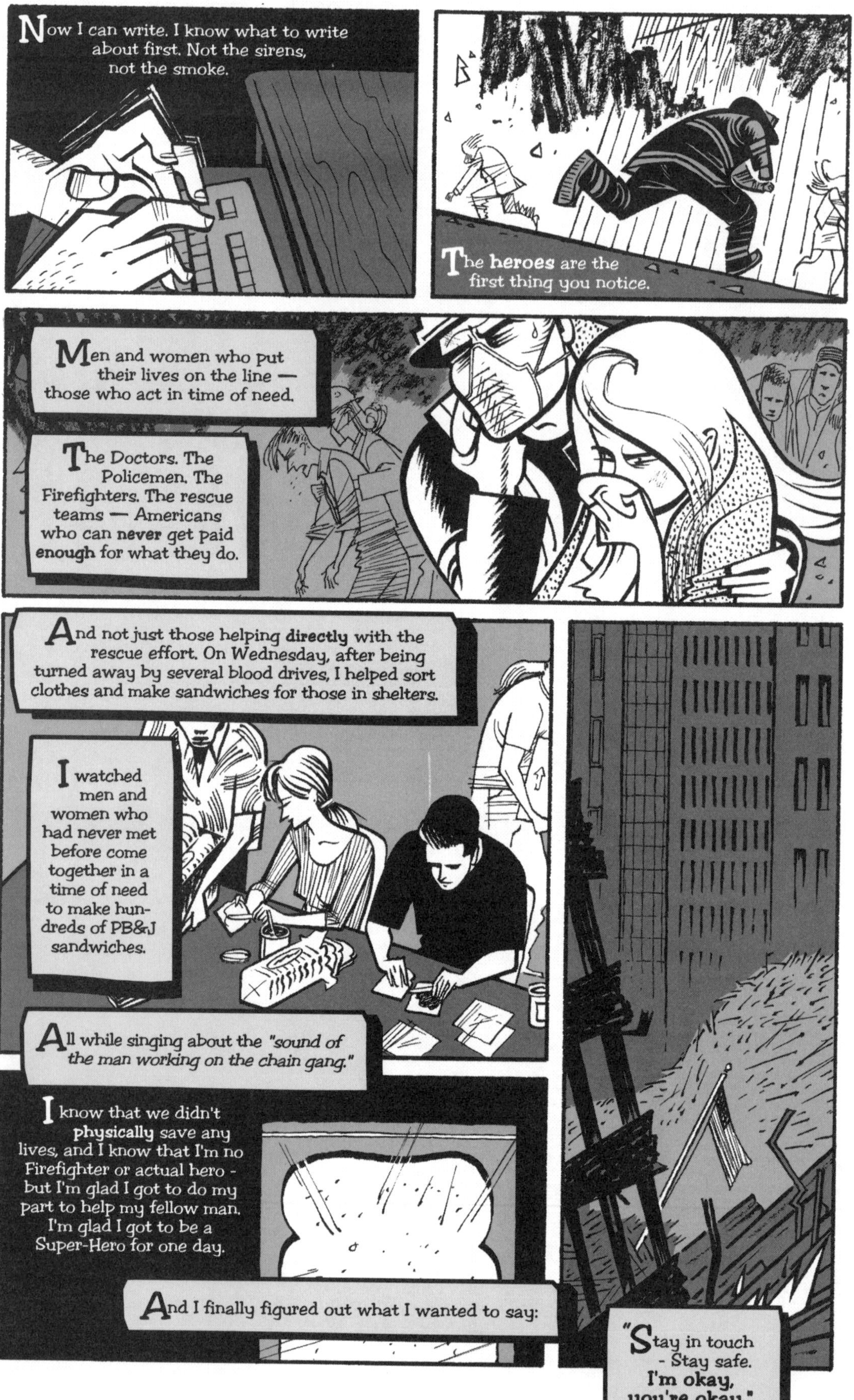
Now I can write. I know what to write about first. Not the sirens, not the smoke.
The heroes are the first thing you notice.
Men and women who put their lives on the line — those who act in time of need.
The Doctors. The Policemen. The Firefighters. The rescue teams — Americans who can never get paid enough for what they do.
And not just those helping directly with the rescue effort. On Wednesday, after being turned away by several blood drives, I helped sort clothes and make sandwiches for those in shelters.
I watched men and women who had never met before come together in a time of need to make hundreds of PB&J sandwiches.
All while singing about the "sound of the man working on the chain gang."
I know that we didn't physically save any lives, and I know that I'm no Firefighter or actual hero - but I'm glad I got to do my part to help my fellow man. I'm glad I got to be a Super-Hero for one day.
And I finally figured out what I wanted to say:
"Stay in touch - Stay safe. I'm okay, you're okay."

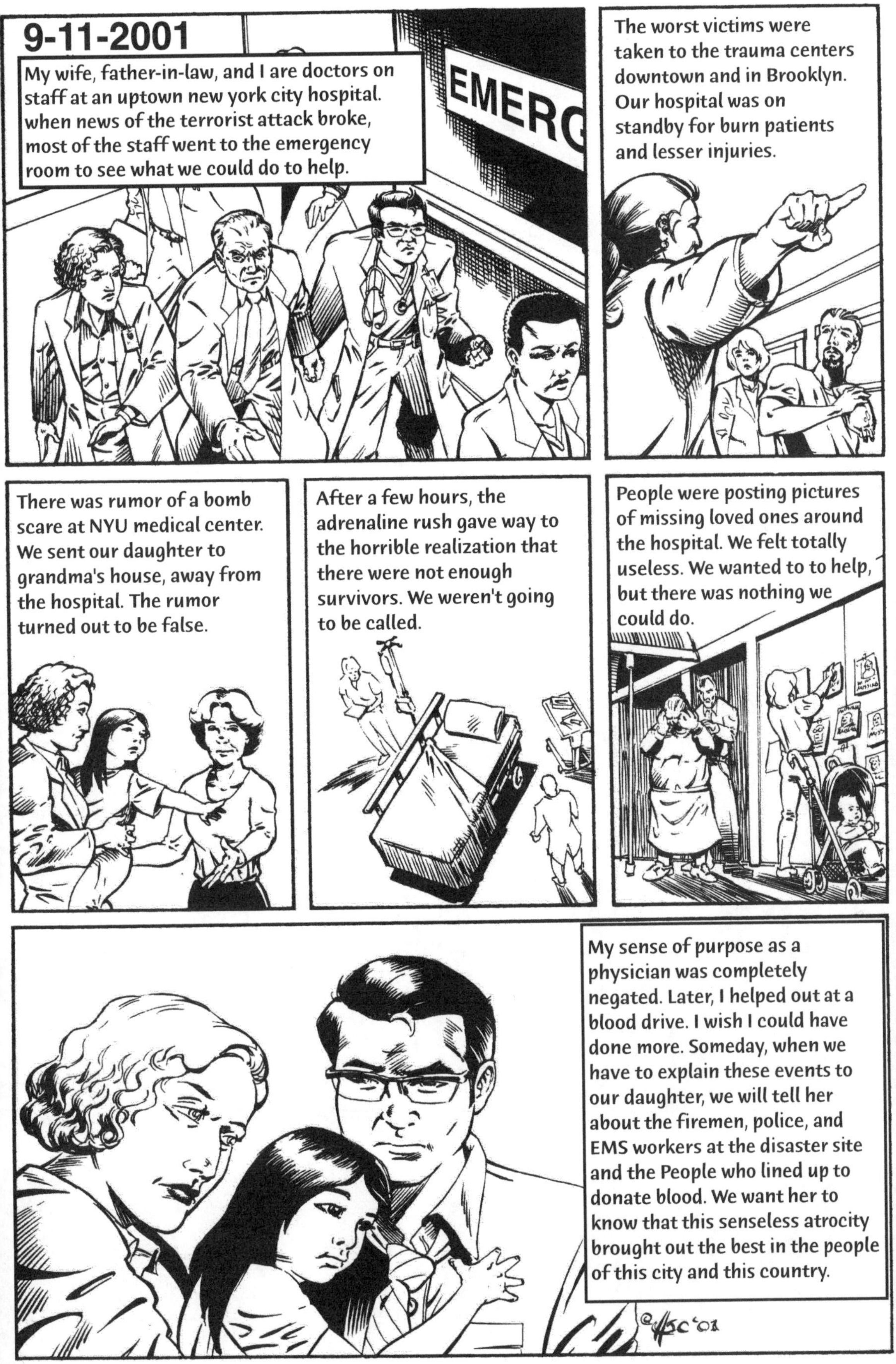
9-11-2001
My wife, father-in-law, and I are doctors on staff at an uptown new york city hospital. when news of the terrorist attack broke, most of the staff went to the emergency room to see what we could do to help.
EMERG
The worst victims were taken to the trauma centers downtown and in Brooklyn. Our hospital was on standby for burn patients and lesser injuries.
There was rumor of a bomb scare at NYU medical center. We sent our daughter to grandma's house, away from the hospital. The rumor turned out to be false.
After a few hours, the adrenaline rush gave way to the horrible realization that there were not enough survivors. We weren't going to be called.
People were posting pictures of missing loved ones around the hospital. We felt totally useless. We wanted to to help, but there was nothing we could do.
My sense of purpose as a physician was completely negated. Later, I helped out at a blood drive. I wish I could have done more. Someday, when we have to explain these events to our daughter, we will tell her about the firemen, police, and EMS workers at the disaster site and the People who lined up to donate blood. We want her to know that this senseless atrocity brought out the best in the people of this city and this country.

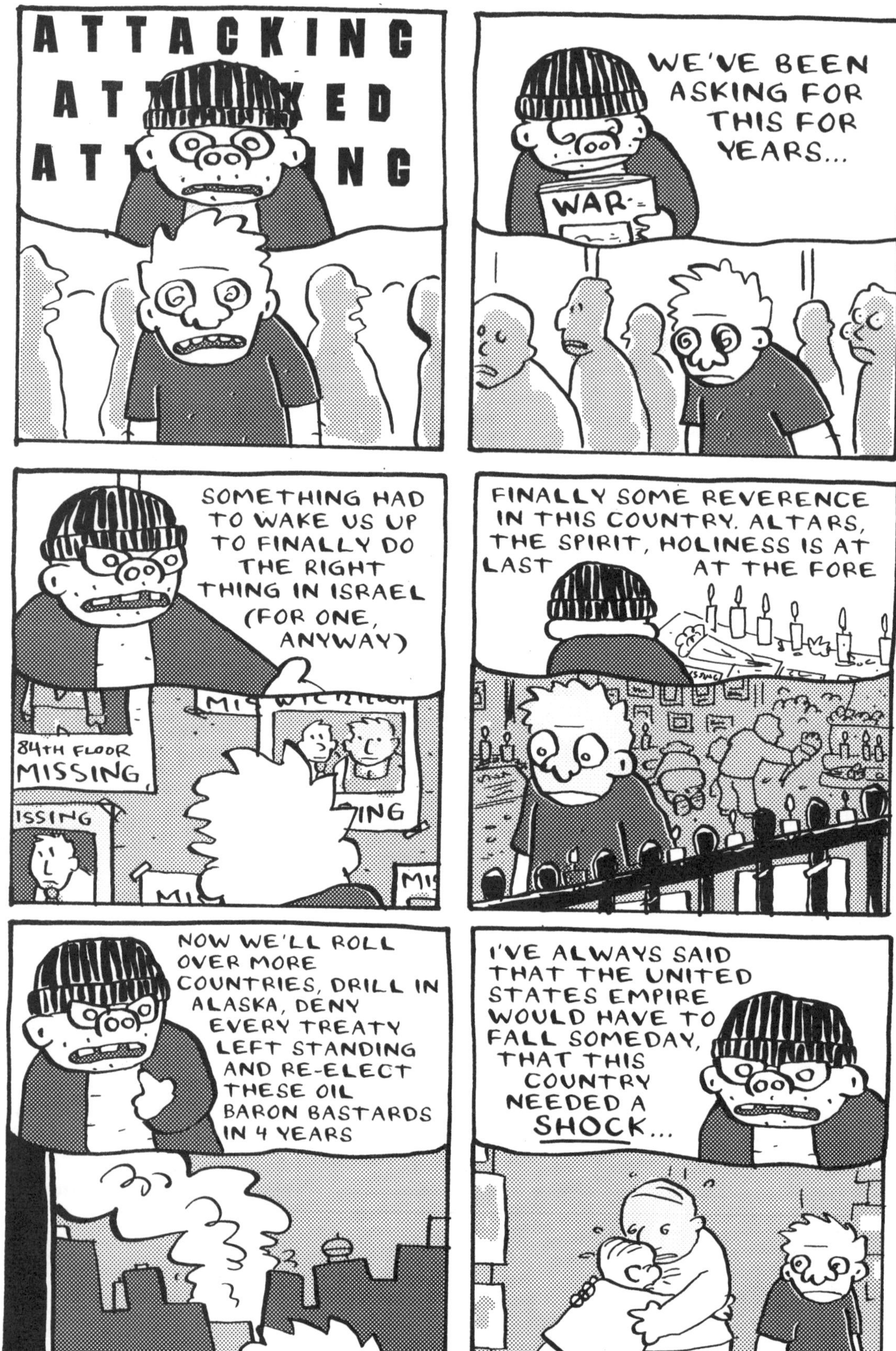
ATTACKING
WE'VE BEEN ASKING FOR THIS FOR YEARS...
WAR
SOMETHING HAD TO WAKE US UP TO FINALLY DO THE RIGHT THING IN ISRAEL (FOR ONE, ANYWAY)
84TH FLOOR MISSING
FINALLY SOME REVERENCE IN THIS COUNTRY. ALTARS, THE SPIRIT, HOLINESS IS AT LAST AT THE FORE
NOW WE'LL ROLL OVER MORE COUNTRIES, DRILL IN ALASKA, DENY EVERY TREATY LEFT STANDING AND RE-ELECT THESE OIL BARON BASTARDS IN 4 YEARS
I'VE ALWAYS SAID THAT THE UNITED STATES EMPIRE WOULD HAVE TO FALL SOMEDAY, THAT THIS COUNTRY NEEDED A SHOCK...

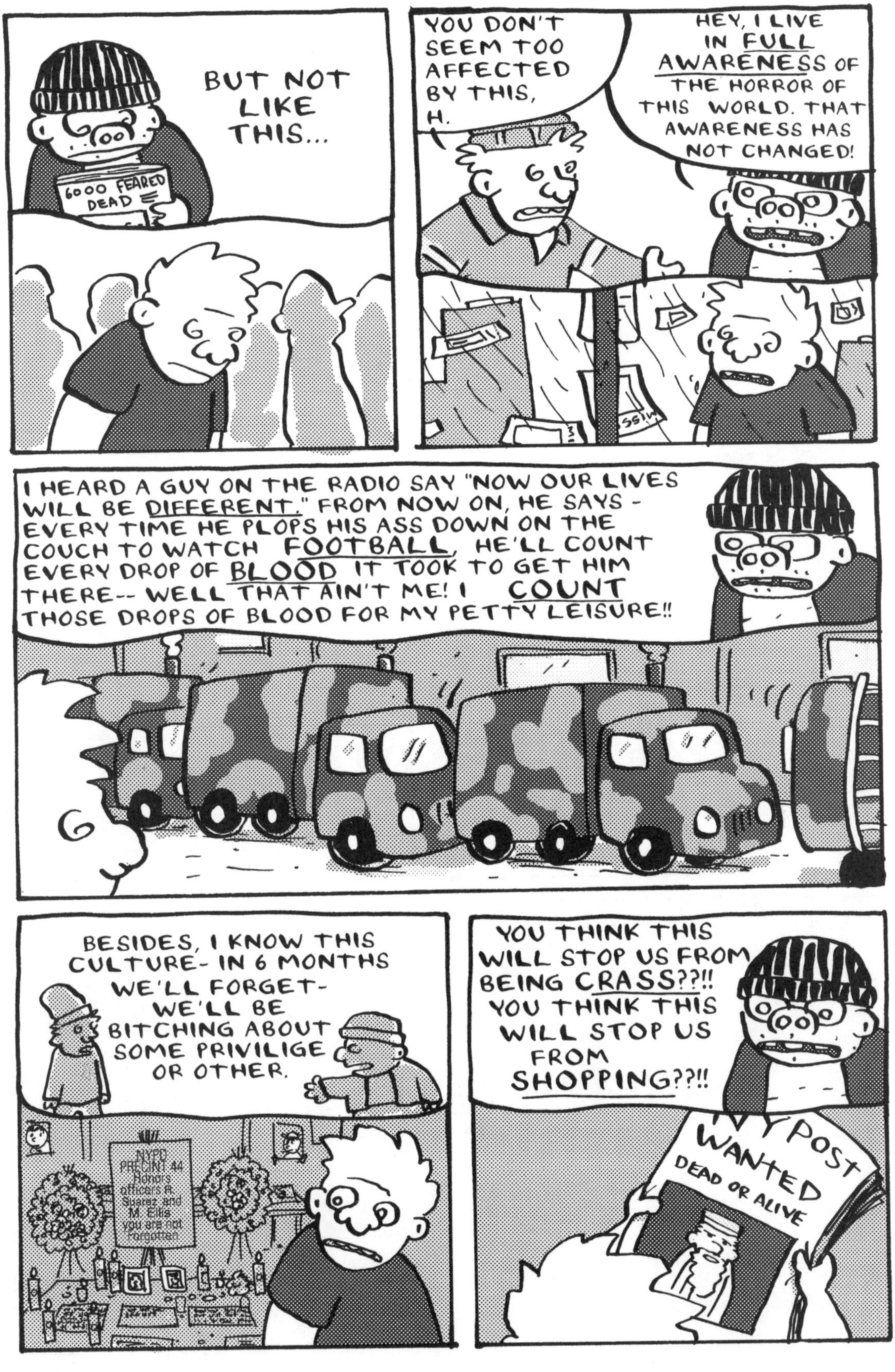
6000 FEARED DEAD
BUT NOT LIKE THIS...
YOU DON'T SEEM TOO AFFECTED BY THIS, H.
HEY, I LIVE IN FULL AWARENESS OF THE HORROR OF THIS WORLD. THAT AWARENESS HAS NOT CHANGED!
I HEARD A GUY ON THE RADIO SAY "NOW OUR LIVES WILL BE DIFFERENT." FROM NOW ON, HE SAYS - EVERY TIME HE PLOPS HIS ASS DOWN ON THE COUCH TO WATCH FOOTBALL, HE'LL COUNT EVERY DROP OF BLOOD IT TOOK TO GET HIM THERE-- WELL THAT AIN'T ME! I COUNT THOSE DROPS OF BLOOD FOR MY PETTY LEISURE!!
BESIDES, I KNOW THIS CULTURE- IN 6 MONTHS WE'LL FORGET- WE'LL BE BITCHING ABOUT SOME PRIVILIGE OR OTHER.
NYPD PRECINCT 44 Honors officers R. Suarez and M. Ellis you are not Forgotten
YOU THINK THIS WILL STOP US FROM BEING CRASS??!! YOU THINK THIS WILL STOP US FROM SHOPPING??!!
NY POST
WANTED DEAD OR ALIVE

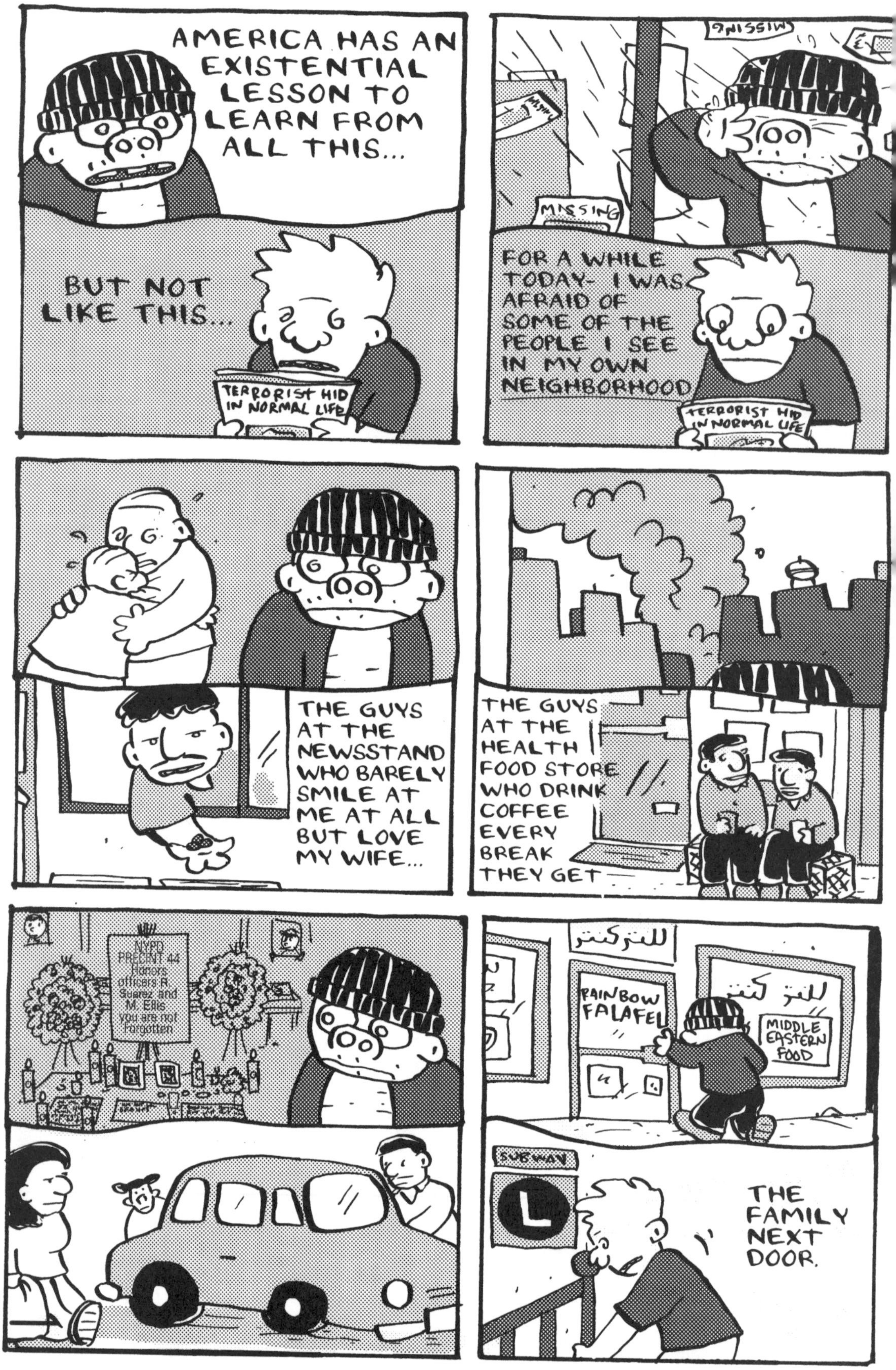
AMERICA HAS AN EXISTENTIAL LESSON TO LEARN FROM ALL THIS...
BUT NOT LIKE THIS...
TERRORIST HID IN NORMAL LIFE
MISSING
FOR A WHILE TODAY- I WAS AFRAID OF SOME OF THE PEOPLE I SEE IN MY OWN NEIGHBORHOOD
TERRORIST HID IN NORMAL LIFE
THE GUYS AT THE NEWSSTAND WHO BARELY SMILE AT ME AT ALL BUT LOVE MY WIFE...
THE GUYS AT THE HEALTH FOOD STORE WHO DRINK COFFEE EVERY BREAK THEY GET
NYPD PRECINT 44 Honors officers R. Suarez and M. Ellis you are not Forgotten
RAINBOW FALAFEL
MIDDLE EASTERN FOOD
SUBWAY
L
THE FAMILY NEXT DOOR.

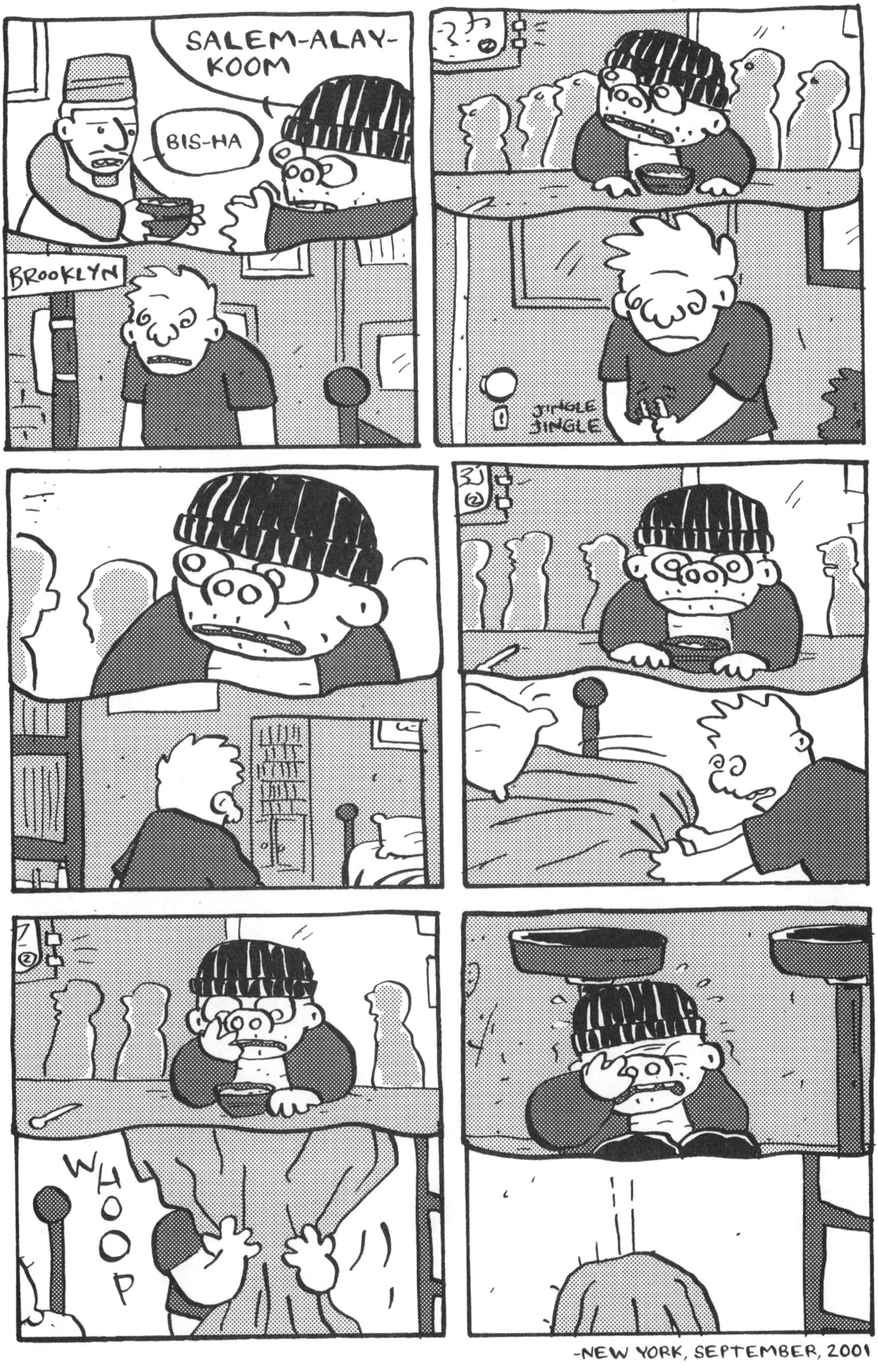
SALEM-ALAY-KOOM
BIS-HA
BROOKLYN
JINGLE JINGLE
WHOOP

-NEW YORK, SEPTEMBER, 2001

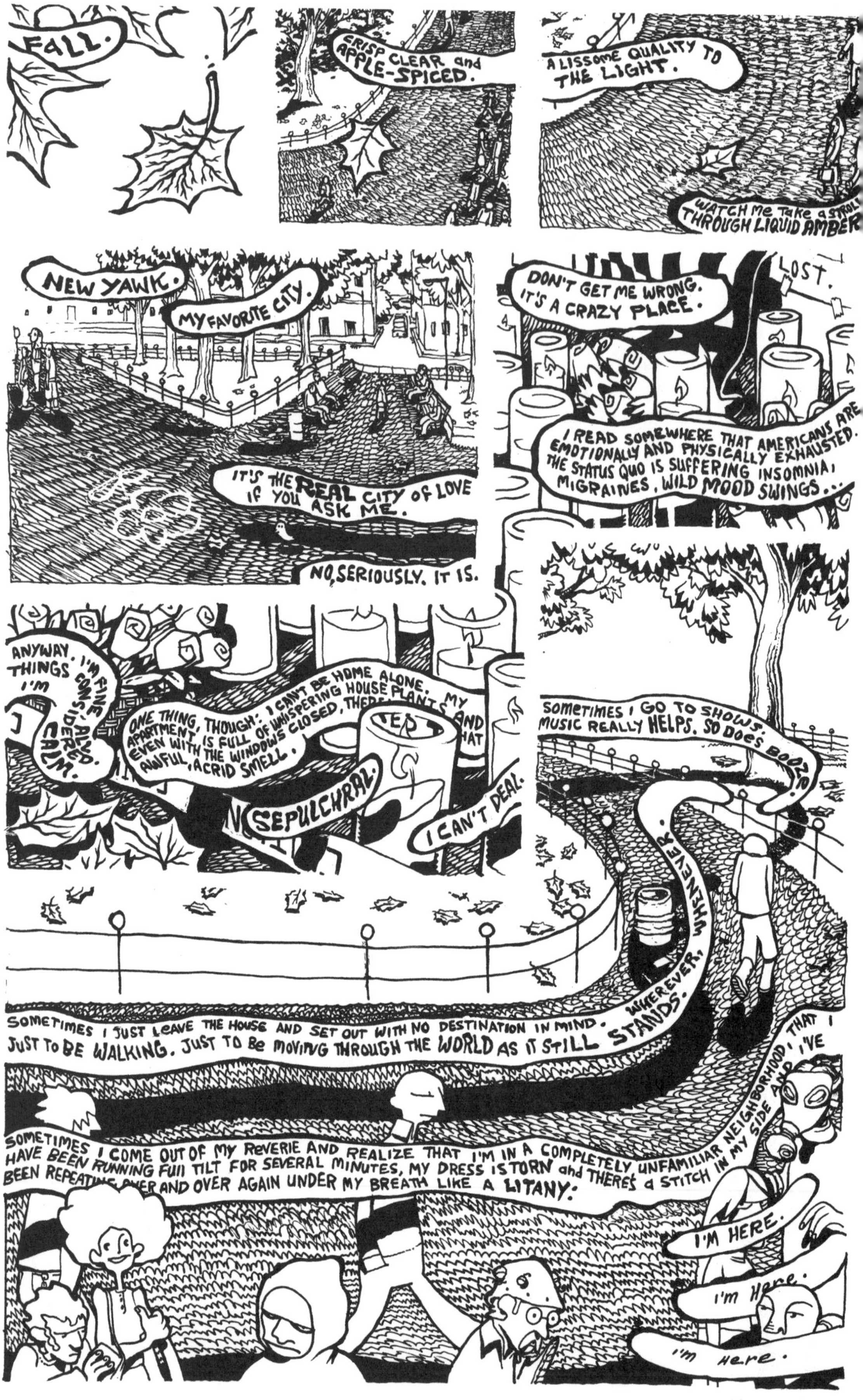
FALL.
CRISP CLEAR and APPLE-SPICED.
A LISSOME QUALITY TO THE LIGHT.
WATCH ME TAKE A STROLL THROUGH LIQUID AMBER
NEW YAWK.
MY FAVORITE CITY.
IT'S THE REAL CITY OF LOVE IF YOU ASK ME.
NO, SERIOUSLY. IT IS.
DON'T GET ME WRONG. IT'S A CRAZY PLACE.
LOST.
I READ SOMEWHERE THAT AMERICANS ARE EMOTIONALLY AND PHYSICALLY EXHAUSTED. THE STATUS QUO IS SUFFERING INSOMNIA, MIGRAINES, WILD MOOD SWINGS...
ANYWAY. I'M FINE. THINGS CONSIDERED. I'M ALSO CALM.
ONE THING, THOUGH: I CAN'T BE HOME ALONE. MY APARTMENT IS FULL OF WHISPERING HOUSE PLANTS AND EVEN WITH THE WINDOWS CLOSED, THERE HAT AWFUL, ACRID SMELL.
SEPULCHRAL.
I CAN'T DEAL.
SOMETIMES I GO TO SHOWS. MUSIC REALLY HELPS. SO DOES BOOZE.
SOMETIMES I JUST LEAVE THE HOUSE AND SET OUT WITH NO DESTINATION IN MIND. WHENEVER, WHEREVER. JUST TO BE WALKING. JUST TO BE MOVING THROUGH THE WORLD AS IT STILL STANDS.
SOMETIMES I COME OUT OF MY REVERIE AND REALIZE THAT I'M IN A COMPLETELY UNFAMILIAR NEIGHBORHOOD, THAT I HAVE BEEN RUNNING FULL TILT FOR SEVERAL MINUTES, MY DRESS IS TORN and THERE'S a STITCH IN MY SIDE AND I'VE BEEN REPEATING OVER AND OVER AGAIN UNDER MY BREATH LIKE A LITANY:
I'M HERE.
I'm here.
I'm here.

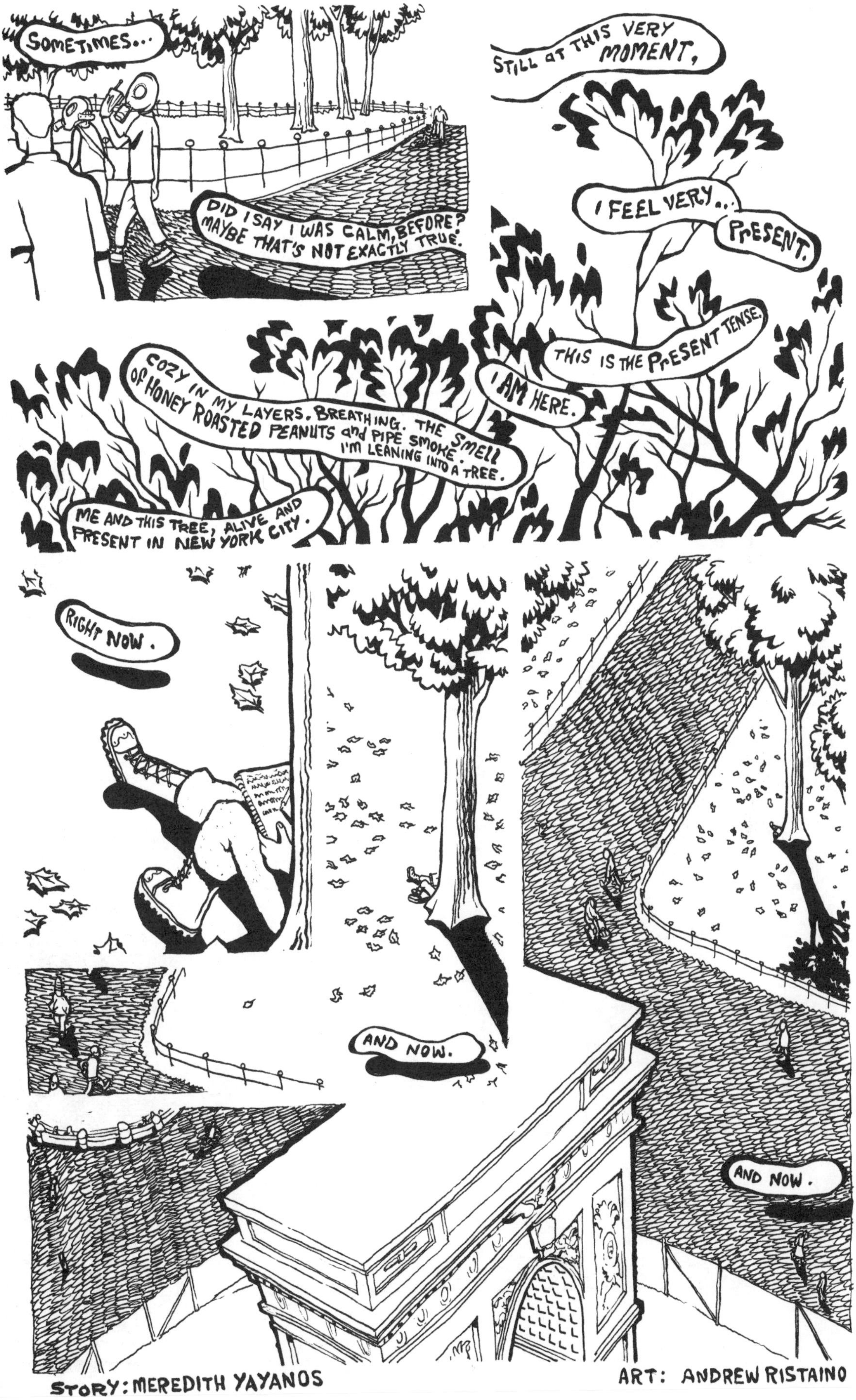

SOMETIMES...
DID I SAY I WAS CALM, BEFORE? MAYBE THAT'S NOT EXACTLY TRUE.
STILL AT THIS VERY MOMENT,
I FEEL VERY...
PRESENT.
COZY IN MY LAYERS. BREATHING. THE SMELL OF HONEY ROASTED PEANUTS and PIPE SMOKE. I'M LEANING INTO A TREE.
I AM HERE.
THIS IS THE PRESENT TENSE.
ME AND THIS TREE, ALIVE AND PRESENT IN NEW YORK CITY.
RIGHT NOW.
AND NOW.
AND NOW.

STORY: MEREDITH YAYANOS

ART: ANDREW RISTAINO

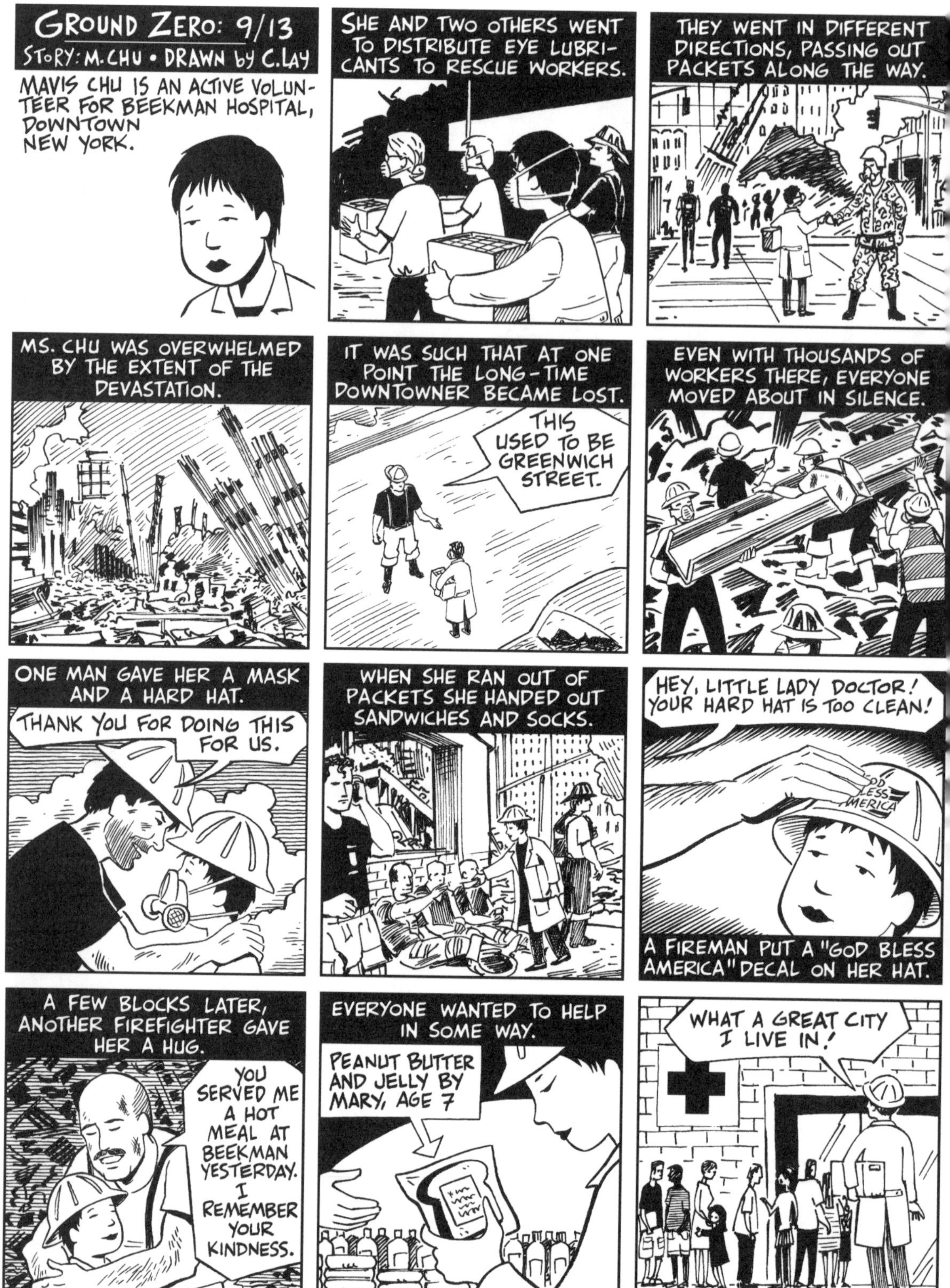
GROUND ZERO: 9/13
STORY: M. CHU • DRAWN by C. LAY
MAVIS CHU IS AN ACTIVE VOLUNTEER FOR BEEKMAN HOSPITAL, DOWNTOWN NEW YORK.
SHE AND TWO OTHERS WENT TO DISTRIBUTE EYE LUBRICANTS TO RESCUE WORKERS.
THEY WENT IN DIFFERENT DIRECTIONS, PASSING OUT PACKETS ALONG THE WAY.
MS. CHU WAS OVERWHELMED BY THE EXTENT OF THE DEVASTATION.
IT WAS SUCH THAT AT ONE POINT THE LONG-TIME DOWNTOWNER BECAME LOST.
THIS USED TO BE GREENWICH STREET.
EVEN WITH THOUSANDS OF WORKERS THERE, EVERYONE MOVED ABOUT IN SILENCE.
ONE MAN GAVE HER A MASK AND A HARD HAT.
THANK YOU FOR DOING THIS FOR US.
WHEN SHE RAN OUT OF PACKETS SHE HANDED OUT SANDWICHES AND SOCKS.
HEY, LITTLE LADY DOCTOR! YOUR HARD HAT IS TOO CLEAN!
GOD BLESS AMERICA
A FIREMAN PUT A "GOD BLESS AMERICA" DECAL ON HER HAT.
A FEW BLOCKS LATER, ANOTHER FIREFIGHTER GAVE HER A HUG.
YOU SERVED ME A HOT MEAL AT BEEKMAN YESTERDAY. I REMEMBER YOUR KINDNESS.
EVERYONE WANTED TO HELP IN SOME WAY.
PEANUT BUTTER AND JELLY BY MARY, AGE 7
WHAT A GREAT CITY I LIVE IN!

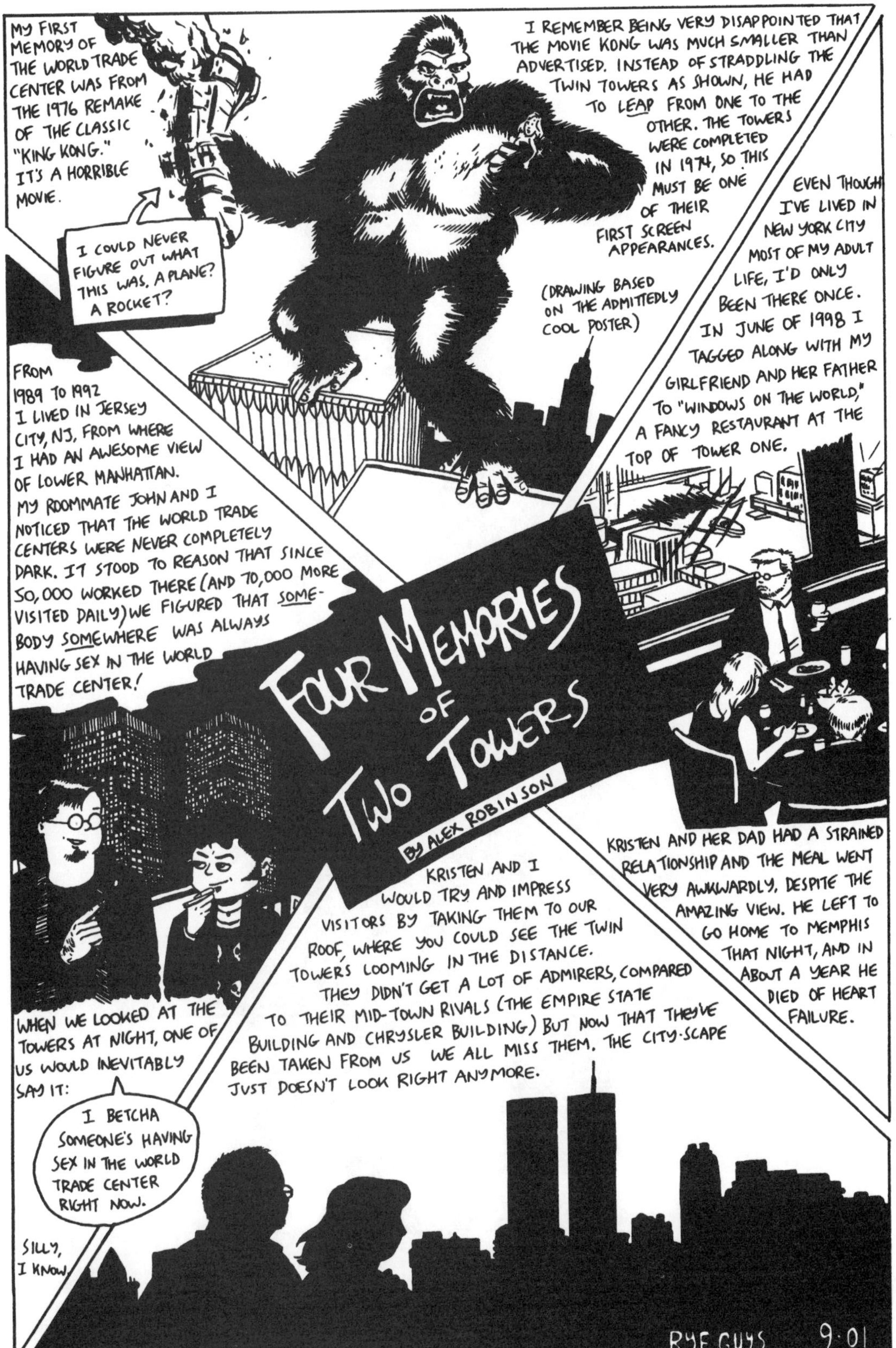
MY FIRST MEMORY OF THE WORLD TRADE CENTER WAS FROM THE 1976 REMAKE OF THE CLASSIC "KING KONG." IT'S A HORRIBLE MOVIE.
I COULD NEVER FIGURE OUT WHAT THIS WAS. A PLANE? A ROCKET?
I REMEMBER BEING VERY DISAPPOINTED THAT THE MOVIE KONG WAS MUCH SMALLER THAN ADVERTISED. INSTEAD OF STRADDLING THE TWIN TOWERS AS SHOWN, HE HAD TO LEAP FROM ONE TO THE OTHER. THE TOWERS WERE COMPLETED IN 1974, SO THIS MUST BE ONE OF THEIR FIRST SCREEN APPEARANCES.
(DRAWING BASED ON THE ADMITTEDLY COOL POSTER)
FROM 1989 TO 1992 I LIVED IN JERSEY CITY, NJ, FROM WHERE I HAD AN AWESOME VIEW OF LOWER MANHATTAN. MY ROOMMATE JOHN AND I NOTICED THAT THE WORLD TRADE CENTERS WERE NEVER COMPLETELY DARK. IT STOOD TO REASON THAT SINCE 50,000 WORKED THERE (AND 70,000 MORE VISITED DAILY) WE FIGURED THAT SOMEBODY SOMEWHERE WAS ALWAYS HAVING SEX IN THE WORLD TRADE CENTER!
FOUR MEMORIES OF TWO TOWERS
BY ALEX ROBINSON
EVEN THOUGH I'VE LIVED IN NEW YORK CITY MOST OF MY ADULT LIFE, I'D ONLY BEEN THERE ONCE. IN JUNE OF 1998 I TAGGED ALONG WITH MY GIRLFRIEND AND HER FATHER TO "WINDOWS ON THE WORLD," A FANCY RESTAURANT AT THE TOP OF TOWER ONE.
KRISTEN AND HER DAD HAD A STRAINED RELATIONSHIP AND THE MEAL WENT VERY AWKWARDLY, DESPITE THE AMAZING VIEW. HE LEFT TO GO HOME TO MEMPHIS THAT NIGHT, AND IN ABOUT A YEAR HE DIED OF HEART FAILURE.
KRISTEN AND I WOULD TRY AND IMPRESS VISITORS BY TAKING THEM TO OUR ROOF, WHERE YOU COULD SEE THE TWIN TOWERS LOOMING IN THE DISTANCE. THEY DIDN'T GET A LOT OF ADMIRERS, COMPARED TO THEIR MID-TOWN RIVALS (THE EMPIRE STATE BUILDING AND CHRYSLER BUILDING) BUT NOW THAT THEY'VE BEEN TAKEN FROM US WE ALL MISS THEM. THE CITY-SCAPE JUST DOESN'T LOOK RIGHT ANYMORE.
WHEN WE LOOKED AT THE TOWERS AT NIGHT, ONE OF US WOULD INEVITABLY SAY IT:
I BETCHA SOMEONE'S HAVING SEX IN THE WORLD TRADE CENTER RIGHT NOW.
SILLY, I KNOW.
BYE GUYS 9·01

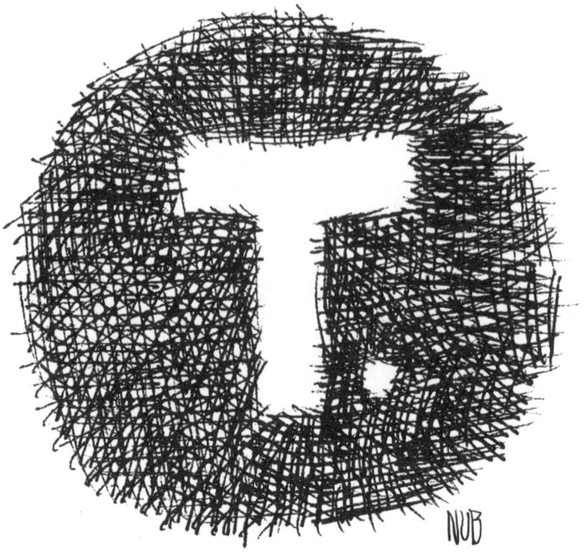
NUB

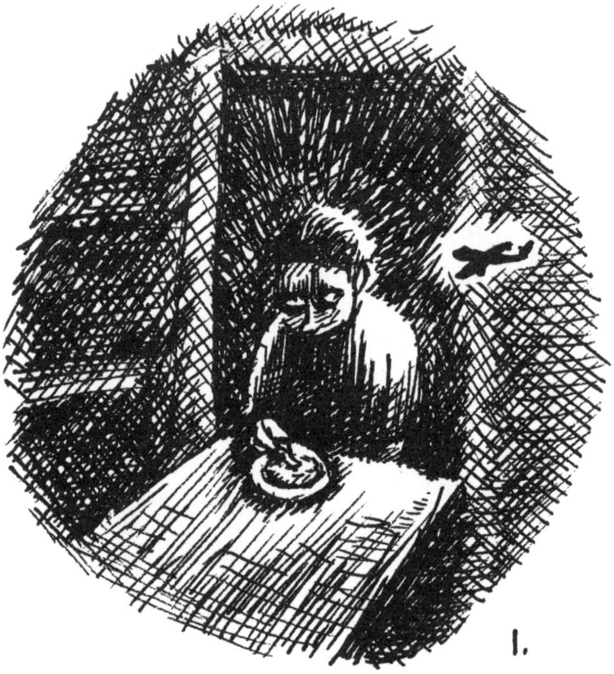

1.

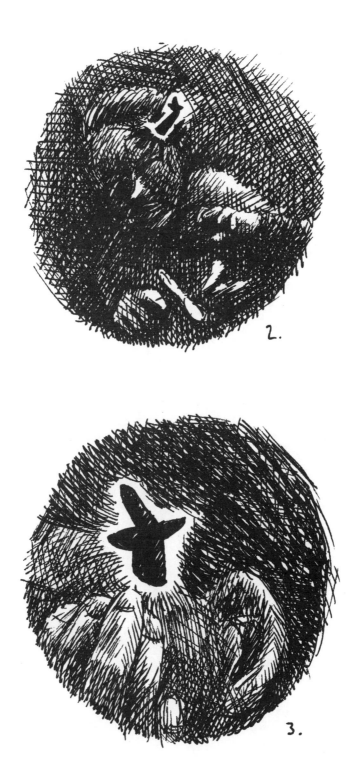

2.

3.

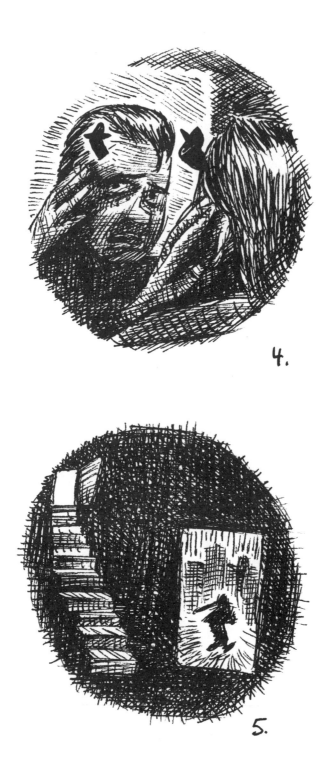

4.

5.

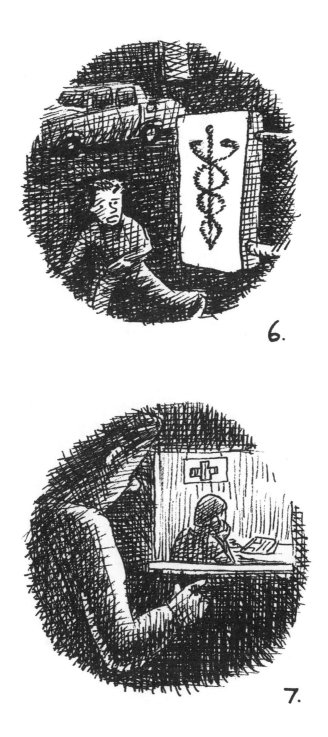

6.

7.

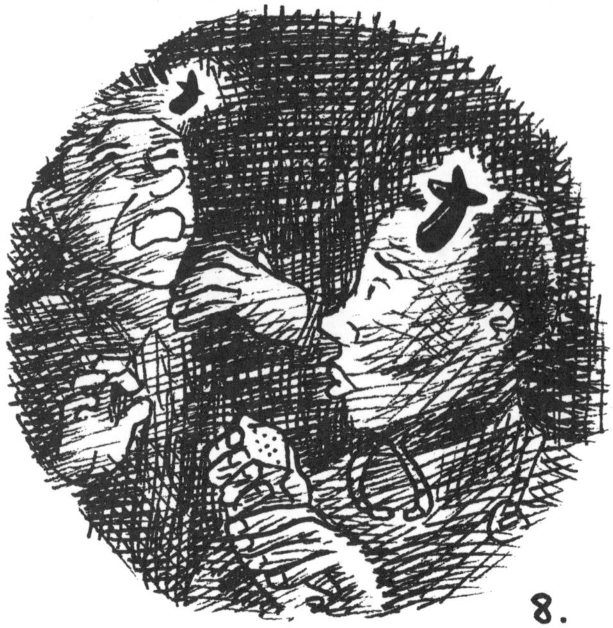

8.

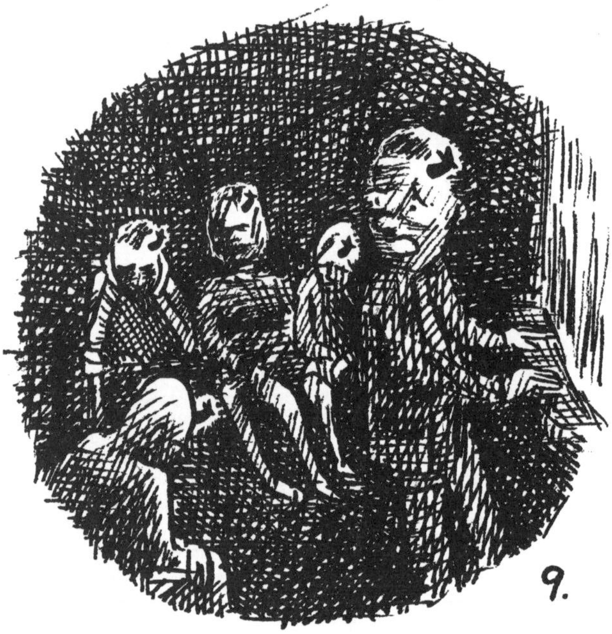

9.

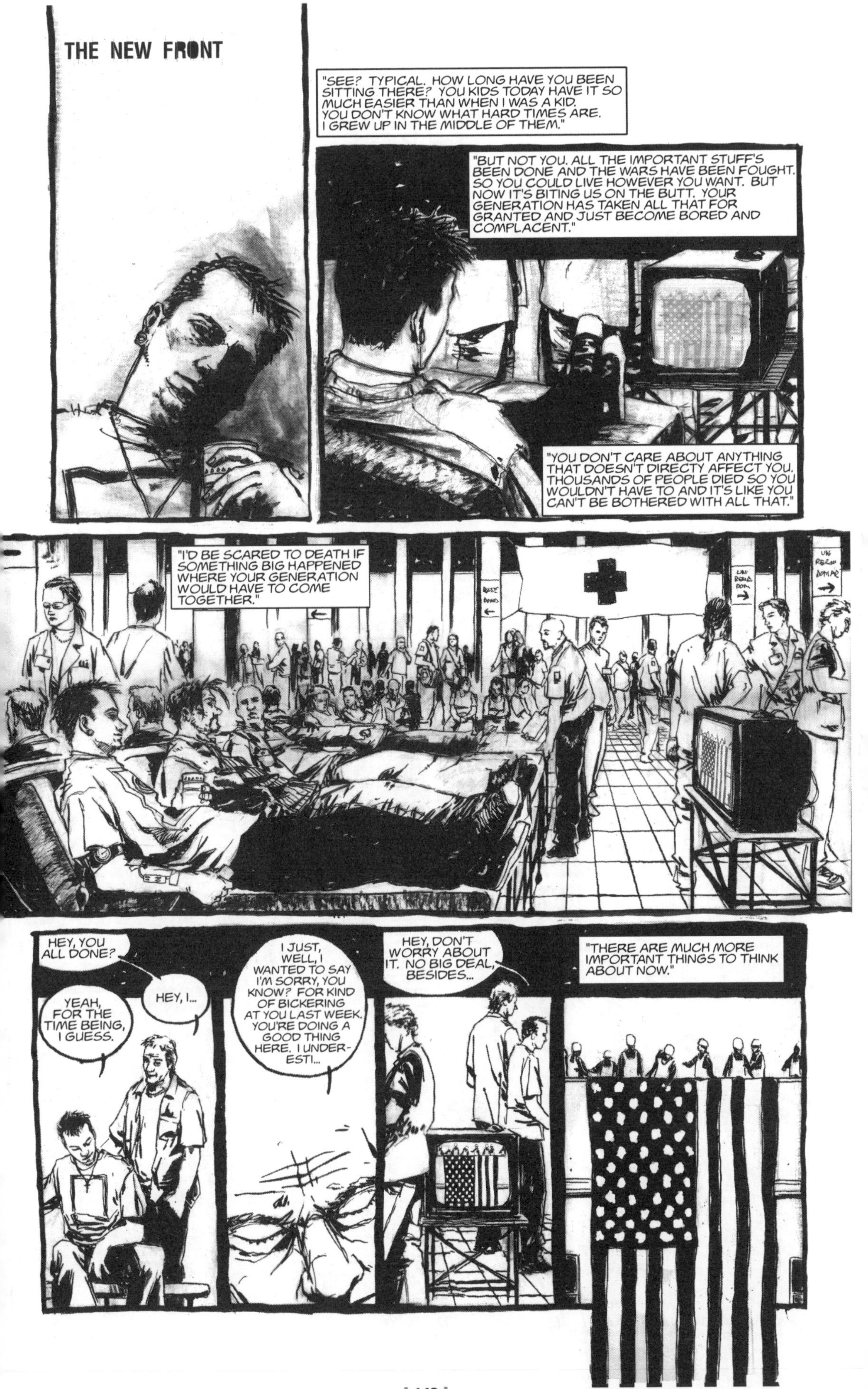
THE NEW FRONT
"SEE? TYPICAL. HOW LONG HAVE YOU BEEN SITTING THERE? YOU KIDS TODAY HAVE IT SO MUCH EASIER THAN WHEN I WAS A KID. YOU DON'T KNOW WHAT HARD TIMES ARE. I GREW UP IN THE MIDDLE OF THEM."
"BUT NOT YOU. ALL THE IMPORTANT STUFF'S BEEN DONE AND THE WARS HAVE BEEN FOUGHT. SO YOU COULD LIVE HOWEVER YOU WANT. BUT NOW IT'S BITING US ON THE BUTT. YOUR GENERATION HAS TAKEN ALL THAT FOR GRANTED AND JUST BECOME BORED AND COMPLACENT."
"YOU DON'T CARE ABOUT ANYTHING THAT DOESN'T DIRECTY AFFECT YOU. THOUSANDS OF PEOPLE DIED SO YOU WOULDN'T HAVE TO AND IT'S LIKE YOU CAN'T BE BOTHERED WITH ALL THAT."
"I'D BE SCARED TO DEATH IF SOMETHING BIG HAPPENED WHERE YOUR GENERATION WOULD HAVE TO COME TOGETHER."
HEY, YOU ALL DONE?
YEAH, FOR THE TIME BEING, I GUESS.
HEY, I...
I JUST, WELL, I WANTED TO SAY I'M SORRY, YOU KNOW? FOR KIND OF BICKERING AT YOU LAST WEEK. YOU'RE DOING A GOOD THING HERE. I UNDER-ESTI...
HEY, DON'T WORRY ABOUT IT. NO BIG DEAL, BESIDES...
"THERE ARE MUCH MORE IMPORTANT THINGS TO THINK ABOUT NOW."

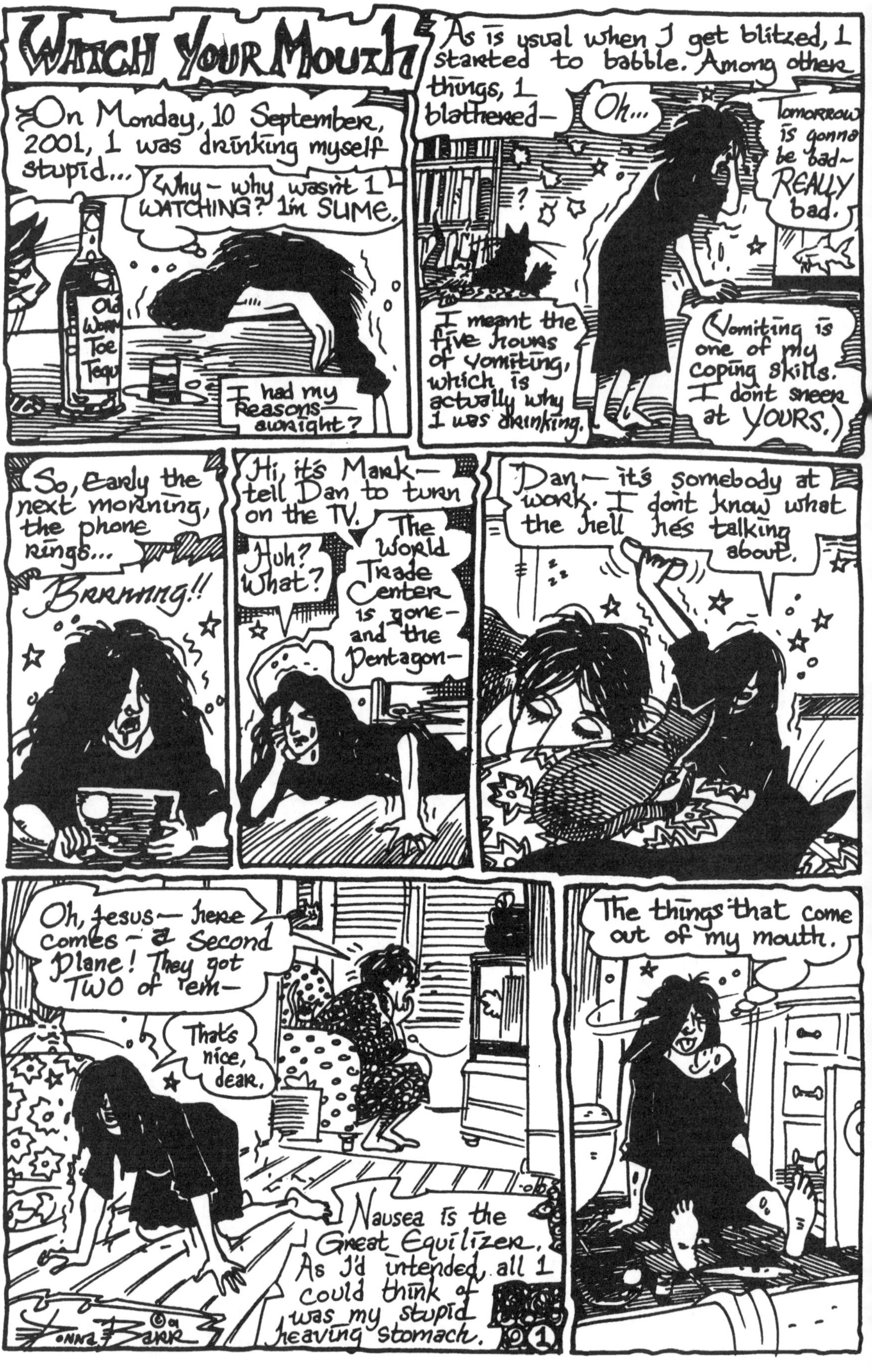
WATCH YOUR MOUTH
On Monday, 10 September, 2001, I was drinking myself stupid...
Why— why wasn't I WATCHING? I'm SLIME.
Old Worm Toe Tequ
I had my Reasons— awright?
As is usual when I get blitzed, I started to babble. Among other things, I blathered—
Oh...
TOMORROW is gonna be bad— REALLY bad.
I meant the five hours of vomiting, which is actually why I was drinking.
(Vomiting is one of my coping skills. I dont sneer at YOURS.)
So, early the next morning, the phone rings...
BRRRNNNG!!
Hi, it's Mark— tell Dan to turn on the TV.
Huh? What?
The World Trade Center is gone— and the Pentagon—
Dan— it's somebody at work. I dont know what the hell hes talking about.
Oh, Jesus— here comes— a second plane! They got TWO of 'em—
That's nice, dear.
Nausea is the Great Equilizer. As I'd intended, all I could think of was my stupid heaving stomach.
Donna Barr ©01
The things that come out of my mouth.

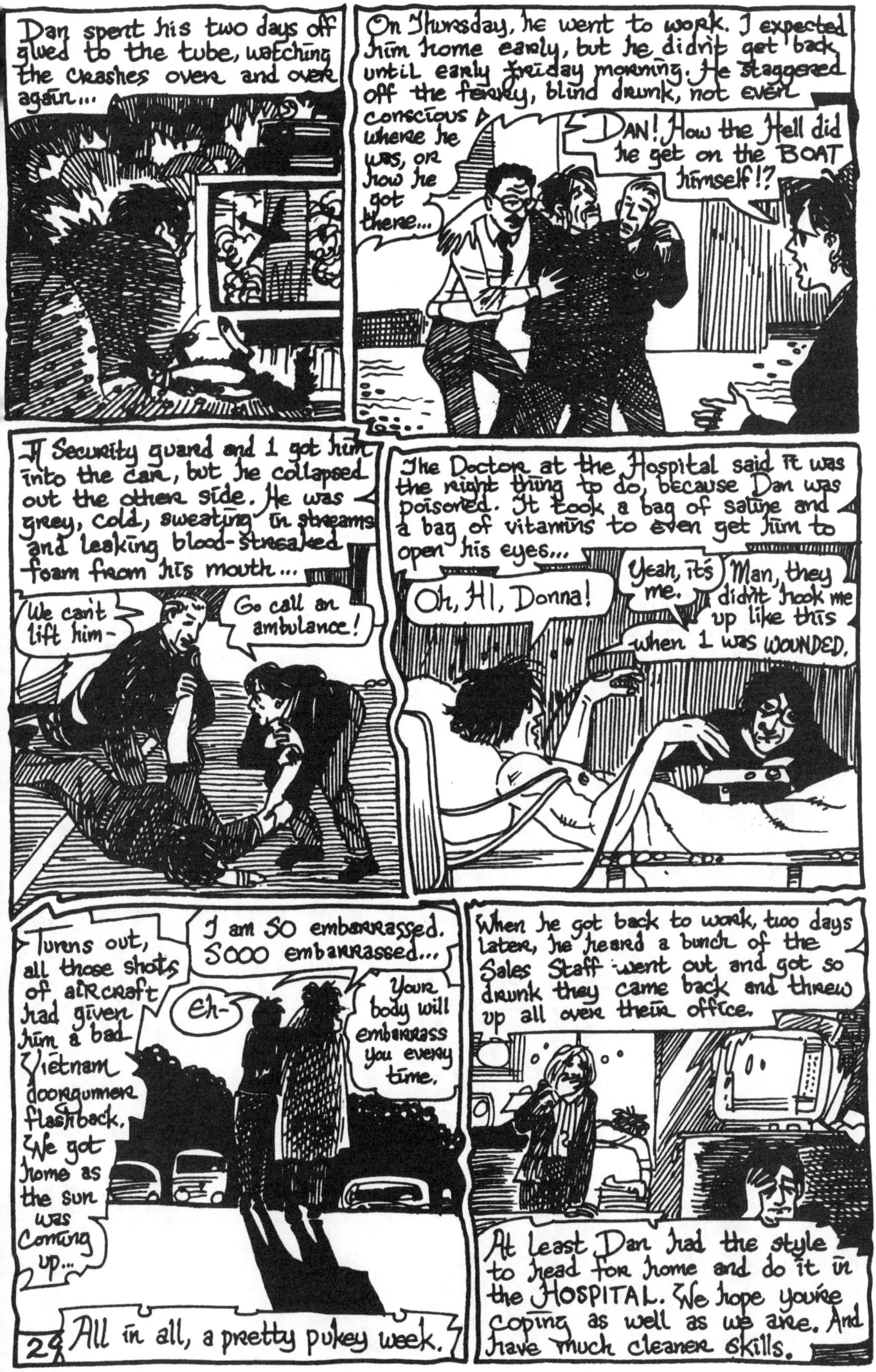

Dan spent his two days off glued to the tube, watching the crashes over and over again...
On Thursday, he went to work. I expected him home early, but he didn't get back until early Friday morning. He staggered off the ferry, blind drunk, not even conscious where he was, or how he got there...
DAN! How the Hell did he get on the BOAT himself!?
A Security guard and I got him into the car, but he collapsed out the other side. He was grey, cold, sweating in streams and leaking blood-streaked foam from his mouth...
We can't lift him-
Go call an ambulance!
The Doctor at the Hospital said it was the right thing to do, because Dan was poisoned. It took a bag of saline and a bag of vitamins to even get him to open his eyes...
Oh, HI, Donna!
Yeah, it's me.
Man, they didn't hook me up like this when I was WOUNDED.
Turns out, all those shots of aircraft had given him a bad Vietnam doorgunner flashback. We got home as the sun was coming up...
I am SO embarrassed. SOOO embarrassed...
Eh-
Your body will embarrass you every time.
29
All in all, a pretty pukey week.
When he got back to work, two days later, he heard a bunch of the Sales Staff went out and got so drunk they came back and threw up all over their office.
At least Dan had the style to head for home and do it in the HOSPITAL. We hope you're coping as well as we are. And have much cleaner skills.

INDOMITABLE HUMAN SPIRIT

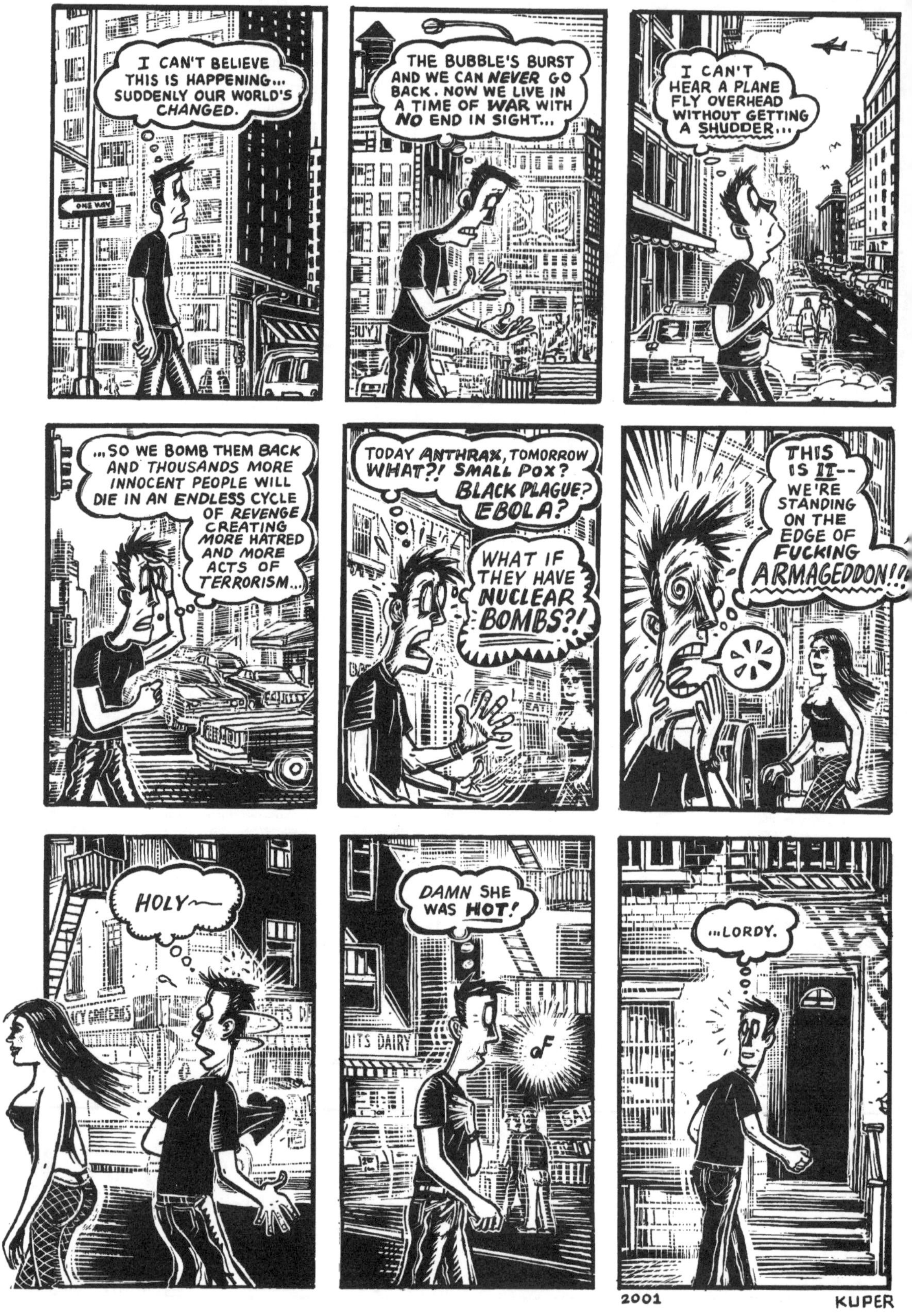
I CAN'T BELIEVE THIS IS HAPPENING... SUDDENLY OUR WORLD'S CHANGED.
ONE WAY
THE BUBBLE'S BURST AND WE CAN NEVER GO BACK. NOW WE LIVE IN A TIME OF WAR WITH NO END IN SIGHT...
I CAN'T HEAR A PLANE FLY OVERHEAD WITHOUT GETTING A SHUDDER...
...SO WE BOMB THEM BACK AND THOUSANDS MORE INNOCENT PEOPLE WILL DIE IN AN ENDLESS CYCLE OF REVENGE CREATING MORE HATRED AND MORE ACTS OF TERRORISM...
TODAY ANTHRAX, TOMORROW WHAT?! SMALL POX? BLACK PLAGUE? EBOLA?
WHAT IF THEY HAVE NUCLEAR BOMBS?!
THIS IS IT-- WE'RE STANDING ON THE EDGE OF FUCKING ARMAGEDDON!!
HOLY—
DAMN SHE WAS HOT!
...LORDY.
2001
KUPER

Clear Skies by Anon Friend

artwork by **Guy Davis**

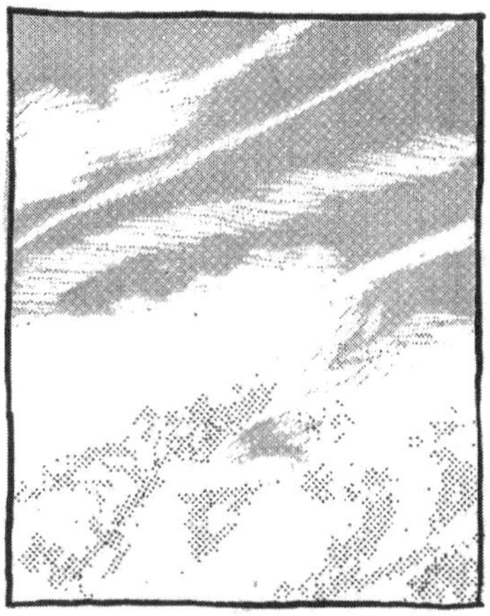

It's funny how sometimes you never notice something was there until it's gone.

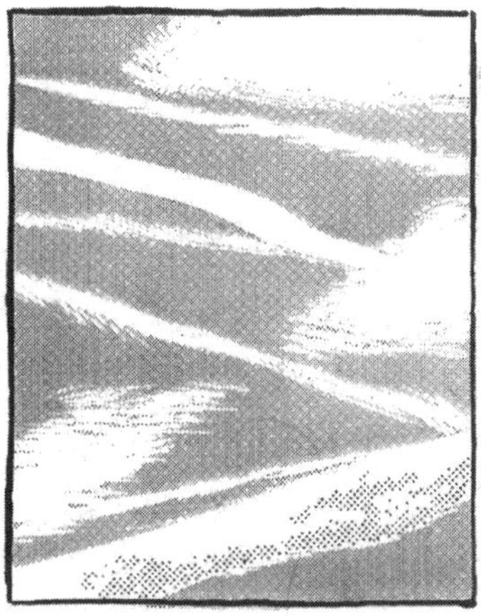

I would often look at the clouds to clear my mind or relax after work, the sky would always be crisscrossed by the days travels.

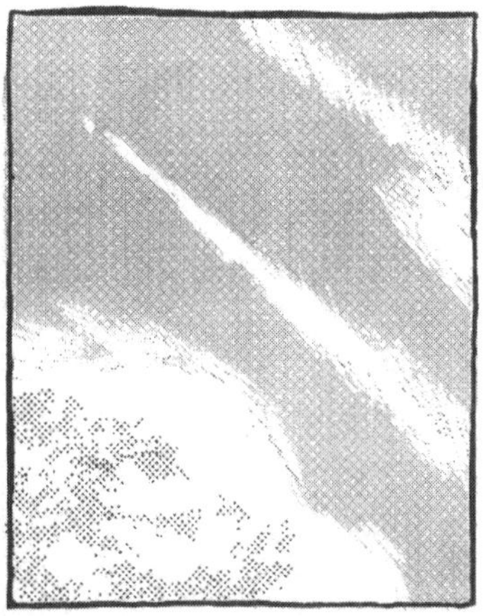

You could never really see the actual jets, only a small dot that would leave a white streak. The distance made you forget that it was a group of people enroute, and it became only an object that made a mark in the sky.

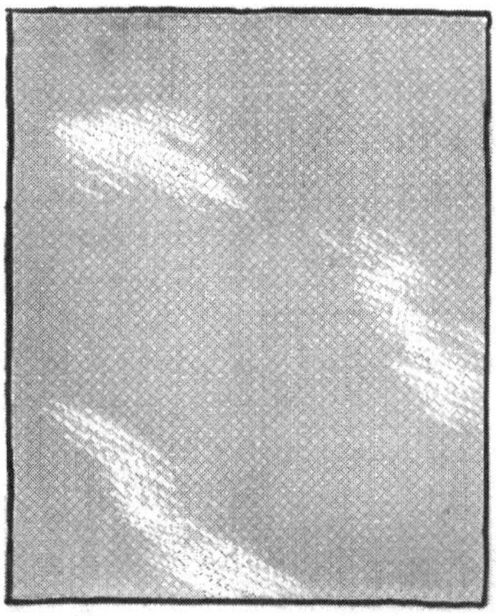

Then came a day when I needed time to get away from the images and news that filled every minute, every thought.

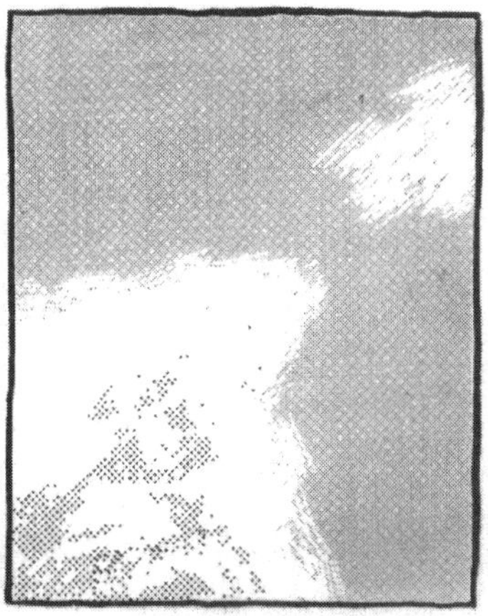

Overwhelmed, I looked to the sky and clouds to clear my mind as I had always done and noticed that the sky was empty of the streaks of jets.

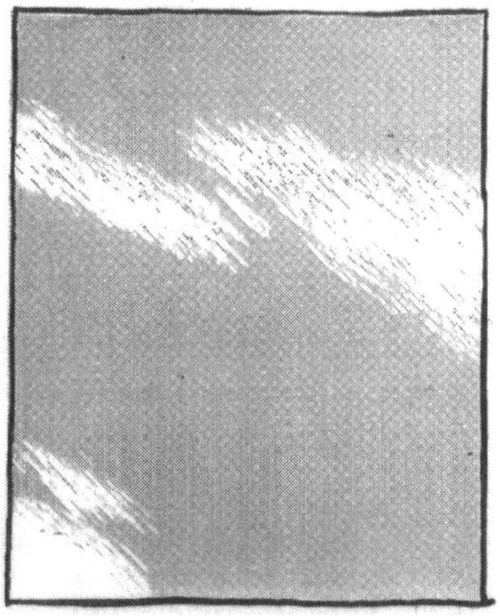

It seemed silly to notice in light of what was happening, but the emptiness seemed ominous and threatening in a way. As if it echoed the mournfulness of the day.

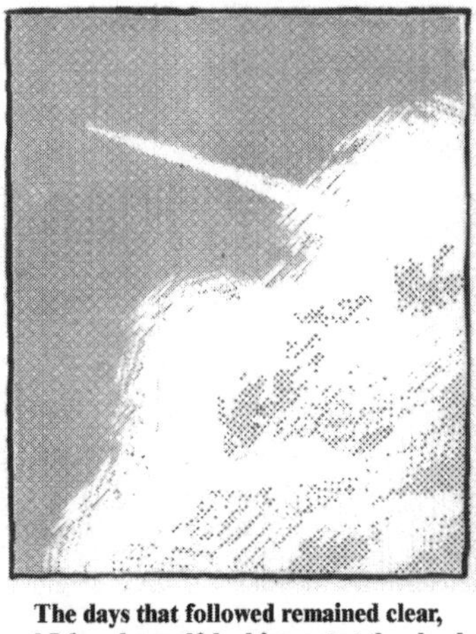

The days that followed remained clear, and I found myself looking out at the clouds more and more, hoping to see the familiar marks in the sky.

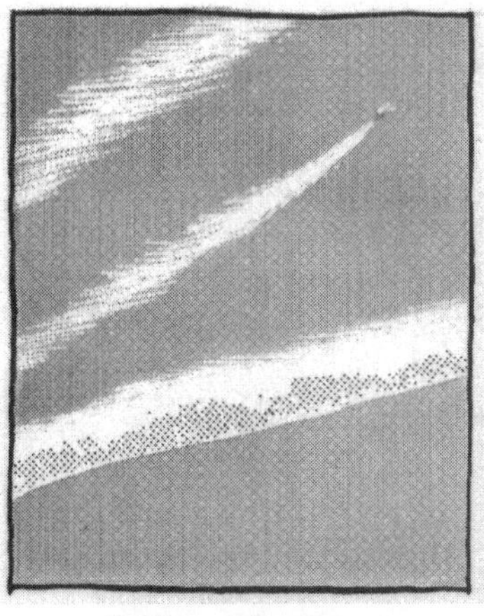

But it was only a pause.
The sky is familiar again,
but it will never seem the same.

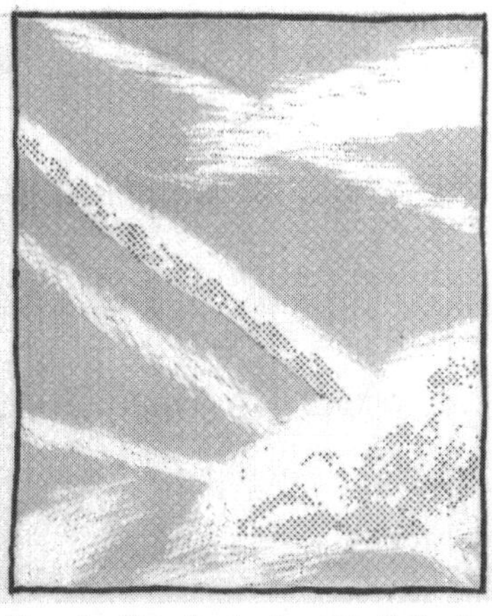

Now when I see the streaks and trails I notice the jets that leave them, I think of the people onboard and wonder where they are headed.
....always remembering the ones that never made it there.

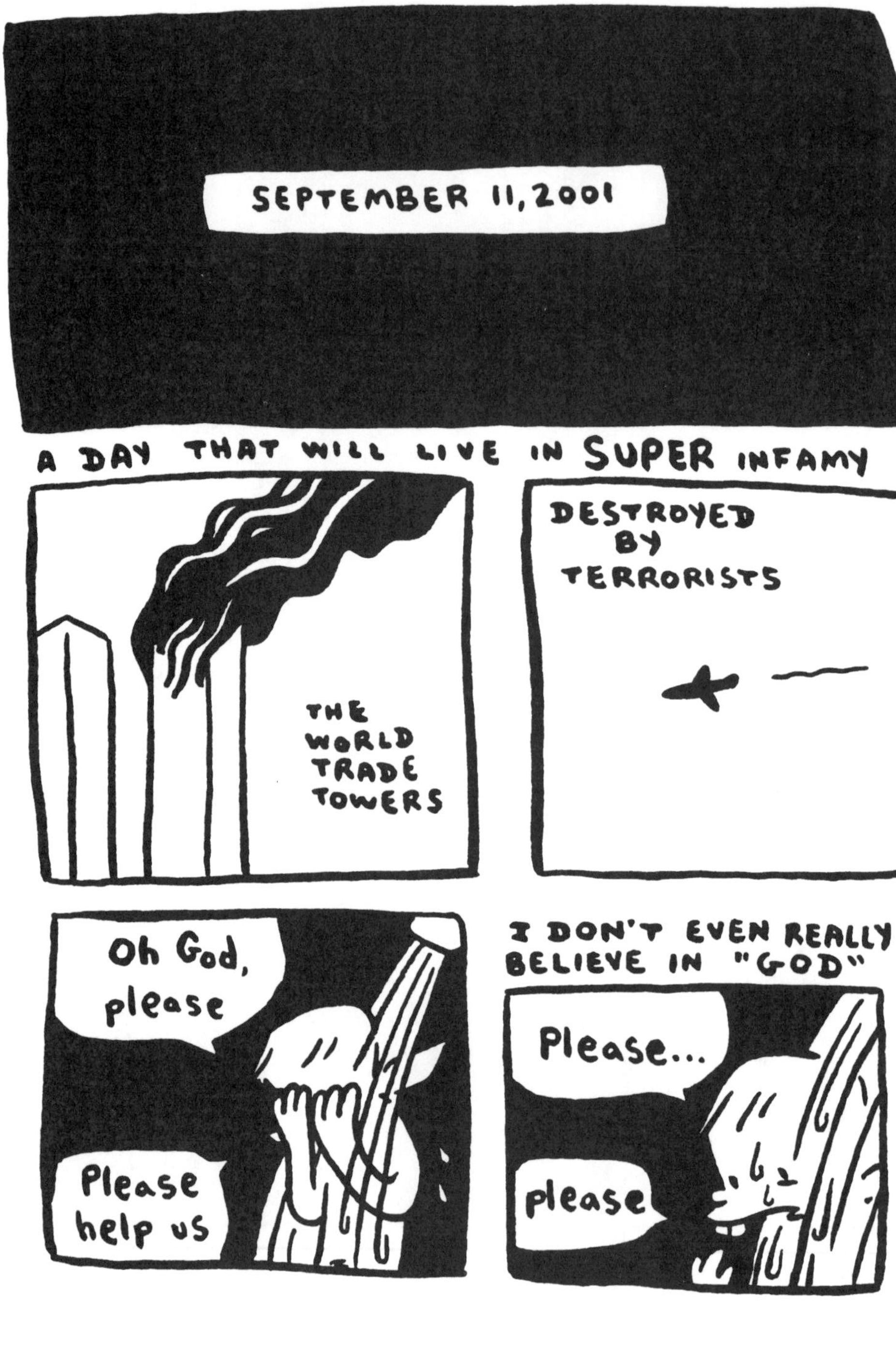
SEPTEMBER 11, 2001
A DAY THAT WILL LIVE IN SUPER INFAMY
THE WORLD TRADE TOWERS
DESTROYED BY TERRORISTS
Oh God, please
Please help us
I DON'T EVEN REALLY BELIEVE IN "GOD"
Please...
please

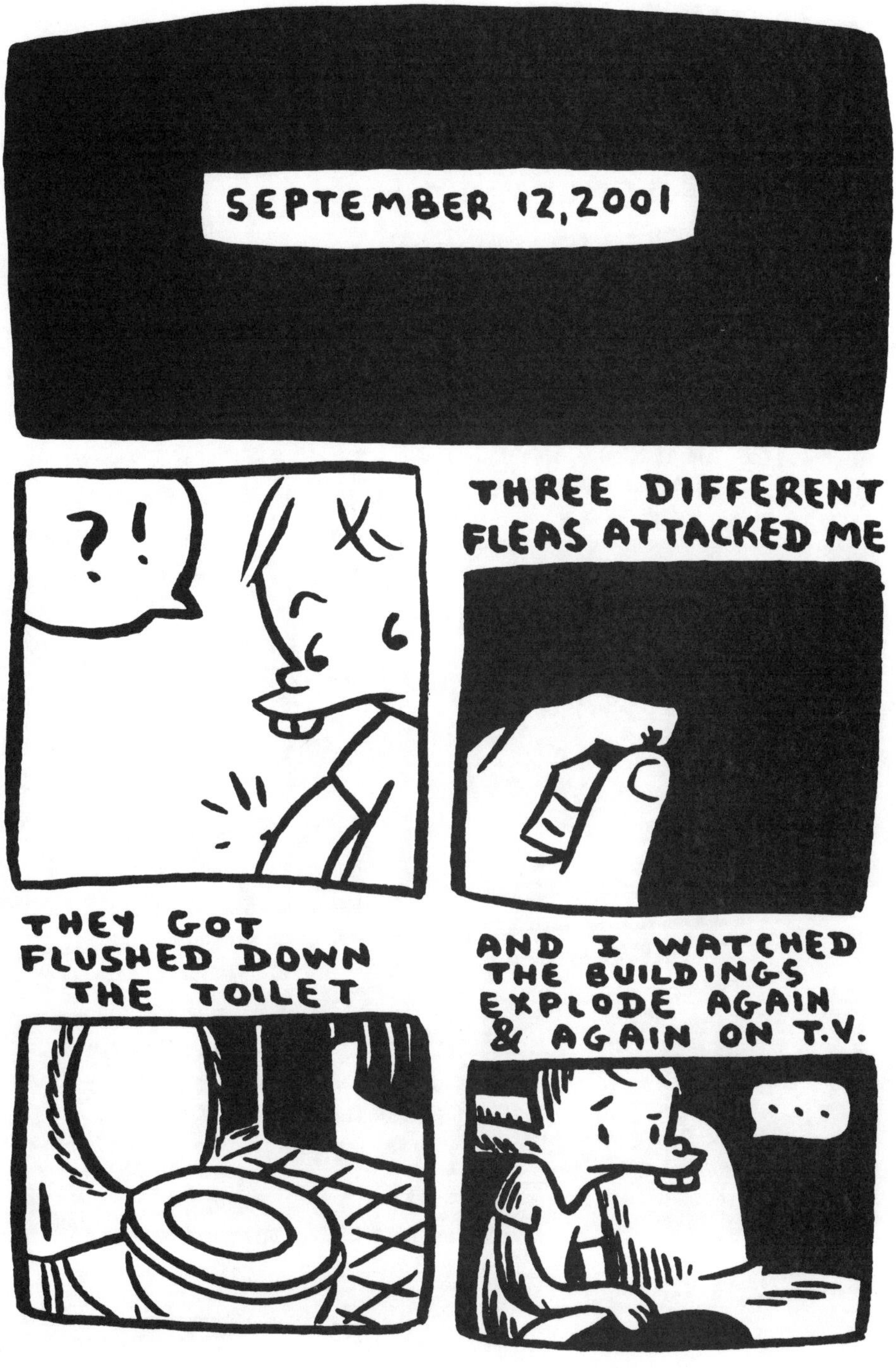
SEPTEMBER 12, 2001
?!
THREE DIFFERENT FLEAS ATTACKED ME
THEY GOT FLUSHED DOWN THE TOILET
AND I WATCHED THE BUILDINGS EXPLODE AGAIN & AGAIN ON T.V.
...

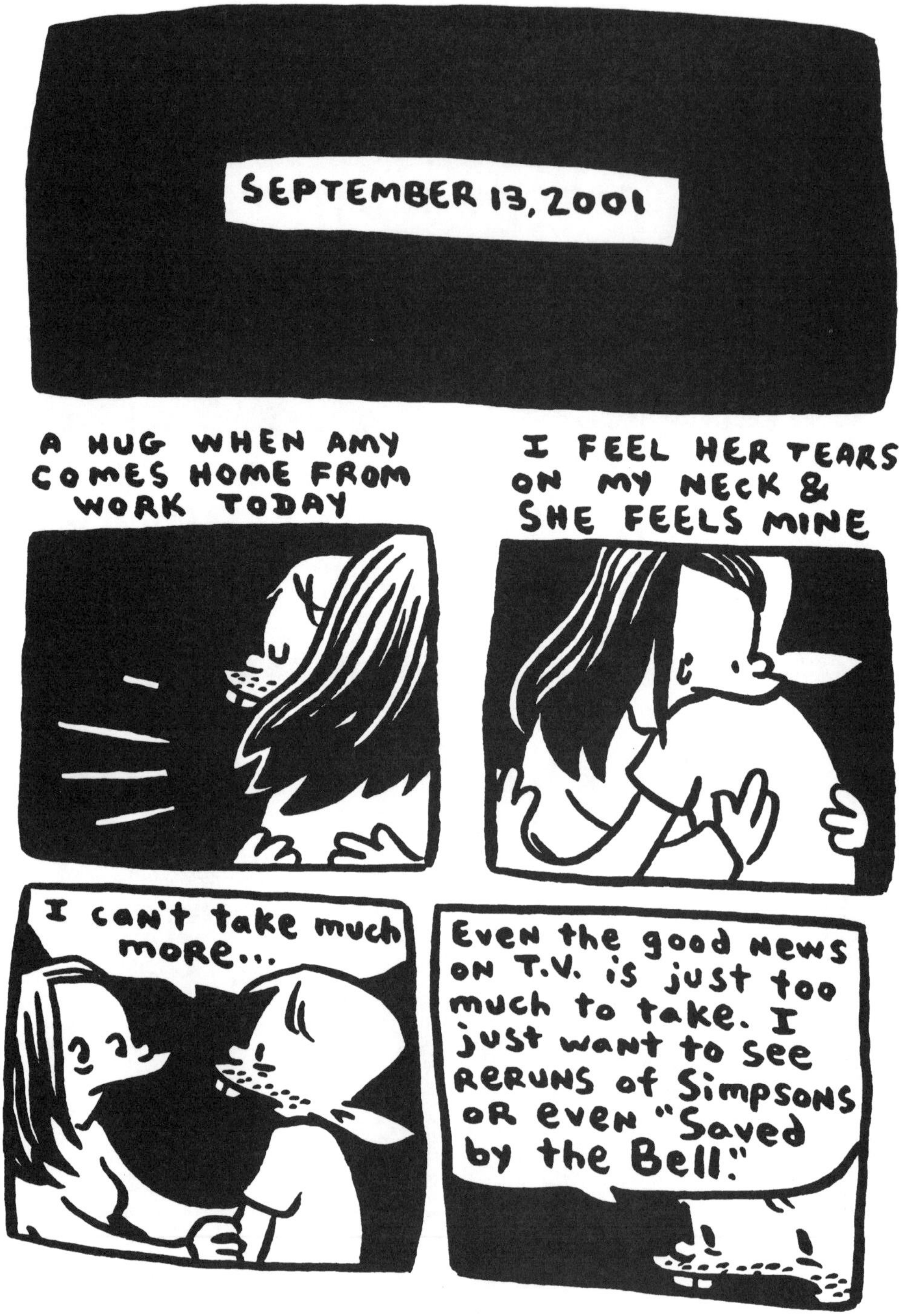
SEPTEMBER 13, 2001
A HUG WHEN AMY COMES HOME FROM WORK TODAY
I FEEL HER TEARS ON MY NECK & SHE FEELS MINE
I can't take much more...
Even the good news on T.V. is just too much to take. I just want to see reruns of Simpsons or even "Saved by the Bell."

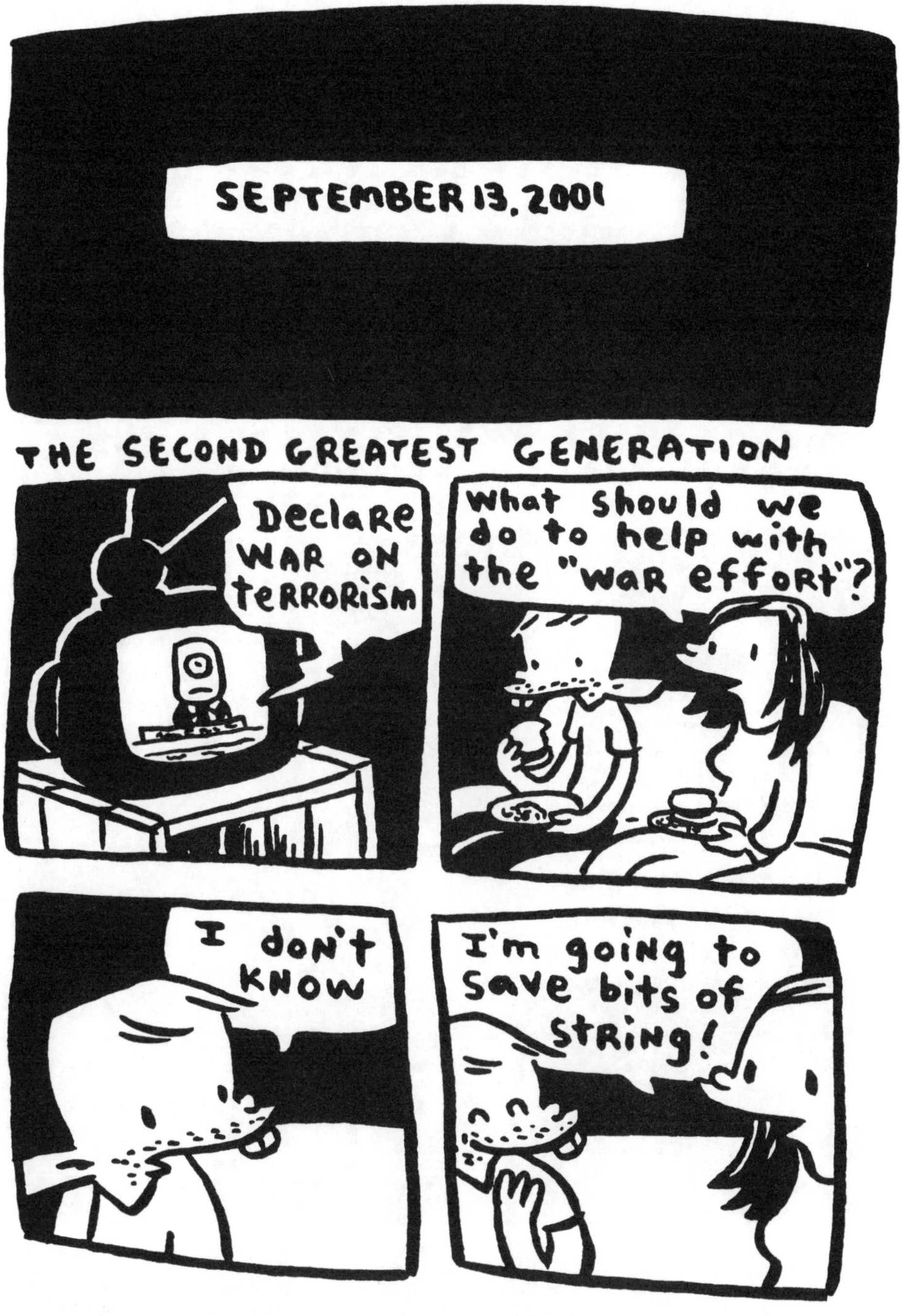
SEPTEMBER 13, 2001
THE SECOND GREATEST GENERATION
Declare WAR ON terrorism
What should we do to help with the "war effort"?
I don't KNOW
I'm going to save bits of STRING!

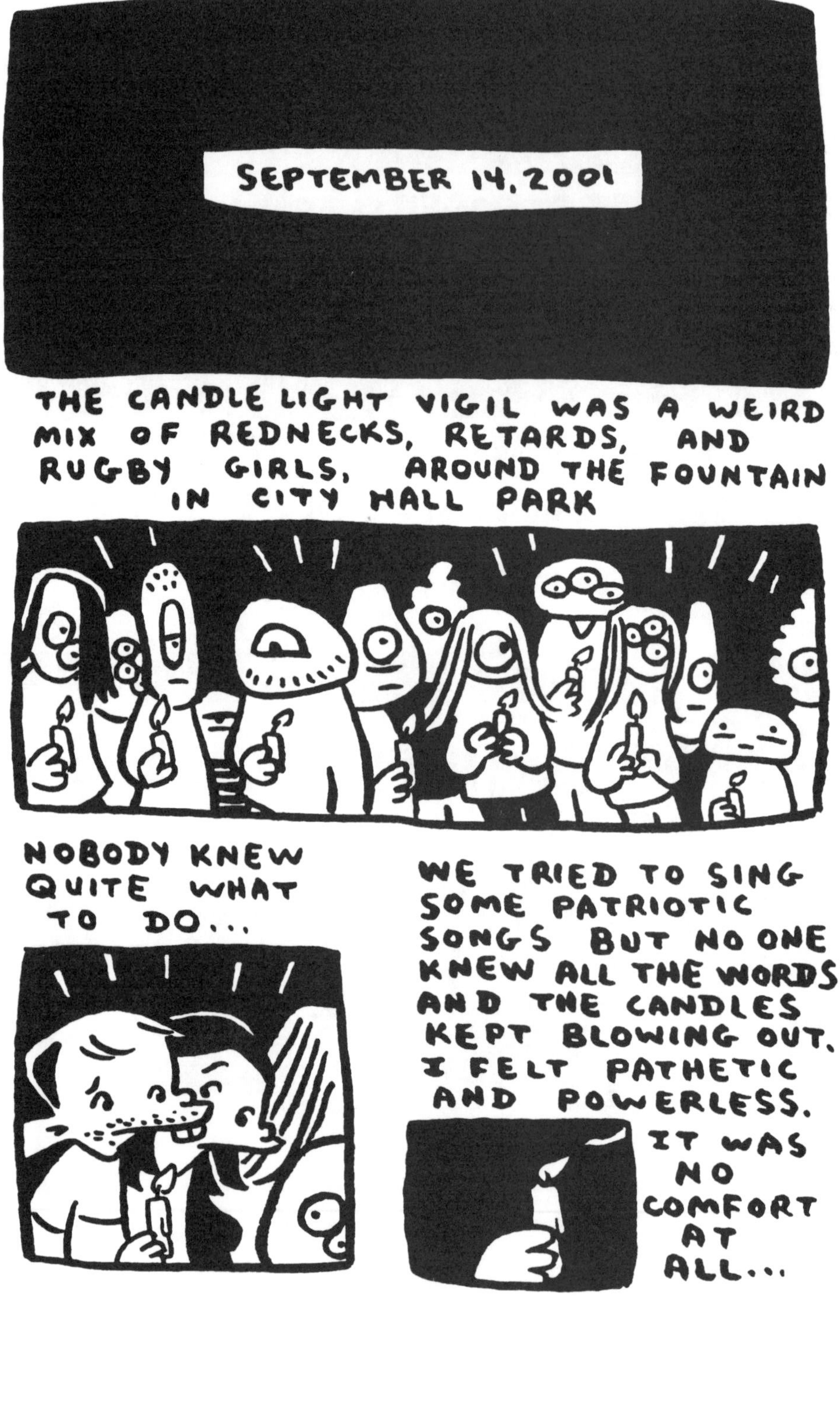
SEPTEMBER 14, 2001
THE CANDLE LIGHT VIGIL WAS A WEIRD MIX OF REDNECKS, RETARDS, AND RUGBY GIRLS, AROUND THE FOUNTAIN IN CITY HALL PARK
NOBODY KNEW QUITE WHAT TO DO...
WE TRIED TO SING SOME PATRIOTIC SONGS BUT NO ONE KNEW ALL THE WORDS AND THE CANDLES KEPT BLOWING OUT. I FELT PATHETIC AND POWERLESS.
IT WAS NO COMFORT AT ALL...

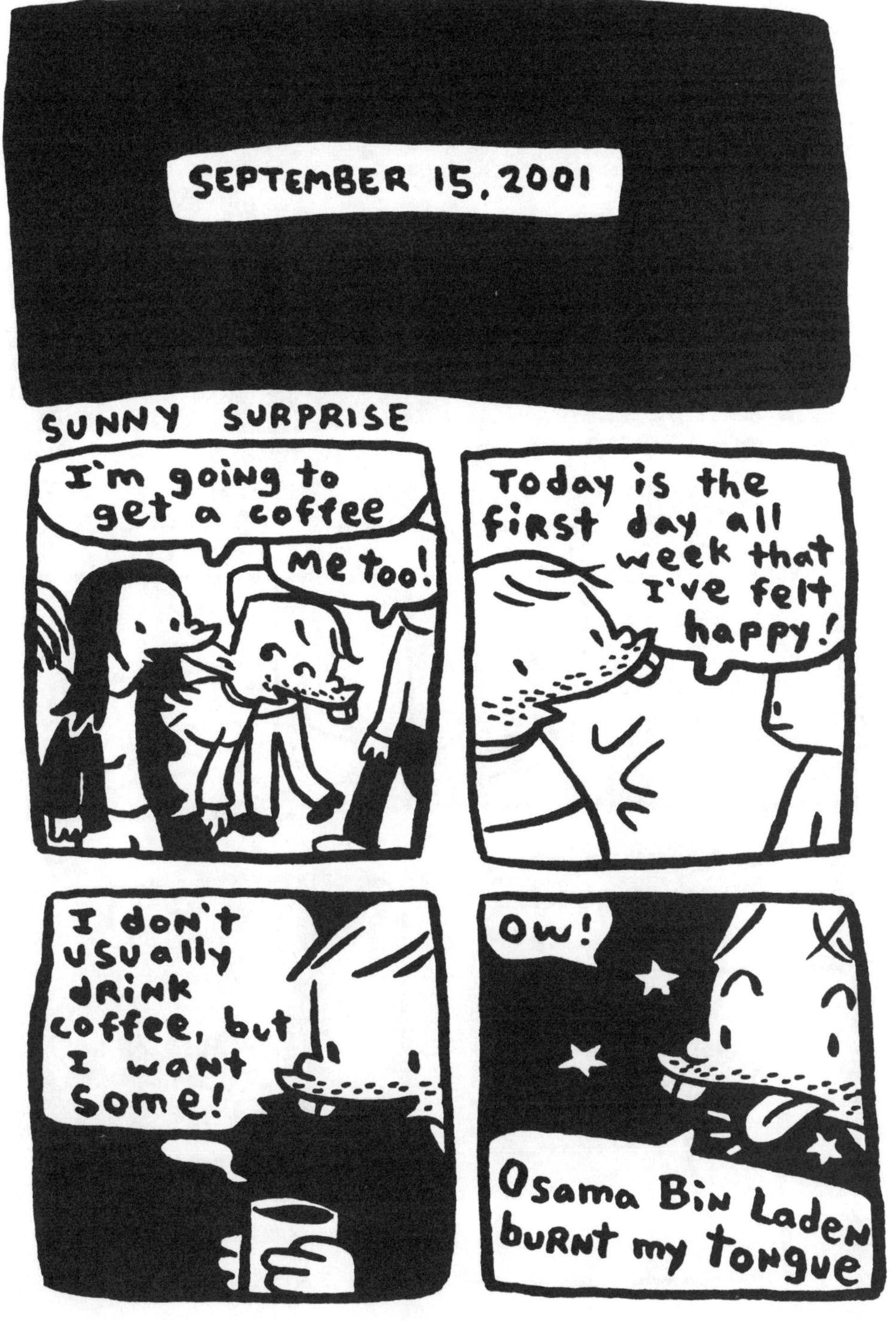
SEPTEMBER 15, 2001
SUNNY SURPRISE
I'm going to get a coffee
me too!
Today is the first day all week that I've felt happy!
I don't usually drink coffee, but I want some!
Ow!
Osama Bin Laden burnt my tongue

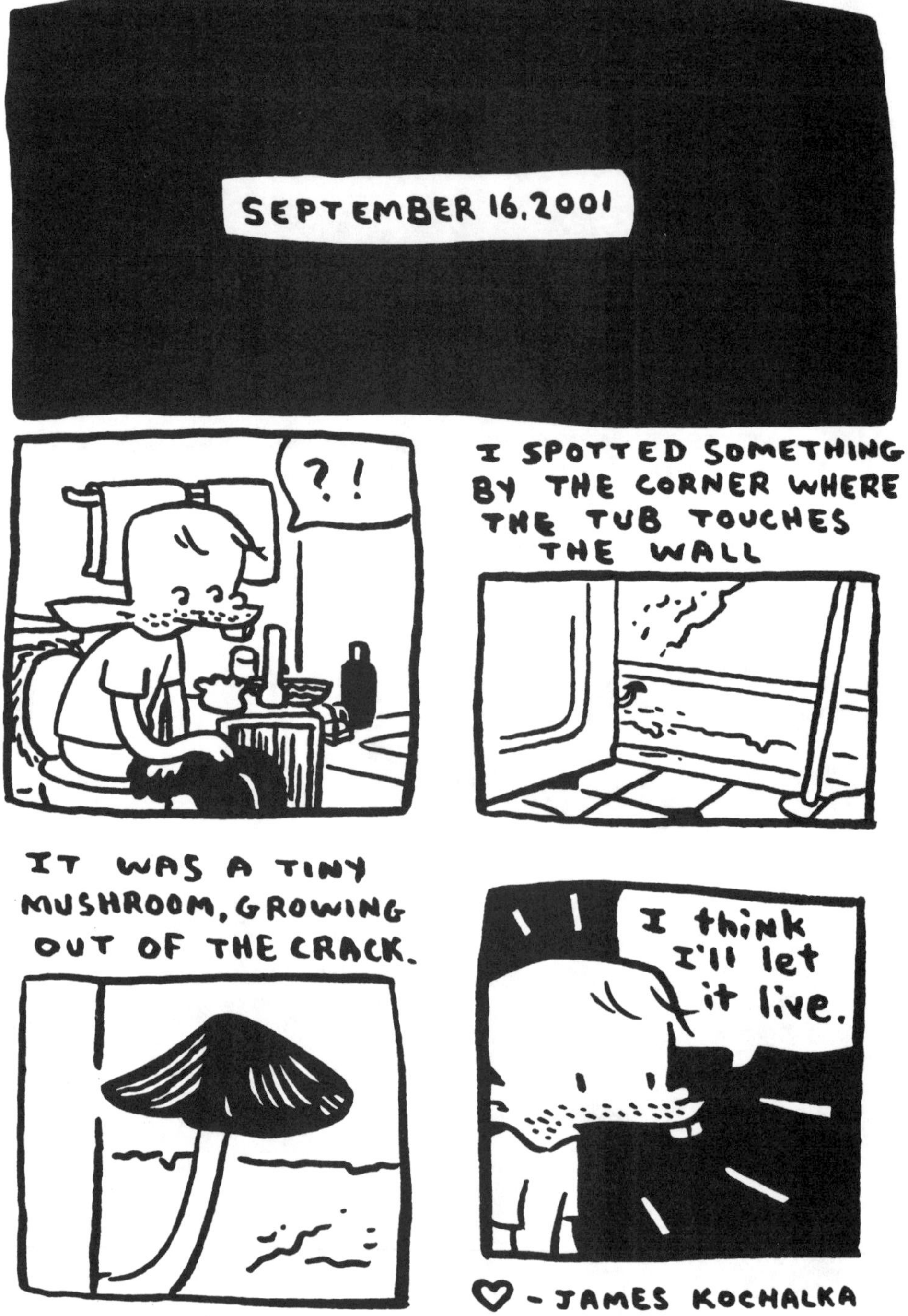
SEPTEMBER 16, 2001
?!
I SPOTTED SOMETHING BY THE CORNER WHERE THE TUB TOUCHES THE WALL
IT WAS A TINY MUSHROOM, GROWING OUT OF THE CRACK.
I think I'll let it live.
♡ - JAMES KOCHALKA

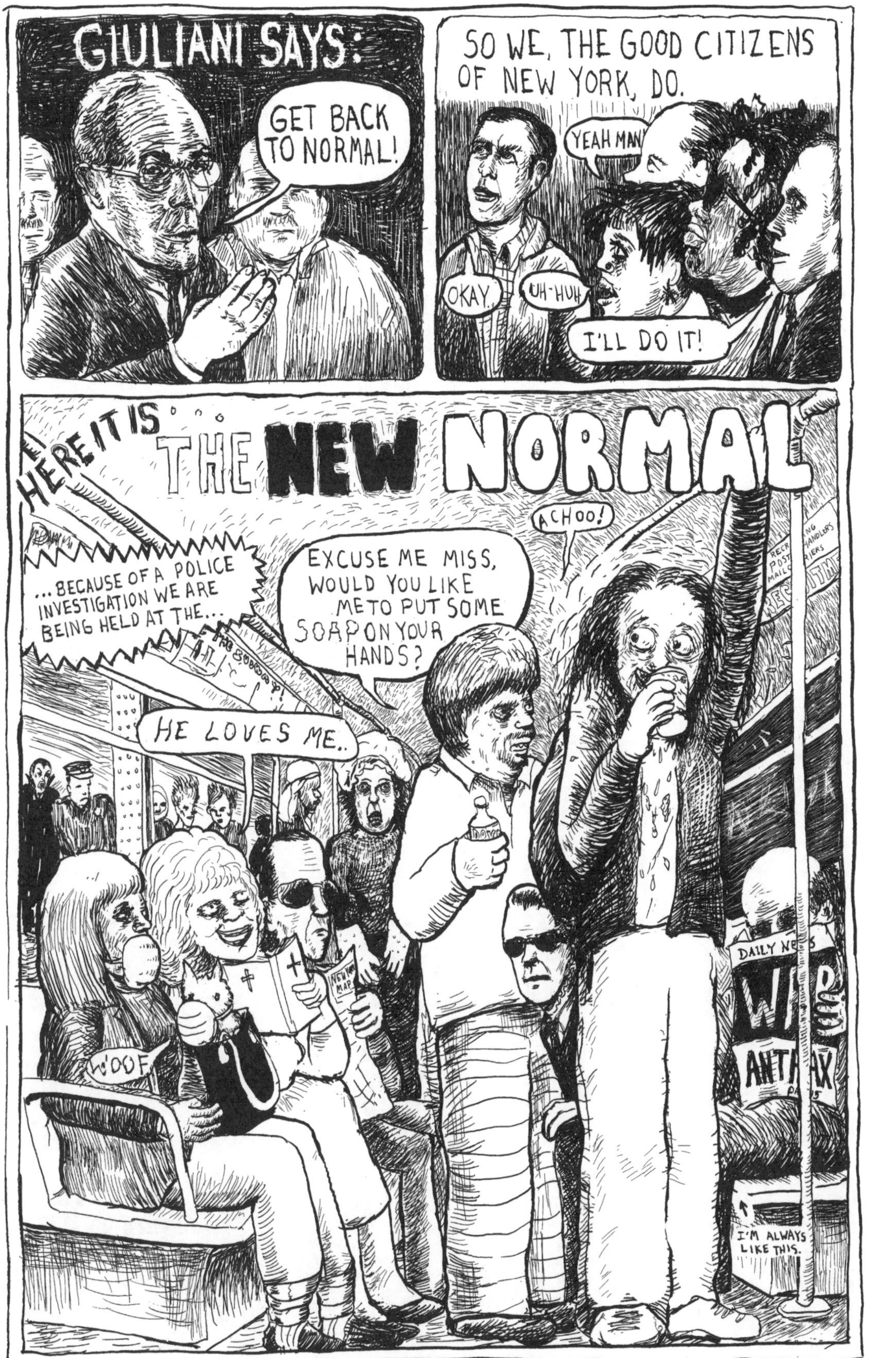
GIULIANI SAYS:
GET BACK TO NORMAL!
SO WE, THE GOOD CITIZENS OF NEW YORK, DO.
YEAH MAN
OKAY.
UH-HUH
I'LL DO IT!
HERE IT IS... THE NEW NORMAL
...BECAUSE OF A POLICE INVESTIGATION WE ARE BEING HELD AT THE...
EXCUSE ME MISS, WOULD YOU LIKE ME TO PUT SOME SOAP ON YOUR HANDS?
ACHOO!
HE LOVES ME..
WOOF
DAILY NEWS
I'M ALWAYS LIKE THIS.

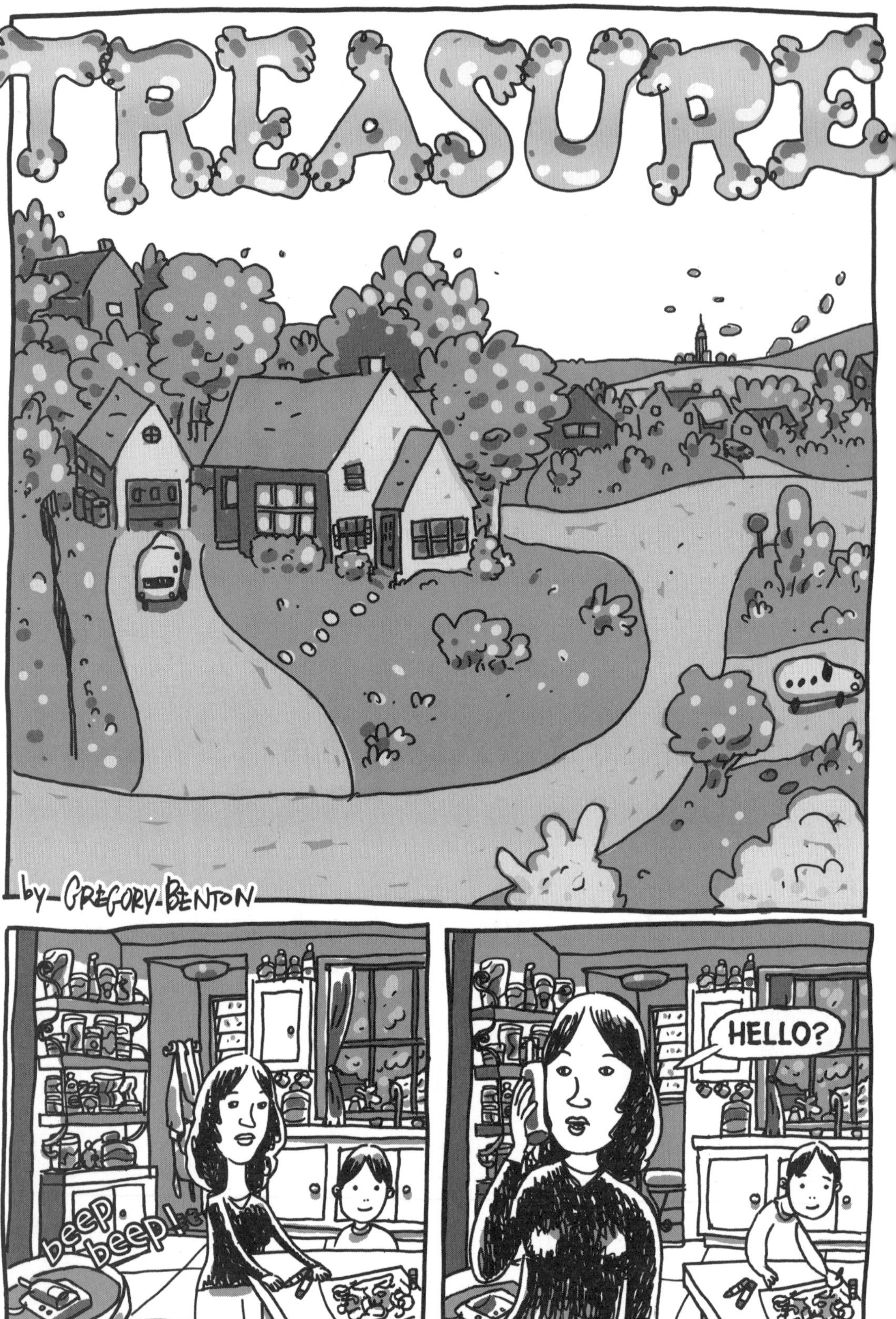
TREASURE
by GREGORY BENTON
beep beep!
HELLO?

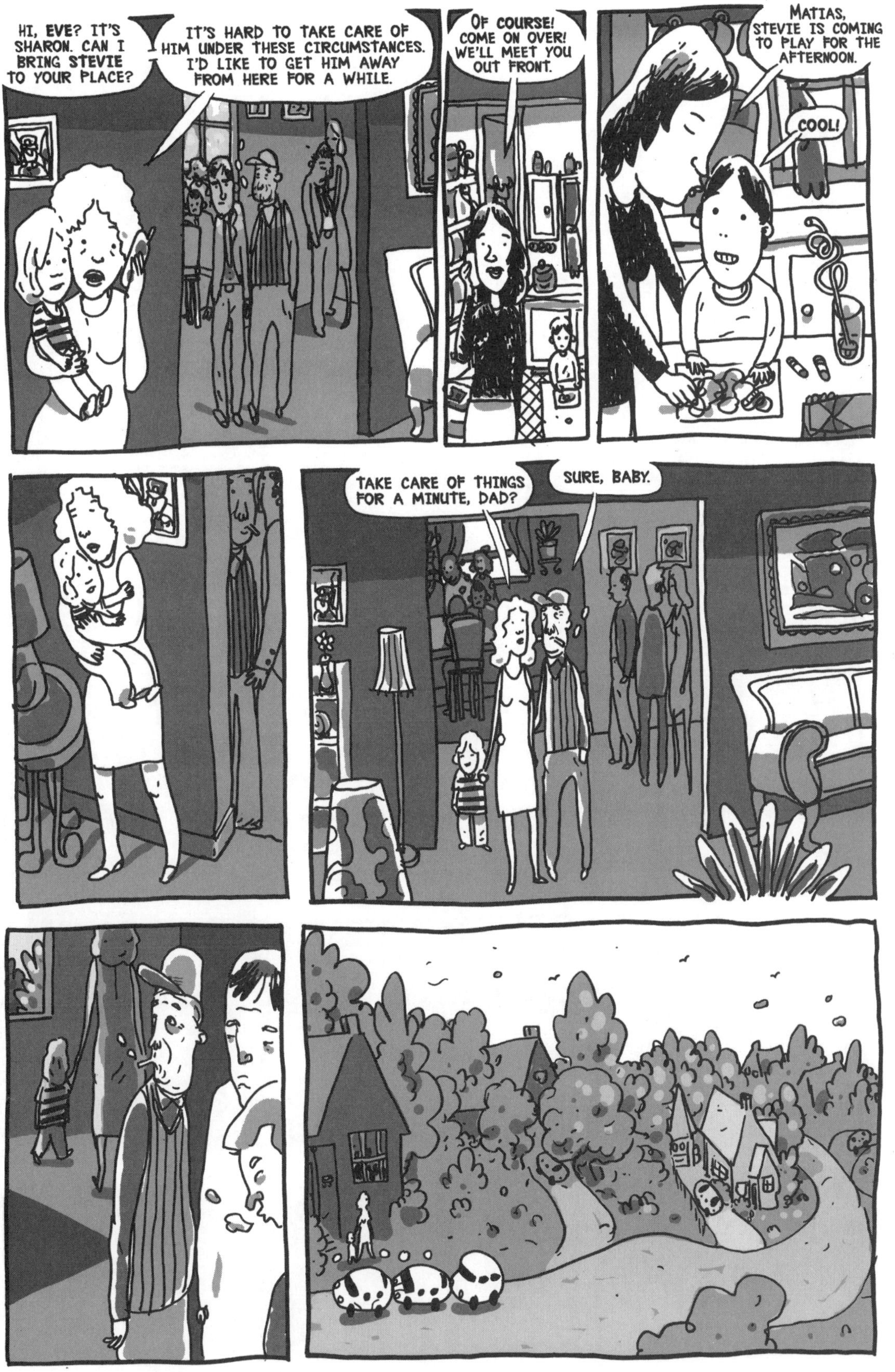
HI, EVE? IT'S SHARON. CAN I BRING STEVIE TO YOUR PLACE?
IT'S HARD TO TAKE CARE OF HIM UNDER THESE CIRCUMSTANCES. I'D LIKE TO GET HIM AWAY FROM HERE FOR A WHILE.
OF COURSE! COME ON OVER! WE'LL MEET YOU OUT FRONT.
MATIAS, STEVIE IS COMING TO PLAY FOR THE AFTERNOON.
COOL!
TAKE CARE OF THINGS FOR A MINUTE, DAD?
SURE, BABY.

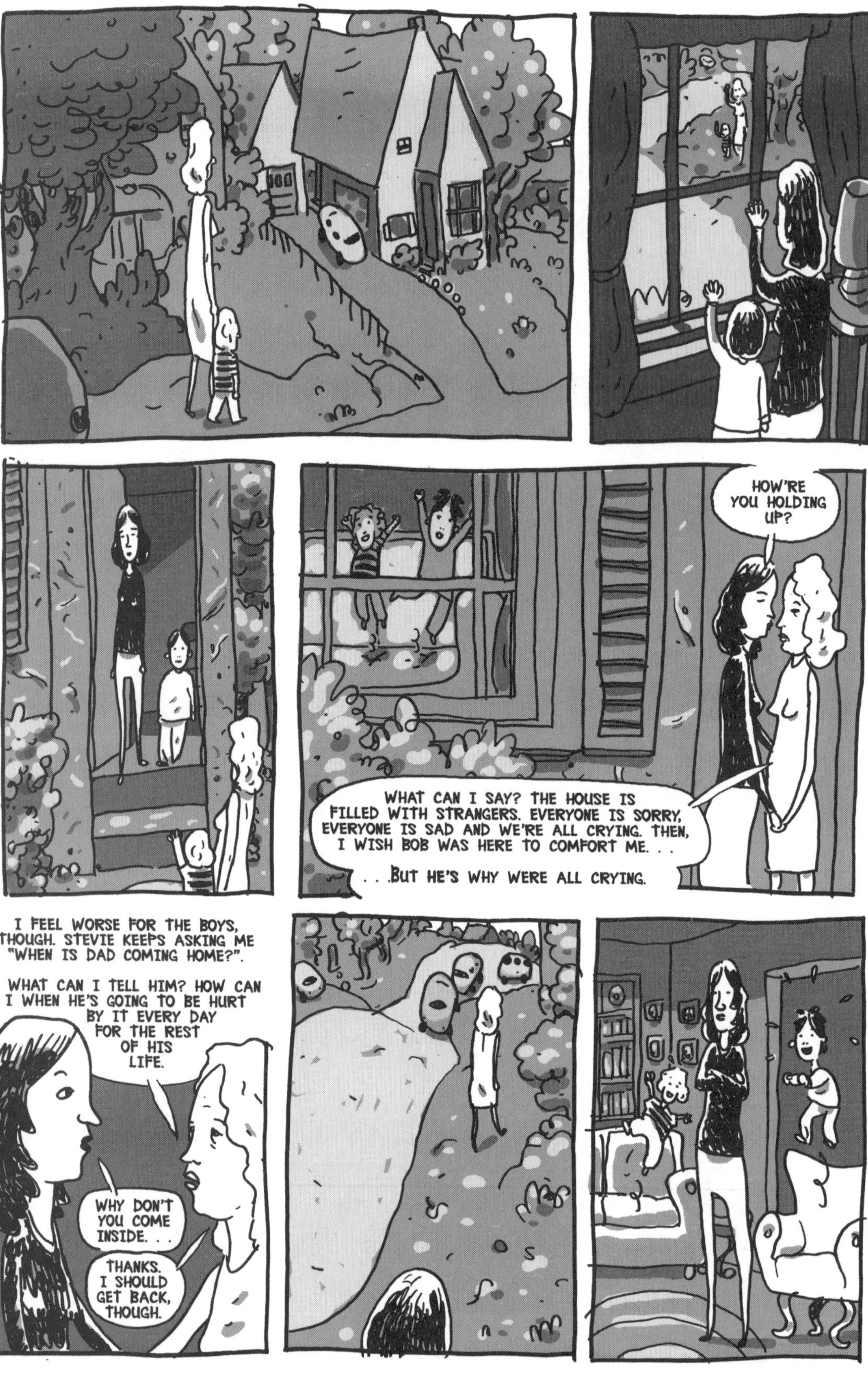
HOW'RE YOU HOLDING UP?
WHAT CAN I SAY? THE HOUSE IS FILLED WITH STRANGERS. EVERYONE IS SORRY, EVERYONE IS SAD AND WE'RE ALL CRYING. THEN, I WISH BOB WAS HERE TO COMFORT ME. . .
. . .BUT HE'S WHY WERE ALL CRYING.
I FEEL WORSE FOR THE BOYS, THOUGH. STEVIE KEEPS ASKING ME "WHEN IS DAD COMING HOME?".
WHAT CAN I TELL HIM? HOW CAN I WHEN HE'S GOING TO BE HURT BY IT EVERY DAY FOR THE REST OF HIS LIFE.
WHY DON'T YOU COME INSIDE. . .
THANKS. I SHOULD GET BACK, THOUGH.

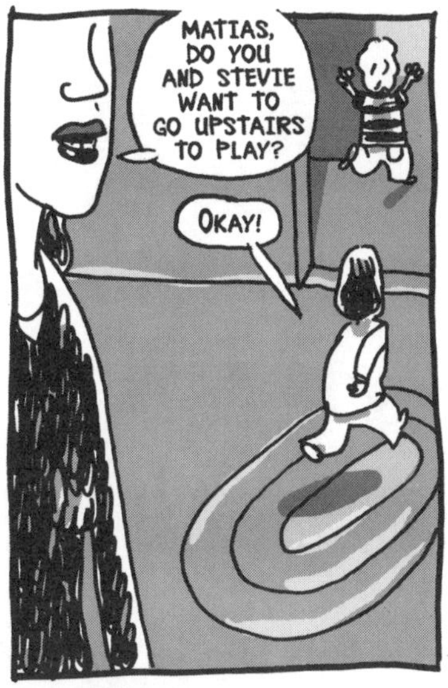
MATIAS, DO YOU AND STEVIE WANT TO GO UPSTAIRS TO PLAY?
OKAY!
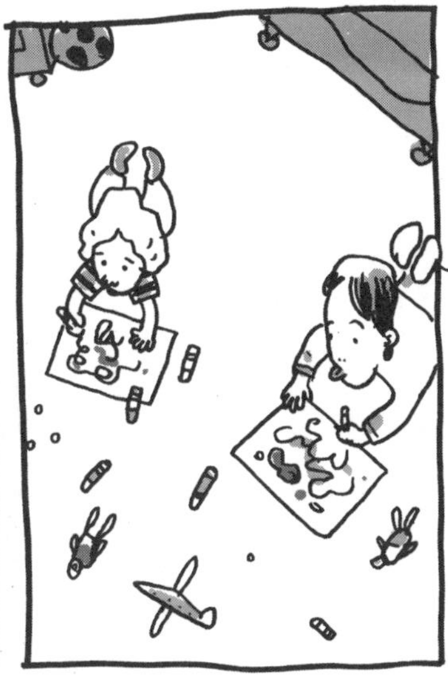
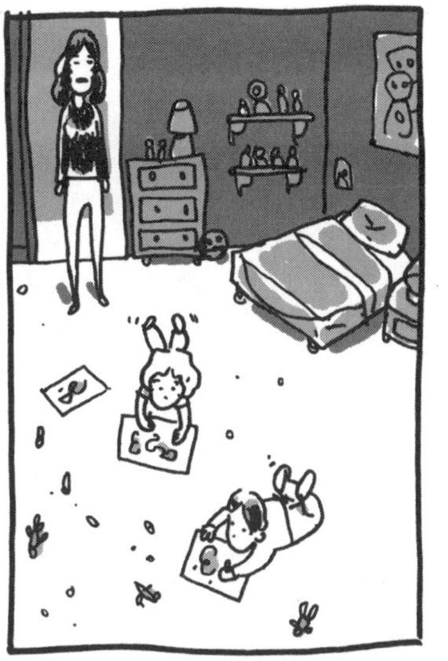
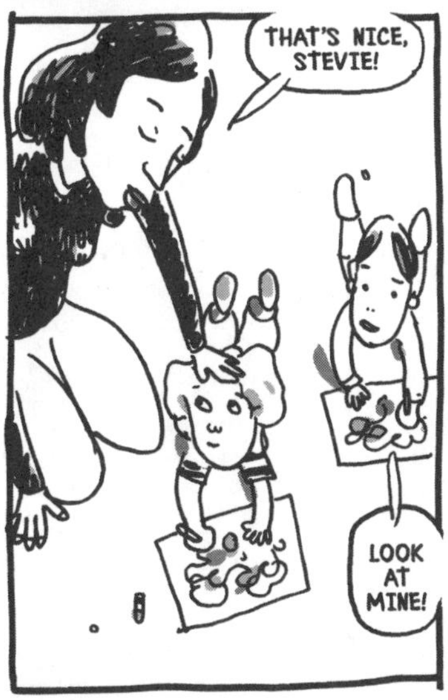
THAT'S NICE, STEVIE!
LOOK AT MINE!
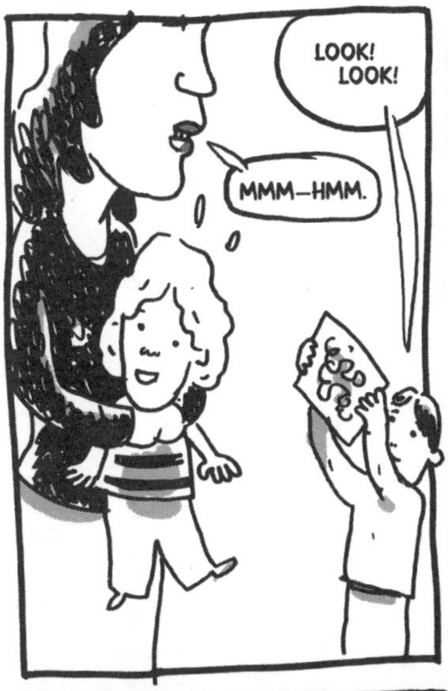
LOOK! LOOK!
MMM–HMM.
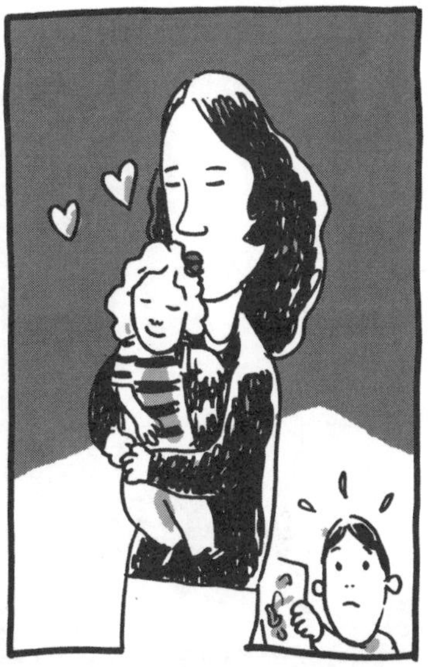
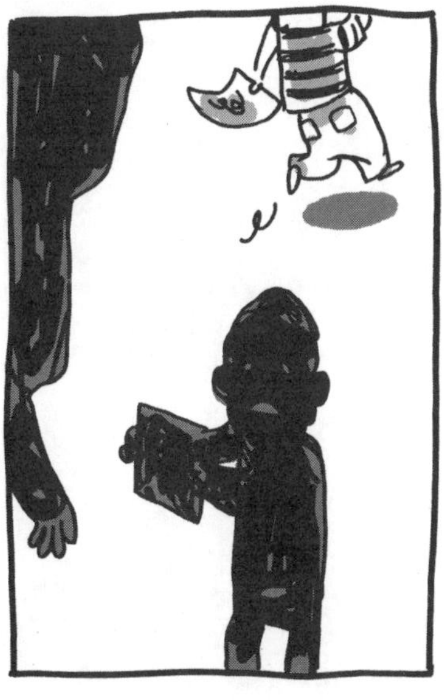
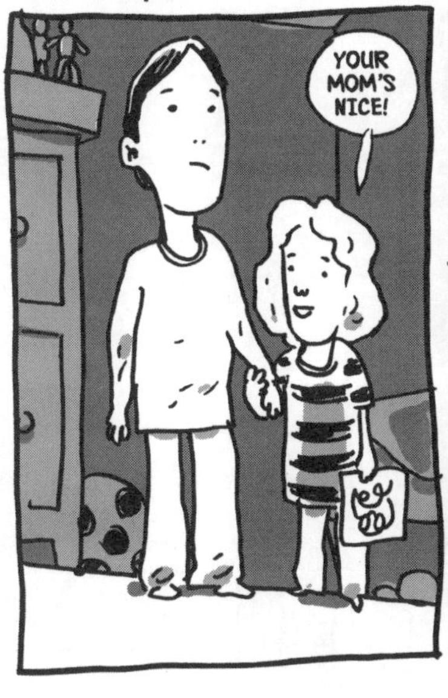
YOUR MOM'S NICE!
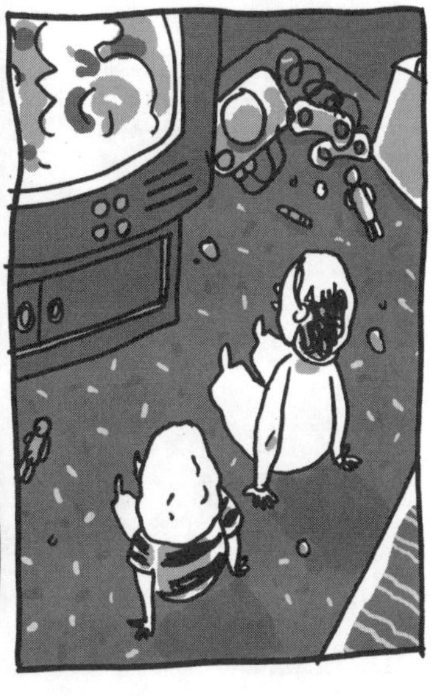

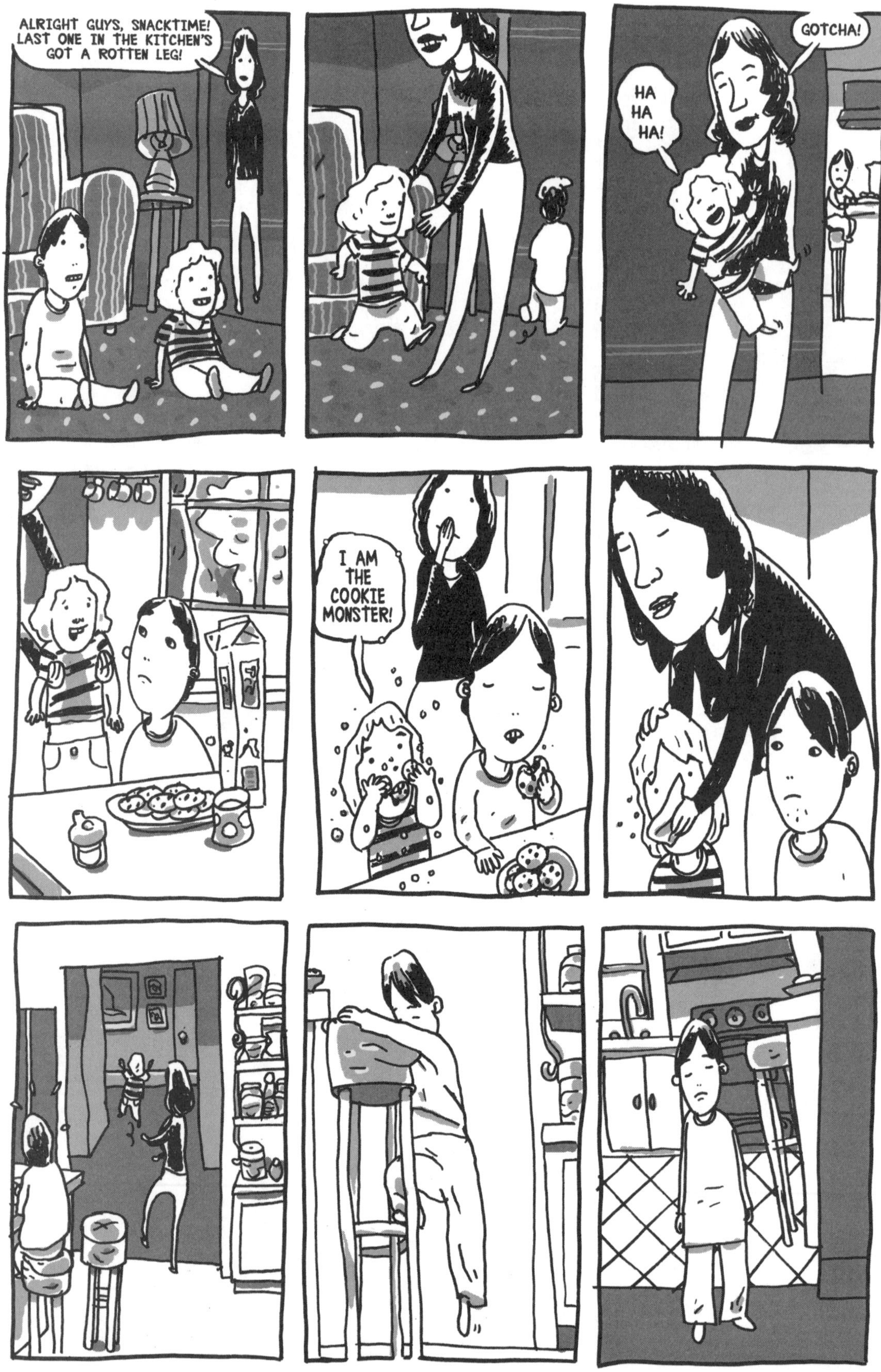
ALRIGHT GUYS, SNACKTIME! LAST ONE IN THE KITCHEN'S GOT A ROTTEN LEG!
GOTCHA!
HA HA HA!
I AM THE COOKIE MONSTER!

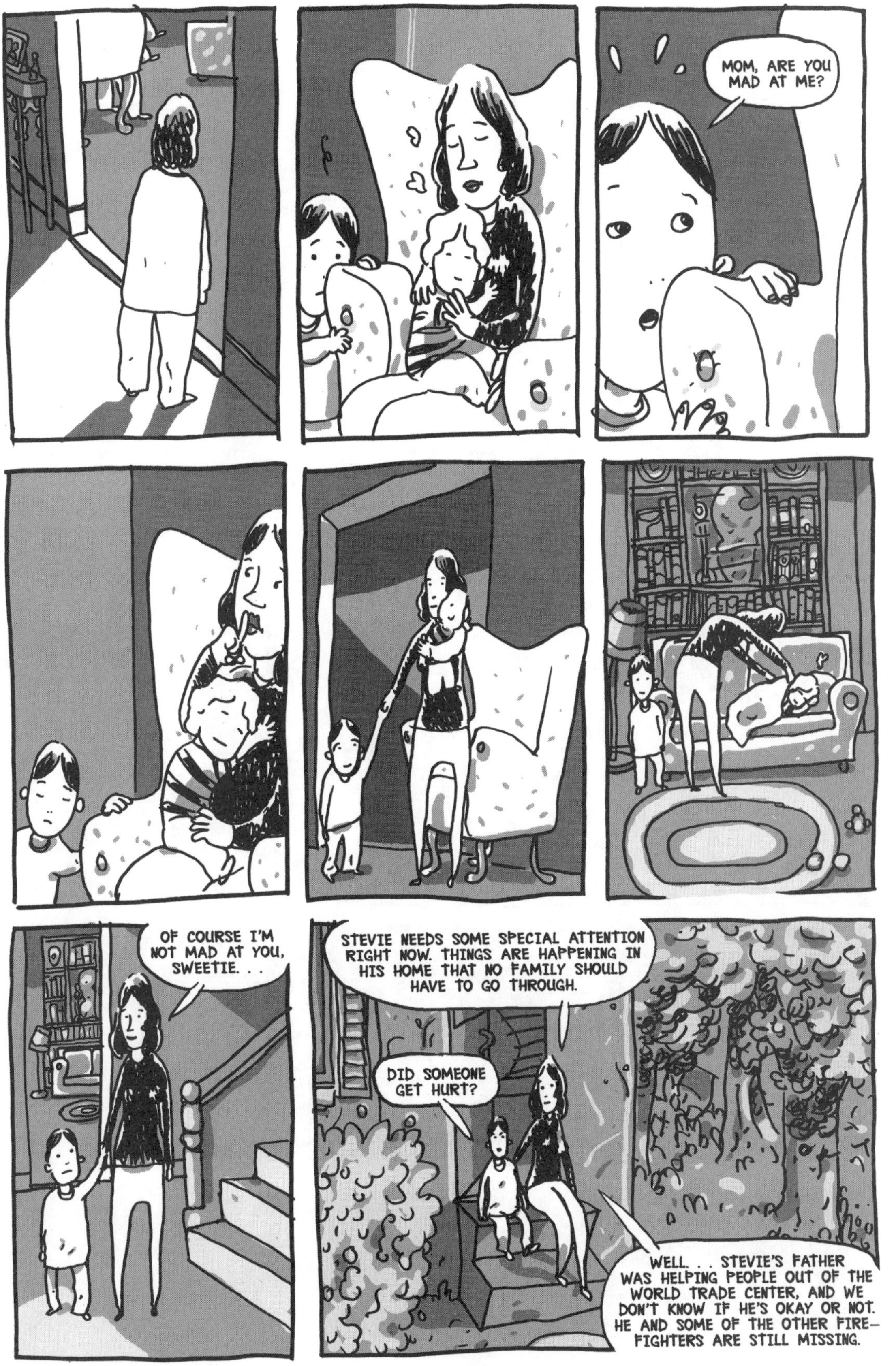
MOM, ARE YOU MAD AT ME?
OF COURSE I'M NOT MAD AT YOU, SWEETIE. . .
STEVIE NEEDS SOME SPECIAL ATTENTION RIGHT NOW. THINGS ARE HAPPENING IN HIS HOME THAT NO FAMILY SHOULD HAVE TO GO THROUGH.
DID SOMEONE GET HURT?
WELL. . . STEVIE'S FATHER WAS HELPING PEOPLE OUT OF THE WORLD TRADE CENTER, AND WE DON'T KNOW IF HE'S OKAY OR NOT. HE AND SOME OF THE OTHER FIRE-FIGHTERS ARE STILL MISSING.

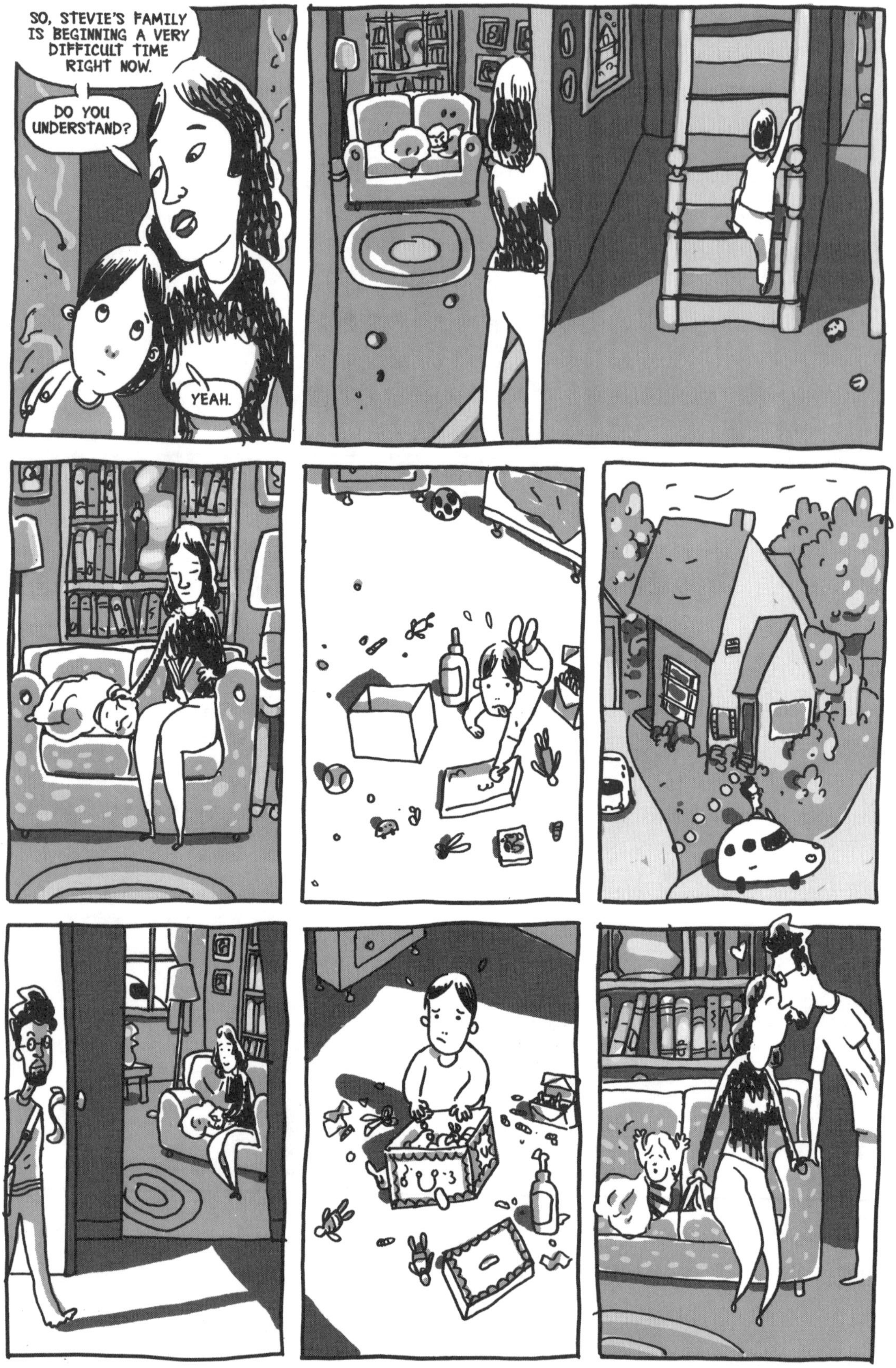

SO, STEVIE'S FAMILY IS BEGINNING A VERY DIFFICULT TIME RIGHT NOW.
DO YOU UNDERSTAND?
YEAH.

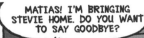
MATIAS! I'M BRINGING STEVIE HOME. DO YOU WANT TO SAY GOODBYE?

IS EVERYONE STILL GOING TO BE SAD WHEN I GET HOME?

MOM! WAIT!

HI, DAD!

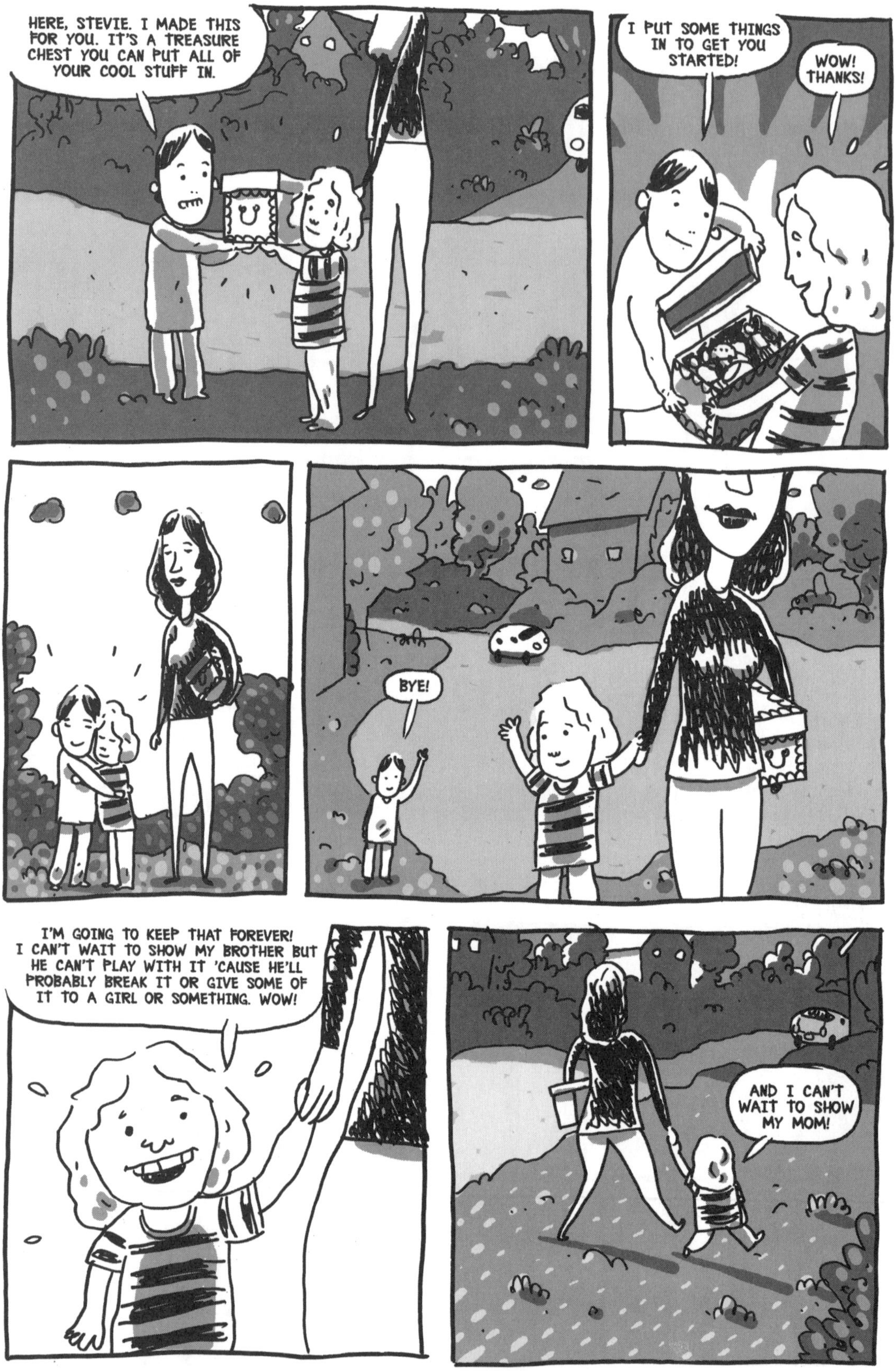
HERE, STEVIE. I MADE THIS FOR YOU. IT'S A TREASURE CHEST YOU CAN PUT ALL OF YOUR COOL STUFF IN.
I PUT SOME THINGS IN TO GET YOU STARTED!
WOW! THANKS!
BYE!
I'M GOING TO KEEP THAT FOREVER! I CAN'T WAIT TO SHOW MY BROTHER BUT HE CAN'T PLAY WITH IT 'CAUSE HE'LL PROBABLY BREAK IT OR GIVE SOME OF IT TO A GIRL OR SOMETHING. WOW!
AND I CAN'T WAIT TO SHOW MY MOM!

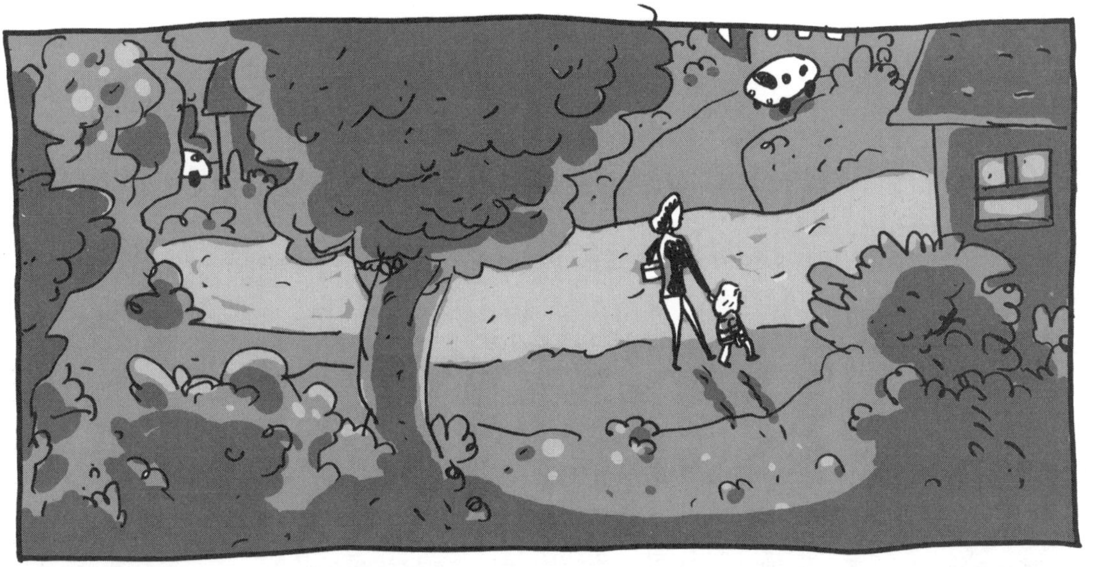

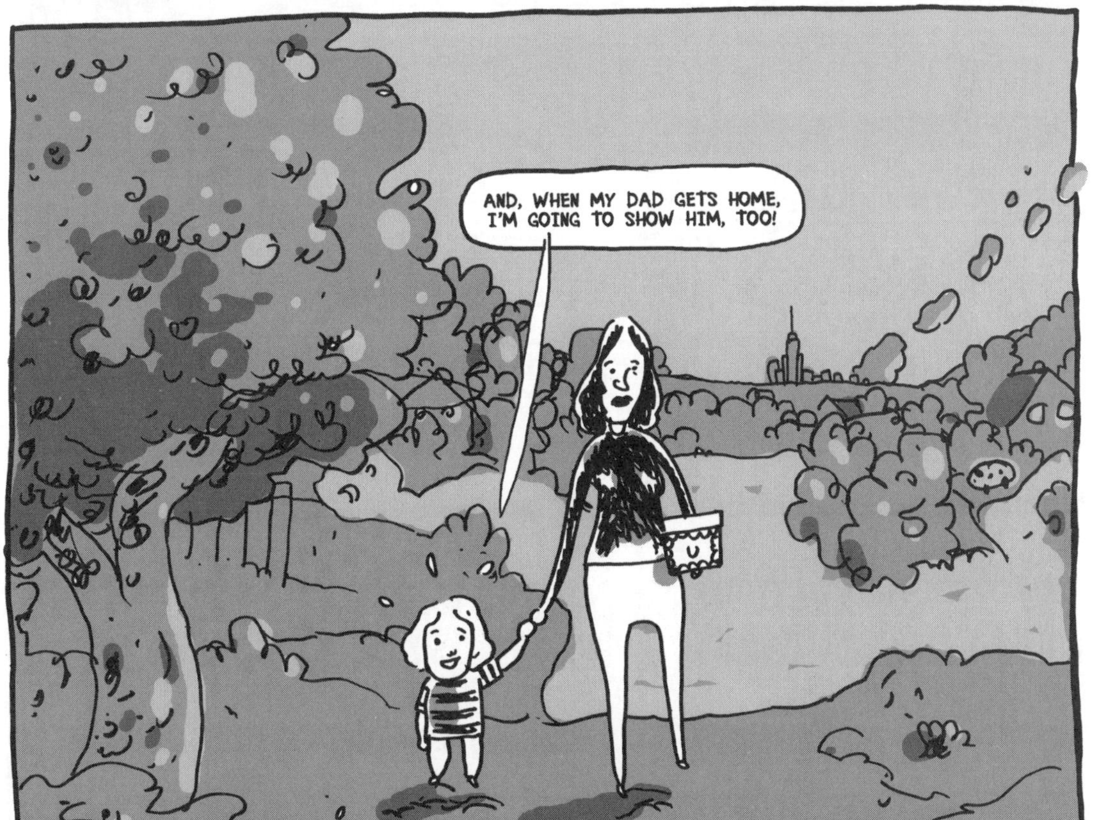
AND, WHEN MY DAD GETS HOME, I'M GOING TO SHOW HIM, TOO!
©2001 GREGORY BENTON
end

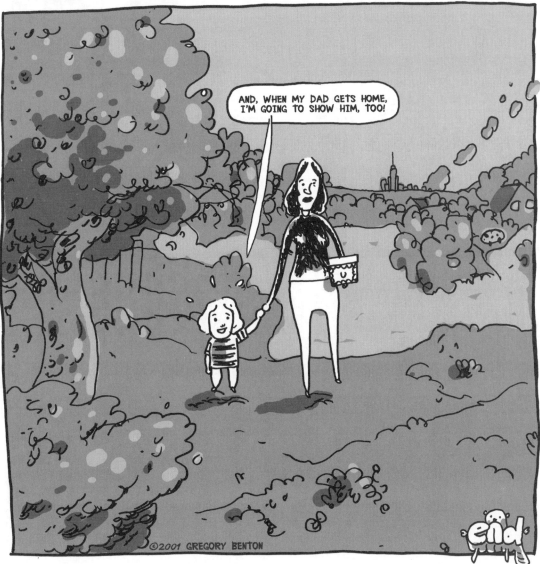

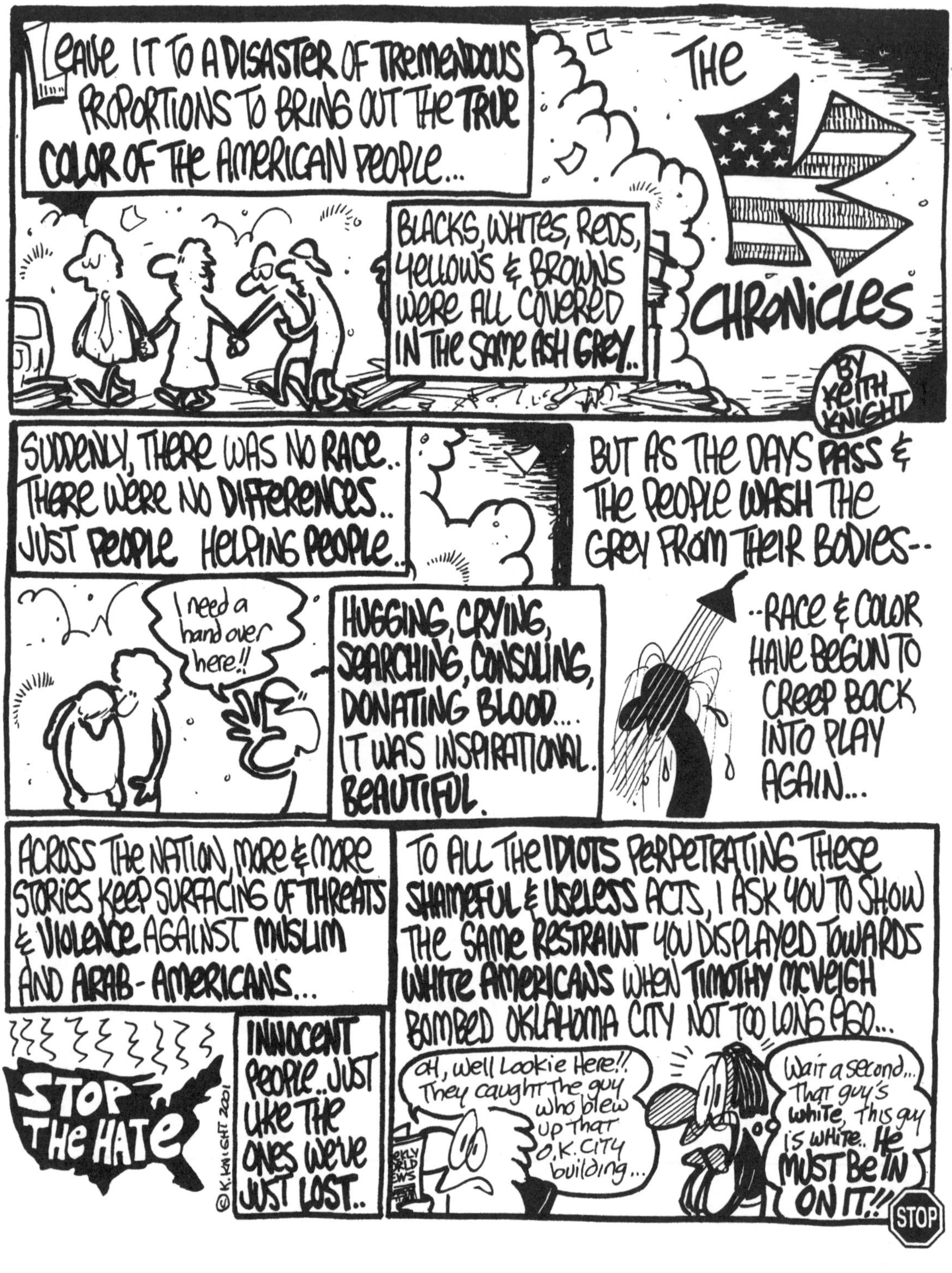
THE K CHRONICLES
BY KEITH KNIGHT
LEAVE IT TO A DISASTER OF TREMENDOUS PROPORTIONS TO BRING OUT THE TRUE COLOR OF THE AMERICAN PEOPLE...
BLACKS, WHITES, REDS, YELLOWS & BROWNS WERE ALL COVERED IN THE SAME ASH GREY..
SUDDENLY, THERE WAS NO RACE.. THERE WERE NO DIFFERENCES.. JUST PEOPLE HELPING PEOPLE..
BUT AS THE DAYS PASS & THE PEOPLE WASH THE GREY FROM THEIR BODIES--
I need a hand over here!!
HUGGING, CRYING, SEARCHING, CONSOLING, DONATING BLOOD.... IT WAS INSPIRATIONAL. BEAUTIFUL.
--RACE & COLOR HAVE BEGUN TO CREEP BACK INTO PLAY AGAIN...
ACROSS THE NATION, MORE & MORE STORIES KEEP SURFACING OF THREATS & VIOLENCE AGAINST MUSLIM AND ARAB-AMERICANS...
TO ALL THE IDIOTS PERPETRATING THESE SHAMEFUL & USELESS ACTS, I ASK YOU TO SHOW THE SAME RESTRAINT YOU DISPLAYED TOWARDS WHITE AMERICANS WHEN TIMOTHY MCVEIGH BOMBED OKLAHOMA CITY NOT TOO LONG AGO...
STOP THE HATE
©K. KNIGHT 2001
INNOCENT PEOPLE.. JUST LIKE THE ONES WE'VE JUST LOST..
OH, Well Lookie Here!! They caught the guy who blew up that O.K. CITY building...
Wait a second... That guy's white, this guy is white.. He MUST Be IN ON IT!!
STOP

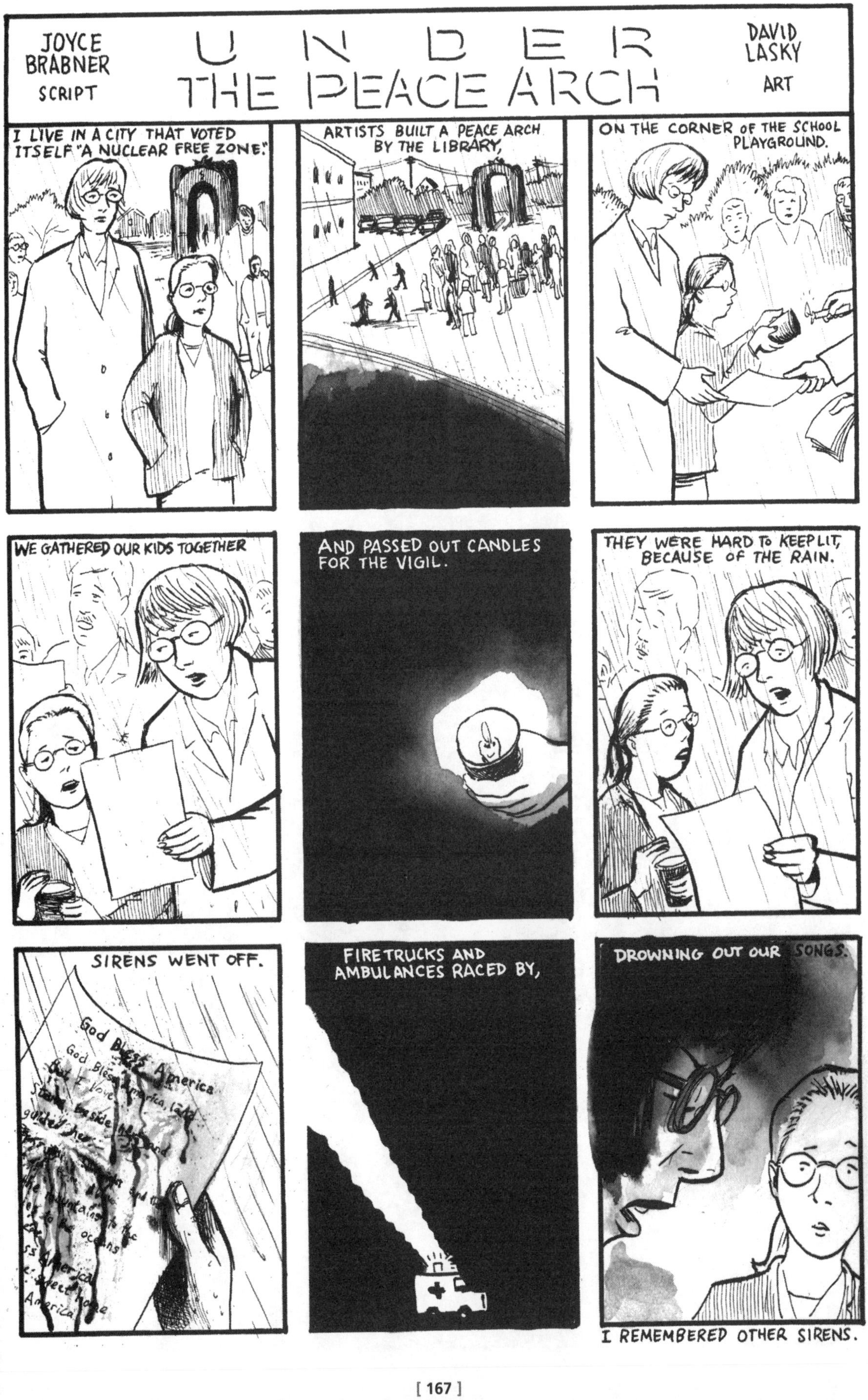

JOYCE BRABNER SCRIPT
UNDER THE PEACE ARCH
DAVID LASKY ART
I LIVE IN A CITY THAT VOTED ITSELF "A NUCLEAR FREE ZONE."
ARTISTS BUILT A PEACE ARCH BY THE LIBRARY,
ON THE CORNER OF THE SCHOOL PLAYGROUND.
WE GATHERED OUR KIDS TOGETHER
AND PASSED OUT CANDLES FOR THE VIGIL.
THEY WERE HARD TO KEEP LIT, BECAUSE OF THE RAIN.
SIRENS WENT OFF.
God Bless America
FIRETRUCKS AND AMBULANCES RACED BY,
DROWNING OUT OUR SONGS.
I REMEMBERED OTHER SIRENS.

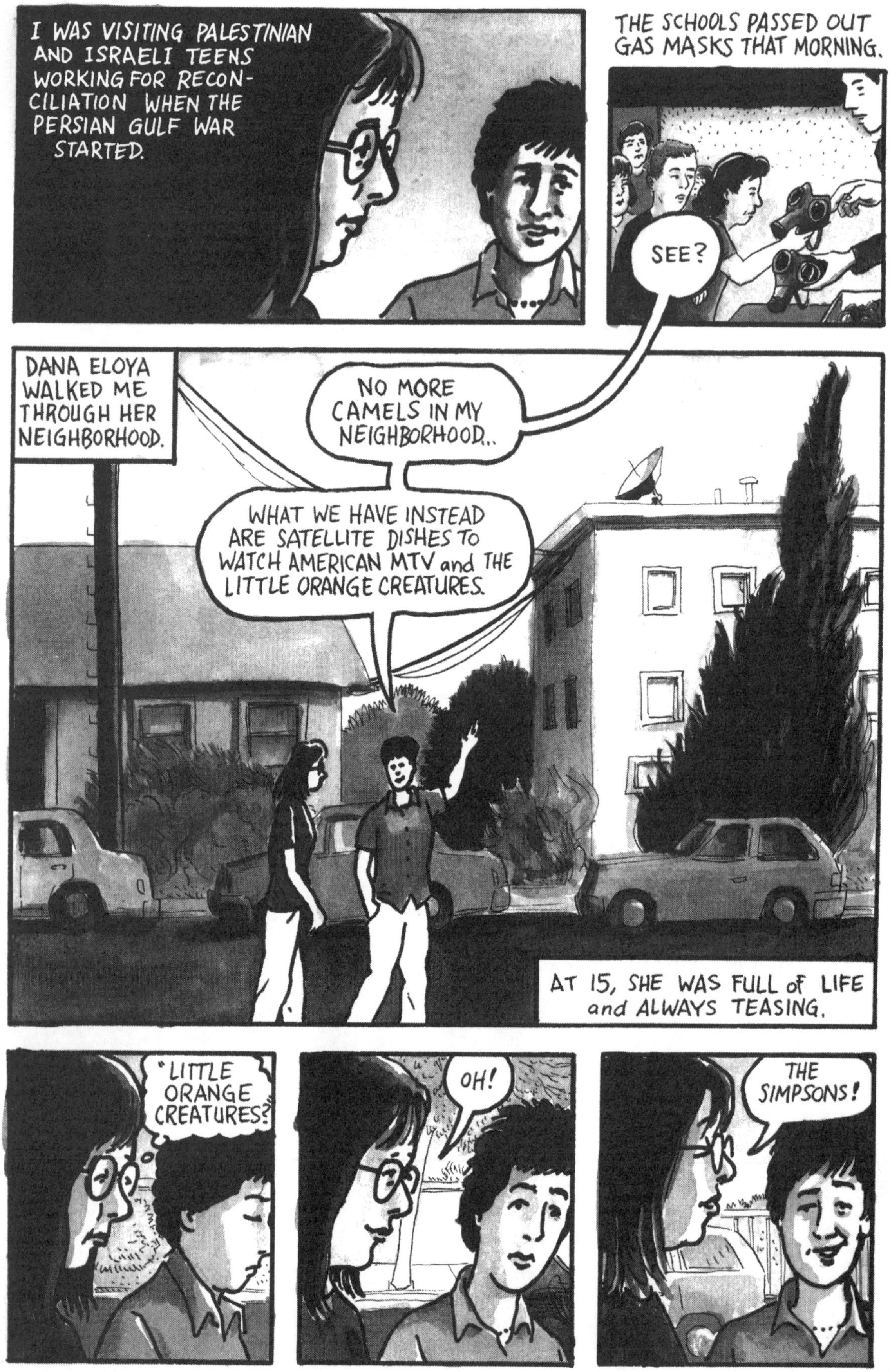
I WAS VISITING PALESTINIAN AND ISRAELI TEENS WORKING FOR RECONCILIATION WHEN THE PERSIAN GULF WAR STARTED.
THE SCHOOLS PASSED OUT GAS MASKS THAT MORNING.
SEE?
DANA ELOYA WALKED ME THROUGH HER NEIGHBORHOOD.
NO MORE CAMELS IN MY NEIGHBORHOOD...
WHAT WE HAVE INSTEAD ARE SATELLITE DISHES TO WATCH AMERICAN MTV and THE LITTLE ORANGE CREATURES.
AT 15, SHE WAS FULL of LIFE and ALWAYS TEASING.
"LITTLE ORANGE CREATURES?"
OH!
THE SIMPSONS!

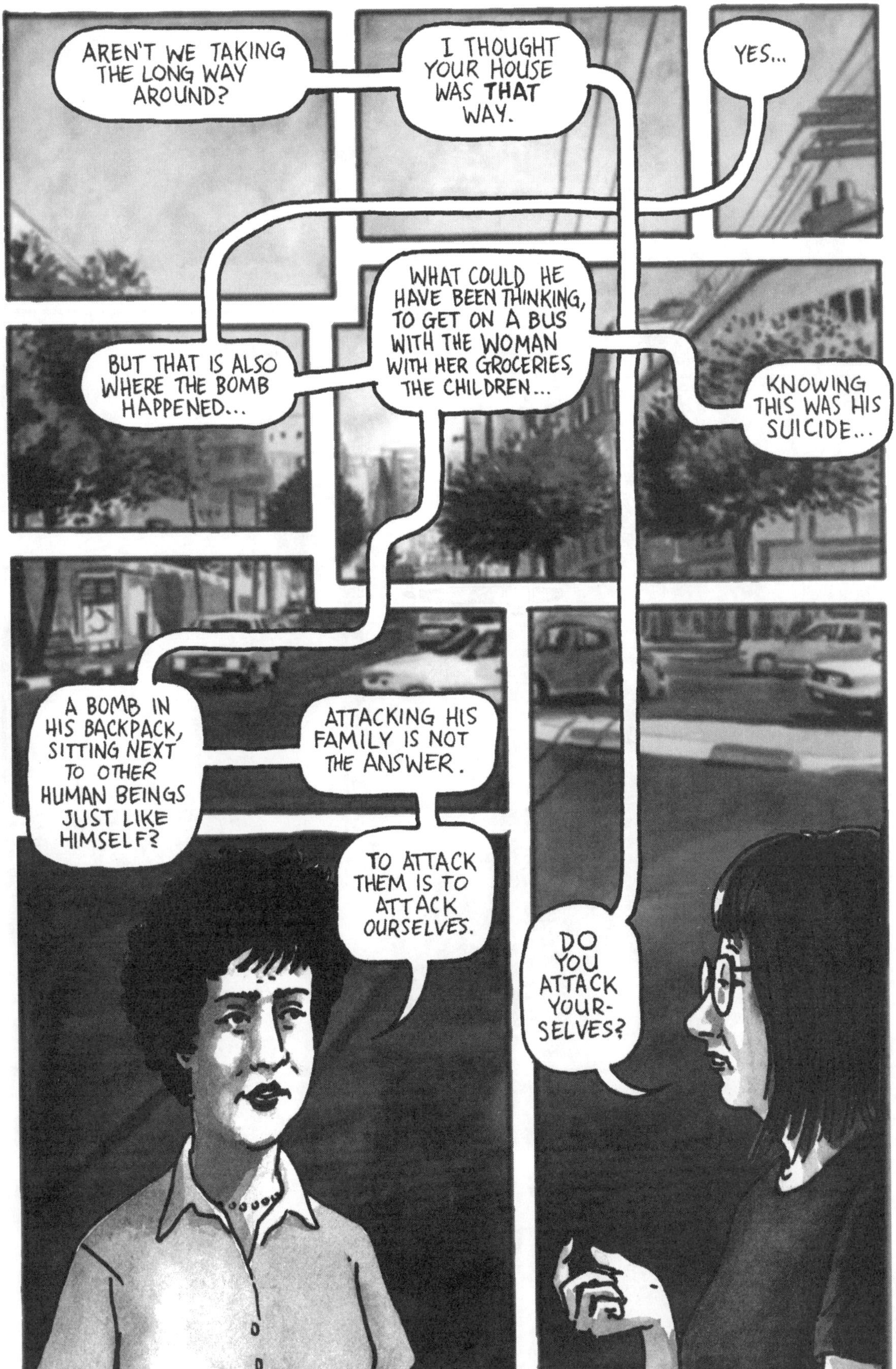
AREN'T WE TAKING THE LONG WAY AROUND?
I THOUGHT YOUR HOUSE WAS **THAT** WAY.
YES...
BUT THAT IS ALSO WHERE THE BOMB HAPPENED...
WHAT COULD HE HAVE BEEN THINKING, TO GET ON A BUS WITH THE WOMAN WITH HER GROCERIES, THE CHILDREN...
KNOWING THIS WAS HIS SUICIDE...
A BOMB IN HIS BACKPACK, SITTING NEXT TO OTHER HUMAN BEINGS JUST LIKE HIMSELF?
ATTACKING HIS FAMILY IS NOT THE ANSWER.
TO ATTACK THEM IS TO ATTACK OURSELVES.
DO YOU ATTACK YOUR-SELVES?

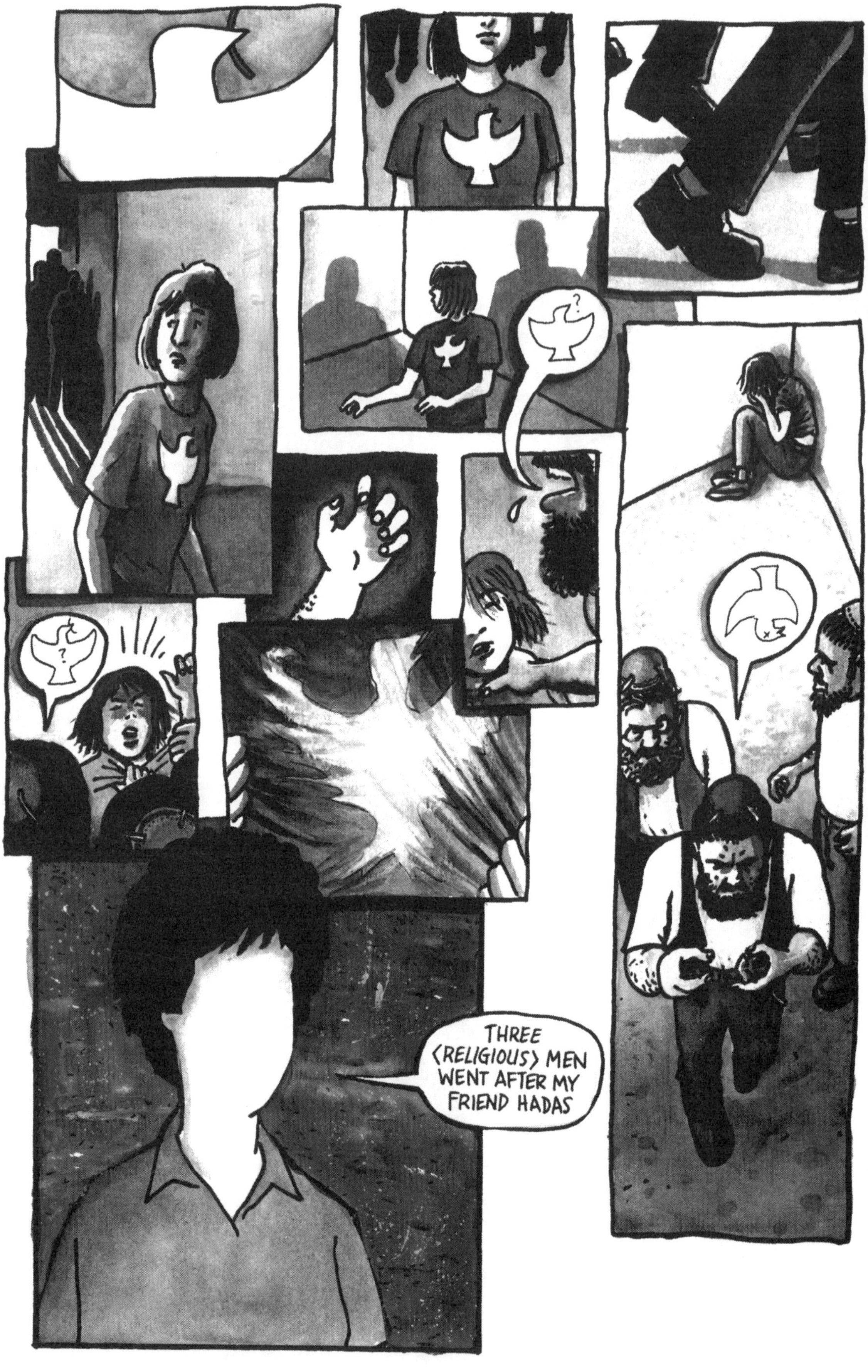
THREE <RELIGIOUS> MEN WENT AFTER MY FRIEND HADAS

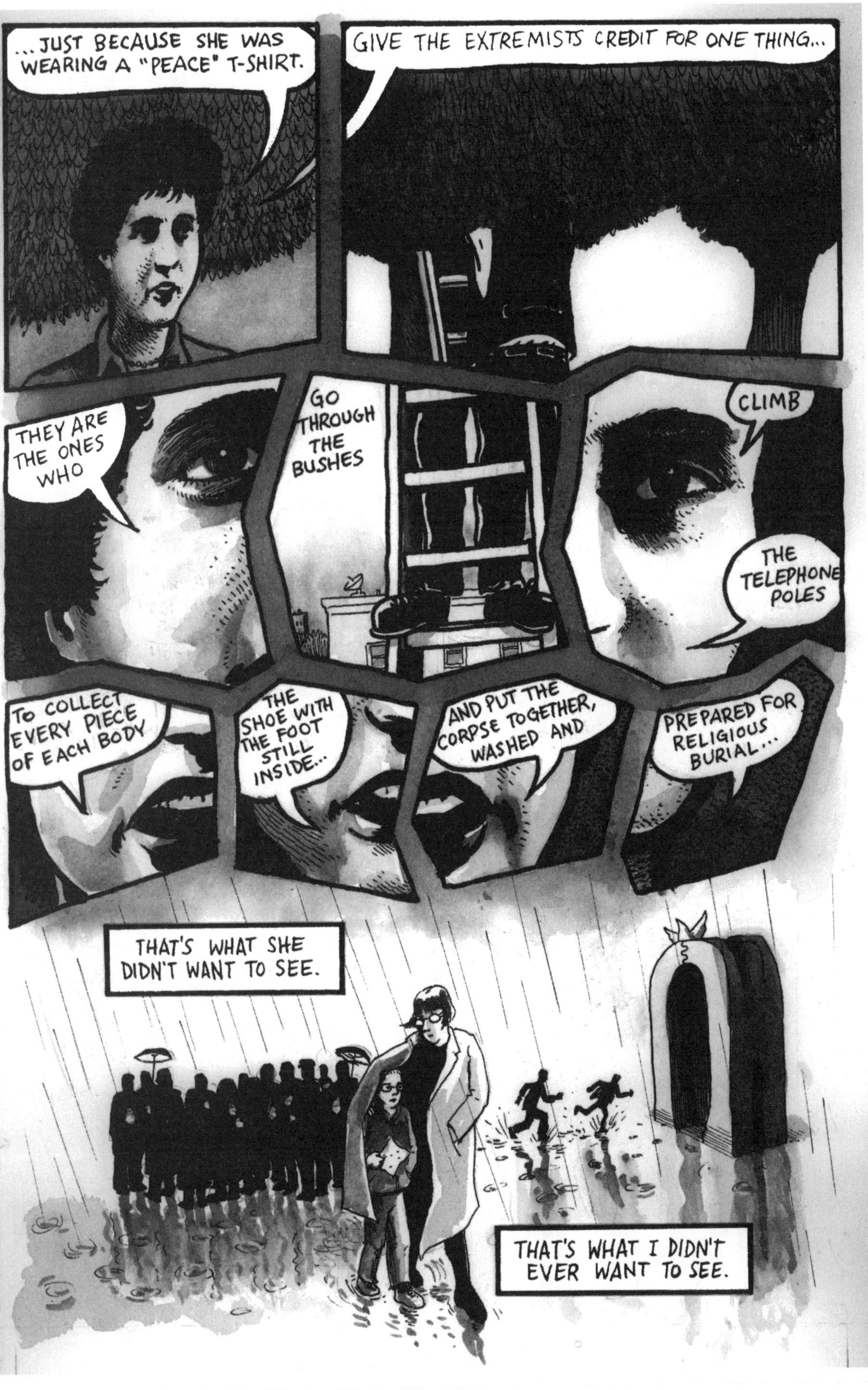
...JUST BECAUSE SHE WAS WEARING A "PEACE" T-SHIRT.
GIVE THE EXTREMISTS CREDIT FOR ONE THING...
THEY ARE THE ONES WHO
GO THROUGH THE BUSHES
CLIMB
THE TELEPHONE POLES
TO COLLECT EVERY PIECE OF EACH BODY
THE SHOE WITH THE FOOT STILL INSIDE...
AND PUT THE CORPSE TOGETHER, WASHED AND
PREPARED FOR RELIGIOUS BURIAL...
THAT'S WHAT SHE DIDN'T WANT TO SEE.
THAT'S WHAT I DIDN'T EVER WANT TO SEE.

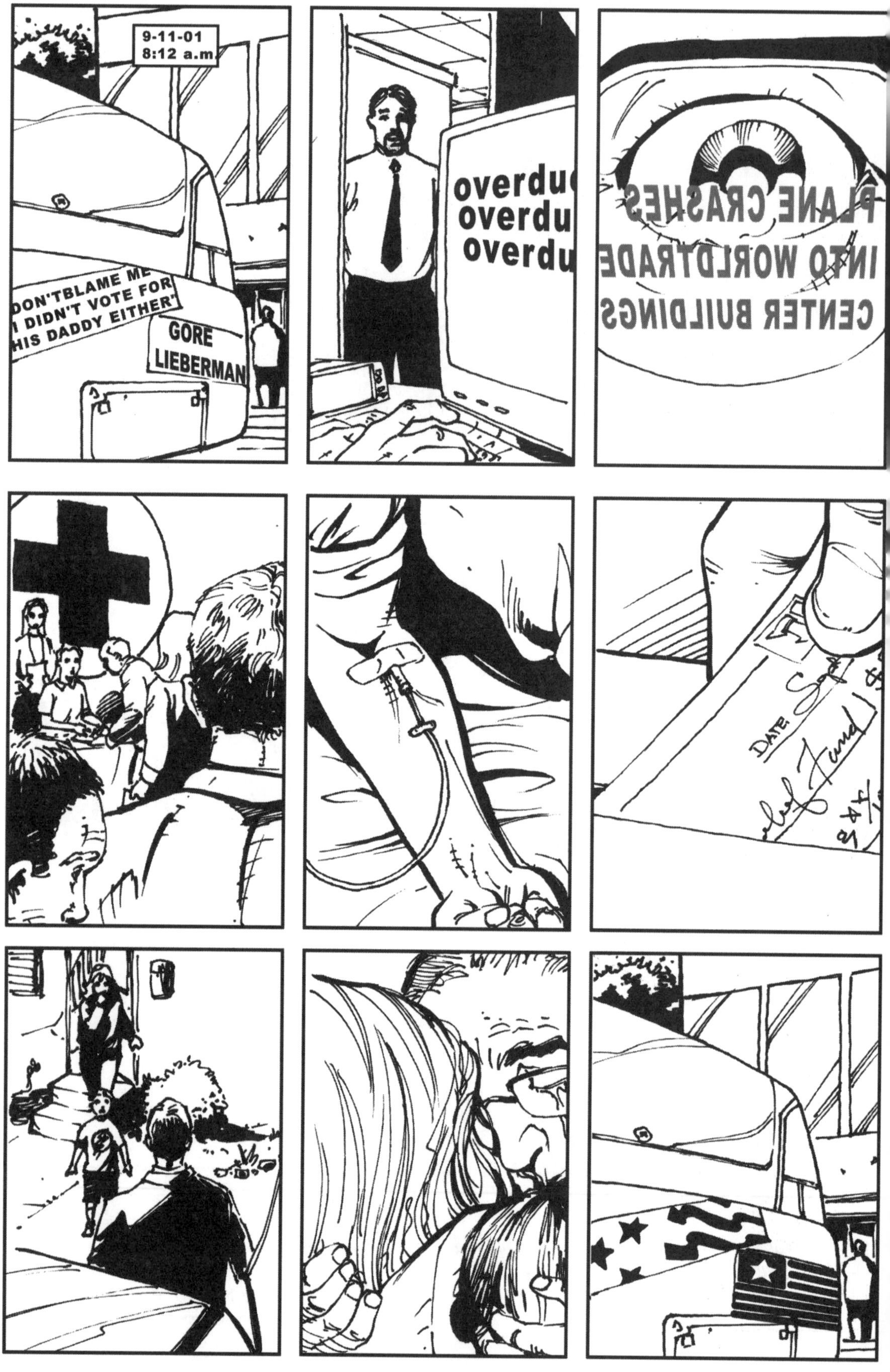
9-11-01
8:12 a.m
DON'TBLAME ME
I DIDN'T VOTE FOR
HIS DADDY EITHER'
GORE
LIEBERMAN
overdue
overdu
overdu
PLANE CRASHES
INTO WORLDTRADE
CENTER BUILDINGS
DATE

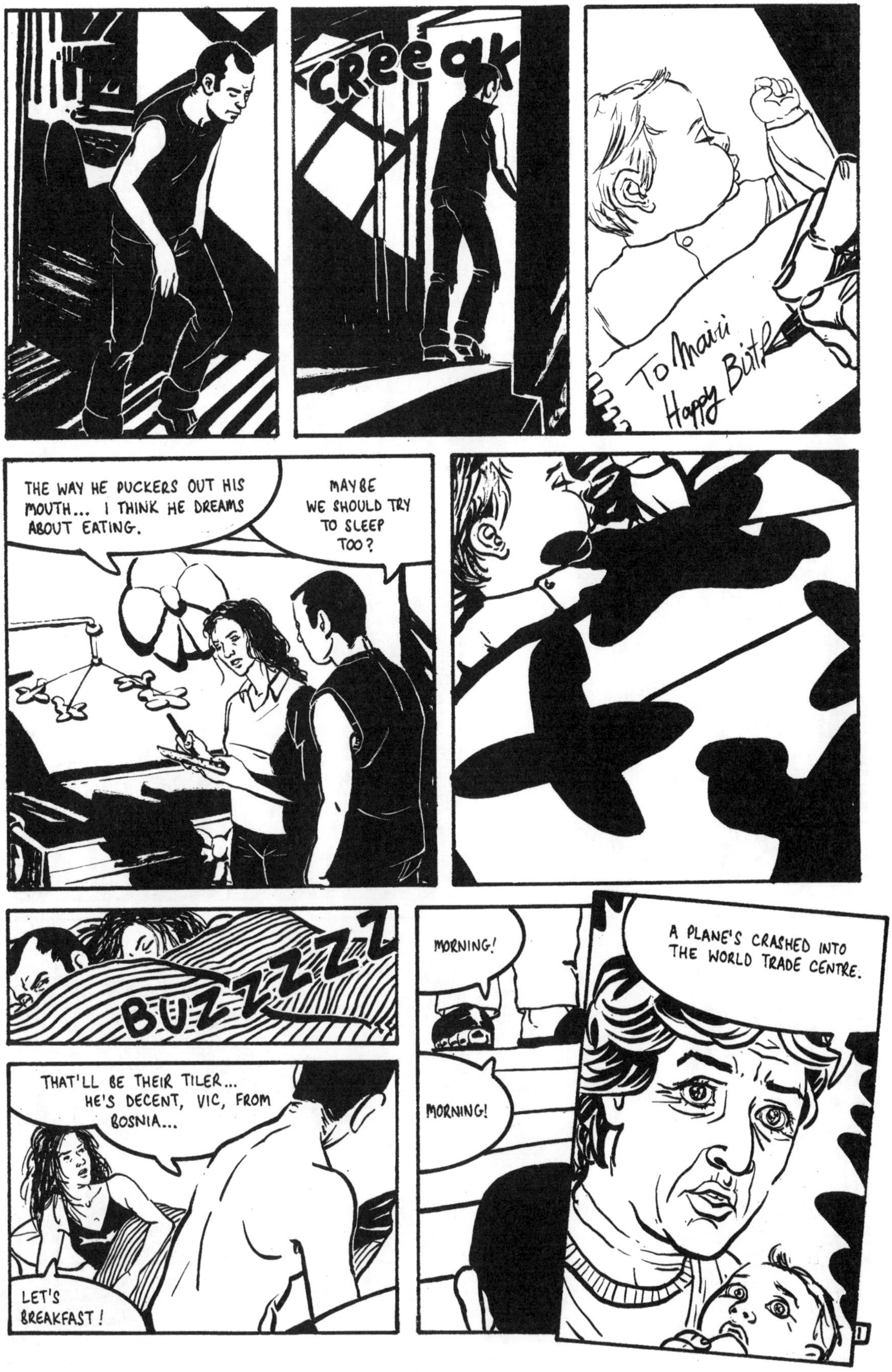
CREEAK
To Mairi
Happy Birth
THE WAY HE PUCKERS OUT HIS MOUTH... I THINK HE DREAMS ABOUT EATING.
MAYBE WE SHOULD TRY TO SLEEP TOO?
BUZZZZZZ
THAT'LL BE THEIR TILER... HE'S DECENT, VIC, FROM BOSNIA...
LET'S BREAKFAST!
MORNING!
MORNING!
A PLANE'S CRASHED INTO THE WORLD TRADE CENTRE.

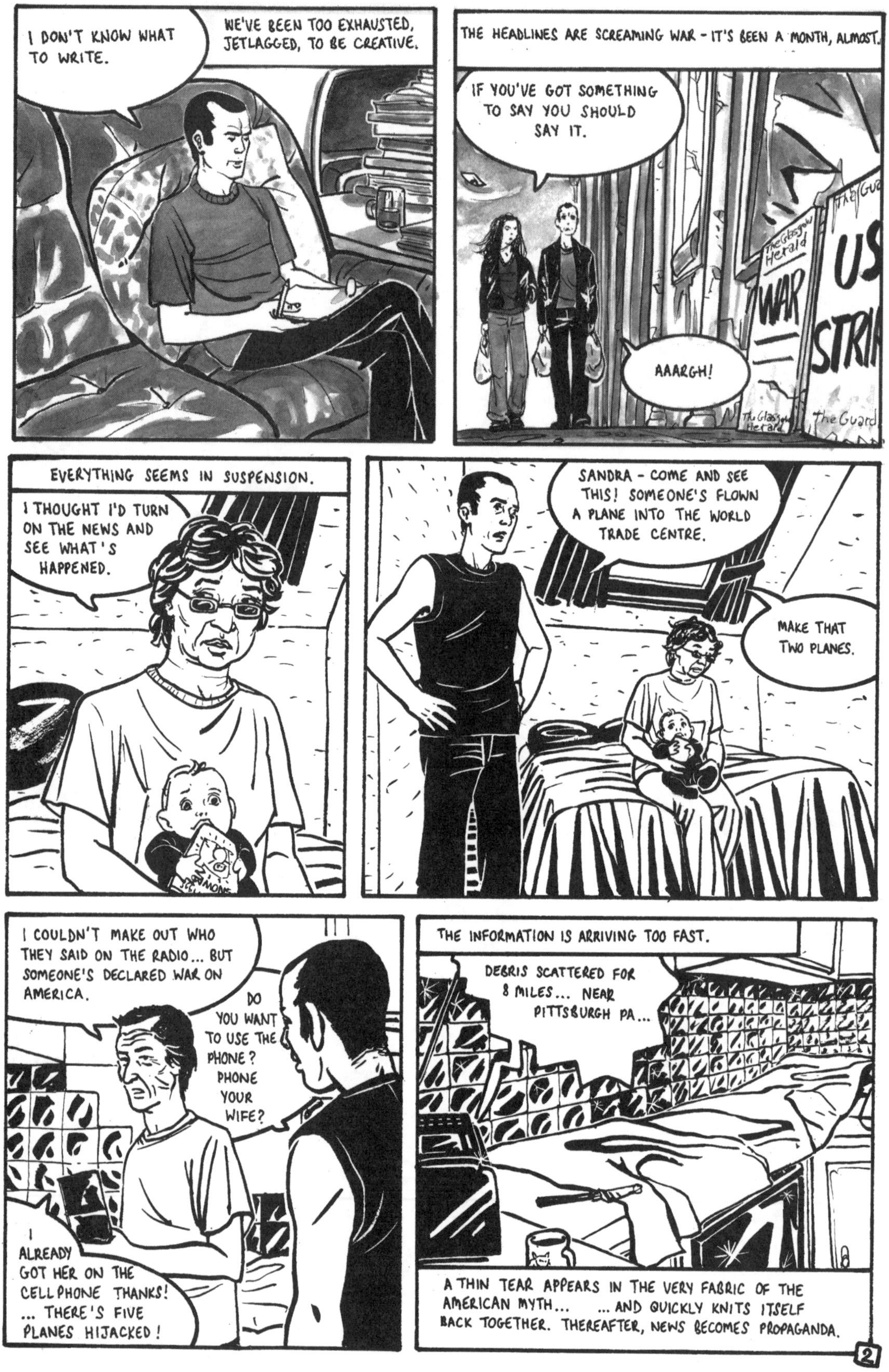
I DON'T KNOW WHAT TO WRITE.
WE'VE BEEN TOO EXHAUSTED, JETLAGGED, TO BE CREATIVE.
THE HEADLINES ARE SCREAMING WAR - IT'S BEEN A MONTH, ALMOST.
IF YOU'VE GOT SOMETHING TO SAY YOU SHOULD SAY IT.
The Glasgow Herald
WAR
AAARGH!
EVERYTHING SEEMS IN SUSPENSION.
I THOUGHT I'D TURN ON THE NEWS AND SEE WHAT'S HAPPENED.
SANDRA - COME AND SEE THIS! SOMEONE'S FLOWN A PLANE INTO THE WORLD TRADE CENTRE.
MAKE THAT TWO PLANES.
I COULDN'T MAKE OUT WHO THEY SAID ON THE RADIO... BUT SOMEONE'S DECLARED WAR ON AMERICA.
DO YOU WANT TO USE THE PHONE? PHONE YOUR WIFE?
I ALREADY GOT HER ON THE CELLPHONE THANKS! ... THERE'S FIVE PLANES HIJACKED!
THE INFORMATION IS ARRIVING TOO FAST.
DEBRIS SCATTERED FOR 8 MILES... NEAR PITTSBURGH PA...
A THIN TEAR APPEARS IN THE VERY FABRIC OF THE AMERICAN MYTH... ... AND QUICKLY KNITS ITSELF BACK TOGETHER. THEREAFTER, NEWS BECOMES PROPAGANDA.
2

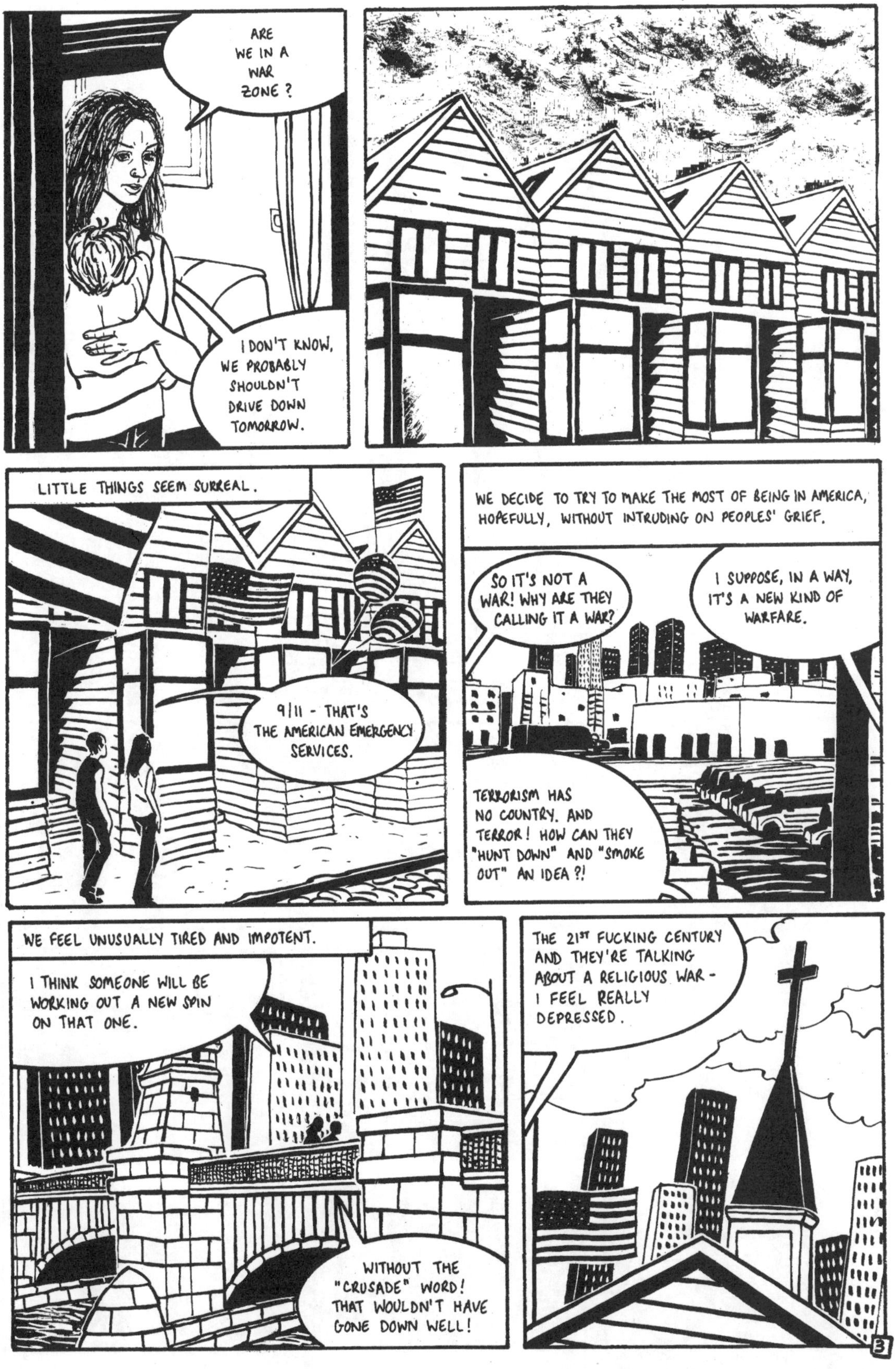
ARE WE IN A WAR ZONE ?
I DON'T KNOW, WE PROBABLY SHOULDN'T DRIVE DOWN TOMORROW.
LITTLE THINGS SEEM SURREAL.
9/11 - THAT'S THE AMERICAN EMERGENCY SERVICES.
WE DECIDE TO TRY TO MAKE THE MOST OF BEING IN AMERICA, HOPEFULLY, WITHOUT INTRUDING ON PEOPLES' GRIEF.
SO IT'S NOT A WAR! WHY ARE THEY CALLING IT A WAR?
I SUPPOSE, IN A WAY, IT'S A NEW KIND OF WARFARE.
TERRORISM HAS NO COUNTRY. AND TERROR! HOW CAN THEY "HUNT DOWN" AND "SMOKE OUT" AN IDEA ?!
WE FEEL UNUSUALLY TIRED AND IMPOTENT.
I THINK SOMEONE WILL BE WORKING OUT A NEW SPIN ON THAT ONE.
WITHOUT THE "CRUSADE" WORD! THAT WOULDN'T HAVE GONE DOWN WELL!
THE 21ST FUCKING CENTURY AND THEY'RE TALKING ABOUT A RELIGIOUS WAR - I FEEL REALLY DEPRESSED.
3

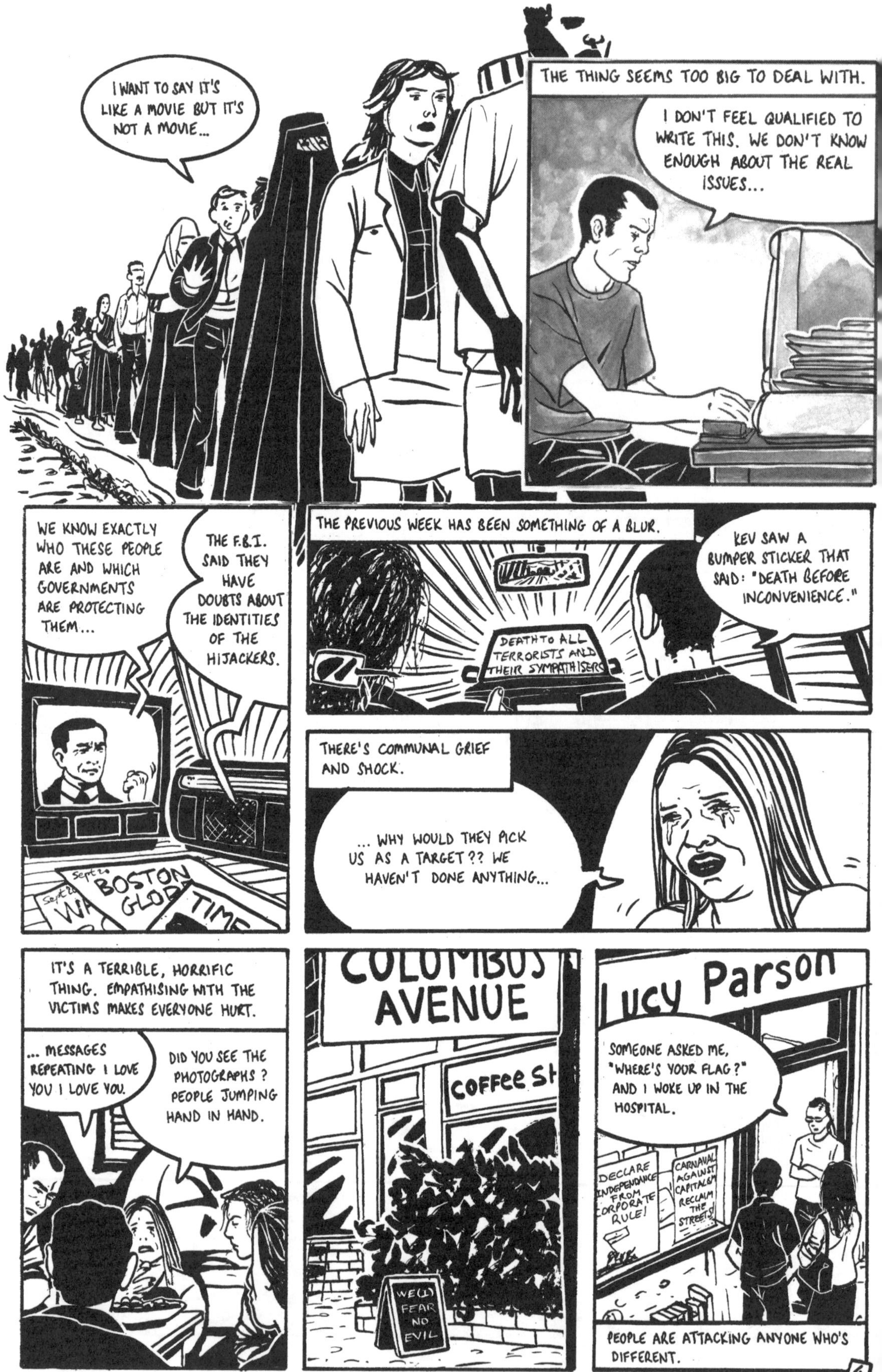
I WANT TO SAY IT'S LIKE A MOVIE BUT IT'S NOT A MOVIE...
THE THING SEEMS TOO BIG TO DEAL WITH.
I DON'T FEEL QUALIFIED TO WRITE THIS. WE DON'T KNOW ENOUGH ABOUT THE REAL ISSUES...
WE KNOW EXACTLY WHO THESE PEOPLE ARE AND WHICH GOVERNMENTS ARE PROTECTING THEM...
THE F.B.I. SAID THEY HAVE DOUBTS ABOUT THE IDENTITIES OF THE HIJACKERS.
BOSTON GLOB
TIME
THE PREVIOUS WEEK HAS BEEN SOMETHING OF A BLUR.
DEATH TO ALL TERRORISTS AND THEIR SYMPATHISERS
KEV SAW A BUMPER STICKER THAT SAID: "DEATH BEFORE INCONVENIENCE."
THERE'S COMMUNAL GRIEF AND SHOCK.
... WHY WOULD THEY PICK US AS A TARGET?? WE HAVEN'T DONE ANYTHING...
IT'S A TERRIBLE, HORRIFIC THING. EMPATHISING WITH THE VICTIMS MAKES EVERYONE HURT.
... MESSAGES REPEATING I LOVE YOU I LOVE YOU.
DID YOU SEE THE PHOTOGRAPHS ? PEOPLE JUMPING HAND IN HAND.
COLUMBUS AVENUE
COFFEE SH
WE(I) FEAR NO EVIL
Lucy Parson
SOMEONE ASKED ME, "WHERE'S YOUR FLAG ?" AND I WOKE UP IN THE HOSPITAL.
DECLARE INDEPENDANCE FROM CORPORATE RULE!
CARNAVAL AGAINST CAPITALISM RECLAIM THE STREETS!
PEOPLE ARE ATTACKING ANYONE WHO'S DIFFERENT.
4

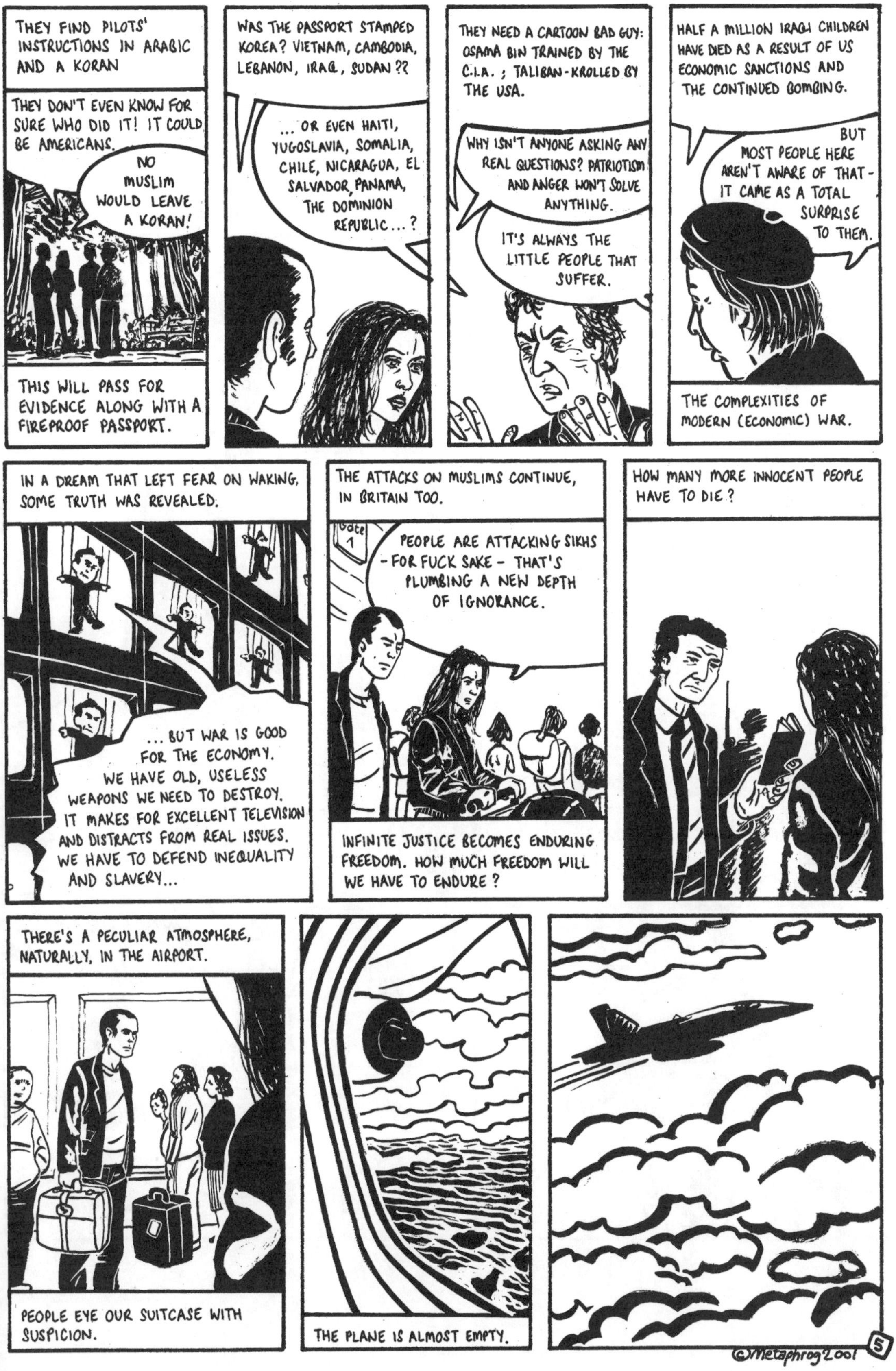
THEY FIND PILOTS' INSTRUCTIONS IN ARABIC AND A KORAN
THEY DON'T EVEN KNOW FOR SURE WHO DID IT! IT COULD BE AMERICANS.
NO MUSLIM WOULD LEAVE A KORAN!
THIS WILL PASS FOR EVIDENCE ALONG WITH A FIREPROOF PASSPORT.
WAS THE PASSPORT STAMPED KOREA? VIETNAM, CAMBODIA, LEBANON, IRAQ, SUDAN ??
... OR EVEN HAITI, YUGOSLAVIA, SOMALIA, CHILE, NICARAGUA, EL SALVADOR, PANAMA, THE DOMINION REPUBLIC ... ?
THEY NEED A CARTOON BAD GUY: OSAMA BIN TRAINED BY THE C.I.A. ; TALIBAN-KROLLED BY THE USA.
WHY ISN'T ANYONE ASKING ANY REAL QUESTIONS? PATRIOTISM AND ANGER WON'T SOLVE ANYTHING.
IT'S ALWAYS THE LITTLE PEOPLE THAT SUFFER.
HALF A MILLION IRAQI CHILDREN HAVE DIED AS A RESULT OF US ECONOMIC SANCTIONS AND THE CONTINUED BOMBING.
BUT MOST PEOPLE HERE AREN'T AWARE OF THAT - IT CAME AS A TOTAL SURPRISE TO THEM.
THE COMPLEXITIES OF MODERN (ECONOMIC) WAR.
IN A DREAM THAT LEFT FEAR ON WAKING, SOME TRUTH WAS REVEALED.
... BUT WAR IS GOOD FOR THE ECONOMY. WE HAVE OLD, USELESS WEAPONS WE NEED TO DESTROY. IT MAKES FOR EXCELLENT TELEVISION AND DISTRACTS FROM REAL ISSUES. WE HAVE TO DEFEND INEQUALITY AND SLAVERY...
THE ATTACKS ON MUSLIMS CONTINUE, IN BRITAIN TOO.
Gate 1
PEOPLE ARE ATTACKING SIKHS - FOR FUCK SAKE - THAT'S PLUMBING A NEW DEPTH OF IGNORANCE.
INFINITE JUSTICE BECOMES ENDURING FREEDOM. HOW MUCH FREEDOM WILL WE HAVE TO ENDURE?
HOW MANY MORE INNOCENT PEOPLE HAVE TO DIE?
THERE'S A PECULIAR ATMOSPHERE, NATURALLY, IN THE AIRPORT.
PEOPLE EYE OUR SUITCASE WITH SUSPICION.
THE PLANE IS ALMOST EMPTY.
©Metaphrog 2001
5

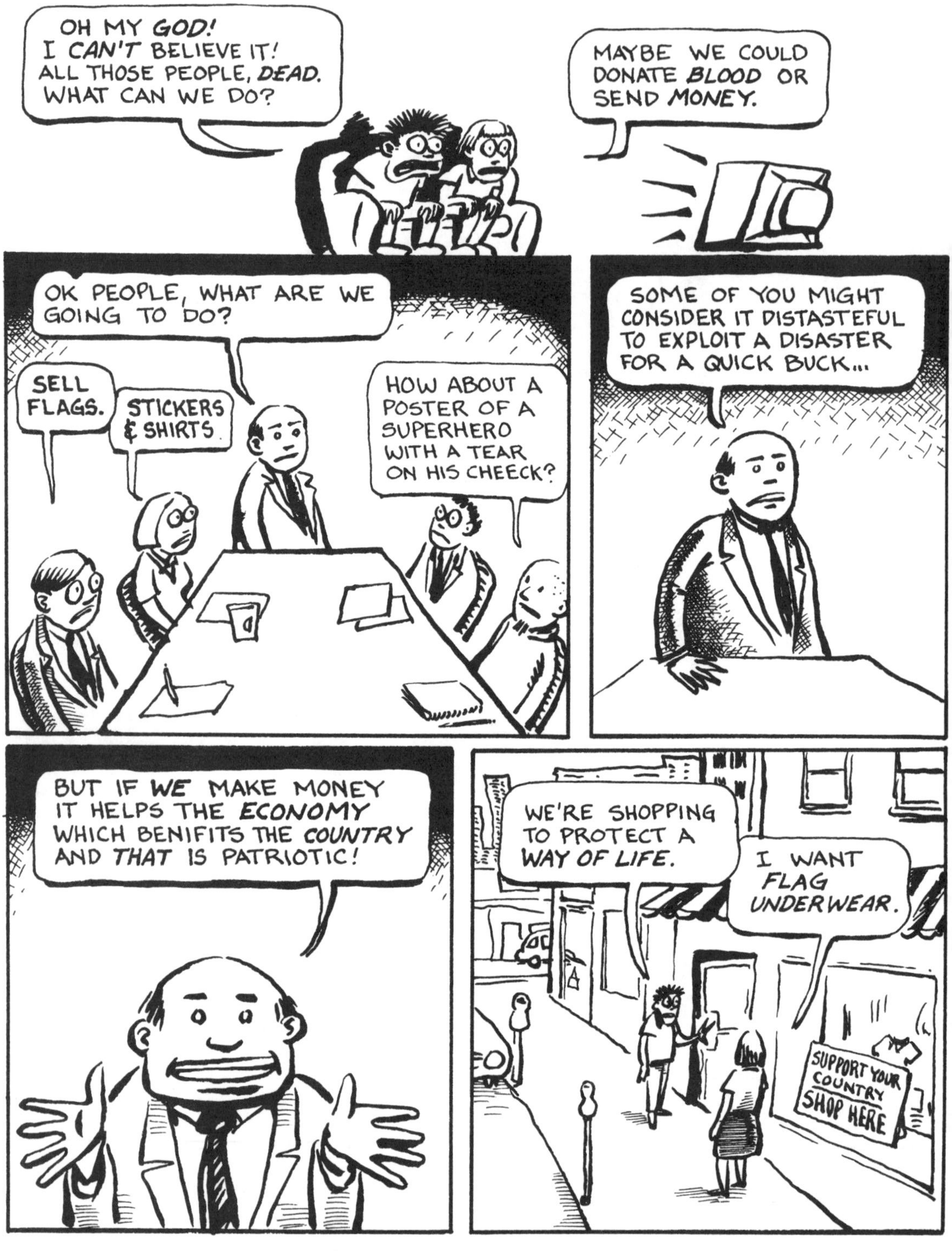
OH MY GOD! I CAN'T BELIEVE IT! ALL THOSE PEOPLE, DEAD. WHAT CAN WE DO?
MAYBE WE COULD DONATE BLOOD OR SEND MONEY.
OK PEOPLE, WHAT ARE WE GOING TO DO?
SELL FLAGS.
STICKERS & SHIRTS
HOW ABOUT A POSTER OF A SUPERHERO WITH A TEAR ON HIS CHEECK?
SOME OF YOU MIGHT CONSIDER IT DISTASTEFUL TO EXPLOIT A DISASTER FOR A QUICK BUCK...
BUT IF WE MAKE MONEY IT HELPS THE ECONOMY WHICH BENIFITS THE COUNTRY AND THAT IS PATRIOTIC!
WE'RE SHOPPING TO PROTECT A WAY OF LIFE.
I WANT FLAG UNDERWEAR.
SUPPORT YOUR COUNTRY SHOP HERE

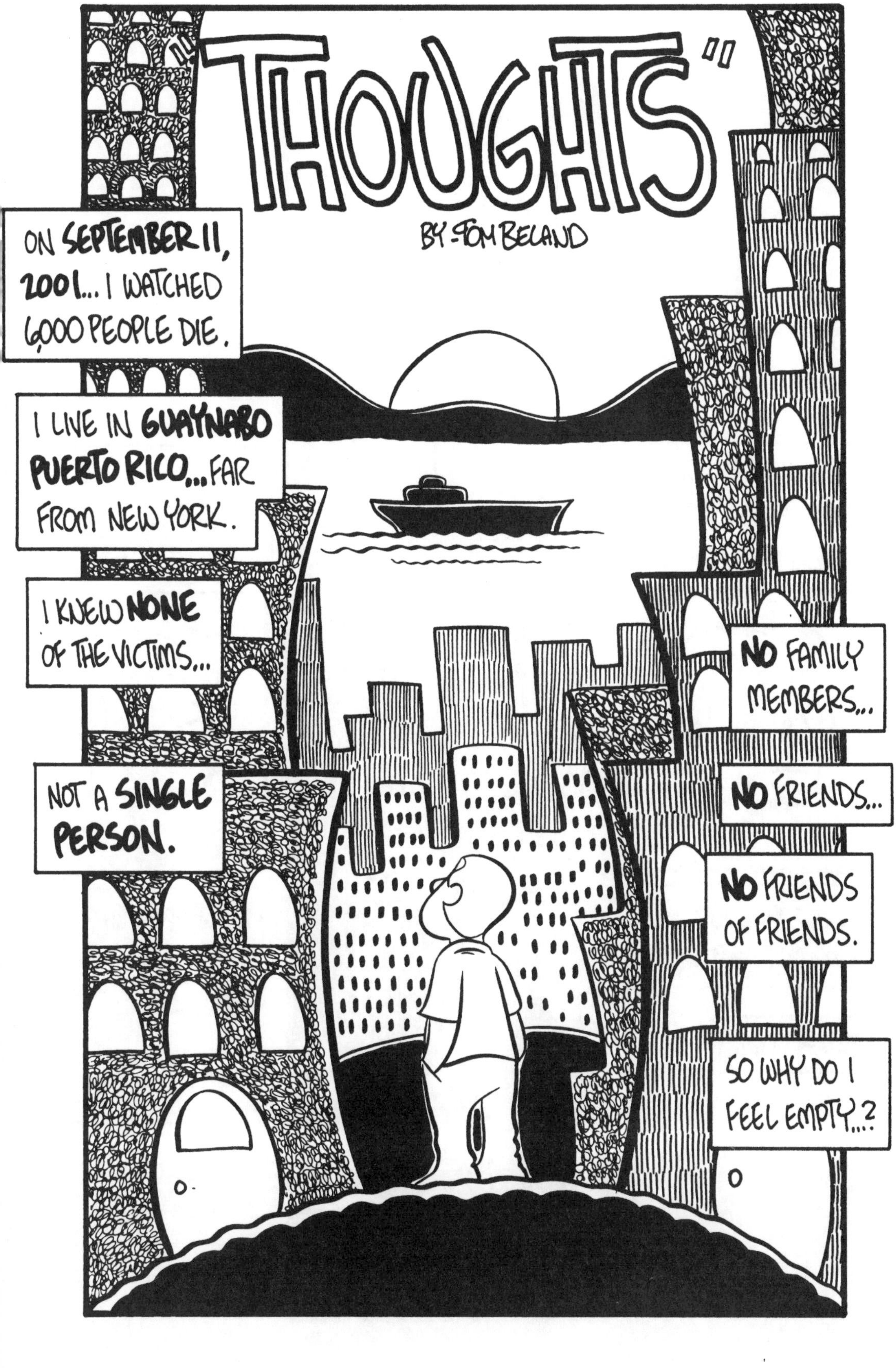
"THOUGHTS"
BY TOM BELAND
ON SEPTEMBER 11, 2001... I WATCHED 6,000 PEOPLE DIE.
I LIVE IN GUAYNABO PUERTO RICO... FAR FROM NEW YORK.
I KNEW NONE OF THE VICTIMS...
NOT A SINGLE PERSON.
NO FAMILY MEMBERS...
NO FRIENDS...
NO FRIENDS OF FRIENDS.
SO WHY DO I FEEL EMPTY...?

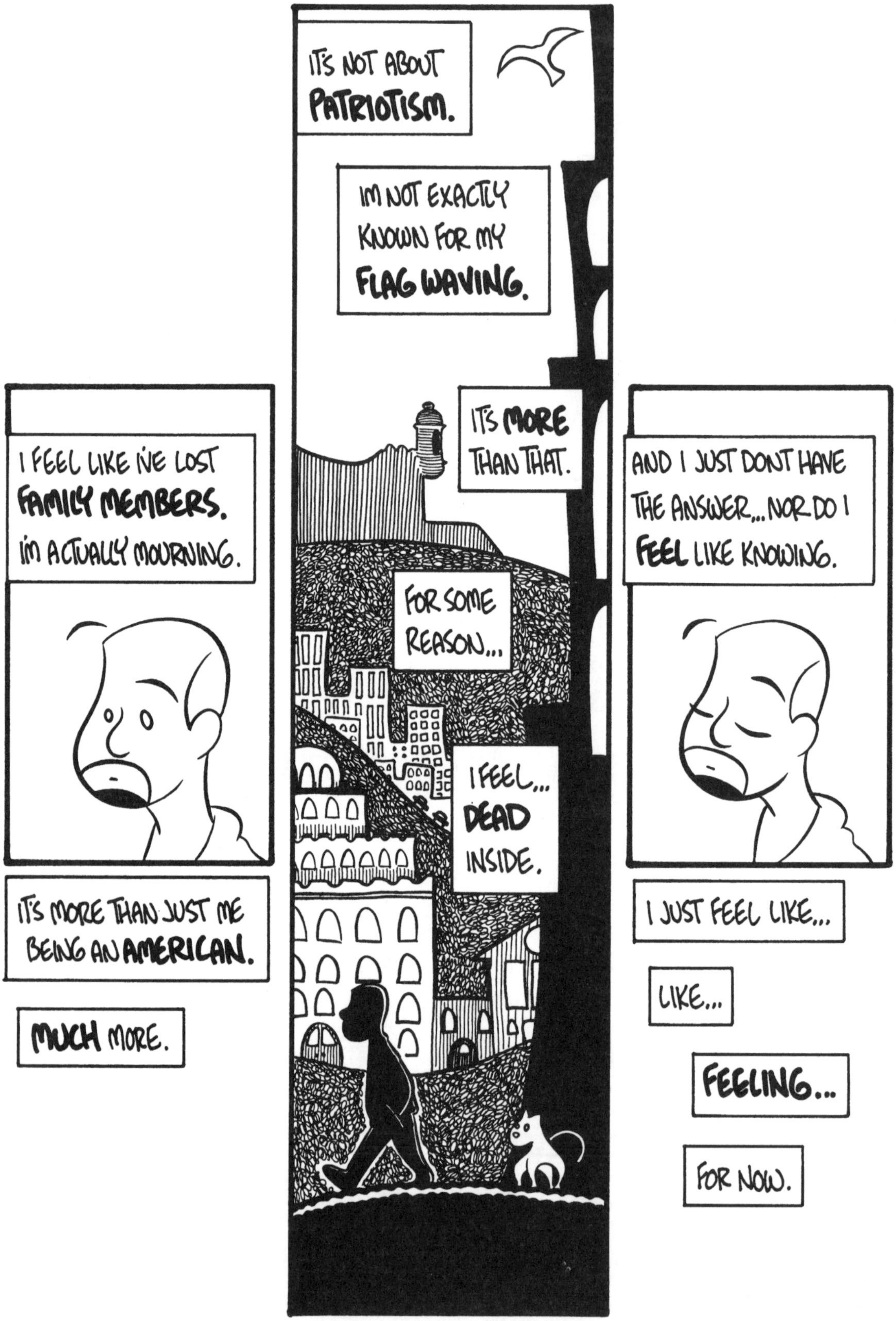
IT'S NOT ABOUT PATRIOTISM.
I'M NOT EXACTLY KNOWN FOR MY FLAG WAVING.
IT'S MORE THAN THAT.
I FEEL LIKE I'VE LOST FAMILY MEMBERS. I'M ACTUALLY MOURNING.
IT'S MORE THAN JUST ME BEING AN AMERICAN.
MUCH MORE.
FOR SOME REASON...
I FEEL... DEAD INSIDE.
AND I JUST DON'T HAVE THE ANSWER... NOR DO I FEEL LIKE KNOWING.
I JUST FEEL LIKE...
LIKE...
FEELING...
FOR NOW.

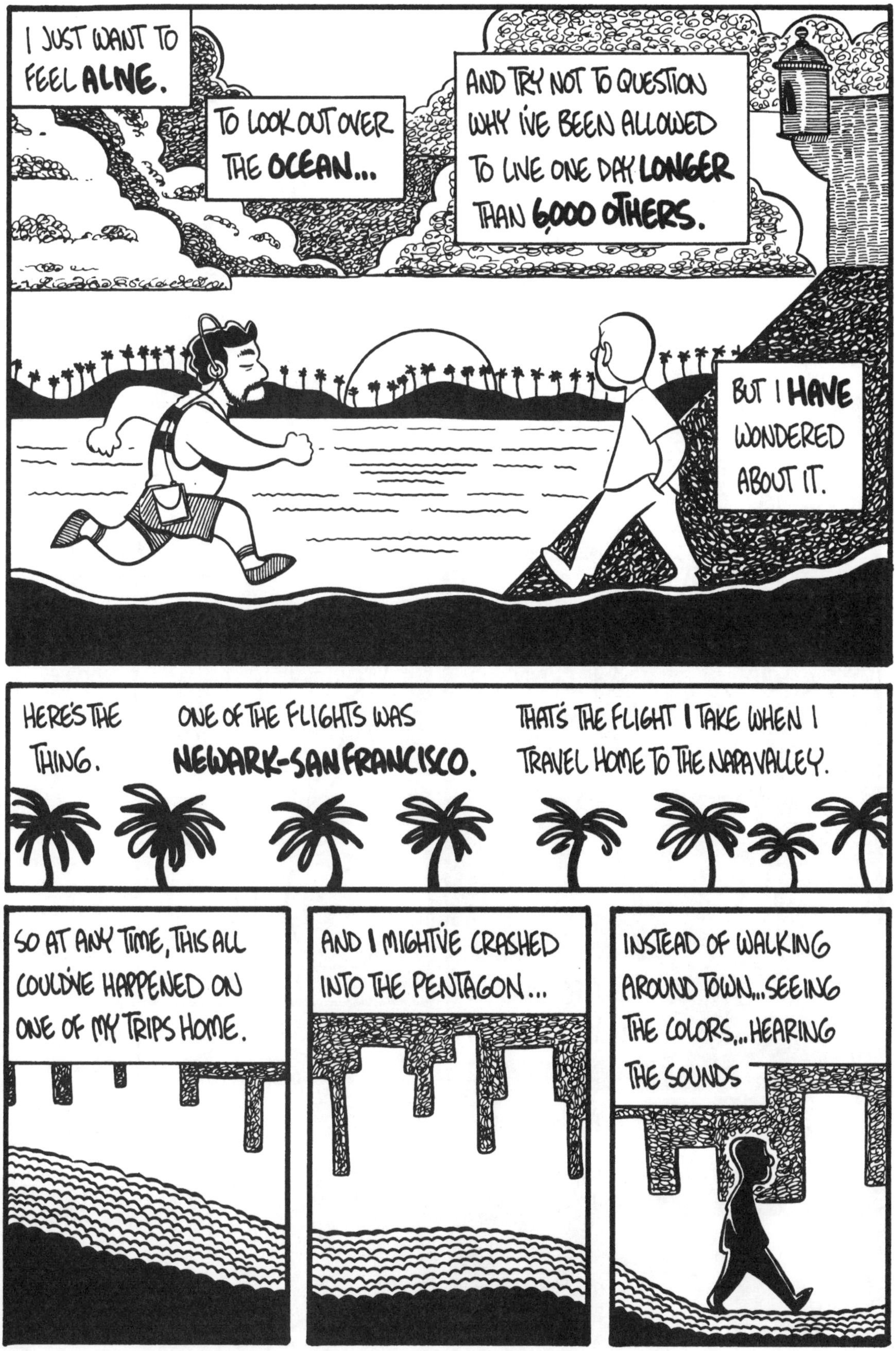
I JUST WANT TO FEEL ALIVE.
TO LOOK OUT OVER THE OCEAN...
AND TRY NOT TO QUESTION WHY I'VE BEEN ALLOWED TO LIVE ONE DAY LONGER THAN 6,000 OTHERS.
BUT I HAVE WONDERED ABOUT IT.
HERE'S THE THING.
ONE OF THE FLIGHTS WAS NEWARK-SAN FRANCISCO.
THAT'S THE FLIGHT I TAKE WHEN I TRAVEL HOME TO THE NAPA VALLEY.
SO AT ANY TIME, THIS ALL COULD'VE HAPPENED ON ONE OF MY TRIPS HOME.
AND I MIGHT'VE CRASHED INTO THE PENTAGON...
INSTEAD OF WALKING AROUND TOWN... SEEING THE COLORS... HEARING THE SOUNDS

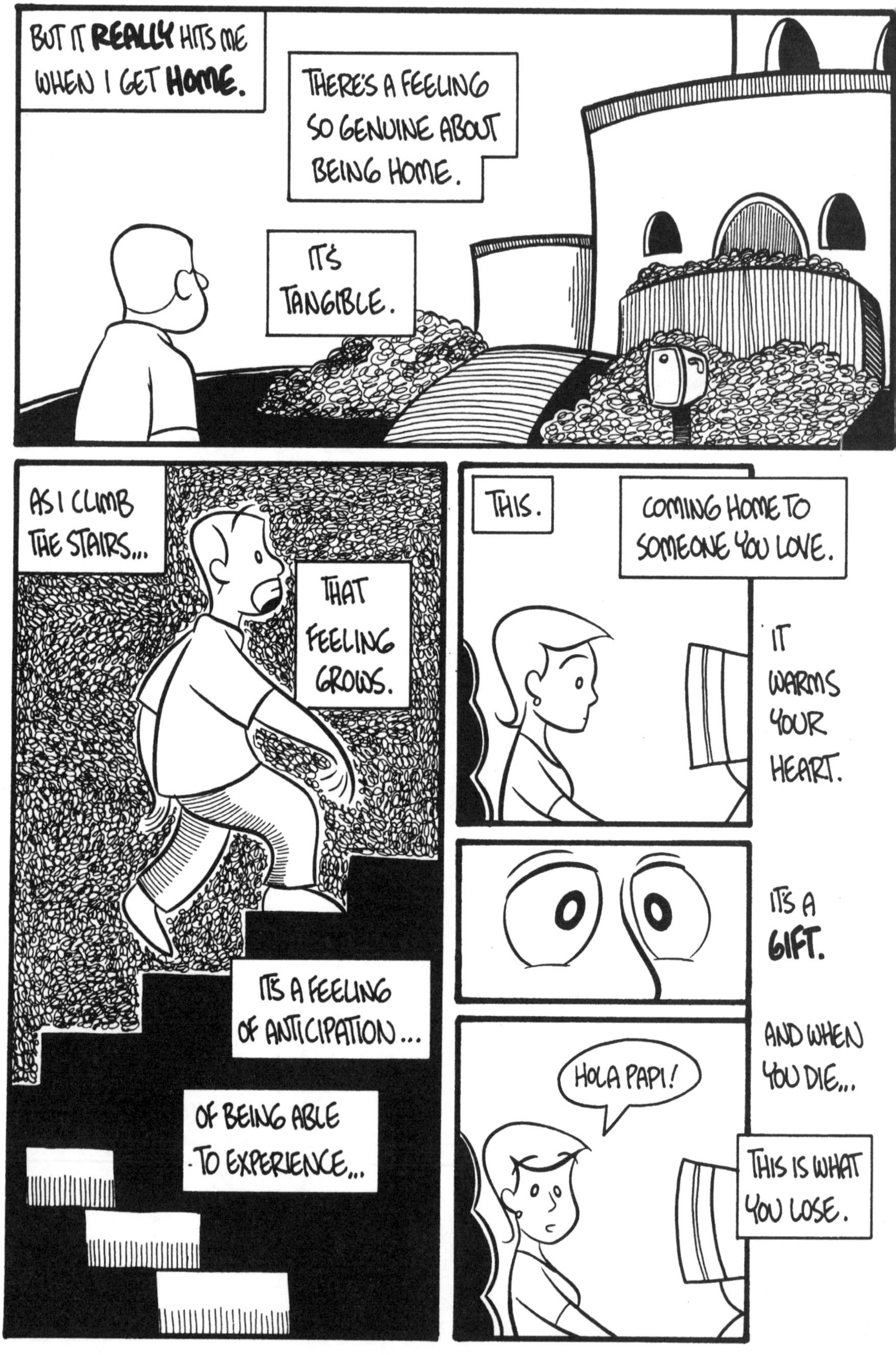
BUT IT REALLY HITS ME WHEN I GET HOME.
THERE'S A FEELING SO GENUINE ABOUT BEING HOME.
IT'S TANGIBLE.
AS I CLIMB THE STAIRS...
THAT FEELING GROWS.
IT'S A FEELING OF ANTICIPATION...
OF BEING ABLE TO EXPERIENCE...
THIS.
COMING HOME TO SOMEONE YOU LOVE.
IT WARMS YOUR HEART.
IT'S A GIFT.
AND WHEN YOU DIE...
HOLA PAPI!
THIS IS WHAT YOU LOSE.

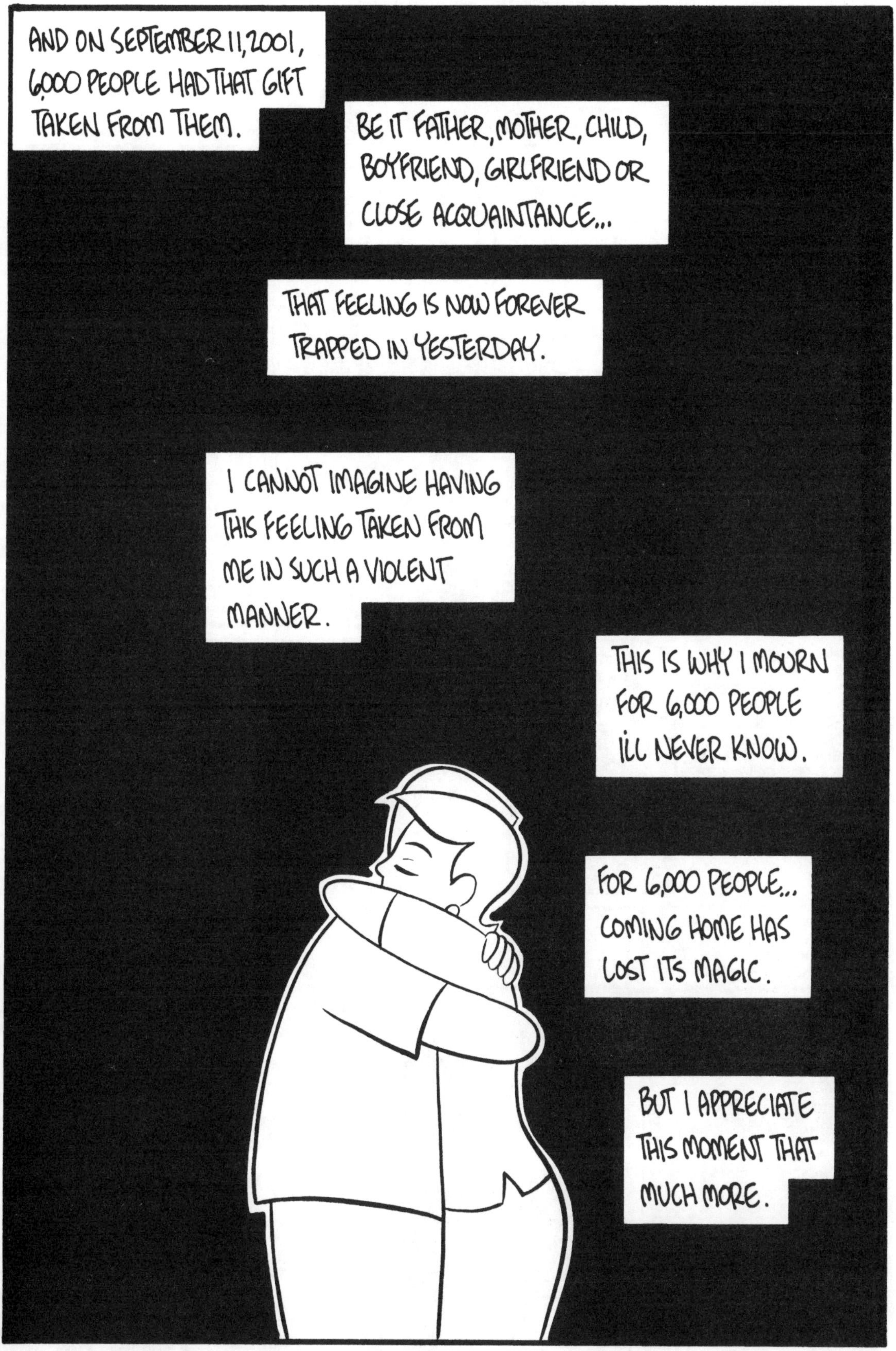
AND ON SEPTEMBER 11, 2001, 6,000 PEOPLE HAD THAT GIFT TAKEN FROM THEM.
BE IT FATHER, MOTHER, CHILD, BOYFRIEND, GIRLFRIEND OR CLOSE ACQUAINTANCE...
THAT FEELING IS NOW FOREVER TRAPPED IN YESTERDAY.
I CANNOT IMAGINE HAVING THIS FEELING TAKEN FROM ME IN SUCH A VIOLENT MANNER.
THIS IS WHY I MOURN FOR 6,000 PEOPLE I'LL NEVER KNOW.
FOR 6,000 PEOPLE... COMING HOME HAS LOST ITS MAGIC.
BUT I APPRECIATE THIS MOMENT THAT MUCH MORE.

The tragedy of the 9-11 terrorist attacks, while having an immediate and visceral effect upon almost everyone watching TV, the events of that morning also had almost the same effect upon my family and the relationship between me and my youngest brother Marc, who is a Muslim. I am not a religious person at all. The tension that would soon boil within my own family, who loves and cares deeply for each other, were echoed only a few short hours later as across America many mosques were attacked and people who looked Arabic, even if they were not, were threatened and harrased.

A TALE OF TWO BROTHERS

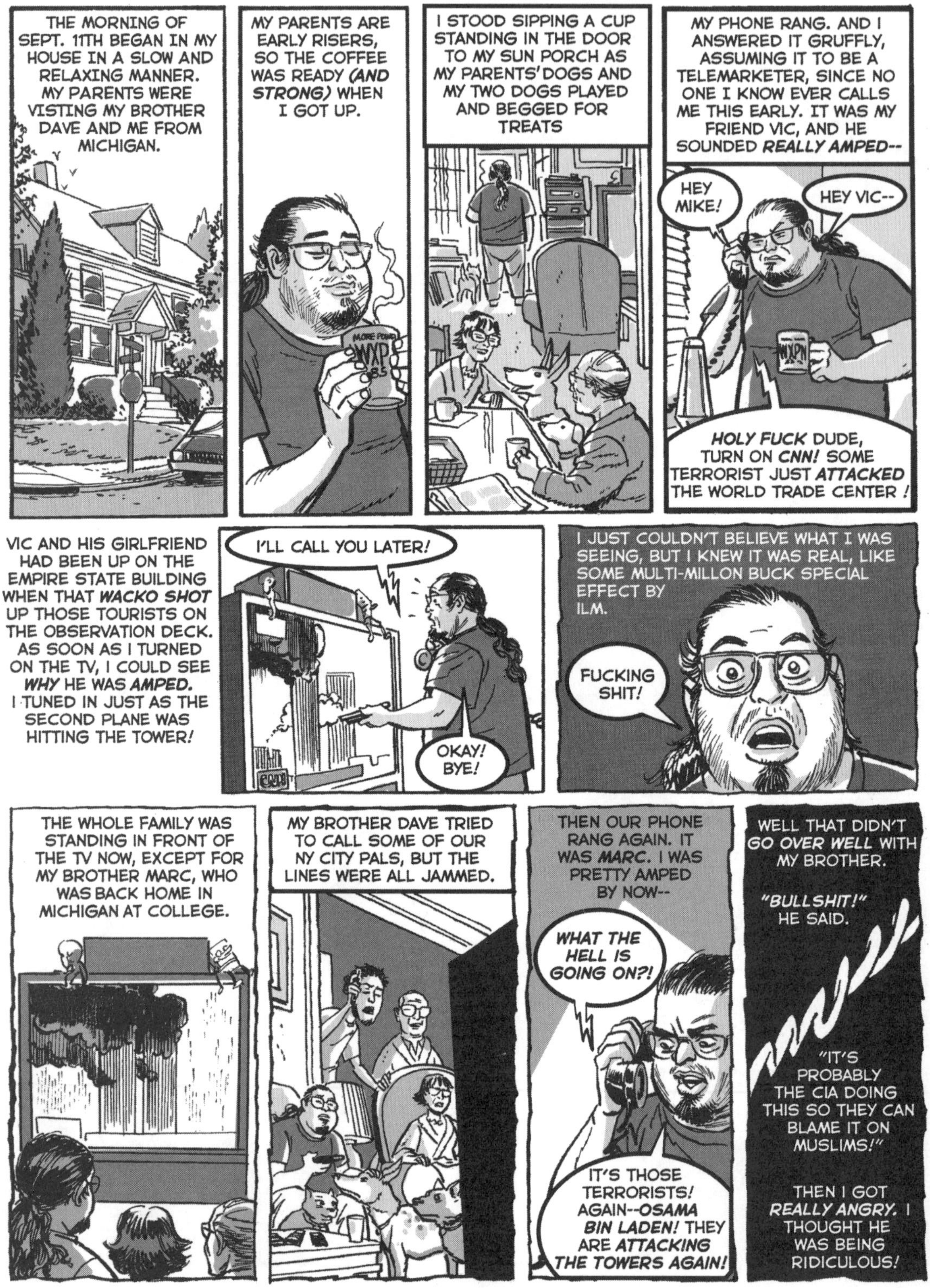
THE MORNING OF SEPT. 11TH BEGAN IN MY HOUSE IN A SLOW AND RELAXING MANNER. MY PARENTS WERE VISTING MY BROTHER DAVE AND ME FROM MICHIGAN.
MY PARENTS ARE EARLY RISERS, SO THE COFFEE WAS READY (AND STRONG) WHEN I GOT UP.
I STOOD SIPPING A CUP STANDING IN THE DOOR TO MY SUN PORCH AS MY PARENTS' DOGS AND MY TWO DOGS PLAYED AND BEGGED FOR TREATS
MY PHONE RANG. AND I ANSWERED IT GRUFFLY, ASSUMING IT TO BE A TELEMARKETER, SINCE NO ONE I KNOW EVER CALLS ME THIS EARLY. IT WAS MY FRIEND VIC, AND HE SOUNDED REALLY AMPED--
HEY MIKE!
HEY VIC--
HOLY FUCK DUDE, TURN ON CNN! SOME TERRORIST JUST ATTACKED THE WORLD TRADE CENTER!
VIC AND HIS GIRLFRIEND HAD BEEN UP ON THE EMPIRE STATE BUILDING WHEN THAT WACKO SHOT UP THOSE TOURISTS ON THE OBSERVATION DECK. AS SOON AS I TURNED ON THE TV, I COULD SEE WHY HE WAS AMPED. I TUNED IN JUST AS THE SECOND PLANE WAS HITTING THE TOWER!
I'LL CALL YOU LATER!
OKAY! BYE!
I JUST COULDN'T BELIEVE WHAT I WAS SEEING, BUT I KNEW IT WAS REAL, LIKE SOME MULTI-MILLON BUCK SPECIAL EFFECT BY ILM.
FUCKING SHIT!
THE WHOLE FAMILY WAS STANDING IN FRONT OF THE TV NOW, EXCEPT FOR MY BROTHER MARC, WHO WAS BACK HOME IN MICHIGAN AT COLLEGE.
MY BROTHER DAVE TRIED TO CALL SOME OF OUR NY CITY PALS, BUT THE LINES WERE ALL JAMMED.
THEN OUR PHONE RANG AGAIN. IT WAS MARC. I WAS PRETTY AMPED BY NOW--
WHAT THE HELL IS GOING ON?!
IT'S THOSE TERRORISTS! AGAIN--OSAMA BIN LADEN! THEY ARE ATTACKING THE TOWERS AGAIN!
WELL THAT DIDN'T GO OVER WELL WITH MY BROTHER.
"BULLSHIT!" HE SAID.
"IT'S PROBABLY THE CIA DOING THIS SO THEY CAN BLAME IT ON MUSLIMS!"
THEN I GOT REALLY ANGRY. I THOUGHT HE WAS BEING RIDICULOUS!

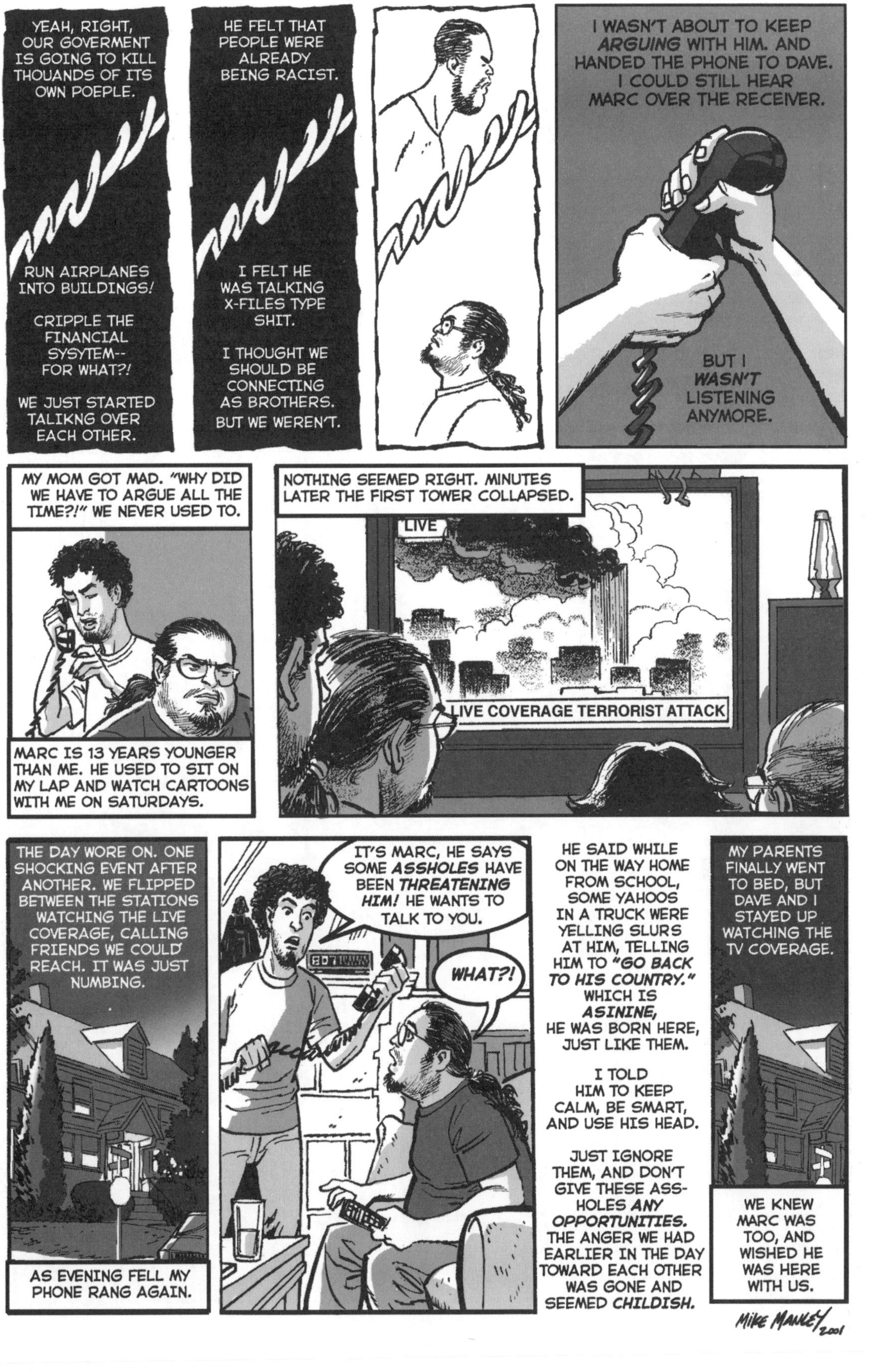
YEAH, RIGHT, OUR GOVERMENT IS GOING TO KILL THOUANDS OF ITS OWN POEPLE.
RUN AIRPLANES INTO BUILDINGS!
CRIPPLE THE FINANCIAL SYSYTEM-- FOR WHAT?!
WE JUST STARTED TALIKNG OVER EACH OTHER.
HE FELT THAT PEOPLE WERE ALREADY BEING RACIST.
I FELT HE WAS TALKING X-FILES TYPE SHIT.
I THOUGHT WE SHOULD BE CONNECTING AS BROTHERS.
BUT WE WEREN'T.
I WASN'T ABOUT TO KEEP ARGUING WITH HIM. AND HANDED THE PHONE TO DAVE. I COULD STILL HEAR MARC OVER THE RECEIVER.
BUT I WASN'T LISTENING ANYMORE.
MY MOM GOT MAD. "WHY DID WE HAVE TO ARGUE ALL THE TIME?!" WE NEVER USED TO.
MARC IS 13 YEARS YOUNGER THAN ME. HE USED TO SIT ON MY LAP AND WATCH CARTOONS WITH ME ON SATURDAYS.
NOTHING SEEMED RIGHT. MINUTES LATER THE FIRST TOWER COLLAPSED.
LIVE
LIVE COVERAGE TERRORIST ATTACK
THE DAY WORE ON. ONE SHOCKING EVENT AFTER ANOTHER. WE FLIPPED BETWEEN THE STATIONS WATCHING THE LIVE COVERAGE, CALLING FRIENDS WE COULD REACH. IT WAS JUST NUMBING.
AS EVENING FELL MY PHONE RANG AGAIN.
IT'S MARC, HE SAYS SOME ASSHOLES HAVE BEEN THREATENING HIM! HE WANTS TO TALK TO YOU.
WHAT?!
HE SAID WHILE ON THE WAY HOME FROM SCHOOL, SOME YAHOOS IN A TRUCK WERE YELLING SLURS AT HIM, TELLING HIM TO "GO BACK TO HIS COUNTRY." WHICH IS ASININE, HE WAS BORN HERE, JUST LIKE THEM.
I TOLD HIM TO KEEP CALM, BE SMART, AND USE HIS HEAD.
JUST IGNORE THEM, AND DON'T GIVE THESE ASS-HOLES ANY OPPORTUNITIES.
THE ANGER WE HAD EARLIER IN THE DAY TOWARD EACH OTHER WAS GONE AND SEEMED CHILDISH.
MY PARENTS FINALLY WENT TO BED, BUT DAVE AND I STAYED UP WATCHING THE TV COVERAGE.
WE KNEW MARC WAS TOO, AND WISHED HE WAS HERE WITH US.
MIKE MANLEY 2001

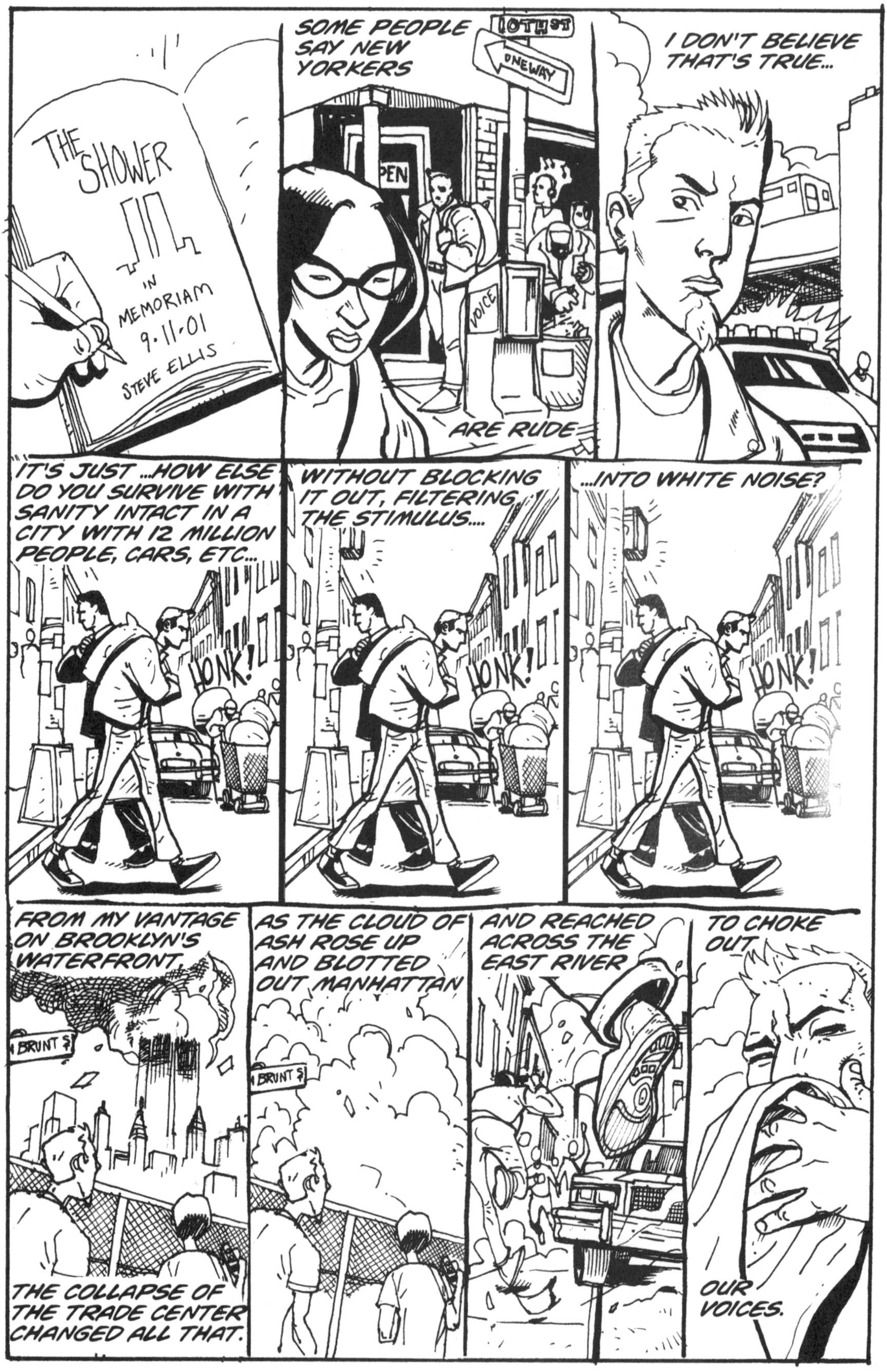
THE SHOWER
IN MEMORIAM 9.11.01
STEVE ELLIS
SOME PEOPLE SAY NEW YORKERS
10TH ST
ONE WAY
OPEN
VOICE
ARE RUDE
I DON'T BELIEVE THAT'S TRUE...
IT'S JUST ...HOW ELSE DO YOU SURVIVE WITH SANITY INTACT IN A CITY WITH 12 MILLION PEOPLE, CARS, ETC...
HONK!
WITHOUT BLOCKING IT OUT, FILTERING THE STIMULUS....
HONK!
...INTO WHITE NOISE?
HONK!
FROM MY VANTAGE ON BROOKLYN'S WATERFRONT,
BRUNT ST
THE COLLAPSE OF THE TRADE CENTER CHANGED ALL THAT.
AS THE CLOUD OF ASH ROSE UP AND BLOTTED OUT MANHATTAN
BRUNT ST
AND REACHED ACROSS THE EAST RIVER
TO CHOKE OUT
OUR VOICES.

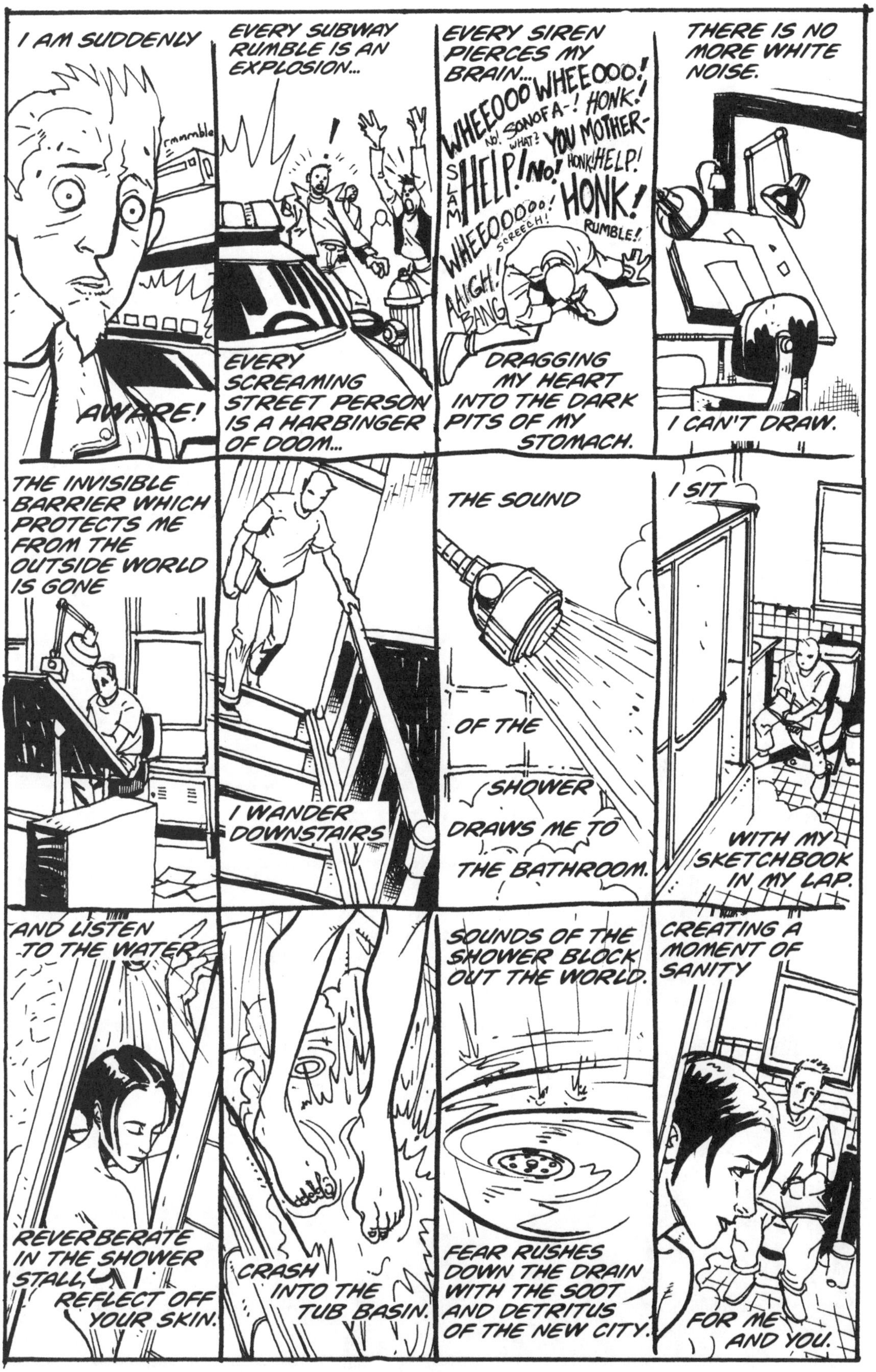
I AM SUDDENLY
rmmmble
AWARE!
EVERY SUBWAY RUMBLE IS AN EXPLOSION...
!
EVERY SCREAMING STREET PERSON IS A HARBINGER OF DOOM...
EVERY SIREN PIERCES MY BRAIN...
WHEEOOO WHEEOOO!
No! SONOFA-! WHAT? HONK!
YOU MOTHER-
SLAM HELP! No! HONK! HELP!
WHEEOOOOO! HONK!
SCREECH! RUMBLE!
AAIGH! BANG
DRAGGING MY HEART INTO THE DARK PITS OF MY STOMACH.
THERE IS NO MORE WHITE NOISE.
I CAN'T DRAW.
THE INVISIBLE BARRIER WHICH PROTECTS ME FROM THE OUTSIDE WORLD IS GONE
I WANDER DOWNSTAIRS
THE SOUND
OF THE
SHOWER
DRAWS ME TO
THE BATHROOM.
I SIT
WITH MY SKETCHBOOK IN MY LAP.
AND LISTEN TO THE WATER
REVERBERATE IN THE SHOWER STALL,
REFLECT OFF YOUR SKIN.
CRASH
INTO THE TUB BASIN.
SOUNDS OF THE SHOWER BLOCK OUT THE WORLD.
FEAR RUSHES DOWN THE DRAIN WITH THE SOOT AND DETRITUS OF THE NEW CITY.
CREATING A MOMENT OF SANITY
FOR ME AND YOU.

the phone call came some time in the morning. i was sleeping.
my husband picked it up.

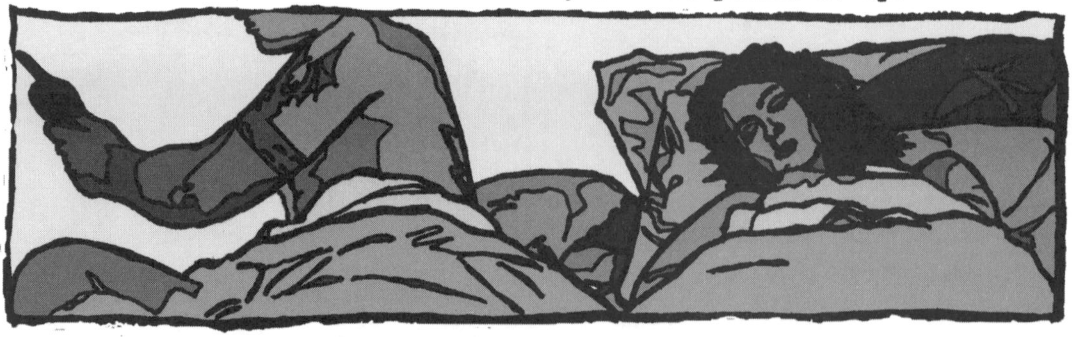

he turned on the television.

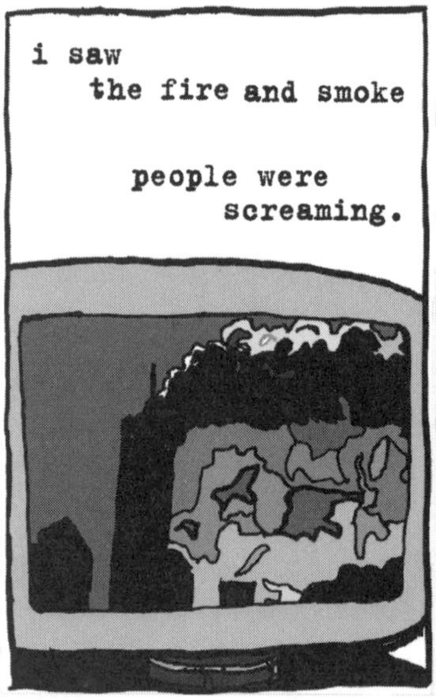
i saw
the fire and smoke
people were
screaming.

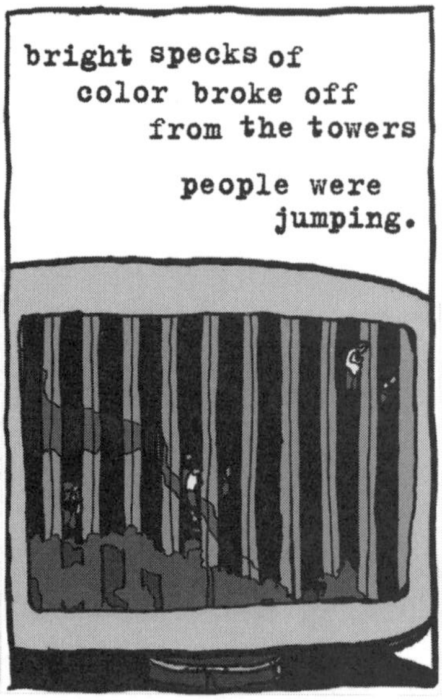
bright specks of
color broke off
from the towers
people were
jumping.

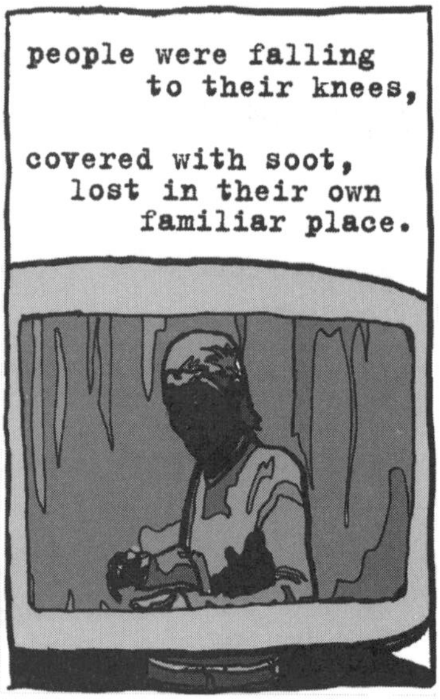
people were falling
to their knees,
covered with soot,
lost in their own
familiar place.

for days i cried for the families of the victims
and watched people around the world crying with me.

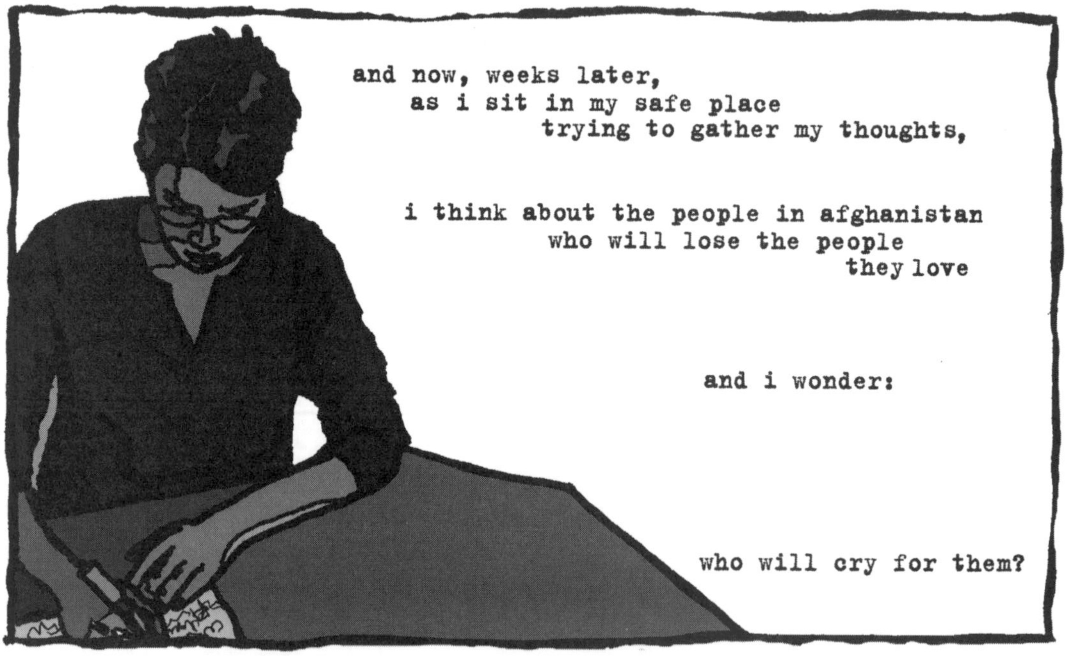
and now, weeks later,
as i sit in my safe place
trying to gather my thoughts,
i think about the people in afghanistan
who will lose the people
they love
and i wonder:
who will cry for them?

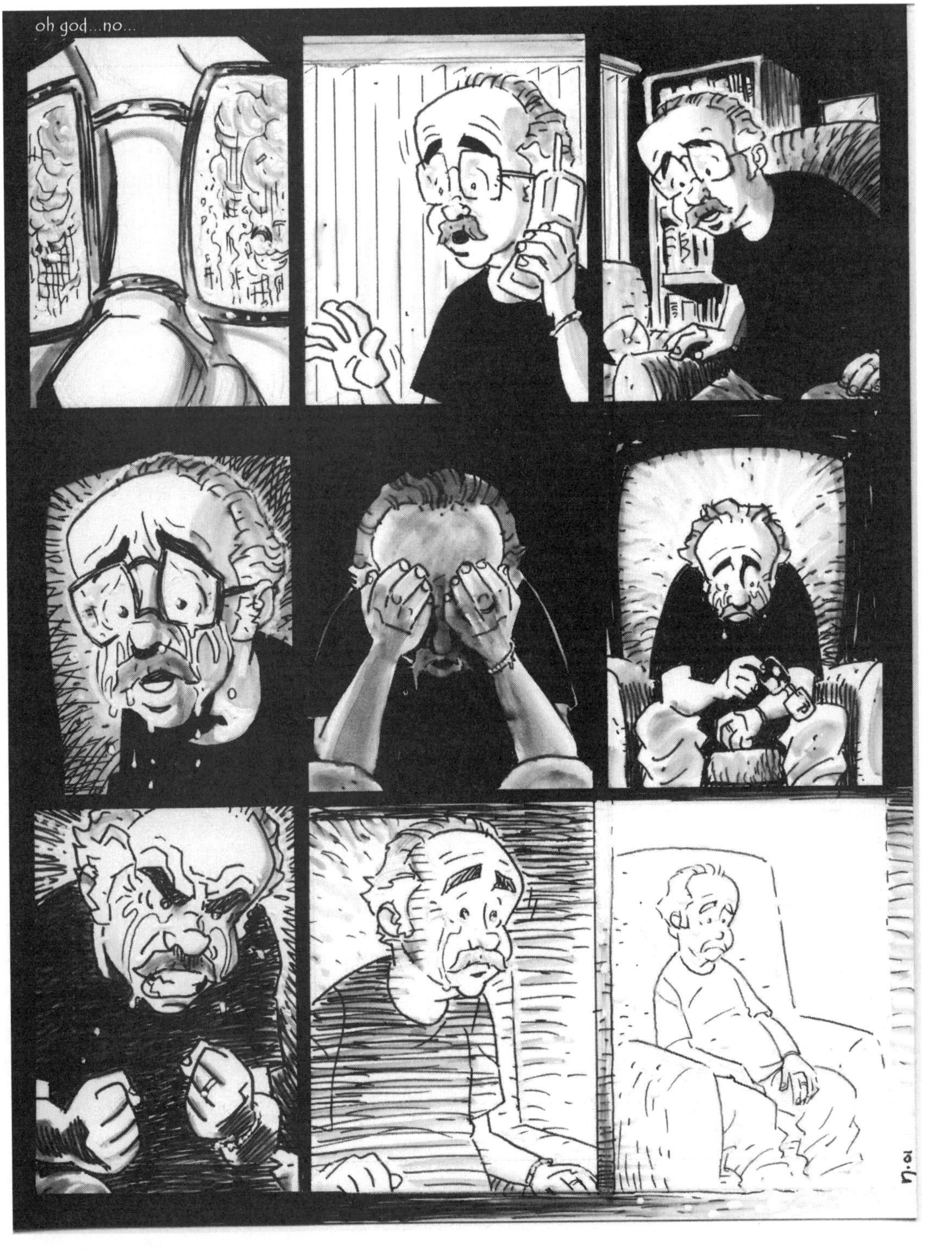
oh god...no...

Nothing fixes a thing

so intensely in the memory

as the wish to forget it.

✳ Michel Eyquem de Montaigne (1533 - 1592)

biographies

Nick Abadzis . . . . [54]
Nick Abadzis is a stalwart of the UK alternative cartooning scene. He moonlights as a children's author, TV scriptwriter and web-toon artist and is best known for his characters Mr Pleebus and the award-winning Hugo Tate. He lives in London with his partner, Angela. Rising Trout Press, PO Box 305, Teddington, Middx. TW11 8WA, UK
nick@nabad.demon.co.uk

Jessica Abel . . . . [13]
Cartoonist and Illustrator Jessica Abel (Chicago, 1969) is best known for her comic-book series of short fiction, Artbabe, and her journalistic comics, such as *Radio: An illustrated Guide.* Her most recent book, a serialized thriller set in Mexico City, is titled *La Perdida,* and is published by Fantagraphics. She lives in Brooklyn, New York with her husband, Matt Madden.
www.artbabe.com

Jason Alexander . . . . . . [143]
The majority of Jason Alexander's career has taken place in the comics medium. It gives him the freedom to do the type of drawing and painting he loves and the opportunity to express himself through his writing. Since self-publishing the *Section8* anthology in 1995, Alexander's work has gone on to appear in numerous small press comics as well as several projects for Sirius Entertainment. Over the past 4 years his work has appeared in *The Best of Crypt of Dawn, Sirius Gallery 2000, Poison Elves, The Waiting Place,* and his own book, *Empty Zone.* Recently he's worked in several White Wolf publications and book illustrations for Dalmatian Press' release of *Alice in Wonderland* and *The Time Machine.* Currently Alexander is working on another *Empty Zone* mini-series, finishing his art stint on *Tower for The Waiting Place,* and his first full-color graphic novel, *Stray Pulse.*
sectioneight@earthlink.net

David Alvarez . . . . [10]
David Alvarez was born, raised and still lives in Puerto Rico. Alvarez started publishing comic strips and cartoons in local newspapers and magazines, and then explored the comic book world by self-publishing a series of a humorous cartoon superhero Changuy and also worked and developed a few local animated projects. Currently, Alvarez is a freelance artist for Warner Brothers Worldwide Publishing and his work can be seen on *Looney Tunes* comics as a penciller.
david01@caribe.net

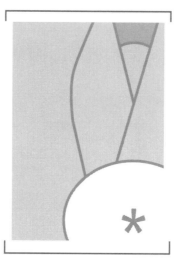

Graham Annable . . . . . . [27]
Graham Annable was classically trained as an animator at Sheridan College in Toronto, graduating in 1992, and has worked as an animator ever since, including work on British children's TV, story boards for Chuck Jones Enterprises, Disney's *A Goofy Movie,* and since 1994 an extended string of computer game projects for Lucas-Arts such as *Full Throttle, The Dig, Afterlife, Outlaws,* and *The Curse of Monkey Island.* Annable was the Lead Animator for the LucasArts video game *Star Wars: Obi-Wan.* His projects have won numerous animation and graphics awards including the ASIFA Annie Award, animation's highest honor, in 1998 for "Outstanding Achievement in an Animated Interactive Program." Graham currently resides in the Bay Area, California where he creates his *Grickle* series of books for Alternative Comics.
www.indyworld.com/grickle
grickle@hotmail.com

Donna Barr . . . . [144]
Donna Barr has been a respected presence in Drawn Books since 1986. Her award-winning, ground-breaking, mind-twisting books, include *Desert Peach* and *Stinz.*
www.stinz.com; barr@stinz.com

Tom Beland . . . . [179]
Tom Beland is a cartoonist from Napa Valley, California now living in Guaynabo, Puerto Rico with his wife, Lily Garcia. His strip, *True Story, Swear to God* is available on-line at www.yunque.net/tom.
tom@yunque.net.

Gregory Benton . . . . [156]
Artist/Writer Gregory Benton was born and lives in New York City.
www.gregorybenton.com
gbenton@nyc.rr.com

Nick Bertozzi . . . . [138]
Nick Bertozzi lives in Brooklyn, NY with his wife and daughter. He is the author of *Boswash* (Luxurious Comics), a map-comic, and *The Masochists* (Alternative Comics), and he is working on a new series for Alternative Comics.
www.indyworld.com/bertozzi
nick@luxcomics.com

Joyce Brabner . . . . [167]
Joyce Brabner first appeared in comics as a character in her husband Harvey Pekar's autobio series, *American Splendor.* She pioneered cause comics and comics as journalism with such titles as *Real War Stories* and *Brought to Light.* With Harvey, she wrote a book length comics memoir, *Our Cancer Year.* Their adventures in marriage are now being turned into a feature film. Together, they're writing the behind scenes story, *Our Movie Year.*
jbrabner@en.com

Frank Cho . . . . [cover]
Frank Cho's comic books sell out, issue after issue with early issues now in later printings. His college comic strip collection, *University2, The Angry Years* is soon to enter its 8th printing. He has won the Charles Schulz Plaque for Excellence in Cartooning, the Scripps-Howard Award for Best College Cartoonist

and the Ignatz Awards for Outstanding Artist and Outstanding Comic for *Liberty Meadows.* He was born Duk Hyun Cho in 1971 in Seoul, South Korea. At the age of six he and his parents came to live in the United States. In college he created *University2.* Upon graduation from the University of Maryland in 1996 with a degree in Nursing, he signed with Creators Syndicate, Inc. for a continuation of *University2* as *Liberty Meadows.* He was married in April of 1999 and lives in the Baltimore area with his wife Cari and his wiener dog, Truman. Insight Studios, 7844 Saint Thomas Drive, Baltimore MD 21236.
www.InsightStudiosGroup.com

Hearn Jay Cho . . . . [129]
Hearn Jay Cho is an oncologist in New York City. In a previous life, he wrote and/or drew *Vengeance of Vampirella, Zen: Intergalactic Ninja,* and *Zorro.* He thanks his wife Cary for providing good ideas to steal.
hjc2001@med.cornell.edu

Brian Clopper . . . . [23]
Brian Clopper, 5th grade teacher, children's book author and cartoonist, is the creator of *The Heebie-Jeebies, Monster Pals, Norton The Vampire, Graham The Gargoyle,* and *Cartoonists in the Classroom.*
www.brianclopper.com
wingnutibh@aol.com

Nikki Coffman . . . . [188]
Nikki Coffman began as a photographer producing primarily self-portraits using experimental processes. She and her husband, Craig, moved to Chicago to teach Graphic Design at Columbia College and attend the School of the Art Institute of Chicago. After taking design and photo classes and spending a semester producing and directing a new modern Opera titled "The Dig," Nikki began collaborating with Laurenn McCubbin, photographing and interpreting her semi-autobiographical stories for Laurenn's beautiful handmade books. Design opportunities drew Nikki to San Francisco where she was soon joined by Laurenn and they began working on *XXX Live Nude Girls.* Nikki and Craig moved back to Omaha, Nebraska to rediscover the good life and to have a baby in February. Laurenn and Nikki continue their work long-distance.
www.xxxlivenudegirls.com
nikki@xxxlivenudegirls.com

Daniel Cooney . . . . [60]
Daniel Cooney, 31, is a graphic designer by day and aspiring comic book illustrator by night. There's no sleep for this aging hipster who is the artist/writer of *Valentine: Assassin For Hire,* published by Red Eye Press.
www.valentine4hire.com.

Guy Davis . . . . [147]
Guy Davis' first creator owned series *Baker Street,* led him to *Sandman Mystery Theatre* for DC Comics/Vertigo. Other works include *The Nevermen, Hellblazer, Grendel: Black, White and Red, The Phantom Stranger, House of Secrets, Brave Old World, Aliens: Survival, Terminator, Batman: Shadow of the Bat, Swamp Thing* and various spot illustrations for White Wolf Games. His current creator owned book *The Marquis* continues through Oni Press.
GDavis3265@aol.com

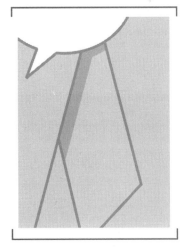

Tom Derenick . . . . [109]
Born 1969 in Scranton PA, Tom Derenick started his career in comics with *Subtle Violents* for Cry For Dawn Productions. Since then he's worked for many companies including Marvel Comics and DC Comics on titles including *Star Trek, Venom* and *X-Men.* He currently works for Marvel Comics on various *X-Men* related projects as well as Marvel's first creator-owned series in many years, *Nightside.* He is also currently co-plotting *Wolverine/ Captain America: The Contingency* for Marvel Comics.
manthing75@aol.com

Danny Donovan . . . . [15]
Born in Portsmouth Virginia, Danny Donovan traveled extensively, just seeing what he could see. He spent three years living in North Yorkshire, England and recently coming back to the states in 1998 where he presently lives in the mountains of North Carolina with plans to head back to his place of birth soon. He began his career in 1998 with his web comic *Hardcore* and working for other small press companies along the way. Currently he works for Committed Comics and Marvel Comics.
www.dannydonovan.com
impulse545@aol.com

Will Eisner . . . . [45]
Will Eisner has been a pioneering force in comics for over sixty years. His career spans groundbreaking work in early newspaper comics to the mature graphic novels that he continues to produce today. In addition to producing a continuing legacy of great work, Eisner taught cartooning at the School of Visual Arts in New York, and is the author of two definitive works examining the creative process, *Comics and Sequential Art* and *Graphic Story-telling.* Each year he presides over the Eisner Awards, established in 1988, presented each year at Comic-Con International in San Diego. Recently, his work was gained wider recognition when it was showcased in the Whitney Museum's 1996 "NYNY: City of Ambition" show. Eisner has been cited as an inspiration by cartoonists from all corners of the genre, and his influence is seen as widely. He remains one of the most active, vital, and prolific forces in the comics' field today.
www.willeisner.com

Steve Ellis . . . . [186]
Steve Ellis has had a varied career in comics working in both the mainstream (Marvel, DC) and the independent area. His favorite projects so far have been his self-published Sci-Fi comic *Tranquility,* and drawing *Lobo* for DC Comics. Recently, he co-created *Jezebelle* for Wildstorm. Ellis does a lot of gaming art too, for Whitewolf Games and his own project "STUPERPOWERS Deluxe: The First Class Game for Third Rate Heroes." Currently, Steve is developing new projects and spends his free time with his wife and cats.
www.hyperactiveart.com
steve@hyperactiveart.com

Fly . . . . [98]
Fly has been living and squatting in the lower East side of Manhattan since 1990. Mostly she paints and draws comix and illustrations. Her work has appeared in the *New York Press, Village Voice, San Francisco Bay Guardian, The Comics Journal, The Bradleys* (Fantagraphics Books), *Raygun, World War 3 Illustrated, Maximumrocknroll,* and numerous others. Fly's first book - *CHRON!IC!RIOTS!PA!SM!* was published by Brooklyn-based Auto-nomedia in 1999. She is currently working on a collection of portraits and stories called *Peops* which will be published by Soft Skull in the fall of 2002. PO Box 1318, Cooper Station, New York, NY 10276.
www.bway.net/~fly
fly@bway.net

Evan Forsch . . . . [100]
Evan Forsch is a tall, quiet and mysterious man, except that he's not all that tall nor mysterious. Five days a week Evan is a corporate drone, sitting in front of a computer and pretending to work while daydreaming of peace on earth in a world where everyone reads his comics.
evan4sh@yahoo.com

Renée French . . . . [35]
Renée French has been writing and illustrating comic books since 1991. She's the creator of the Fantagraphics Books series *Grit Bath,* the Dark Horse graphic novels, *The Ninth Gland* and *Corny's Fetish,* the Oni Press book, *Marbles in My Underpants: The Renée French Collection,* and the recently released picture book, *The Soap Lady,* published by Top Shelf Productions. She lives in New Jersey with her husband and a hermit crab.
www.reneefrench.com
renee@mightycheese.com

Jenny Gonzalez . . . . . . [114]
Jenny Gonzalez currently resides in Brooklyn, New York, where she divides her time between cartooning, fronting her band Mz. PakMan, and other projects. Her work has appeared in various places such as The ComicStore.com, *Legal Action Comics,* and gURL.com, as well as gracing T-shirts at the Anna Sui boutique and the pages of NY Metropolis. PO Box 22477, Brooklyn, NY 11202-2477.
www.angelfire.com/ny3/devildoll
lilrenoir@aol.com

Derek Gray . . . . [56]
Living in the UK, Derek Gray works as a freelance illustrator at the Scottish Cartoon Art Studio in Glasgow. The page he created for this book is his first professionally published comics work for a number of years as he is now concentrating on illustration, caricaturing and storyboarding. Scottish Cartoon Art Studio, Ladywell, 94 Duke Street, Glasgow, G4 0UW, United Kingdom.
www.scottishcartoons.com

Eric Wolfe Hanson . . . . . [15]
Eric Wolfe Hanson has illustrated *G.I.Joe* and *Tellos: Sons & Moons* for Image Comics. Hanson lives in Richmond, Virginia with his lovely wife, Trish, and their three cats.
ericwolfehanson@aol.com

Tomer Hanuka . . . . [112]
Tomer Hanuka was born in Israel. After three years of mandatory Army service he moved to New York. He works as a freelance illustrator for publications such as *the New Yorker, The New York Times, Rolling Stone,* and *TIME.* He was awarded the gold and silver medals from the Society of Illustrators, and is featured in *Print* magazine. Also, he has been self-publishing a comic book called *Bipolar* with twin brother Assaf. He lives in Brooklyn.
www.thanuka.com
tomer@thanuka.com

Jim Harrison . . . . [39]
Jim Harrison is a noted graphic designer and illustrator with DECA Design in Gainesville, Florida. His comics work includes various freelance assignments as well as 4 issues of his creation *Humongous Man,* with partner Dan Stepp.
InkPotJim@aol.com

Tom Hart . . . . [130]
Many of Tom Hart's comics feature the confrontational pariah, Hutch Owen, squaring off within and against the forces of multi-nation-alism and corporate hegemony. His stories often examine issues with an uncommon objectivity and emotional depth. Tom Hart was born in upstate New York and lived in Seattle, Texas, Morocco, Florida and Boston before settling in New York City.
www.newhatstories.com
tomhart@newhatstories.com

Dean Haspiel . . . . [92]
Dean Haspiel is the author of semi-autobiographical comix and super-psychedelic romances. Haspiel's aggro-moxie appears regularly in *The Billy Dogma Experience* (Top Shelf); heart-charming tales about the last romantic anti-hero, and *Opposable Thumbs* (Alternative Comics); episodic tales about a native New Yorker.
www.DeanHaspiel.com
dino@cobite.com

Jon "Bean" Hastings . . . . [57]
Jon "Bean" Hastings is the creator of *Smith Brown Jones: Alien Accountant* and *Mad Science.* His Lovely wife Terry is a former fire fighter and he spent most of 9/11 thinking what it would be like to lose her. He didn't like it at all. This was the hardest story he's ever had to write.
www.beantoons.com
kiwistudios@compuserve.com

Phillip Hester . . . . [76]
Phillip Hester was born in Iowa, 1966 where he still lives with his wife and two children. Past credits (Artist): *Swamp Thing, The Crow:Waking Nightmares, Brave Old World, Fringe;* (Writer): *The Coffin;* (Writer & Artist): *The Wretch, Taboo, Deadline USA, Negative Burn.* Current and upcoming work: *Green Arrow* and *The Brave and The Bold* for DC Comics, *Deep Sleeper* for Oni Press, and *The Wretch* for Slave Labor Graphics.
pahester@netINS.net

Sam Hester . . . . [4]
Sam Hester has been picturing her life as a comic strip for as long as she can remember, so she was very glad to be able to contribute to this project. Sam is a Calgary-based artist, and her autobiographical comic strip can be found at thedrawingbook.com.
sam_silvio@hotmail.com

Marc Hempel . . . . [119]
A native of Chicago, Marc's work first appeared in *Epic Illustrated, Heavy Metal* and *Questar.* After moving to Baltimore to join forces with Mark Wheatley at Insight Studios, the two collaborated on the acclaimed series *MARS* and *Breathtaker.* Marc is perhaps best known for his work on *The Sandman,* and for his own humor books, *Gregory* and *Tug & Buster.* Insight Studios, 7844 Saint Thomas Drive, Baltimore MD 21236.
www.InsightStudiosGroup.com

K. Thor Jensen . . . . [28]
K. Thor Jensen, 25, is a New York resident currently traveling around America gathering material for his next book, *Red Eye, Black Eye.* PO Box 250593, New York, NY 10025.
www.shortandhappy.com
kthor@portalofevil.com

Neil Kleid . . . . [119]
A Detroit native, Neil Kleid moved to Manhattan in 1999, where he created "Stand Up Comics" – forums designed to elevate awareness of the comics medium. He co-founded the Third Eye Publishing Anthology and writes *Bit City* for *Committed Comics,* as well

as features for the on-line PopImage.com. Kleid is working on perfecting the art of "rant" comics with *Singles Night,* his upcoming autobiographic novel.
thirdeyepublishing.homestead.com /Neil.html
slashr3@aol.com

Keith Knight . . . . [156]
Keith Knight is a cartoonist, rapper, teacher and media activist. His two comic strips, *(th)ink* and *the k chronicles* can be found in various newspapers, magazines, and websites around the world. His hip-hop/garage band, The Marginal Prophets, isn't very popular at all. PO Box 591794, San Francisco, CA 94159-1794.
keeflix@hotmail.com

Chris Knowle . . . . [28]
Chris Knowle is a walking repository of odd stories, tall tales, and embarrassing memories. He works as a graphic designer and illustrator in Washington DC.

James Kochalka . . . . [148]
James Kochalka has been keeping a daily diary in comic strip form since October of 1998. His contribution to this book consists of his diary entries from September 11 and the days immediately following the tragedy. They vary in tone from being heartfelt to being snotty and flippant, but they accurately reflect the range of emotions that he, and many others (one presumes), went through that week. Kochalka's diary strips are being collected by Top Shelf Productions and published in a series titled *The Sketchbook Diaries.* The first volume is currently available from www.topshelfcomix.com.
www.indyworld.com/kochalka
james@indyworld.com

James A. Kuhoric . . . . . . [172]
James Anthony Kuhoric is a seven-year professional in the comic book industry with a degree in psychology and sociology from the University of Maryland. He has written over two-dozen comics including the sci-fi mainstays *Battlestar Galactica* and *First Wave.* Currently he is writing the

upcoming series Roger Corman's *Black Scorpion* with artist Greg LaRocque and is developing a creator owned series with artist Neil Vokes. His most important role in life is being the father of two very special boys – James "Jay" Anthony and Zachary Allen Kuhoric.
james_kuhoric@hotmail.com

Peter Kuper . . . . [146]
Peter Kuper's work has appeared in, among others, *TIME, Newsweek, The New York Times,* and *Mad,* where he illustrates "Spy vs. Spy." In 1979, Kuper co-founded the political comix magazine *World War 3 Illustrated* and is currently co-editing issue #32. His comics have been translated into German, Italian, Portuguese, Swedish, Spanish and Greek and his artwork has been exhibited around the world. His most recent book *Speechless* is a coffee table art book covering his career to date published by Top Shelf Productions.
www.peterkuper.com
kuperart@aol.com

Michael Kupperman . . . . [73]
Michael Kupperman is a cartoonist and illustrator whose work has appeared in *The New Yorker, Fortune, The New York Times, Heavy Metal, LA Weekly,* and the *Oxford American.* His book *Snake'N'Bacons Cartoon Cabaret* was published in September 2000 by Harper Collins, and his work was adapted for the Comedy Central show TV Funhouse. He lives and works in New York City.
mkupperman@earthlink.net

Greg LaRocque . . . . [172]
Greg LaRocque is a twenty plus year veteran of comics. His career began in 1980 and has included stints with both DC Comics and Marvel Comics on titles including *Legion of Superheroes, Marvel Team Up, The Avengers,* and *Web of Spider-Man.* His kinetic storytelling style was epitomized in the classic *Flash* story arc "Return of Barry Allen." Through Exiled Studios Greg was able to unleash his creator-owned projects *Crybaby* and *The Exiled.*
exstudio@aol.com

David Lasky . . . . [167]
Originally from the Virginia suburbs, David Lasky moved to Seattle in 1992, where he joined the ranks of a new wave of young "alternative cartoonists." He has since produced a number of experimental comic books, including a nine page adaptation of Joyce's *Ulysses. Urban Hipster,* his collaboration with Greg Stump, was nominated for a Harvey Award in 1999.
www.indyworld.com/uh
davidlasky@yahoo.com

Layla Lawlor . . . . [78]
A graphic artist, illustrator, mini-comic creator and former Alaskan hippie-child now living in Illinois, Layla Lawlor self-publishes *Raven's Children,* a graphic novel serialized in chapters. She also writes for the comics webzine Sequential Tart and has been known to refer to herself in the third person. Shadowgrass Design, PO Box 3283, Champaign, IL 61826-3283.
www.ravenschildren.com
llayla@ravenschildren.com

Carol Lay . . . . [136]
Carol Lay has been in the comics racket for quite some time. Her weekly strip, *Story Minute,* appears in several daily and weekly papers in the United States and abroad.
www.waylay.com

A. David Lewis . . . . [60]
A. David Lewis hails from Boston, a graduate of Brandeis University. Now at Georgetown University, Dave has presented conference papers on comic books across the continent and is working with Committed Comics, The Third Eye Group, and other collaborators on upcoming projects. He thanks his loved ones for their support.
adl6@georgetown.edu

Ellen Lindner . . . . [84]
Ellen Lindner is an emerging wit in the New York City comix scene. In her zine/comix compilation *little white bird/MEGACOM,* comix *Beatnik Love* and *The Egg Mysterious,* Ellen explores the malaise of relationships, rubbernecking boys through the dual lens: patriarchy

and pleasure. Her brazenly introspective humor, rock-fashion edge and graphic styling meld subversive context with romantic content while revealing the mystery of female orgasm. She's a sista.
littlewhitebird@fantasticteam.com

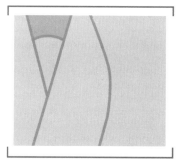

Mike Manley . . . . [184]
Mike Manley was born in Detroit, Michigan. His powerful and expressive drawings, dynamic inks and strong story telling skills, have made him an in-demand artist for some of comics' top titles for all of the major publishers and animation studios from Marvel, DC, Warner Bros, Disney to the Cartoon Network.
www.actionplanet.com

Jason Martin . . . . [60]
All around inker Jason Martin has worked on a wide variety of books for Marvel Comics, DC Comics, Dark Horse, Wildstorm and Image. Contributing to this comic was something he felt strongly about, and was glad to do.
www.artplayboy.com
artplayboy@hotmail.com

Jeff Mason . . . . [editor]
Jeff Mason is the publisher of Alternative Comics, a company billed as "publishers of cool comic books." When Jeff is not working on Alternative Comics' latest release, he is working diligently to protect everyone's rights as a criminal defense lawyer in Gainesville, Florida.
www.indyworld.com/comics
jmason@indyworld.com

Laurenn McCubbin . . . . . [12]
Laurenn McCubbin has done a little bit of everything. She's been a retail slave, an office drone, a stripper, a

teacher, a successful graphic designer and a broke art student. A California native, she moved to Chicago to attend the School of the Art Institute on a scholarship, then scurried back to her beloved Bay Area as soon as she graduated. She and Nikki Coffman began collaborating as students in Chicago, and on moving to San Francisco they resumed their collaboration in *XXX Live Nude Girls.* She continues doing freelance design, lettering translations of Japanese comics and silk-screening postcards and prints.
www.xxxlivenudegirls.com
laurenn@xxxlivenudegirls.com

Darren Merinuk . . . . [60]
Darren Merinuk's internationally obscure artwork has appeared on dozens of releases by punk /rock'n'roll bands from all over North America, Europe and Japan. His comic art and stories have appeared in *Rockin' Bones, 3-D Space Zombies* and others even less well-known. His future plans are built around the probability of continued obscurity. Merinuk lives in Winnipeg, Manitoba, Canada.
merinuk@aol.com

Metaphrog . . . . [173]
Metaphrog are a Franco-Scottish duo comprising Sandra Marrs, art, and John Chalmers, words and lettering. Their publications include *The Maze, Vermin, Strange Weather Lately* and the *Louis'* series. The scary cute *Louis – Red Letter Day* received multiple Eisner and Ignatz Award nominations.
www.metaphrog.com.

Tony Millionaire . . . . [1]
Tony Millionaire lives in Los Angeles. His comic strip *MAAKIES* can be seen in weeklies across the country, with collections published by Fantagraphics Books. His comic book *Sock Monkey* is published by Dark Horse Comics and *Sock Monkey – A Children's Book* is available in book stores now.
www.maakies.com
millionaire@mindspring.com

Gray Morrow . . . . [119]
Sadly, Gray Morrow passed away

shortly after completing his work on this book. Gray Morrow was part of the generation that broke into comics in the 1950s, and he mastered a distinctive "fantastic realist" style that was tailor-made to science fiction and horror. Morrow worked for almost every comic book publisher in the United States during his long career, and was probably best known for his lush wash work on the Warren horror books *Creepy* and *Eerie*. He was also a regular cover artist at Warren. In the late 1970s, Morrow turned in what many say is his greatest work, on *The Illustrated Roger Zelazny*. He was a regular contributor to science fiction magazines such as *If* and *Galaxy*. Gray Morrow's cover paintings for paperback books, as well as his many posters for motion pictures established him as a popular illustrator outside of the comic book field. He also had a career in animation, with the fondly remembered *Spider-Man* television series to his credit. He was a master illustrator who had the respect and friendship of his peers. His wealth of talent, which enabled him to build an astonishingly deep catalog of work in different areas of illustration, serves as a fitting legacy for his diverse career.

Scott Morse . . . . [46]
Scott Morse is the Eisner and Ignatz Award nominated creator of *Soulwind, Visitations,* and *Volcanic Revolver*. His comics work also includes *The Simpsons Treehouse of Horror, Star Wars Tales,* and the comic book companion to the Jim Jarmusch film *Ghost Dog*. His current work includes the series *Magic Pickle* for Oni Press, and *Ancient Joe* for Dark Horse. In animation, Morse has worked as an art director and storyboard artist for Universal and Cartoon Network, most notably on the Emmy Award nominated *Cow and Chicken*.
www.crazyfish.net
crazymorse@earthlink.net

Jason Narvaez . . . . [60]
Raised in the Bronx, Jason Narvaez would lose himself in his comic collection for hours, if not days, at a time. He attended the High School of Art & Design and mostly credits any lessons learned to other students. In the early to mid-1990s, he visited the offices of DC Comics and received invaluable advice on how he could improve his artwork. Narvaez currently manages the graphics department for a top consulting company and has continued to pursue his life-long passion of drawing comics.
earthlink.net/~bidexx
jncomix@arghstudios.com

Josh Neufeld . . . . [89]
Josh Neufeld has been drawing comics since he was four years old. With writer R. Walker, Josh has recently published *Titans of Finance* (Alternative Comics), a satire comic of the financial world featuring true tales of money & business. Josh also co-created *Keyhole,* where he does stories about his travel experiences in Southeast Asia and Central Europe. He has contributed artwork to Harvey Pekar's *American Splendor,* the EXPO anthologies, and many other comics. Josh resides in Brooklyn and makes a living mixing freelance illustration with web design.
www.josh.neufeld.com
joshn@mindspring.com

Phil Noto . . . . [110]
Phil Noto is the cover artist for DC Comics' *Birds Of Prey* and the artist for the upcoming miniseries *Beautiful Killer* from Black Bull. He is also currently an assistant animator at Disney, where his credits include *Lion King, Pocahontas, Hunchback, Tarzan, Mulan* and the upcoming film *Lilo and Stitch*.
www.notoart.com
phil@notoart.com

Mike Avon Oeming . . . . [111]
Mike Avon Oeming began his career inking for Innovation Comics at the age of 14. He has inked *Daredevil, Avengers* and various titles for Marvel Comics, pencils/inks on *Judge Dredd* and the *Big Books* at DC Comics. After stumbling into *Foot Soldiers* at Dark Horse, Mike and writer/partner Bryan J.L. Glass, created *Ship of Fools* as a six issue mini-series originally published by Caliber Press. He is co creator of Eisner Award winning book *Powers* with Brian Bendis and currently creates his *Hammer of the Gods* comic book series with Mark Wheatley and Insight Studios. Mike lives in New Jersey with his wife and son.
oeming@aol.com

Peter Palmiotti . . . . [60]
Peter Palmiotti has been inking comic books for years including *Aquaman* for DC Comics, many titles for Marvel Comics, Crusade Comics, Acclaim, and is currently working on *Valentine* with Daniel Cooney for Red Eye Press and his *Penance* series for Red Anvil.

Ande Parks . . . . [76]
Ande Parks has been employed in the glamorous world of comic book inking for over a decade, working on such titles as *Superman, Wonder Woman* and *Catwoman*. He has often been teamed with his long-time friend, Phil Hester. The duo has won acclaim for their bold, graphic style. Parks has also created his own characters, *Uncle Slam and Fire Dog*. He is currently continuing his work on *Green Arrow,* and writing a gangster graphic novel. He lives in Kansas with his lovely wife and daughter.
www.uncleslam.com
ande@uncleslam.com

Harvey Pekar . . . . [1]
With his mostly autobiographical stories, Pekar has fearlessly pursued the mundanities of life: going to the market, shoveling snow, talking with co-workers, and elevated them to a work of art. Pekar uses a simple but induplicable device to hold the reader's interest — sheer force of personality. Most every-thing in his seminal auto-biographical comic book "American Splendor" revolves around Harvey Pekar. From outright auto-biography to essays (or "rants" as he calls them) on subjects he cares about, over the twenty-five years Pekar has created a remarkable hot/cold effect with his self-portrayal. PO Box 1847; Cleveland Heights, OH 44118.
hpekar@aol.com

Chris Pitzer . . . . [38]
Chris Pitzer's first memory of comics was a *House of Mystery,* which had a monster breaking out of a box in the attic. Pitzer has worked at Eclipse Comics (as their Art Director), and Wildstorm and IDW in the capacity of freelance designer and colorist. Currently, Pitzer likes to publish minis every now and again.
pitzerboy@aol.com

Evan Quiring . . . . [60]
Evan Quiring lives, draws, plays guitar and sleeps occasionally in Winnipeg, Manitoba, Canada. Previous work includes the self-published, small print runs of *Insane World* (1996) and *Midnight Comics* (1998).
smokescreen_ii@hotmail.com

Ted Rall . . . . [80]
Ted Rall, 38, is an editorial and social-commentary cartoonist for Universal Press Syndicate. A Pulitzer Prize finalist and two-time RFK Journalism Award winner, Rall is the author of seven books, including the graphic novels *My War With Brian* and *2024,* as well as the Gen X manifesto *Revenge of the Latchkey Kids.*
www.rall.com

Andy Ristaino . . . . [134]
Andy Ristaino is a freelance animator/illustrator from Massachusetts. Ristaino is currently working on the two titles *Life of a Fetus* and *The Babysitter* for Slave Labor Graphics.
rashanko@yahoo.com.

Alex Robinson . . . . [137]
Alex Robinson's graphic novel *Box Office Poison* was released by Top Shelf Productions in 2001, and he is hard at work at his second book, tentatively titled *Sophomore Slump.* He is a little over six feet tall and he lives with his girlfriend Kristen in New York City.
members.aol.com/ComicBookAlex
ComicBookAlex@aol.com

Harry Roland . . . . [119]
During the 1970s Harry Roland contributed cover paintings for Warren Publication's *Famous*

Monsters of Filmland, cover paintings and line art for *Amazing* and *Fantastic* and other similar projects. Since then he has been involved in non-comic corporate and agency art assignments. In 2001 Harry joined the gang of creators at Insight Studios. Insight Studios, 7844 Saint Thomas Drive, Baltimore MD 21236.
www.InsightStudiosGroup.com

David Roman . . . . [86]
Dave Roman is the writer/co-creator of the comic book series *Quicken Forbidden,* which is published by Cryptic Press. He works for *Nickelodeon Magazine* and is the comics editor for *Nicktoons Specials.* Roman has also written a few stories for DC Comics' *Dexter's Laboratory* series based on the popular Cartoon Network show and he secretly draws his own comics when no one is looking.
www.realmsend.com
deviated2@aol.com

Gail Simone . . . . [10]
Gail Simone got started in the comics business as a humorist for comicbookresources.com. Since then, she's written numerous *Simpsons* comics and Sunday strips, *Killer Princesses* for Oni Press, and is currently writing *Night Nurse* and *Deadpool* for Marvel Comics. PO Box 485, Florence, OR 97439.
gailcbr@yahoo.com

Jeff Smith . . . . [2]
Born and raised in the American mid-west, Jeff Smith learned about cartooning from comic strips, comic books, and watching animation on TV. After four years of drawing comic strips for Ohio State's student newspaper, Smith co-founded the Character Builders animation studio in 1986. In 1991, he launched a

company called Cartoon Books to publish his independent comic book *Bone,* a comedy/adventure about three lost cousins from Boneville. Against all odds, the small company flourished, building a reputation for quality stories and artwork. Word of mouth, critical acclaim, and a string of major awards, which continues to this day, helped propel Cartoon Books and Bone to the forefront of the comic book industry - an industry not known for its openness to non-action heroes. In the American comic book direct market (the largest system of comic book retail stores) Bone has risen to the #1 spot for humor. Jeff Smith's work is published in thirteen languages and has won the highest awards in Germany, France, Italy and at home. Jeff Smith currently works and resides in Columbus, Ohio. PO Box 16973, Columbus, OH 43216
www.boneville.com

Tommy Sommerville . . . . [56]
Co-creator of the Scottish humour comic *Electric Soup,* and co-founder of the Scottish Cartoonist & Comic Artist Members Club, Tommy Sommerville has been drawing cartoons for as long as he can remember. He lives in Glasgow, and works at the Scottish Cartoon Art Studio, particularly as a caricaturist. Scottish Cartoon Art Studio, Ladywell, 94 Duke Street, Glasgow, G4 0UW, United Kingdom.
www.scottishcartoons.com

Jen Sorensen . . . . [22]
Jen Sorensen is the creator of *Slowpoke,* a weekly comic strip that appears in several alternative newspapers throughout the US, for which she was nominated twice for the Friends of Lulu Kimberly Yale Award for Best New Talent. *Slowpoke,* which serves up political and social commentary with an absurdist twist, grew out of a popular daily strip she drew while a student at the University of Virginia. Jen was recently awarded a Xeric Grant to publish *Slowpoke: Cafe Pompous.* Jen Sorensen's work has also appeared in several other publications, including *The Big Book of the '70s* (DC/Paradox Press),

Action Girl Comics, Dignifying Science, Empty Love Stories, the EXPO anthologies, and will be featured alongside such luminaries as Matt Groening and Tom Tomorrow in Ted Rall's upcoming book on alternative political cartoonists. Jen Sorensen lives in Charlottesville Virginia, where she also does web design.
www.slowpokecomics.com
jls6c@virginia.edu

John Staton . . . . [119]
An independent illustrator with a flair for the technical, John Staton has worked on everything from aircraft concept renderings for military engineering contracts, to production sketches for all the weird machines depicted in computer and role playing game manuals, to manga girl comic strips. Marvel Comics has benefitted from his dramatic depictions of *Spider-Man* and the *Punisher,* and his art has appeared in syndicated newspaper strips nationwide and on CNN. Presently, John works as a production manager at Insight Studios Group, where he lends his considerable talents to the publication of such popular comic books as *Liberty Meadows,* and *Hammer of the Gods,* and online comics such as *Doctor Cyborg.* Insight Studios, 7844 Saint Thomas Drive, Baltimore MD 21236.
www.InsightStudiosGroup.com

Steve Stegelin . . . . [59]
Steve Stegelin is best known as the creator of the cult comic book *Boondoggle,* currently running in strip form at www.popimage .com/boondoggle and in various anthologies. He resides in coastal Charleston, South Carolina with his wife and daughter.
stevesteglin@juno.com

Eric Thériault . . . . [36]
Thériault has been a published cartoonist in the Québec area since 1982. He debuted on the American market by publishing in *Melody* (Kitchen Sink Press), *Real Stuff* (Fantagaphics) and *The Jam* (Dark Horse, Slave Labor). In 1999, *Veena,* his mini-comic about nostalgia, time travel and other personal topics became a self-published comic book.
www.cam.org/~veena
veena@cam.org

Robert Ullman . . . . [100]
Robert Ullman has been diligently pumping out issues of his mini-comic *From the Curve* for six years, and his spot illustrations appear weekly in several alternative newspapers on the East coast. A resident of North Carolina, his comics work includes *Signifying Nothing,* a collection of his best cartoons from 1994 to 1998, *Atom-Bomb Bikini,* and *World's Apart.* The first issue of the all-new, big time *From the Curve* is slated to debut in 2002 from Alternative Comics.
www.lurid.com/chappy
fromcurve@yahoo.com

Neil Vokes . . . . [189]
Neil Vokes is a middle aged Hammer film fan with a Dr. Pepper addiction who has drawn comic books for 17 years. Vokes has a wife who supports him, a daughter who is the light of his life, and a job that makes him feel young every time he sits at his drawing table.
ndv45@home.com.

Lauren Weinstein . . . . . [155]
Lauren R. Weinstein was born in 1975. Then she went to school. Now, for some reason, they let her do a weekly comic in Seattle's *The Stranger.* She also gets to corrupt teenage girls' minds with her comics for gURL.com. She likes that.
vineshtein@mindspring.com

Mark Wheatley . . . . [119]
Mark Wheatley is known inter-

nationally as an accomplished illustrator, writer, editor, and publisher. He has won the Inkpot, Speakeasy, Gem and Mucker awards and been nominated for the Harvey and Ignatz awards for his comic book and pulp creations that include *Breathtaker, Radical Dreamer, MARS* and *Titanic Tales.* His illustration work, chosen for inclusion in the annual *Spectrum* selection of the best in fantasy and science fiction art, has also appeared in magazines, books, comic books and on games. He has written books, comic books and television shows. Currently he is writing Michael Avon Oeming's *Hammer of the Gods* comic book series and acting as publisher for Insight Studios Group. Insight Studios, 7844 Saint Thomas Drive, Baltimore MD 21236.
www.InsightStudiosGroup.com

Shannon Wheeler . . . . . [178]
Shannon Wheeler was born a while back and went to various schools. None of the schools managed to knock enough sense into him to keep him from becoming a cartoonist. Currently he draws a comic strip called *Too Much Coffee Man* and contributes his efforts to a magazine of the same name.
www.tmcm.com
wheeler@tmcm.com

Ashley Wood . . . . [74]
Ashley Wood was born in Western Australia and now lives with his wife and children in Arizona. An award winning artist and illustrator his work has contributed towards and appeared in numerous movie, television and music industry projects, comic books and graphic novels, children's books and book covers.
www.ashleywood.com

Meredith Yayanos . . . . . [134]
Meredith Yayanos is a professional violinist who lives and works in lower Manhattan. She has performed at countless downtown venues including Tonic, the Knitting Factory, the Bowery Ballroom, CBGB's, and the F-train platform at 2nd Avenue.
mabqueenie@yahoo.com

Special thanks to the
companies that helped make
this book possible...
Diamond Comic Distributors,
Quebecor Printing,
Wizard: The Guide to Comics,
Comic Shop News, Oni Press,
Comic-Con International,
Worlds of Westfield,
MegaCon, TJs Print Shop
and many others.

American Red Cross
To donate blood, call
1-800-GIVE-LIFE.
To donate money, call
1-800-HELP-NOW.
www.redcross.org